A Pilgrim's Treasury

A Pilgrim's Treasury

366 daily devotional
Bible studies

Alec Taylor

 BOOKS

EP BOOKS
Faverdale North
Darlington
DL3 0PH, England

www.epbooks.org
sales@epbooks.org

EP BOOKS are distributed in the USA by:
JPL Fulfillment
3741 Linden Avenue Southeast,
Grand Rapids, MI 49548.

E-mail: sales@jplfulfillment.com
Tel: 877.683.6935

First published 2013

British Library Cataloguing in Publication Data available
ISBN: 978-0-85234-952-6

Contents

There are 207 readings from the Old Testament
and 159 readings from the New Testament

Preface

I began to produce daily Bible notes in 1989 to meet a need in my own congregation at Chelmsley Wood Reformed Baptist Church. The notes were later taken by other churches and are now circulated throughout the United Kingdom, South Africa, Zambia and Malaysia. *Pilgrim Bible Notes* have been published on a monthly basis in English, French and Slovak. They are also translated into Tagalog by Necy Ellis of Cubao Reformed Baptist Church, Manilla. Some undated notes are also available in German. It is hoped to make them available from a dedicated web site.

My wife, Beverley, faithfully supports me in this work, helping me to simplify them and to make them more accessible to those who have English as their second language. The popularity of the notes in other countries owes much to her work.

In the *Pilgrim Bible Notes* daily readings scheme I take over eight years to cover the whole of the Bible. The notes are continually revised to include insights from contemporary writers. My selection of readings for *A Pilgrim's Treasury* omits many important chapters of the Bible. I am not able to compress eight years of readings into a single year.

Scripture contains *some things hard to understand* (2 Peter 3:16) and some may understand some of the difficult things differently from myself.

Alec Taylor

Introduction

There is no other book like the Holy Bible, which is God's word. God has much to say to us and he has spoken through his prophets, apostles and through the Lord Jesus Christ. The Bible is the inspired, inerrant and authoritative word of God; it is a library of sixty-six books divided into two sections, the Old Testament and the New Testament.

We will go wrong in many ways if we are ignorant of the teaching of the Bible, or if we fail to obey what God has to say to us through this sacred book. I am inviting you to travel through the pages of the Bible in a year. I cannot possibly cover every chapter of every book, but I will introduce you to each book and bring select readings from each one. Readings will generally alternate between Old Testament and New Testament books. Many Christians know little of the Old Testament except for a few well-known passages. The Old Testament is very important because it speaks of the Lord Jesus Christ before he was born into the world (Luke 24:25-27, 44-45).

This book is not intended for use as a brief daily devotional. It is for those who are earnest in their desire to know God and his holy word. Those who train for competitive sport or who are serious about physical fitness spend hours every day in pursuit of their goal. Can we be less enthusiastic about our own spiritual well-being? Spiritual fitness is far more important than physical fitness (1 Timothy 4:8).

The Bible is a gold mine of spiritual truth but it takes time and effort to find and to enjoy its treasure. To obtain the best from these readings each day you will need to spend at least twenty minutes reading God's holy word slowly, reverently, thoughtfully and prayerfully. Before you read this most holy book, ask God to open your eyes to see wonderful things in his word and to speak to you (see Psalm 119:18). Pray and read aloud (or in a whisper where this is not possible); this will help your concentration. You will remember more of what you read, if you repeat your reading later in the day.

When you use these notes, do turn to the Scripture references in brackets and read them; they will throw further light on the verses you are reading.

I feel that it is important to have a sense of biblical geography as well as biblical history and for this reason maps are provided throughout the notes.

My aim is to give you, the reader, a basic knowledge of the Bible and its teaching. I want you to love the word of God and to be serious about obeying what God says to us through the Bible. If at the end of the year, you not only know this holy book better, but also know God better, and love the Lord Jesus Christ more, I will have succeeded.

Key to notes

- All Scripture quotations are taken from the New King James Version unless stated otherwise; they are printed in italics. **If you have a different translation of the Bible, you will still be able to use these notes.**

- The number in brackets e.g. (6) refers to the verse number in the passage that we are reading; (23:16) refers us to another chapter and verse in the book of the Bible from which we are reading. When we read from Matthew, this would be Matthew chapter 23, verse 16.

- Where verses from other books of the Bible are brought to our attention, the name of the book is also indicated in the brackets e.g. (Psalm 19:1).

- Where I ask you to compare another verse of Scripture, I prefix the reference with cp. (e.g. cp. Psalm 1:1). I prefer this to the more common abbreviation cf. which relates to the obsolete word 'confer'.

The word 'Lord' in the Old Testament

The Hebrew words translated '*Lord*' are:

- 'Adon', which is used with reference to men (Genesis 42:33; 45:8-9), and with reference to God (Joshua 3:11,13; Psalm 8:1).

- 'Adonai', literally 'my Lord' (Exodus 4:10; Psalm 68:19).

- 'Yahweh' ('Jehovah'), the sacred name for God, considered by many Jews as too sacred to utter. They regularly used 'Adonai' in its place. '*Yah*' is a contracted form of 'Yahweh' (Isaiah 12:2; 26:4). The word '*Alleluia*' or '*Hallelujah*' (Revelation 19:1-6) means 'Praise Yah'.

Dale Ralph Davis writes with reference to Exodus 3:12,14: 'In light of verse 12, God does not here stress his being or existence so much as his presence and "Yahweh" captures and summarizes that thought — **he is the God who will be present to be all that his people need him to be**. "Yahweh" means the God who is present to help ... "Yahweh" is a personal name, while "the LORD" is a title ... there's a devotional warmth in a personal name that a title can't convey' (*The way of the righteous in the muck of life — Psalms 1-12*, page 8). NB. Our Bible translators have made it possible for us to recognize when 'Yahweh' is used in the Old Testament. 'Yahweh' is printed 'LORD', whereas 'Adon' or 'Adonai' are printed '*Lord*'.

GENESIS

God used Moses to write the first five books of the Bible which are known as the Pentateuch (cp. Luke 24:27). We need to know and to understand the contents of Genesis, the first of these books, if we are to understand the rest of the Bible, especially the New Testament.

The title 'Genesis' means 'origin' or 'beginning' and was given to the book by the translators of the Septuagint (or LXX).* Genesis is a book of beginnings — the beginning of the universe, of life, of man, of human sin, of death, of families, of cities, of nations, of languages, of covenants and of redemption. There is one beginning that we do not read of — God never had a beginning. He planned and made ours.

Outline of Genesis

The beginning of history (chapters 1 to 11)

Creation:	1:1 - 2:25
The coming of sin into the world:	3:1-24
The progress of sin:	4:1 - 5:32
The wickedness of men and the Flood:	6:1 - 8:22
A new beginning with Noah:	9:1 - 10:32
The rebellion at Babel:	11:1-32

The beginning of the Hebrew race (chapters 12 to 50)

The life of Abraham:	12:1 - 25:18
The life of Isaac:	25:19 - 26:35
The life of Jacob:	27:1 - 37:1
The life of Joseph:	37:2 - 50:26

---

* The Septuagint is the earliest version of the Old Testament in the Greek language; the translation was sponsored by Ptolemy II of Egypt towards the end of the third century BC for use by Greek-speaking Jews in Alexandria. Seventy Jewish scholars who were fluent in the Greek language undertook this work.

In the beginning God created the heavens and the earth

The opening words of the Bible are the key to understanding life; if we leave God out of our thinking, we will certainly go wrong. *In the beginning God created the heavens and the earth.* Godless men promote the theory of evolution to explain beginnings without reference to God. Many non-Christian scientists have shown that this theory does not answer the question of origins. Our universe did not come about by accident or by chance. It is the handiwork of God who is absolutely sovereign, powerful and wise (1 Timothy 1:17).

Did God really create everything in six days? Some understand a day in Genesis 1 to represent a long period of time but I cannot agree with them. The almighty God spoke and creation came into being, e.g. *Then God said, 'Let there be light'; and there was light* (3). In the fourth commandment the same Hebrew word is used to describe the six days in which we should work as well as the six days of creation (Exodus 20:8-11). After each day of creation we read of '*the evening and the morning*' (5,8, etc.).

All that God made was '*very good*' (31). Life does have purpose and meaning. Man was made in the image of God (26-27) to worship, love and serve him. To be without God is to be without true hope and purpose (Ephesians 2:12). To know that our great Creator loves us and delights in us is comfort indeed for every child of God (Psalm 121; Isaiah 40:25-31).

In the beginning God ... **Let us now worship him with reverence and with awe.** '*When I consider your heavens, the work of your fingers, the moon and the stars, which you have ordained, what is man that you are mindful of him, and the son of man that you visit him? ... O LORD, our Lord, how excellent is your name in all the earth!*' (Psalm 8:3-4,9).

'*You are worthy, O Lord, to receive glory and honour and power; for you created all things, and by your will they exist and were created*' (Revelation 4:11).

Then God blessed the seventh day and sanctified it

God's work of creation was a completed work; there is not a hint of any process of evolution. *The heavens and the earth, and all the host of them, were finished* (1). 'The host' not only refers to the sun, moon and stars (cp. Deuteronomy 4:19), but also to all things and creatures God made (cp. Psalm 148). God did not rest on the seventh day because he was weary after his work of creation. He never grows weary (Isaiah 40:28). God's rest was a rest of accomplishment, of satisfaction and of joy. *Then God blessed the seventh day and sanctified it* (3). God set apart the Sabbath as a special day at creation and we must not despise the fourth commandment (Exodus 20:8-11). The first day of the week, the Lord's Day, has become the Christian Sabbath (Acts 20:7; 1 Corinthians 16:2; Revelation 1:10).

Adam is not a myth, but a real man whose existence is endorsed in the New Testament (e.g. Romans 5:12-19; 1 Corinthians 15:45; 1 Timothy 2:13-14). This chapter gives us more details of the creation of man. God formed both man and animals from the dust of the ground but man is different in that God breathed into him *the breath of life; and man became a living being* (or *soul*; 7).

God planted the garden of Eden and placed Adam in this perfect environment to cultivate the garden and to care for it (8,15). Adam was immortal and death had no power over him as long as he heeded God's word concerning the tree of the knowledge of good and evil (16-17). Adam lacked just one thing and God said, *'It is not good that man should be alone; I will make him a helper comparable to him'* (18-23). Just a word to readers who are married. God ordained marriage for companionship and procreation (24). Adam needed a companion and a helper. Are you a good companion to your spouse? Do you encourage him (her) in the Christian life? Do you give support in difficult times? Are you loyal and faithful? **Let those of us who are married prayerfully seek at all times to work for a marriage where the Lord is always loved, honoured and obeyed.**

Has God indeed said ... ?

If God's creation was very good (1:31) why is the world in such a mess? We have the answer in this chapter of Genesis. We are not told here that the serpent is Satan, but the New Testament confirms that this is so (2 Corinthians 11:3,14; Revelation 12:9; 20:2). Satan is the father of lies (John 8:44). He cast doubt on God's word, asking Eve, *'Has God indeed said ... ?'* (1). His question suggested that God had forbidden them to eat the fruit of every tree in the garden. That was not true! The forbidden fruit was from only one tree. He then contradicted what God has plainly declared, telling Eve, *'You will not surely die'* (1,4).

The devil makes sin appear attractive. He enticed Eve by promising, *'You will be like God, knowing good and evil'* (5). He also made the fruit of the tree of the knowledge of good and evil appear to be more desirable than the fruit of the other trees, though they were also *pleasant to the sight and good for food* (2:9). *So when the woman saw that the tree was good for food, that it was pleasant to the eyes, and a tree desirable to make one wise, she took its fruit and ate ...* (5-6). **Sin is always more attractive in the imagination than in reality**. Satan promised them so much but they soon proved him to be a liar.

The grace of God is wonderful! He sought the rebels and called to Adam, *'Where are you?'* (9). They tried to shift the blame for their sin. Adam blamed Eve and she blamed the serpent (12-13). Adam's disobedience brought ruin, misery and death into the world (16-19; Romans 5:12; 8:20-23). God promised a coming deliverer who would bruise Satan's head (15). This is the first of many promises in the Old Testament which speak of the coming of Christ into the world, who would destroy the works of the devil (Romans 16:20; cp. 1 John 3:8).

Everyone should know the three Rs of the gospel, the first of which is found in this chapter: Ruin (Genesis chapter 3); Redemption (Romans chapter 3); and Regeneration (John chapter 3). **Adam and Eve were driven out of Eden, but let us thank God that he has provided the way of reconciliation to himself through the blood of the cross.**

Blood cries out

Sin brought a bitter harvest into the lives of Adam and Eve. Cain, their first son, became a murderer, slaying his younger brother. Both sons had been taught about the Lord and we find them bringing offerings to God. God requires blood sacrifice to atone for sin (Hebrews 9:22). The Lord accepted Abel's offering which fulfilled his requirements but he rejected Cain's offering of the fruit of the ground. An angry Cain refused to do as God required and in his jealous rage he shed blood by murdering his brother rather than by animal sacrifice (1-7).

Many people still have not learned that we must come to God on his terms. They vainly imagine that their good works and their honest way of life will gain them acceptance with him. They do not understand that we are all sinners who fall short of God's holy standards. There is only one way to God and that is through the Lord Jesus Christ (John 14:6; Acts 4:12). The message of the cross may seem foolish (1 Corinthians 1:18) but it is only through the shed blood of Jesus that there is forgiveness and cleansing from sin (Ephesians 1:7; 1 John 1:7).

Cain pleaded ignorance when God challenged him. The Lord then said to him, 'What have you done? The voice of your brother's blood cries out to me from the ground' (10). Abel's blood cried out for justice and revenge but the blood of the Lord Jesus speaks better things than that of Abel (Hebrews 12:24). 'Blood cries out!' **The blood of Jesus speaks mercy, forgiveness, peace and eternal life. Hallelujah!**

Cain was cursed and he feared for his own life (14). He said to the Lord, 'My punishment is greater than I can bear! Surely you have driven me out ... I shall be hidden from your face' (13-14). He was much wiser than most sinners today! He realized that to be hidden from the smile and protection of God made life too dreadful to bear. Then Cain went out from the presence of the LORD and dwelt in the land of Nod (which means 'wandering', 16). Adam and Eve's other son, Seth (25-26), had godly descendants, including Enoch, Noah and Abraham.

Noah walked with God

The population of the world had multiplied by the time of Noah (1) but wickedness was rampant. *The wickedness of man was great in the earth ... every intent of the thoughts of his heart was only evil continually* (5). We read later that the earth was corrupt and filled with violence (11-12). Why were the godly unable to stem the tide of wickedness? *The sons of God* from the godly line of Seth* intermarried with women from the godless line of Cain because those women were beautiful (2).

The LORD was sorry ... and he was grieved in his heart (6). Does this mean that God has regrets or disappointment over thwarted plans? Does it mean that he made a mistake in creating man? No, not at all! God's purposes can never be frustrated (Isaiah 14:24,27) and he knew that Adam would sin before he created him. He also decreed before he made the world, that Christ would die for sinners (Acts 2:23). When we sorrow and grieve, it is with a sense of helplessness, but not so with God. John Currid points out that 'Moses is employing expressions of human pain and sorrow to demonstrate God's attitude towards mankind's sin' (*Genesis*, volume 1, page 179).

Noah found grace in the eyes of the LORD (8). We are saved because of the grace of God (Ephesians 2:8-9). Grace is the undeserved favour of God and it was this that made Noah different from his contemporaries. Though he had the privilege of coming from a godly line and would have been instructed in the things of God, he *walked with God* because he *found grace in the eyes of the LORD. Noah was a just man, perfect in his generations. Noah walked with God* (8-9). He had a good testimony in the dark world around him. Like his great-grandfather Enoch, Noah *walked with God* (5:22). **Those who walk with God obey him and enjoy fellowship with him. Do you?**

---

*   Some commentators believe that 'the sons of God' in verse 2 refer to fallen angels who married into the human race and produced offspring who were 'giants' (4). I cannot agree with such speculation. It is true that angels are called 'sons of God' (e.g. Job 1:6; 2:1) but they are incapable of reproduction (Matthew 22:30). See John Currid's commentary on *Genesis*, volume 1, pages 173-175.

And the LORD shut him in

God told Noah that he was going to destroy the earth and its wicked people with a worldwide flood. He promised, '*I will establish my covenant with you*' (6:11-18). Noah was to build an ark to preserve his family. We must recognize that it was a miracle for such a vast number of birds and beasts to be brought into the ark and kept there. God brought the animals and birds to Adam to be named (2:19) and it is certain that he brought the animals to Noah to be taken into the ark. Noah was six hundred years old when he took his household into the ark at the command of God (7:1-9). You will have noticed that the civilization that lived before the Flood enjoyed a very long lifespan; this was greatly reduced in the civilization to follow.

The world has suffered some terrible floods but there has never been anything like the Flood described here. *The fountains of the great deep were broken up* (7:11). There were great tidal waves and the earth was totally submerged after forty days and nights of torrential rain (7:11-12). The water began to recede after one hundred and fifty days (24), but Noah was in the ark for more than a year (7:11; cp. 8:13-14). Why did God send the Flood? It was his judgment on wicked people (6:13) who rejected the preaching of Noah (1 Peter 3:20; 2 Peter 2:5). The Lord Jesus said that before he comes again, the same godless conditions will prevail in the world as they did in the time of Noah. His second coming will be a wonderful event for those who belong to him, but it will be a dreadful day for unbelievers (Matthew 24:36-44).

And the LORD shut him in (7:16). Noah and his family were safe in the ark but it was too late for those outside because God had shut them out. If your heart is right with God you can look forward to the return of Christ with great joy and longing. You can say in the words of Scripture, '*Even so, come, Lord Jesus*' (Revelation 22:20). Heaven and endless bliss await you. **You will be shut in and safe with God for ever! If you are not a true Christian, you will be shut out for ever.** The Lord Jesus warns, '*Be ready*' (Matthew 24:44). Are you?

I will remember my covenant

Noah had taken seven pairs of clean animals and birds into the ark; when he left, he built an altar to the Lord, sacrificing from each of them (7:2-3; 8:20). The Lord was pleased with the *'soothing aroma'* (21). These verses foreshadow the great offering of the Lord Jesus Christ on the cross which was a pleasing aroma to God (Ephesians 5:2). God commanded Noah, *'Be fruitful and multiply, and fill the earth'* (9:1-3, 7; cp. Genesis 1:28-30). He also told Noah that he could now eat the flesh of animals, whereas before the Flood man was only allowed a vegetarian diet (9:2-3; cp. 1:29-30). Though it was permitted to kill animals, God stressed to Noah the sanctity of human life. Man is made in the image of God and murder is an offence which must be punished by death. This is the just punishment for a terrible crime (9:5-6).

The word *'covenant'* is found seven times between verses 9 and 17 of chapter 9. A covenant is a binding agreement between two or more persons, bringing them into a special relationship with each other. The Lord made a covenant with Noah for all mankind and for all the animal kingdom. In this covenant God promised that he would never again destroy the earth by a flood (8-11). He said, *'I will remember my covenant'* (15).

Noah planted a vineyard and he brewed wine from his vintage. *Then he drank of the wine and was drunk, and became uncovered in his tent* (9:21). His son, Ham, discovered him naked and in a drunken stupor. Ham did nothing to cover his father but went and told his two brothers. They went backwards into Noah's tent so as not to see his nakedness, and they covered him. When Noah found out what had happened, he cursed Ham's son, Canaan. Why did he curse Canaan rather than Ham? We are not told, but he may have been involved with Ham in some immodest deed when Noah was drunk (9:22-25). Noah had remained faithful when civilization around him was wicked and violent but he fell into sin through brewing his own wine. **Noah did not intend to sin, but Satan was waiting for the unguarded, careless moment.**

There he built an altar to the LORD

Abram came from a family who worshipped false gods (Joshua 24:2). His life was changed after God appeared to him in Ur and told him to leave his country and his relatives and go to a land that he would show to him (1; cp. Acts 7:2-4). Abram faced a costly choice that required great faith when he left his country and family to follow where God would lead him. God promised, '*I will make you a great nation; I will bless you and make your name great; and you shall be a blessing ... and in you all the families of the earth shall be blessed*' (2-3). All these promises were fulfilled.

Abram was a tent-dweller and a pilgrim who *waited for the city ... whose builder and maker is God* (a city in heaven; Hebrews 11:10, 13-16). Abram did not build cities. He built altars where he offered sacrifices to God and worshipped him. As he travelled from one place to another, we read, *There he built an altar to the* LORD (7-8). These altars were a testimony which proclaimed the name of the Lord to the heathen around him. The sacrifice of the Lord Jesus has put an end to animal sacrifices, but we must offer the sacrifice of praise to God (Hebrews 13:15; 1 Peter 2:9).

We have already seen from Noah's experience that even great men can fall into sin. Famine drove Abram to Egypt where he lied about his relationship to Sarai who was very beautiful despite her advancing years. He feared that the Egyptians would kill him if they found out that Sarai was his wife and then claim her for Pharaoh. Sarai was his stepsister (20:12) but he told the Egyptians that she was his sister (13). The half-truth was a lie which was intended to deceive. Pharaoh took Sarai into his palace and he treated Abram well for her sake but the Lord intervened by sending diseases on Pharaoh and his household. When the king discovered the truth about Sarai, he rebuked Abram and sent them away (14-20). **Abram did not build an altar in Egypt. Was he forgetting the faithfulness and promises of God?**

Sketch maps to show journeys of Abram
(Genesis 11:27 - 13:18)

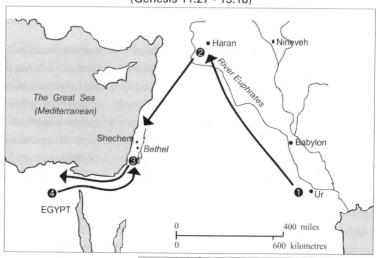

1. Abram and Sarai leave Ur for Canaan with Terah his father, and Lot. They settle in Haran.

2. After the death of Terah Abram leaves Haran for Canaan (about 2090 BC). He builds altars to the Lord at Shechem and Bethel.

3. Abram goes to Egypt (about 2089 BC) because of famine in Canaan.

4/5. He returns to Canaan and settles near Bethel but insufficient pasture land leads to strife between his herdsmen and those of Lot.

6. They separate. Lot chooses the fertile plain of Jordan leaving Abram with the hill country.

7. God renews his promise to Abram. He moves to Hebron and builds an altar to the Lord.

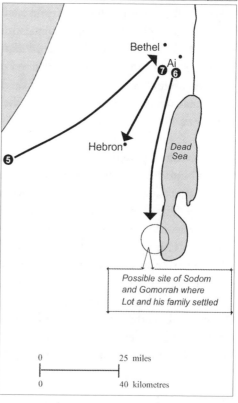

The LORD *made a covenant with Abram*

Abram had just enjoyed a great victory (chapter 14), but it appears that after this he was troubled by fear (1). Satan often attacks us following times of blessing, for it is at such times that we are least on our guard. It was after his great victory over the prophets of Baal that Elijah experienced an attack of the devil (1 Kings 19:1-4). God reassured his servant, '*Do not be afraid, Abram. I am your shield, your exceedingly great reward*' (1). God was his protector ('*shield*'), why should he fear? We all have fears from time to time and need the Lord's assurance (e.g. Joshua 1:9; Luke 1:13,30; Acts 18:9).

Abram may have been afraid because he was still childless and God's promise had not yet been fulfilled (2-3; cp. 12:1-3). The Lord told him that he would father a child who would be his heir (4-5). Though he was an old man, Abram believed God's promise and trusted in the Lord who *accounted it to him for righteousness* (6). The apostle Paul quotes this verse to show that salvation is not of works, but comes from trusting in the Lord Jesus who died and rose from the dead for our forgiveness and justification (Romans 4:1-4,19-25).

The Lord not only promised Abram that he would have an heir in his old age, but also that he would give him the land of Canaan as an inheritance (7). Abram asked, '*Lord* GOD, *how shall I know that I will inherit it?*' (8). The Lord instructed Abram to bring clean animals and birds as a sacrifice. He cut in two the carcases of the heifer, goat and ram, but not the two birds. The dividing of the animals (10) was the normal way of sealing a covenant (cp. Jeremiah 34:18).

God deals with us by covenant. We saw earlier this month that he made a covenant with Noah (chapter 9). We read in this chapter, *The* LORD *made a covenant with Abram* (18). **Every Christian is joined to God in the new covenant which has many precious and wonderful promises from God who is totally committed to all who belong to him (Hebrews 8:6; 2 Peter 1:4).**

My covenant I will establish with Isaac

God had promised Abraham a son but the years passed without the promise being fulfilled. Sarai reasoned that Hagar, her maidservant, could bear children on her behalf, if Abraham took her as a concubine. Abraham foolishly listened to Sarai's plea and Ishmael was born (chapter 16).

The Lord again appeared to Abram when he was ninety-nine years of age, and thirteen years after the birth of Ishmael. The Lord said to Abram, '*I am Almighty God; walk before me and be blameless*' (1). The Lord confirmed his covenant and repeated his promise that Abram would have many descendants. The Lord changed his name from Abram (which means 'high father') to Abraham (meaning '*a father of many nations*') and gave circumcision as the sign of the covenant (5-14). God also changed the name of Sarai to *Sarah* (both names mean 'princess'). Abraham had been promised a son, and the Lord now tells him that Sarah would bear this son. She would be a mother of nations and kings would descend from her (15-16).

Abraham fell prostrate on his face in response to the words of God. He said in his heart, '*Shall a child be born to a man who is one hundred years old? And shall Sarah, who is ninety years old, bear a child?*' He then said to God, '*Oh, that Ishmael might live before you!*' (17-18). The Lord knew what Abraham was thinking and told him that Sarah would indeed bear him a son who was to be named, '*Isaac*' (meaning 'he laughs'). He promised, '*I will establish my covenant with him for an everlasting covenant, and with his descendants after him*' (19) and said that Isaac would be born the following year. Isaac, and not Ishmael, was the child of the covenant but Ishmael would not be forgotten. God had blessed him and a great nation would descend from him, but the Lord repeated that he had established his covenant with Isaac (20-21).

Abraham obeyed the command of God and circumcised himself and all the males in his household (23-27). **Obedience to the word of God is a vital evidence of faith in God.**

God has made me laugh

This chapter records the fulfilment of God's promise to Abraham that Sarah would bear him a son. *And the* LORD *visited Sarah as he had said, and the* LORD *did for Sarah as he had spoken* (1). God is faithful and he always keeps his promises (2 Corinthians 1:20). It is impossible for God to lie (Titus 1:2). The promises of God's word are always a great comfort and encouragement. Satan wants us to doubt Scripture and thus to doubt the faithfulness of God. He questioned Eve in Eden, asking her, '*Has God indeed said?*' (3:1). The great missionary, Hudson Taylor, once said, 'God means what he says, and he will do all that he promises.'

Sarah conceived and bore Abraham a son in his old age, at the set time of which God had spoken to him (2). **God is never in a hurry, but he is never too late! He will surely work out his wise and sovereign purposes!** Sarah had laughed with unbelief and a sense of helplessness a year earlier (18:12-13). The long years of yearning and of bitter disappointment had crushed her hopes. In the later years of life it is all too possible to sink into despair because of heartache and disappointment. Here is Sarah at ninety years of age exclaiming, '*God has made me laugh*' (6). The meaning of Isaac is 'he laughs' and the elderly parents were given much joy.

Ishmael was now sixteen or seventeen years old and he showed his antagonism to Sarah and Isaac by scoffing at them. Sarah was angry and demanded of Abraham, '*Cast out this bondwoman and her son; for the son of this bondwoman shall not be heir with my son, namely with Isaac*' (10). The patriarch was displeased (Hebrew could be translated 'distressed') when he heard the words of Sarah. The Lord told Abraham not to let this distress him but to do as Sarah wished in the matter. The life of Isaac, the son of promise, was in danger as long as Ishmael was living with them. God said that he would make a great nation of Ishmael's descendants because he was of Abraham's seed (9-12). That nation became the Arab race.

Take now your son, your only son Isaac, whom you love

Abraham was truly outstanding in his faith and obedience when the Lord called on him to do the unimaginable — to sacrifice his beloved son, Isaac. *'Take now your son, your only son Isaac, whom you love'* (2). Abraham's anguish on that lonely three-day journey to Moriah must have been almost unbearable. He must have been sorely tempted to turn back in order to preserve his beloved son. **How did Abraham triumph in testing?**

- He trusted in God's wisdom believing that God knew what he was doing with him.
- He trusted in God's promises which can never fail (God had promised descendants through Isaac, 21:12).
- He trusted in God's power that, to fulfil his promise, he would raise Isaac from the dead (Hebrews 11:17-19). He was expecting to return with Isaac (5).

Isaac knew that they needed an animal to sacrifice to God and he asked where it was. His father replied that God would *provide for himself the lamb for a burnt offering* (7-8). After Abraham had built an altar for the sacrifice, he bound Isaac and was ready to kill him when the angel of the Lord intervened telling him not to harm Isaac (12). He then saw a ram which was *caught in a thicket by its horn*s. He offered up the ram *for a burnt offering instead of his son*. He named the place, 'Jehovah Jireh' which means, *'the-*LORD*-will-provide'* (or 'see' 13-14).

Scripture locates Mount Moriah at Jerusalem (2 Chronicles 3:1). There is even greater significance in those words, *'In the Mount of the* LORD *it shall be provided'* (or 'it shall be seen', 14). There is a hill in the mountains of Moriah called Calvary. It was there that God did not spare his only begotten Son, whom he loved. *He who did not spare his own Son, but delivered him up for us all, how shall he not with him also freely give us all things?* (Romans 8:32). **Christian! That is the measure of God's love for you.** God made the provision for our salvation in giving his Son to die on the cross.

As for me, being on the way, the LORD led me

After the death of Sarah Abraham was concerned that Isaac, now approaching forty, should find a wife from his own people (1-4). He did not want his son to be unequally yoked with a Canaanite. This vital principle still holds — we must not marry an unbeliever (2 Corinthians 6:14; cp. 1 Corinthians 7:39 — *'only in the Lord'*). Abraham entrusted his chief servant to find a wife for Isaac and solemnly charged him not to take a woman from among the Canaanites. He said, *'You shall go to my country and to my family, and take a wife for my son Isaac.'* The servant was fearful that any prospective bride would refuse to return with him, but Abraham was confident that God would send his angel ahead of him (2-8).

The servant went to the city of Nahor in Mesopotamia (Haran — 27:43; 29:4) and arriving at a well he did the essential thing: he prayed for God's success in his venture (12). He also asked for a token to confirm his choice of a bride for Isaac (14). Notice that he wasn't so much concerned to look for someone with outward beauty, but for someone with a thoughtful and kind character. God answered him before he finished praying (15). He watched in amazed silence as Rebekah, a beautiful young woman, showed herself to be the answer to his prayer (16-21). He was also surprised to discover that Rebekah was related to Abraham (24; cp. 11:27). God had wonderfully answered him and the man *bowed down his head and worshipped the LORD* (26).

Worship and prayerful dependence upon God are essential if we would prove him in our lives (12,27). Isaac was also involved in spiritual exercise when he first met Rebekah (63). The servant blessed God for his goodness and exclaimed, *'As for me, being on the way, the LORD led me to the house of my master's brethren'* (27). **Oh, the joy and happiness that God bestows on those who walk in the way of trust and obedience!** The servant's journey was successful because he had committed his way to the Lord (cp. Psalm 37:5). May we do likewise.

I shall seem to be a deceiver to him

Chapter 26 ends by reporting that Isaac and Rebekah were grieved because Esau had taken two Canaanite wives (26:34-35; 27:46; 28:8). When Isaac was old and blind he was determined to give his blessing to Esau, despite the disobedience of the elder twin. This blessing was important because the son receiving it ruled over his brothers (see verse 29). Isaac and Rebekah knew that God had decreed that Esau would serve Jacob (25:23) and this should have kept them from following their own opposing schemes. Isaac was wrong to go against the revealed will of God in his plan to bless Esau. When we disobey the word of God we invite trouble into our lives! We should always keep in mind the admonition, '*Trust in the LORD with all your heart, and lean not on your own understanding*' (Proverbs 3:5-6).

Rebekah overheard Isaac making his plans with Esau and she hastened to involve Jacob in a scheme of deception to obtain the blessing. Their behaviour was inexcusable and they should have waited on God and trusted in him to bring his purposes to pass. We must never use the ends to justify sinful means! Jacob had serious misgivings concerning his mother's scheme and was troubled at the possibility of his father's recognizing his deception. He said to his mother, '*Perhaps my father will feel me, and I shall seem to be a deceiver to him; and I shall bring a curse on myself and not a blessing*' (12).

Jacob was to pay dearly for his sin, being forced to leave the home he loved, and worse was to follow. God's word warns us: '*Do not be deceived, God is not mocked; for whatever a man sows, that he will also reap*' (Galatians 6:7). Jacob the deceiver was himself to become the victim of cruel deception — in marriage (29:25); in work (31:7,41); and by his own sons (37:20,31-35). **Let us be careful of the things we sow. If we resort to sinful scheming, we too will reap a bitter harvest.**

How awesome is this place!

Isaac readily agreed with Rebekah's wish to send Jacob away to find a wife from her own family and he blessed Jacob before sending him on his journey (1-5). Esau realized that his marriage to Canaanite women had upset his parents and heard his father instructing Jacob that he must not marry a Canaanite. He hoped that by marrying a daughter of Ishmael (who was descended from Abraham) he would please Isaac (8-9).

Jacob not only left home to find an acceptable wife (1-2,6-7) but also to escape Esau's wrath and revenge (27:42-43). The Lord appeared to him in a dream and repeated the covenant promises made to Abraham and to Isaac (14-15; cp. 22:17-18; 26:3-5). Jacob did not deserve such kindness from God, but the Lord is full of grace and he bestows on us favour which we do not deserve. Among our great privileges as Christians is the promise that God is with us and that he watches over us. *'Behold, I am with you and will keep you wherever you go'* (15).

True spiritual experience brings with it a reverent fear of the Lord.

Jacob exclaimed: *'How awesome is this place! This is none other than the house of God, and this is the gate of heaven!'* (17). Oh, that we reminded ourselves more often of this as we come to worship each Lord's Day. Do we feel that we are on the threshold of heaven when we come to the house of God? (cp. Hebrews 12:22-24,28-29).

Jacob made a vow that if the Lord would be with him to keep him and provide for him, then he would serve him and give him back a tenth of everything that God gave him (22). Should Christians tithe (give a tenth of their income) to God? If Jacob tithed as a token of his love to the Lord, dare we give less? (cp. Malachi 3:8-10). If we rob God of our tithes and offerings, we impoverish his work and deprive ourselves of the blessings that he so freely bestows on those who are bountiful. **Is the Lord waiting for you to prove him in this matter?** *God loves a cheerful giver* (2 Corinthians 9:7).

Into a pit

Seventeen-year-old Joseph helped the sons of Bilhah and Zilpah (Dan, Naphtali, Gad and Asher; 30:3-7,9-12) in their work as shepherds. He gossiped about them to his father and if they were aware of this, it would not have endeared him to them. Jacob loved Rachel more than Leah, and Joseph, son of Rachel, was his favourite son. This favouritism led to Joseph's brothers hating and resenting him (1-4). We shall be seeing that dreams, and a God-given ability to interpret them, played a very significant part in Joseph's life. He was immature enough to relate the two dreams concerning his future greatness to his hostile brothers. *They hated him even more* and Jacob rebuked him (5-10). *His brothers envied him, but his father kept the matter in mind* (11). Their nickname for Joseph, *'this dreamer'*, is an indication of the strong resentment of his brothers (19).

They plotted to kill Joseph when he arrived on an errand from his father. Reuben was the exception and he planned to deliver Joseph from the pit into which they had cast him (20-22). His plan was thwarted while he was away, when the others sold Joseph into slavery (28-30). Jacob had killed *two choice kids of the goats* to deceive Isaac (27:9) and now his own sons killed *a kid of the goats* to deceive him into believing that Joseph had been torn to pieces by a wild animal (31-33). Jacob was shattered with grief and God, whom he had seen face to face (32:30), was silent! **God had wise purposes for Jacob and for Joseph, and he was to bring much blessing out of this trial.**

Things seemed to go horribly wrong for Joseph. He was thrown *into a pit* (24) and then taken to Egypt as a slave. His comfortable, pampered world was swept away in an instant, but the Lord had planned it all to refine his character and to bring a great deliverance to his people (50:20). **God chastises us because he loves us and uses trials to produce spiritual fruit in our lives (Job 23:10; Hebrews 12:5-11).** When our circumstances do not seem to make sense, we need to encourage ourselves in the Lord and in his word (Jeremiah 29:11-13).

The LORD was with Joseph

Joseph maintained a great testimony, even in adversity. He was a slave and a prisoner but *the LORD was with Joseph*, and this could be seen by those who did not know God (2-3,21,23). God promises to be with every Christian (Hebrews 13:5). Having the presence of God does not spare us from temptation or suffering. **When God is with us, Satan is never far away.** The devil used Potiphar's wife in one attempt after another to seduce Joseph who refused to sin against his master and against God (9). Joseph behaved wisely and avoided the wicked woman as much as possible to escape temptation (10). When she took hold of him, he fled outside (12). Joseph's example teaches us never to linger with temptation. The outcome was most distressing for Joseph who was falsely accused of the very sin that he had so steadfastly avoided. He was thrown into prison, but God was with him and had a work for him to do there.

Pharaoh's chief butler and chief baker had offended him and the angry king imprisoned them. The captain of the guard (Potiphar?) ordered Joseph to serve them (40:1-4). The 'chance' meeting with these two men was to set in motion a train of events which were to see God raise Joseph to esteem and greatness. **God lovingly cares for us and watches over us (Isaiah 41:10); there are no 'chance' happenings in our lives.** Both men were troubled by dreams which they were unable to interpret. Joseph interpreted their dreams which prophesied a happy outcome within three days for the butler and a terrible end for the baker (40:5-19). The chief butler promised Joseph that he would seek justice for him but he forgot his promise and he forgot Joseph (23).

James Philip comments: 'The story of Joseph began with a man intent upon interpreting his own dreams, and preoccupied with his own interests, but now he is interpreting the dreams of others. Nothing could be more significant. He has been freed from the tyranny of self-centred living, and it is worth a dozen imprisonments and humiliations to know such an emancipation' (*Holyrood Bible Notes*).

31

A man in whom is the Spirit of God

The chief butler cannot be excused for his ingratitude and forgetfulness but God was in control of all these events and his timing is always perfect. The Lord prepared the way for Pharaoh to call on Joseph for help rather than for Joseph to need to seek favours from the king. Two years later, Pharaoh had two dreams which troubled him, and baffled his magicians and wise men (1-13). The chief butler then told the king about Joseph who had interpreted his dream and that of the chief baker after they had been sent to prison.

Pharaoh sent for Joseph to interpret his dreams. Joseph shaved and changed his clothing, putting off his prison garments. Joseph was not ashamed to own his Lord in a heathen palace. He gave God the glory for his ability to interpret the dreams (16,25,28,32). He told the king that the dreams had the same interpretation. God had given two dreams because he had established the events prophesied and would soon bring them to pass. Pharaoh recognized that Joseph was *a man in whom is the Spirit of God* (38). Pharaoh worshipped many gods but he was forced to acknowledge the true and living God (39).

Joseph had endured thirteen perplexing and difficult years. He was seventeen when sold into slavery (37:2) and thirty when elevated to power in Egypt (46). His father had given him a special tunic of many colours which his brothers had stripped from him (37:23). Pharaoh now clothed Joseph in fine linen and put a gold necklace around his neck (42). What an amazing change of circumstances in Joseph's life! He began the day as a prisoner and ended it as a powerful ruler, second only to Pharaoh. **Are you feeling impatient in some trial which appears to be unending? Do you feel forgotten? Men may forget you, but God never will. He will work out his purpose in your life.** The seven years of plenty came as Joseph had prophesied and he organized the storage of the huge surplus of grain. His authority in Egypt was consolidated when the years of famine came and he was in control of the sale and distribution of the grain (47-57).

All these things are against me

When Joseph's brothers arrived in Egypt to purchase grain, he recognized them but they did not recognize him. He would have been dressed as an Egyptian ruler and it had been more than twenty years since they had seen him. When he saw his brothers, he *remembered the dreams which he had dreamed about them* (9). They had hated him and taunted him about those dreams (37:8,20), but now he saw them fulfilled. God had given Joseph those dreams and he ordains all that will happen. His brothers were deeply troubled by his apparent hostility towards them and by his accusation that they were spies. They protested that they were honest men, which was hardly true when their past record is considered (9-12). They remembered their wicked deeds little realizing that Joseph understood their conversation because he spoke to them through an interpreter (21-23).

Joseph sent his brothers away with supplies to sustain them on their journey and he commanded that the money used to purchase the grain should be placed in their sacks. When one of them later opened his sack to feed his donkey, he was puzzled and afraid to find the bundle of money he had handed over to the Egyptians in the mouth of the sack (25-27). The troubled conscience of Joseph's brothers was again revealed by their reaction to this discovery. They were afraid, believing that this was a sign that God was punishing them for the way they had treated Joseph years earlier. They asked: '*What is this that God has done to us?*' (28).

Jacob was shocked to hear of the harsh Egyptian governor who was holding Simeon hostage. The demand that Benjamin be taken on the next trip to Egypt was too much for him to accept. He uttered in anguish: '*All these things are against me*' (36). The old man, wounded by bitter and bewildering experiences, had lost sight of the wisdom and goodness of God in his providence. '***All these things***' **were not against him, but for him, if only he had faith to see it.** We know Romans 8:28: *All things work together for good to those who love God* in our heads, but it needs to be impressed on our hearts.

It was not you who sent me here, but God

Though Joseph was overcome with emotion when he met Benjamin (43:30), he still concealed his identity from his brothers. He wanted further proof of their change of character. Before the brothers set out on their journey to Canaan he told the steward to put his silver cup into Benjamin's sack. Soon after their departure he sent his steward after them to accuse them of theft and of repaying his goodness with evil. They were horrified and humbled when Joseph's cup was discovered in Benjamin's sack (1-13).

Judah had a murky history; he had been the ringleader in selling Joseph into slavery (37:26-27) and he had been quite heartless in his attitude to Tamar (chapter 38). It was a chastened and humbled Judah who eloquently pleaded with Joseph, offering himself as a slave instead of Benjamin (33). Tribulation had developed godly character (Romans 5:3-4) in the life of Joseph and it did the same for Judah. He had been heartless and uncaring, but now he was different. He was a broken man, but a better man. Jacob was later to bless him with the words, *'Judah, you are he whom your brothers shall praise'* (49:8).

Joseph could not help but be deeply moved by the urgent, selfless plea from the 'new' Judah. The brothers were stunned into silence and dismay as a weeping Joseph revealed his identity and enquired after Jacob (45:3). Joseph freely forgave them, telling them that God had overruled all their evil deeds (5-9). He assured them, *'It was not you who sent me here, but God'* (8). God had planned it all. He had sent Joseph to Egypt and had made him lord of all the land (5,7-9). This did not lessen the guilt of his brothers but it must have helped Joseph forgive them. **It is a great source of comfort in bitter experiences to know that God is in control. He uses hostile acts against us to further his purposes.** The apostle Paul knew this when thrown into prison at Philippi (Acts 16:22-34). That foul dungeon rang with praise to God, and the jailer and his family were saved. May we learn to see God's hand in the darkest providence.

The sceptre shall not depart from Judah ... until Shiloh comes

Jacob and all his family migrated to Egypt (chapters 46 and 47). Just before he died, he called his twelve sons to him to bless them. He also prophesied concerning them and the tribes which were to descend from them. These prophecies were all fulfilled. Jacob also said something about their character. Reuben is described as being '*unstable as water*' (3-4). He had no depth of character and he did not excel. Scripture has no mention of a single ruler, prophet or judge who descended from him. **Christian, you must have stability in your life if you are to be kept from sin and error (Psalm 1).**

Jacob described Simeon and Levi as '*instruments of cruelty*' who were unable to control their fierce anger which he cursed (5-7). There is a righteous anger (Ephesians 4:26) reserved for a just cause, which must never be allowed to go out of control. **Let us seek to be instruments of kindness and never to be cruel in thought, word or deed.**

Jacob prophesied of the coming of the Messiah (Shiloh) through the line of Judah whose name means 'praise' (8-10). He said, '*The sceptre shall not depart from Judah ... until Shiloh comes; and to him shall be the obedience of the people.*' The sceptre is a symbol of kingly rule. The Lord Jesus is '*the Lion of the tribe of Judah*' (Revelation 5:5).

Dan, '*a serpent*' (16-17), was not to be trusted (his descendants were treacherous; see Judges 18).

Naphtali was a giver of '*beautiful words*' (21). We should follow his example. *Let your speech always be with grace* (Colossians 4:6).

Jacob reserved the longest blessing for Joseph (22-26). He had been hated by his brothers and grieved, but the Lord had strengthened him and had made him fruitful (cp. 41:52). Let us strive to develop a mature and godly character. We must be stable in our lives and gracious in our speech. **If we would be fruitful like Joseph, we must persevere and trust in the Lord when we are afflicted.**

You meant evil against me; but God meant it for good

When he was dying, Jacob made Joseph and his brothers promise to bury him in Canaan (49:29-33). Joseph rightly honoured this promise and there was an impressive funeral in Canaan after the mourning ritual (1-14).

Joseph's brothers were very fearful after their return to Egypt. They had not forgotten their wicked treatment of their young brother when he was a teenager. They expected him to avenge himself now that Jacob had died. They sent a message to Joseph in which they claimed that Jacob had left a plea that Joseph would forgive them. Joseph wept when he received this message. They could not accept that Joseph had really forgiven them for the evil they had done to him. He must have been hurt by their attitude, for he had already shown them his love and forgiveness (45:15-20).

Joseph was a great man. He told his brothers, '*You meant evil against me; but God meant it for good*' (20). God sovereignly works out his purposes and he cannot be thwarted (Isaiah 14:27). It is wonderful to know that the Lord even uses the malice of our enemies for our good. **When we remember that the Lord has good purposes in the evil done against us, it helps us to forgive those who have wronged us.** Joseph comforted his brothers with kind words (21). Joseph's experiences wonderfully illustrate the words of Scripture: *We know that all things work together for good to those who love God, to those who are the called according to his purpose* (Romans 8:28). **Let us worship and adore the almighty, all-wise God. Let us thank him for watching over us at all times, and for bringing good out of evil.**

Joseph lived until he was one hundred and ten years old. Before he died, he prophesied that God would surely visit the Israelites and bring them back to the promised land. He also charged the Israelites on oath that they should take his bones with them for burial in Canaan when they returned to the promised land (22-26; cp. Exodus 13:19).

MATTHEW and MARK

Matthew was one of the twelve apostles (10:3; Acts 1:13). He was a tax-collector before he followed Christ (9:9; cp. Mark 2:14 and Luke 5:29 where he is called Levi). He wrote his Gospel (good news) to convince his Jewish readers that the Lord Jesus was indeed the Messiah promised in the Old Testament. He refers to the fulfilment of over sixty Old Testament prophecies concerning Jesus (e.g. 27:35).

Matthew's Gospel is sometimes called 'The Gospel of the Kingdom' because of its frequent references to the kingdom of heaven. There are five great teaching passages which are followed by *when Jesus had ended these sayings*' or similar words (7:28; 11:1; 13:53; 19:1; 26:1). These passages are contained in chapters 5 to 7; 10; 13; 18; and 24 to 25. They are linked by action passages found in chapters 8 to 9; 11 to 12; 14 to 17; and 19 to 22.

The Gospel of Mark is the shortest of the four Gospels. The name of its author is not mentioned within its pages, but the early church fathers recognized Mark as the author (also called John Mark) His mother, Mary, lived in Jerusalem and the church sometimes met in her house (Acts 12:12). Mark was a cousin of Barnabas (Colossians 4:10). He accompanied Paul and Barnabas at the start of the first missionary journey, but he turned back (Acts 13:13; 15:37). He later became a worker whom Paul valued (Colossians 4:10-11; 2 Timothy 4:11; Philemon 24). Peter regarded him as his spiritual son (1 Peter 5:13) and was probably the main source of Mark's material for his Gospel. Papias (AD 70-130) wrote, 'Mark, having become the interpreter of Peter, wrote down accurately all that he remembered of the things said and done by the Lord, but not however, in order.'

Mark is concise, brisk and vivid in his style (notice how many times the word *immediately*' is used). Peter's words in the house of Cornelius provide a fitting summary of the contents of Mark's Gospel (Acts 10:37-43).

He will save his people from their sins

In Bible times betrothed couples did not live together as man and wife until after the wedding feast which was usually held several months after the betrothal. It was during this interval that Joseph discovered that Mary was pregnant. Can you imagine the shock and shame that Joseph must have felt? (19). His attitude changed when an angel told him in a dream that Mary had conceived by the Holy Spirit (20). Joseph exercised great faith and obedience to God in taking Mary into his home as commanded by the angel (24-25). Both Mary and himself would have to face the reproach of being branded as immoral (cp. John 8:41).

The angel told Joseph that Mary would bear a son, saying, '*You shall call his name JESUS, for he will save his people from their sins*' (21). The name '*Jesus*' is from the Greek '*Iesous*' which is taken from the Hebrew '*Jeshua*', meaning 'Jehovah is salvation'. The Lord Jesus is also called '*Immanuel — God with us*' (23). **He came to save poor sinners so that God would be with us and for us instead of being against us.** It is important that we understand that though the Lord Jesus is the '*Saviour of the world*' (i.e. Jew and Gentile; 1 John 4:14), not everyone will be saved. He came to save his people (described in the Bible as his '*elect*'; e.g. Romans 8:33). The Good Shepherd gave his life for his sheep (John 10:11,15).

The birth of the Lord Jesus was welcomed by the wise men, but not by King Herod, a power-crazed tyrant who ruthlessly ruled Palestine for forty years. Anyone who posed a threat to him was exterminated (2:16-18). The wise men were diligent in their search to find the Lord Jesus. God helped them by providing the star which ultimately led them to their destination. If you are not a Christian and if you are really eager to find the Lord, he will not send a star to guide you, but he will bring people into your life and order your circumstances so that you will be led to him. When they found him, *they ... fell down and worshipped him* (11). **Jesus is God and he is worthy of our worship.**

Let your light so shine before men

In the Sermon on the Mount (chapters 5 to 7) the Lord Jesus teaches us how Christians should live. The Beatitudes (verses 3 to 12) describe the blessedness of those who belong to God's kingdom. The only people who find true and lasting happiness are the godly (Psalm 1). **The Lord Jesus places the emphasis on 'being' rather than 'doing'.** Our attitude is all important! The Beatitudes do not stand in isolation from each other, but are inter-connected, e.g. If we are to *mourn* over sin, we must be *poor in spirit* (humble) and meek (gentle and submissive; see verses 38-42 for examples of meekness). Those who *mourn* over sin will surely *hunger and thirst for righteousness* and they will be satisfied (6). Are you *merciful* and *pure in heart* (7-8)? Do you seek to be a *peacemaker* (9)?

The '*righteousness*' of God's kingdom is very different from that of the scribes and the Pharisees whose '*righteousness*' was all outward show (20; cp. 23:5,27-28). Christian '*righteousness*' is heart '*righteousness*' according to the promise of Ezekiel 36:26-27. It is not our own but comes through faith in Christ (Philippians 3:9). Jesus shows that murder and adultery can be committed in the heart even though the outward act is missing (21-28). The sanctity of marriage is upheld in God's kingdom and we must always keep our word (33-37). Do we really love our enemies and pray for them (44)? If we love the Lord, we will want to be like him; we will aim for perfection though we know that we will never attain it until we reach heaven (48).

Read this chapter again slowly, thoughtfully and prayerfully. Examine your own heart and repent of any sin lurking there. Seek, with God's help, to live so that your light will shine in this dark world. Christians are '*children of light*' (Ephesians 5:8; 1 Thessalonians 5:5). **Your light is desperately needed in this dark world.** *Let your light so shine before men, that they may see your good works and glorify your Father in heaven* (16).

Do not worry

The Lord Jesus now shows how we should practise our righteousness. The problem with the Pharisees was that they wanted to be seen and praised by men when they gave to the poor (2-4), when they prayed (5-8) and when they fasted (16-18). Jesus teaches us how to pray in 'The Lord's Prayer' (9-13). True prayer involves worship, adoration, a desire for the glory of God, the increase and coming of his kingdom; it displays humble dependence on God and submission to his will.

Anxiety brings weariness and distress to many people and may make a child of God weak and prayerless. The words '*Do not worry*' are found three times in these verses (25,31,34). You may be free from the tyranny of seeking to heap up riches for yourself, but be over-anxious about providing for your basic needs. What is the answer to such worry? Jesus says, '*Your heavenly Father knows that you need all these things*' (32). Life is more than food, drink and clothes. Will not God who has given you a body provide for its needs? (25).

The unbeliever often shrugs his shoulders when perplexed and carelessly utters, 'God knows.' The Christian can rejoice that his heavenly Father really does know, and that he loves him and cares for him (1 Peter 5:7). God did not spare his beloved Son but gave him up to die a terrible death to meet our greatest need which is forgiveness of sin and peace with God (Romans 8:32). Do you really think that he will let us down? Worrying will not improve our circumstances (26,31) but will so distract us that we may turn our eyes away from our heavenly Father.

Are you beset by fears and care? Turn your care into prayer (Philippians 4:6-7,19). Trust your Father in heaven. He will never fail you. We are less likely to be burdened with worry if we are first and foremost concerned for our souls and the interests of God's kingdom. Look at the promise in verse 33: '*But seek first the kingdom of God and his righteousness, and all these things shall be added to you.*' **What are your priorities?**

Beware of false prophets

One of the most misunderstood verses in the Bible is *'Judge not, that you be not judged'* (1).We must beware of judging the faults of others while ignoring our own (2-5) but we must not turn a blind eye to wickedness. We are to use our judgment regarding those who continually reject the *'pearls'* of gospel truth (6) and those who are false teachers (15-23). The apostle Paul reminds the Corinthian church, *'He who is spiritual judges all things'* (1 Corinthians 2:15).

There are many voices and influences which seek to entice us to go on the broad way that leads to destruction (13). Many on that way are very religious but they are not true Christians. Satan wrecks many a promising life through the evil influence of false teachers. Jesus warns us: *'Beware of false prophets, who come to you in sheep's clothing, but inwardly they are ravenous wolves'* (15). How can we recognize false prophets and teachers? Jesus said, *'You will know them by their fruits'* (16). They teach error and they do not lead holy lives. The true servant of God is more concerned with the fruit of the Holy Spirit than with spectacular gifts — both in his own life and in the lives of those whom he teaches. It has been rightly said, 'The face of error is highly painted and powdered so as to render it attractive to the unwary.' Do not allow false teachers to deceive you. *'Beware of false prophets.'*

False teachers often claim to be able to work miracles. Our reading contains a solemn and terrifying warning. On the day of judgment *many* will claim that they have prophesied, cast out demons, and done many wonders in the name of the Lord Jesus, but they will be cast out of his presence. There are many false teachers and we observe that they often outnumber the genuine servants of God. These false teachers deceive themselves as well as deceiving others (21-23). The day of judgment will be a day of shocks! The most important thing for every Christian is to do the will of God (21). **Are you seeking to obey God's will as it is revealed in his word?**

Good ground

This chapter contains seven parables about the kingdom of God. After he had told the parable of the sower, the Lord Jesus told the twelve and a wider group of disciples the reason that he spoke in parables. We may think that he told these stories to make his message more clear to his hearers. This was not the case. It was to conceal the meaning of his message from them as a judgment from God (10-15). He explained the meaning of the parables to his disciples, not to the crowds (11,18,36).

We are only going to look at the parable of the sower, in which the crucial factor is not the seed but the ground into which the seed is sown. **The state of the ground determines the fate of the seed.** In this parable the seed is the word of God (19; cp. Mark 4:14). The preaching and teaching of God's word is most important in the work of the kingdom. If we neglect our private reading and meditation of God's word, or if we attend a church where the Bible is not faithfully taught, we will be weak and unstable in our Christian life. The word of God falls on different types of heart. The '*wayside*' hearer does not understand God's word and Satan snatches it away from his heart (4,19). The '*stony places*' hearer has a shallow heart. Though there is an appearance of new life in Christ, there is no depth and his profession of faith soon evaporates when trouble comes (5-6, 20-21). The '*thorns*' hearer has a worldly heart that chokes the word of God so that it becomes unfruitful (7,22). The '*good ground*' hearer (8,23) is '*he who hears the word and understands it, who indeed bears fruit*'.

What kind of ground does your heart provide for the word of God as you hear it taught week by week? Do you seek to understand it? Are you shallow or worldly? If you want to bear precious spiritual fruit in your life, you will make every effort to prepare yourself to hear God's word. To obtain the best from preaching, we must come to services fresh in body and in mind, with a prayerful and submissive heart. '*He who has ears to hear, let him hear!*' (9).

This is my beloved Son ... Hear him!

The transfiguration of Jesus was to make a lasting impression upon the three disciples who were with him. John wrote, '*We beheld his glory, the glory as of the only begotten of the Father, full of grace and truth*' (John 1:14). Peter records, '*We ... were eyewitnesses of his majesty*' (2 Peter 1:16-17). The Lord Jesus spoke to Moses and Elijah at his transfiguration. Luke tells us in his Gospel that they were speaking of the death of Jesus (Luke 9:31). Moses represented the Law, and Elijah the Prophets. The Lord Jesus has fulfilled the teaching of the Law and the Prophets (Luke 24:25-27). Moses had seen the majesty of God on Mount Sinai (Exodus 24:9-10), and later his face shone, reflecting the glory of God (Exodus 34:29-35). **The Lord Jesus did not merely reflect the glory of God — he is God!** The brilliance and the majesty seen by the three disciples was that of God himself.

The voice of God was heard coming from the cloud which overshadowed the Lord Jesus and the three disciples. '*This is my beloved Son, in whom I am well pleased. Hear him!*' (5). The disciples were filled with fear and fell on their faces. Jesus then came and touched them, telling them to get up and not be afraid. He told them not to tell anyone about what they had seen until he had risen from the dead (9). Jesus told them that just as John the Baptist who came '*in the spirit and power of Elijah*' (Luke 1:17) suffered, so he too would suffer (12, 22-23). They could not take it in that their beloved Master had to die and that he would rise from the dead. When he was betrayed and arrested, they were scattered in helpless confusion because they had not remembered what he had taught them (26:56).

Jesus came down from the mountain to find that the other disciples had failed to exorcise a demon from a boy. The distraught father of the boy pleaded with him to deliver his son from the demon (14-16) and Jesus graciously answered his prayer. The disciples were concerned at their failure to help the boy. Jesus told them that they were lacking in prayer, in fasting and in faith (20-21).

A *den of thieves*

Why did the Lord Jesus go into Jerusalem, riding on the young donkey?

- He was welcomed as the messianic King to fulfil Scripture. Matthew informs us that these events were foretold by the prophet, Zechariah (4-5; cp. Zechariah 9:9). The waving of the leafy branches from palm trees is associated with joy (Leviticus 23:40).
- Jesus went to Jerusalem to die. He warned his disciples on three separate occasions that he was going to Jerusalem to die (16:21; 17:22-23; 20:17-19). '*Hosanna*' (9) means 'save now'. The words of the crowd, '*Hosanna! Blessed is he who comes in the name of the* LORD!' are taken from Psalm 118. The same passage in the psalm also speaks of his rejection by the people and of a sacrifice being bound to the altar (Psalm 118:22-27).

The Jews had become so corrupt in their religion that the temple precincts were more like a market-place than a place of worship. Foreign money was not accepted in the temple, and temple tax (cp. 17:24-27; Exodus 30:13) had to be paid in Jewish coin. Moneychangers charged exorbitant rates and sacrificial animals were sold at very high prices. A place of religious worship had become a '*den of thieves*' (13). The Lord Jesus is merciful. His visit was traumatic for the thieves in the den but it was a great day for the blind and lame who were healed, and for the children who rejoiced and praised him (14-15).

Jesus cursed the fig tree because it should have had its early crop of small figs growing from the previous year's shoots, but he found none (18-19). The barren fig tree provides a solemn lesson. Israel, a 'fig tree' planted by God and cared for as no other nation, was barren and was ripe for judgment. **If our religion is all outward show, not bearing the fruit of love to God and obedience to his word, we must question its reality.** The promise of verse 22 is an encouragement to trust God when we pray, but it must be qualified by 1 John 5:14: '*according to his will*'.

Be ready

The disciples were admiring the beauty and the grandeur of the temple and were shocked to hear the Lord Jesus say that it would be destroyed (1-2). They left for the Mount of Olives, where they asked him two questions (3):

1. '*When will these things be?*' (i.e. the destruction of Jerusalem).
2. '*What will be the sign of your coming, and of the end of the age?*'

Some of the events leading to the destruction of Jerusalem and to the second coming of Christ are similar, and there is a certain amount of overlap in the verses of this chapter; some verses may refer to both events. In AD 66 the Jews revolted against the Romans who besieged Jerusalem, destroying the city and the temple in AD 70. More than a million Jews were slaughtered, many of the victims being women and children. Many Christians remembered the warning of Jesus (15-20) and left Jerusalem as the Romans approached, so escaping the massacre.

The conditions which preceded AD 70 are not a sign of the end of the world. They are to be found in any age. There have always been false teachers (5,11,23-24), wars, rumours of wars, earthquakes, famines (6-8), and persecution of God's people (9-10). **How are we to react to all that is happening and will happen?**

- We must be on our guard against deceivers. Jesus said, '*Take heed that no one deceives you*' (4).
- We are not to let fear and trouble overcome us (6). Remember, God is sovereign and he is in control of all these things.
- We are to beware of growing cold in our love for the Lord (12).
- We are to be encouraged because '*the gospel ... will be preached in all the world as a witness to all the nations*' (14).
- We are to be on our guard and ready for the Lord's return. He will come unexpectedly: '*Therefore you also be ready, for the Son of Man is coming at an hour when you do not expect*' (42-44). **If Jesus returned today, would you be ready?**

Faithful over a few things

This chapter continues to emphasize the need to be ready for the return of Christ. In the parable ten virgins were to carry the lamps but five were ill-prepared with insufficient oil for their lamps. While they were away buying oil, *the bridegroom came, and those who were ready went in with him to the wedding; and the door was shut* (10). When the foolish virgins returned with oil, it was too late. They went on to the feast, but it was in progress and they were shut out. They pleaded in vain, '*Lord, Lord, open to us!*' (11). All ten virgins appeared to be ready, but five were not. **We may appear to be Christians, but is our experience genuine? If we are careless about our spiritual state, we too will be shut out of heaven.** '*Watch therefore, for you know neither the day nor the hour in which the Son of Man is coming*' (13).

The parable of the ten virgins warns us to be vigilant and that of the talents stresses the need for diligence. Before he went away to a distant country, a man entrusted each of his servants with varying amounts, '*according to his own ability*' (15). Two of the servants '*were faithful over a few things*'. The third servant did not do anything with his talent except to hide it in the ground and his master punished him (21-30).

When the Lord Jesus returns, he will judge every one who has ever lived, from every nation (31-32; cp. Revelation 20:11-15). Many religious people will be shocked to find themselves shut out of heaven. They will be condemned because the vital evidence of true faith is missing from their lives (41-45). Good works are important. *Faith without works is dead* (James 2:14-26; cp. 1 John 3:17-19). **It is not only what we profess that counts but also what we practise.** The Lord Jesus warned many times of the wrath of God and of hell. He teaches here that those who are lost will be punished eternally for their sins in the everlasting fires of hell, '*prepared for the devil and his angels*' (41,46). **Are you a genuine, true Christian? Examine your own heart. You cannot afford to be mistaken. It is a matter of life or death, of heaven or hell.**

He took the cup

Religion can be a cloak for great wickedness. This can be seen in the case of the Jewish leaders (3-5,59-60) and in the case of Judas Iscariot (14-16,47-49). As Jesus celebrated the Passover meal with the twelve disciples, he warned them that one of them would betray him. He said, *'It would have been good for that man if he had not been born'* (21-25). Judas was on the slippery slope to hell! Peter sincerely believed that he would never deny his Lord and that he would die rather than do such a thing (31-35). He didn't know his own heart. **We must beware of a self-confidence that reckons without the need to lean on the Lord at all times (cp. 1 Corinthians 10:12).**

Jesus gave bread and wine to his disciples as a remembrance of his body and blood given for us at Calvary (26-29; 1 Corinthians 11:24-25). Jesus said of the wine that we take at the communion service, *'This is my blood of the new covenant, which is shed for many for the remission of sins'* (28). At this service we especially remember how our Saviour was tortured and slain to save us. Salvation is free, but we must never forget that it was purchased at tremendous cost.

The Lord Jesus *took the cup* and after giving thanks gave it to the disciples (27). That cup is for us *'the cup of blessing'* (1 Corinthians 10:16). Jesus, however, had to drink a 'cup' of terrible suffering and sorrow in order to save us. In Gethsemane he was overwhelmed with anguish as he contemplated this 'cup' which he had to drink. He said to Peter, James and John, *'My soul is exceedingly sorrowful, even to death'* (36-39). He was in such agony that his sweat became like great drops of blood falling down to the ground (Luke 22:44). His love for us is so great that he submitted to the Father's will to be punished for our sin. He said to God the Father, *'If it is possible, let this cup pass from me; nevertheless, not as I will, but as you will'* (39). He drank that terrible cup in order to give us a cup of blessing, a cup of salvation. **When we think of what it cost him to save us, we should shudder at the very thought of sinning.**

47

He saved others; himself he cannot save

We are not covering all of this important chapter in our notes, but do read the rest of it. Pilate marvelled greatly that Jesus did not seek to defend himself against the charges made against him (11-14). He knew that Jesus was innocent (18,24) and he sought to embarrass the Jews by offering to release either Barabbas, a murderer (15-17; cp. Luke 23:18-19), or Jesus. Pilate's plan failed and the crowd pressed for the release of the notorious criminal (20-23).

Ponder the suffering of our Lord Jesus. The scourge was a whip with several thongs into which were knotted small pieces of metal or bone. When a victim was lashed, his flesh was torn away. Jesus was then handed over to the soldiers who made fun of him, putting a mock royal robe of scarlet over his bleeding, lacerated body. The crown of thorns ripped into his brow and scalp, and they put a reed (a piece of wood) into his right hand as an imitation royal sceptre. They spat on him as they knelt in mock worship and beat him over the head with the reed. All this before he was led away to be crucified! He suffered so much that he was too weak to bear his cross (26-32).

Jesus was taunted by those around the cross and by the robbers on the other two crosses. The chief priests, scribes and elders mocked him, saying, *'He saved others; himself he cannot save'* (42). Those words had a far deeper significance than his enemies realized. He could have saved himself and come down from the cross, but he would not. He was *obedient to the point of death* (Philippians 2:8) to fulfil the Father's plan to save sinners (Acts 2:23). *By one Man's obedience many will be made righteous* (Romans 5:19). He plumbed the depths of suffering as he felt the utter desolation and loneliness of being forsaken by God the Father (46). The Roman centurion and his companions at the cross were convinced that Jesus was the Son of God as they saw him dying in agony (54). **Are you having problems with obedience to God? Meditate upon Christ's great love and obedience to save us. If you love him, surely you will want to obey him.**

Go quickly and tell his disciples that he is risen from the dead

There was an earthquake when Jesus rose from the dead. An angel of the Lord came and rolled back the stone which had sealed the tomb. Some faithful women wanted to anoint the body of Jesus but had waited until the Sabbath ended (the Jewish Sabbath runs from sunset on Friday to sunset on Saturday). They went to the tomb early on Sunday morning and were the first to discover that it was empty. They saw the angel and heard him announce that Jesus had risen from the dead. He said to them, *'Go quickly and tell his disciples that he is risen from the dead'* (1-7).

The women were then met by the risen Saviour and they worshipped him (9). Jesus repeated the message of the angels, *'Do not be afraid. Go and tell'* (10). Christ's resurrection declares him to be the Son of God with power (Romans 1:4). Death could not hold him (Acts 2:24). He triumphed over the grave and his resurrection is a guarantee that all who belong to him will be raised at his coming to have new bodies which will be immune to weakness, pain, ageing and suffering (John 14:19; 1 Corinthians 15:20-28; Philippians 3:20-21; 1 John 3:1-3). The chief priests knew that the terrified guards were not lying about the resurrection, but they bribed them to say that the disciples had stolen the body of Jesus (11-15).

The Lord Jesus had instructed the disciples to go to Galilee where they would see him (10,16). They later returned to Bethany in Judea where they saw him ascend to heaven (Luke 24:50-53).

The Father has given all authority to the Lord Jesus (18). We are to *'make disciples of all the nations, baptizing them in the name of the Father and of the Son and of the Holy Spirit'* (19). Disciples obey God's word and submit to its teaching. How do you do as a disciple? **We have a wonderful message and an almighty Saviour.** He is with us and always will be with us. Let us persevere in our God-given task of reaching men, women, boys and girls with the gospel of Christ.

I will make you become fishers of men

Mark does not tell us anything about the birth of Jesus but begins his Gospel with the ministry of John the Baptist. John was the messenger sent to prepare the way for Christ as foretold by the prophets, Isaiah and Malachi (2-3). He preached about someone mightier than himself who would come after him. He would baptize with the Holy Spirit (7-8).

Mark deals very briefly with the baptism and temptation of Jesus (see Matthew 3:13 to 4:11 for a more detailed account). John baptized those who had repented of their sin (4). **Why then did the Lord Jesus submit to baptism when he is sinless and has no need to repent?** In taking human flesh, he identified himself with sinful mankind. Our sin was laid upon him (Isaiah 53:6; 2 Corinthians 5:21). The Lord Jesus also spoke of a baptism which was a cup of suffering that he had to endure (10:38; Luke 12:50). His baptism not only symbolized his identification with us but also his suffering and death to take away our sin. God the Father said at the baptism of Jesus, *'You are my beloved Son, in whom I am well pleased'* (11). The Father loves the Son (John 3:35) and accepts him as the perfect substitute to die for sinners so that, as Christians, we are accepted in the Beloved (Ephesians 1:6).

Following his baptism the Lord Jesus was driven by the Holy Spirit into the wilderness, where he was tempted by Satan for forty days. Though weak in body through lack of food, he did not yield to the enticements of the devil (12-13). Herod cut short John's ministry by putting him in prison, but the ministry of Jesus began to flourish (14-15,28).

Jesus called on Simon Peter, Andrew, James and John to leave their fishing business to devote all their time to serve him. He promised them, *'Follow me, and I will make you become fishers of men'* (17). We may feel inadequate in our attempts to witness to others, but let us take heart from this statement. If we commit ourselves into his loving hands, he will mould us and fit us for his service, enabling us to become fishers of men.

Herod feared John ... and heard him gladly

This is a chapter of miracles with accounts of the feeding of the five thousand (30-44), the stilling of the storm after Jesus had walked on a rough sea (45-52) and of many healings (53-56). The people of Nazareth were astonished at the wisdom of Jesus. They had heard of his mighty works but did not understand how someone from a humble family could have such wisdom and power (1-2). They did not follow him however, but *were offended at him* (3; i.e. 'they were caused to stumble because of him') and Jesus did no mighty work among them, except a few healings (5).

The fame of Jesus reached Herod Antipas (a son of Herod the Great, the tyrant who had sought to kill the infant Jesus). Antipas ruled over Galilee and Perea and was living in adultery with Herodias, wife of his brother, Philip. John the Baptist had fearlessly denounced Antipas for his sin and the enraged king had him thrown into the dungeon at his palace. The evil, scheming Herodias wanted to kill John but was thwarted because Herod respected John. He also feared the reaction of the people who recognized John as a prophet (19-20; Matthew 14:5). Herod also *feared John ... and when he heard him, he did many things, and heard him gladly* (20). He did many things (better translated, *'was greatly perplexed'*) but he did not repent of his sin. Herodias later had her revenge when Herod made a rash promise to her daughter. John was executed *and the king was exceedingly sorry* (26), but he did not have a godly sorrow which produces repentance (cp. 2 Corinthians 7:10).

Many people thought that Jesus was the prophet Elijah or the promised prophet (15; cp. Deuteronomy 18:15-19). When Herod heard about Jesus, he thought that John had risen from the dead (14-16). **He had silenced John but he could not silence his own conscience.** He wanted to speak to Jesus, but when the opportunity came, the Lord had nothing to say to him (Luke 23:8-9). He had squandered his opportunities to repent. **It is not enough to be sorry for our sin; we must forsake it and obey God.**

Whoever desires to come after me, let him deny himself

The Lord Jesus had compassion on the hungry crowds who had been with him for three days (1-3). The disciples had not learned from the feeding of the five thousand (6:30-44) and they thought it impossible to feed the multitude with the seven loaves that they had. Jesus fed them all and there were *seven large baskets of leftover fragments.*

The disciples were puzzled by the warning of Jesus, *'Beware of the leaven* (yeast) *of the Pharisees and the leaven of Herod'* (15). He was warning them against their doctrine and against hypocrisy (Matthew 16:12; Luke 12:1). The hypocritical Pharisees were more concerned for their unbiblical tradition than for loving God and obeying his word. The Herodians were a political party who supported Herod and their leaven was worldliness. We must not allow our thinking or behaviour to be shaped by the world (Romans 12:2).

Why did the Lord Jesus lead the blind man out of Bethsaida before healing him? Why did he instruct him not to tell any in that town of his healing (22-26)? Perhaps that city which had seen so many mighty works had become so hardened in unbelief that no further testimony would be given to it (cp. Matthew 11:20-21).

Peter's great confession (27-30) that Jesus is the Christ (Messiah) was followed by a stern rebuke from the Lord. Peter wanted to turn Jesus from his mission of suffering and death; such thoughts came from Satan (31-33). The Lord Jesus said, *'Whoever desires to come after me, let him deny himself, and take up his cross'* (34). **Self-denial means total submission to the lordship of Christ. If he is not lord of all, he is not lord at all.** Self-denial does not bring misery, but great liberty and joy in following our blessed Saviour who gave his life to save us! Discipleship is costly but the alternative is too dreadful to contemplate. *For what will it profit a man if he gains the whole world, and loses his own soul? Or what will a man give in exchange for his soul?* (36-37). **The world and its pleasures will pass away but to lose one's soul is to suffer eternal loss.**

EXODUS

'The book of Exodus is the book of redemption. The Greek name "Exodus" [lit. "going out"] here describes how God brought the children of Israel out of bondage in Egypt. By redemption we understand that the Redeemer not only delivers his people out of bondage but also brings them into a special relationship with himself, making them his own purchased possession, his "peculiar treasure" (19:5)' (*New Bible Commentary*, 1958, page 106).

The Old Testament Scriptures testify of Christ (John 5:39; cp. Luke 24:27). In the book of Exodus Christ is foreshadowed as our passover Lamb (12:5,21-27; cp. 1 Corinthians 5:7; 1 Peter 1:18-19). The blood of the covenant (24:8) foreshadows the blood of the Lord Jesus in the new covenant (cp. Matthew 26:28). The worship and sacrifices of the tabernacle were a shadow of the good things to come (Hebrews 10:1).

The Israelites were in Egypt for 430 years, from the time of Jacob's emigration (Genesis chapter 46) until they left after the first Passover (12:40). Moses lived for 120 years (Deuteronomy 34:7). The first forty years of his life were spent as a prince in Egypt; the second forty as a fugitive in the land of Midian. He was eighty years of age when he led the people of Israel out of Egypt (7:7; cp. Acts 7:23,30,36). The birth of Moses was therefore some 350 years after Jacob, his sons and their families moved to Egypt.

Outline of Exodus

1. The Exodus from Egypt — the power of God (chapters 1 to 18);
2. The Law — the precepts of God (chapters 19 to 24);
3. The Tabernacle — the presence of God (chapters 25 to 40) .

But the midwives feared God

The population of the Hebrews who went to Egypt during the famine greatly increased in the years following the death of Joseph. They prospered and the Egyptians began to felt threatened by their presence (7-10; cp. Genesis 46:8-27). The new king over Egypt was possibly the first of a new dynasty of Pharaohs. He may have vaguely heard of Joseph but he felt no sense of gratitude to the Hebrews for saving their nation from famine some centuries earlier (see introduction to Exodus). Pharaoh was determined to halt the population explosion among the Israelites so he enslaved them and forced them to toil on his building projects (9-11).

The Egyptians made the lives of the Israelites *bitter with hard bondage* (14), but the more they afflicted them the more the Israelites increased in number (12). Pharaoh then ordered the Hebrew midwives to kill every male child at birth (16). By doing this, he knew that the Hebrew race would die out as the remaining women would be absorbed by marriage into Egyptian families. *But the midwives feared God* (17). That 'but' changed everything, and the tyrant's cruel plans were frustrated. The Lord honoured those brave women who feared him more than the king of Egypt (20-21). They had saved families and God rewarded them with families of their own.

The answer to the fear of man is to have a healthy fear of God (Psalm 34:9; Proverbs 29:25). Such godly fear produces boldness and an obedience to God's word that is undaunted by the threats of men (cp. Acts 5:28-29). We must have that same fear of God if we are to know blessing and usefulness in our Christian lives (Hebrews 12:28-29).

Pharaoh was determined to destroy the Hebrews and he ordered his own people to massacre the male babies born to the Israelite women (22). Let us remember that the promised Saviour was to come through the Hebrews and Satan was determined to destroy them. The devil was behind the persecution of the Israelites, but he cannot thwart the purposes of almighty God.

God heard ... God remembered

Moses' parents, like the midwives, were fearless in the face of the command of wicked Pharaoh and God richly rewarded their faith (cp. Hebrews 11:23). When they could no longer hide their baby at home, his mother hid him inside an ark of bulrushes among the reeds by the bank of the River Nile (3). Pharaoh's daughter found the baby and though he was a Hebrew, *she had compassion on him* (6). God arranged that Moses be brought up in the palace of Pharaoh, with the tyrant's daughter paying Moses' mother to nurse her own son (9). Moses was later given the finest education in Egypt and prepared for leadership — all at Pharaoh's expense. Our sovereign God laughs at the puny efforts of the wicked in their opposition to him (Psalm 2:4).

There is a daring element in God's sovereignty. The Lord, having preserved Moses from death, kept him from all the evil influences of the court of Pharaoh when he was taken there (10). We must not overlook the influence of a godly mother upon Moses in his early years. What a challenge and an encouragement this is to Christian parents. **We must never underestimate the influence of a godly home as we seek to train our children in a hostile, godless world.** *Train up a child in the way he should go, and when he is old he will not depart from it* (Proverbs 22:6).

Moses made himself aware of the wretched condition of his own people and was not indifferent to the cruel actions of an Egyptian whom he saw beating a Hebrew. He killed the Egyptian and was obliged to flee for his life. He went to the land of Midian where he met his wife and worked for his father-in-law as a shepherd (12-22). Forty years were to pass before he led Israel out of Egypt. The bitter suffering of the Israelites continued year after year, but God had not forgotten his people, nor his promises. *So God heard their groaning, and God remembered his covenant* (24). Although God's activity was not obvious to human eyes, he was working all the time, overruling the wickedness of Pharaoh, and preparing a deliverer (Moses) to bring his people out of their bondage.

Holy ground

'The Angel of the LORD' is more than an angel — he is God. He is identified with God in today's reading (2,4). Many Bible commentators believe that *'the Angel of the LORD'* describes the Lord Jesus appearing to men before he came to earth at Bethlehem. At Mount Horeb (also called Mount Sinai), Moses was attracted by the strange phenomenon of a burning bush which was not consumed by the fire. The Bible describes God as *a consuming fire* (Hebrews 12:29). Fire is a symbol of his blazing purity and of his glorious holiness. God told Moses that he was standing on *'holy ground'* (5). In such a place, he was overwhelmed with awe and fear (5-6). **A sense of the majesty and awesomeness of God is often missing from our worship.** A. W. Tozer describes worship as 'a humbling but delightful sense of admiring awe and astonished wonder and overpowering love' (*Worship — the missing jewel of the evangelical church*).

The Lord assured Moses that he had seen the oppression of his people and that he had heard their cry. He promised that he would deliver them from the Egyptians and bring them into a good fertile land, rich in pasture. Though God told him that he was to lead the people out of Egypt, Moses felt very much his own inadequacy (7-11). The Lord did not give him a crash course to improve his self-esteem. What Moses needed was a greater esteem of God!

Do you feel inadequate to serve God? You are quite correct. You are inadequate. You cannot do anything without his grace and strength to help you (cp. John 15:5). You must learn to depend on him at all times, and learn more of our great God and of his faithfulness. This was the lesson that Moses had to learn. When he asked God his name (13), he was requesting that God would reveal to him something of his character. *'I AM WHO I AM'* (14) reveals God as the 'be'-ing One, the God who is sovereign in all his purposes and power; the God who can be relied upon to do exactly as he promises. Moses and the Israelites were soon to prove the great faithfulness and power of their covenant God.

Please send by the hand of whomever else you may send

Moses, despite his privileged upbringing, was painfully aware of the greatness of the task to which God was calling him (3:11). He was unbelieving and reluctant, wanting God to send someone else (13). Look at his excuses:

- *'But suppose they will not believe me or listen to my voice; suppose they say, "The LORD has not appeared to you"'* (1). God had already told him that the people would heed his voice (3:18). Moses dared to contradict God, such is the evil of an unbelieving heart. The Lord equipped him with the ability to perform certain miracles, so that the people would believe him (2-9).
- *'I am not eloquent ... I am slow of speech and slow of tongue'* (10). God promised Moses that he would take care of this problem (11-12), but he still asked God to send someone else: *'O my Lord, please send by the hand of whomever else you may send'* (13). Is it any wonder that the Lord was angry with him? (14).

Is God calling you to serve him at home or abroad? Can you be content to leave all the work in the church to 'the faithful few'? If you really love the Lord, your love will be seen in willing, joyful and sacrificial service for him. **Do not make excuses or suggest that God send someone else.** He wants you and who he calls, he equips.

The call of God did not mean that Moses could disregard his family responsibilities. Moses sought Jethro's blessing for his return to Egypt and it was given (18). The Lord assured Moses that his enemies in Egypt were dead but warned him that he would harden Pharaoh's heart. The king of Egypt would not let the people go despite the wonders that he would see Moses perform (20-21). Moses was to give Pharaoh a stern warning — if he refused to release Israel, God's *son,* God's *first-born,* then God would kill his first-born son (22-23).

Moses' earlier fears were unfounded. *The people believed; and when they heard that the LORD had visited the children of Israel ... then they bowed their heads and worshipped* (31).

Why is it you have sent me?

The trial of strength between Moses and Pharaoh was more than a battle between two men. It was a conflict between God and Satan, between light and darkness. As Moses acted in obedience to God, the dark powers of Satan and the forces of hell were ranged against him. Pharaoh dismissed the request of Moses and Aaron with arrogant defiance: *'Who is the LORD, that I should obey his voice to let Israel go? I do not know the LORD'* (2). The proud tyrant was soon to discover the greatness of our sovereign God. He was soon to find that there is nothing 'false' about God's word (9; cp. 7:5).

The pathway of obedience to God is rarely smooth. Satan sees to that. Pharaoh accused the Israelites of laziness and made impossible demands upon them. He was obviously determined to teach Moses and Aaron a lesson. He summoned his taskmasters and the Hebrew officers (or foremen) the very same day. He commanded that they were not only to produce the same quota of bricks, but also to gather the straw which was necessary to bind together the mud used in their manufacture. When the quotas were not met, the officers were beaten. They went to Pharaoh to beg an easing of the burden, but he refused to change his conditions and dismissed them. They left the palace and turned on Moses and Aaron, blaming them for the trouble that had befallen them (6-19). Moses now had his own people against him as well as Pharaoh (19-21). He did the right thing, the thing the foremen had failed to do — he went to God in prayer (22-23). Do you first pray to the Lord when you are in trouble, before you complain to others?

Many a servant of God has asked: *'Why is it you have sent me?'* (22). **Satan knew the answer and was doing all in his power to keep Moses from pursuing the path of obedience to God.** Moses' faith was to be sorely tried in his leadership of God's people. We must never be surprised at seeming setbacks as we seek to serve God. He will bring us through and we will be all the stronger in faith and in our knowledge of him (1 Peter 1:6-7; 4:12-14).

Now you shall see what I will do

This chapter contains a genealogy of the Levites (verses 14-27) but we will restrict our comments to the narrative in the other verses. God graciously reassured his discouraged servant with precious promises, reminding Moses of his covenant commitment to Israel (3-5). He said, *'Now you shall see what I will do to Pharaoh'* (1). The One making these promises was the LORD. God repeated to Moses, *'I am the LORD'* (2,6,7,8). The wicked Pharaoh was daring to fight the Lord. God reinforced his promise to Moses seven times with the words *'I will'* (6-8). **There is no hint of possible failure in the promises of God. They are certain and reliable:** *'I am the LORD ... I will ... I will.'* Never forget that even the most hopeless circumstances make no difference whatever to the promises of God. God promised Moses that he would take the Israelites to himself for a people and that he would be their God (7). Matthew Henry comments: 'More than this we need not ask, we cannot have, to make us happy.'

The people of Israel, broken in spirit and weary from toil, would not listen to Moses (9). The Lord told him to go to Pharaoh with the same message as before, but Moses was still full of apprehension and doubt. If the enslaved Israelites would not listen to him why should the Egyptian king? (11-13,28-30). There was to be no change in the method or the message because of setbacks. There is a vital lesson for us here, for we live in times when many crave quick results in God's work. We must not abandon the preaching of God's word or the unremitting toil of faithful service because we lack success. **We need grace from God to persevere. We will then see what he will be pleased to do.**

Therefore, my beloved brethren, be steadfast, immovable, always abounding in the work of the Lord, knowing that your labour is not in vain in the Lord (1 Corinthians 15:58).

I will harden Pharaoh's heart

Moses was not convinced that Pharaoh would listen to him (6:30). The Lord then told him that he had made him *'as God'* to Pharaoh, with Aaron as his prophet (7:1). There was a contest to be fought with Moses representing God and Pharaoh representing Satan. The Egyptian king would refuse to heed Moses but in God's time he would have to release the Israelites. The Egyptians would have to acknowledge the Lord (3-5). Moses and Aaron were old men, but age did not keep them from obedience to God (6-7).

What are we to make of the statement, *'I will harden Pharaoh's heart'*? (3). The book of Exodus demonstrates the truth of God's absolute sovereignty again and again, and this can be seen in the hardening of Pharaoh's heart (3; cp. 4:21; 9:12; 10:1,20,27; 11:10; 14:4,8). God sovereignly controls kings (Deuteronomy 2:30; Proverbs 21:1) and nations (Joshua 11:19-20; Psalm 105:25). Why did God harden Pharaoh's heart? The answer is found in Exodus 9:16 and Romans 9:17-18. God did so for his own glory, to make known his power and his name (i.e. his character) in overthrowing the tyrant. It is important to notice that Pharaoh was not an unwilling puppet in the hands of God. Though God hardened his heart, we also read that Pharaoh hardened his own heart (8:15,32; 9:34-35).

The power of Satan lies behind all false religion (cp. Leviticus 17:7; Deuteronomy 32:17). Egyptian religion was not lacking in miracles. The sorcerers and magicians were able to imitate the first three miracles that God worked through Moses and Aaron. They turned their rods into serpents (11-12), turned water into blood (20-22) and brought on a plague of frogs (8:6-7). **We must always remember, however, that Satan is limited in what he is able to do.** The Egyptian magicians were confronted by a far greater power. They were unable to turn their serpents back into rods, or blood back into water, or to get rid of the frogs. They were unable to imitate any of the remaining plagues or to reverse them. They acknowledged: *'This is the finger of God'* (8:19).

There is no one like the LORD our God

The Egyptian gods were connected with the forces of nature. They had a Nile god, and frogs were the symbol of Hekhet, a goddess of fertility. These plagues were a judgment upon the gods of Egypt (cp. 12:12). The River Nile became so polluted in the first plague that the Egyptians loathed its water (7:18). When Pharaoh refused to allow the Israelites to go, he was warned that his land would be plagued by frogs. The frogs invaded every part of the Egyptians' homes, getting into their food and into their beds (1-4).

Pharaoh was driven to send for Moses and Aaron to ask them to pray that God would remove the frogs. He also promised that he would *let the people go, that they might sacrifice to the LORD* (8). Moses wanted the king to know that the removal of the frogs would be no coincidence, but an answer to prayer. He gave Pharaoh the option of saying just when the frogs should be removed (9). Pharaoh had defiantly said, *'Who is the LORD, that I should obey his voice?'* (5:2). He was now finding out *'that there is no one like the LORD our God'* (10).

The magicians knew that they were beaten when they failed to produce lice with their enchantments. They acknowledged *'the finger of God'* in the plagues, but Pharaoh would not admit defeat (17-19). He would have needed his early morning dip in the Nile to give him some relief from the lice (20). God then plagued Egypt with flies (20-24) and Pharaoh promised to allow the Israelites to go to sacrifice to God. He went back on his promises after Moses prayed for the removal of the flies (31-32). He wanted to be rid of the plagues which were causing so much physical discomfort, but he was not willing to see the plague of his own sinful rebellion removed and he hardened his heart (32).

'There is no one like the LORD our God.' **Think about the great power, the unsearchable wisdom and the majestic holiness of God. Worship him with adoration and with joy and encourage yourself in the face of trials and difficulties.** *Happy are the people whose God is the LORD!* (Psalm 144:15).

I know that you will not yet fear the Lord God

If Pharaoh had entertained any lingering doubts about the supremacy of Jehovah (*'the Lord God'*) over his gods, they were quickly dispelled with the next three plagues. Moses told him, *'The Lord will make a difference between the livestock of Israel and the livestock of Egypt'* (4). God sent a plague upon the livestock of the Egyptians which killed many of the animals. Pharaoh sent to Goshen (where the Hebrews lived) and found that the livestock of Israel had been completely protected from the plague which had devastated the Egyptian livestock (7). Goshen had also been free of the previous plague (8:22).

There is a grim humour in the judgment of God as he vindicates his people. Pharaoh saw the humiliation of his magicians, when the next plague (of boils) so affected them that they were unable to stand before Moses (11). The Egyptian king, himself suffering from boils, was able to see and experience the difference that the Lord had made between the Egyptians and the Hebrews.

Moses warned Pharaoh that the next plague of very heavy hail would be more severe than anything ever seen in Egypt. He told the king the precise time of the plague — *'tomorrow about this time'*. God would destroy what was left of the Egyptian livestock unless the animals were taken indoors for protection. The word of God spoken through Moses was now inspiring fear among some of the Egyptians and those of them who believed God's word spoken by Moses took the appropriate action and thus their animals were spared (18-20). The foolish ones disregarded God's word and suffered the consequences (21-25). There was no hail in Goshen, where the Hebrews lived (26).

Pharaoh seemed to repent when he acknowledged his sin and the righteousness of God (27) but he grew more defiant in his sin (34). Moses was not deceived by his fine sounding words and he declared: *'I know that you will not yet fear the Lord God'* (30). Those who defy God forget that he knows our hearts and our thoughts (Hebrews 4:12-13).

I will never see your face again

Moses and Aaron had asked Pharaoh to let the Israelites go three days' journey into the desert to sacrifice to God (5:1-3). The king had refused this request until after the fourth plague when he suggested that they should remain in Egypt to sacrifice. Moses refused to accept this compromise. Pharaoh then said that they could go, but not very far away (8:25-28); he then went back on his promises (8:32; 9:28,35).

When Moses warned him of the plague of locusts, Pharaoh suggested another compromise — that only the men of Israel go on the three-day journey to sacrifice (8-11). After the ninth plague (of darkness), Pharaoh gave permission for the Israelites to go, but on condition that they left behind all their livestock (24). Moses refused this compromise and demanded that Pharaoh should also provide the sacrifices and burnt offerings (25). The Egyptian, angry and irritated, told Moses that he never wanted to see his face again (28-29). Moses retorted: '*I will never see your face again*' (29). **The Egyptian king had despised many God-given opportunities to repent, and this, his last chance, was also wasted.**

John Currid takes the view that God spoke to Moses during his audience with Pharaoh (11:1-3), writing that the Hebrew appears to indicate that this was the case (*Exodus*, Evangelical Press Study Commentary, volume 1, page 231). Moses warned Pharaoh of the last plague, before leaving him *in great anger* (11:8). The promise given to Moses at the burning bush (3:21-22) was about to be fulfilled, as *the* LORD *gave the people favour in the sight of the Egyptians* (11:2-3; 12:35-36). **God's sovereignty is truly wonderful!** He so worked in the hearts of the Egyptians, that they freely gave their gold and silver to the Israelites. Pharaoh's daughter had paid for Moses' princely upbringing (2:9), and now the Egyptians were to sponsor the Israelites' journey into freedom. Moreover, Moses, the leader of a despised and cruelly treated people, became very great in the land and was respected by Pharaoh's servants and subjects (11:3).

When I see the blood, I will pass over you

The first Passover feast was to be for the Israelites, the beginning of months (2) when God brought them out of bondage (13:3). A lamb without blemish was killed for each household, and its blood sprinkled on the lintels and door posts of the house (7). The lamb was to be roasted in fire and then eaten in haste with unleavened bread and bitter herbs. The people were to be prepared for a quick departure from Egypt (8-12). The sprinkled blood was to protect Israel's first-born against the judgment of the Lord. God said, '*When I see the blood, I will pass over you*' (13).

At a Passover feast almost 2000 years ago the Son of God was crucified at Calvary. We read in the New Testament that Christ our Passover was sacrificed for us (1 Corinthians 5:7). He is the Lamb of God, without blemish and without spot (John 1:29; 1 Peter 1:19). **Just as a lamb was a substitute for the first-born of each Hebrew household, so the Lord Jesus died as a substitute for sinners (Isaiah 53:4-6; 1 Peter 3:18).** We have redemption through the blood of Christ, *the forgiveness of sins, according to the riches of his grace* (Ephesians 1:7).

The judgment of God upon the Egyptians was so great that there was a death in every household (29-30). Pharaoh had refused to pay attention to the warning of the Passover judgment (11:4-8). The consequences for him and his people were terrible. The distraught Egyptians had had enough and wanted the Israelites to leave their land immediately, even though it was not yet daybreak (31-33).

God keeps his promises as well as his threats. He gave the Hebrews favour in the eyes of the Egyptians exactly as he had promised (35-36; cp. 3:21-22). They left Egypt with great wealth. Justice was done, for the Egyptians had oppressed and exploited them for many years. The Lord also kept his promise to bring his people out of Egypt *with great judgments* (6:6; 7:4).

The LORD went before them

The Lord commanded Moses that the first-born of man and animal must be set apart to him (*'sanctified'*; 1-2; 11-16). The Feast of Unleavened Bread was to be kept by the Israelites each year (3-9) and the practice of sacrificing a lamb to redeem the first-born was also to continue (13-15). The first-born had escaped divine judgment because a lamb had died in his place. God said of the first-born, *'It is mine'* (2). Christian, you are not your own, for *you were bought at a price* (1 Corinthians 6:19-20). We have been redeemed by the precious blood of Christ (1 Peter 1:18-19) and we are to live for him (Romans 12:1-2; 2 Corinthians 5:15).

The importance of instructing our children is again emphasized. Moses said to the people, *'And you shall tell your son in that day, saying, "This is done because of what the LORD did for me when I came up from Egypt"'* (8,14; cp. Deuteronomy 4:9-10; 6:6-7). All parents have a God-given responsibility to instruct their children. The instruction of Timothy as a child bore much fruit (2 Timothy 1:5; 3:15). Both parents must be involved in teaching their children about the Lord (cp. Proverbs 1:8). Timothy was instructed by his mother and grandmother, but it appears that his father was not a Christian (cp. Acts 16:1).

The Lord graciously provided a pillar of cloud and of fire for the Israelites. It was a token of:

- God's leading (21). The Lord knew all about their weaknesses. The Philistines were a fierce, warring nation, and God did not want his people so discouraged that they would want to return to Egypt (17).

- God's presence with them day and night. *The LORD went before them* (21). They were protected by his presence, the cloud sheltering them by day (Psalm 105:39), coming between them and their enemies (14:19-20). **It is a tremendous source of comfort and encouragement to know that God is with us** (cp. 33:14; Joshua 1:5,9; Hebrews 13:5-6). We have no cloud today, but God leads us by the Holy Spirit (Romans 8:14). The Lord goes ahead of us, we have no need to fear.

Stand still, and see the salvation of the Lord

Hardened hearts are not receptive to the warnings which God graciously gives to them and Pharaoh led his army in hot pursuit of the Israelites (3,8-9). Humanly speaking the Hebrews were in an impossible situation. The Red Sea lay ahead of them, the Egyptian army was behind them; there were rocky crags to the one side and to the other Egyptian fortresses. They were well and truly hemmed in. They panicked and cried out in bitter complaint against the Lord and against Moses (10-12). How soon they had forgotten the great displays of God's almighty power. When faith gives way to fear, we turn our eyes away from the Lord; we then look at our troubles and problems as if God doesn't care for us, or as if he does not exist.

Moses remained calm in the crisis and encouraged the people, *'Do not be afraid. Stand still, and see the salvation of the* Lord*'* (13). **The Red Sea, which they saw as the great obstacle to any hope of escape, was God's instrument to destroy the pursuing Egyptians.** Are you facing problems or difficulties that would appear to overwhelm you? Is your faith in God failing? *'Stand still* [that is, 'Stand firm, don't panic'] *and see the salvation of the* Lord.*'*

The wind which God sent made a pathway through the water and dried out the sea bed enough for the Israelites to cross by foot. When the Egyptians followed in hot pursuit, the Lord troubled them (24). Their chariots became bogged down on the soft bed of the sea and they said, *'Let us flee from the face of Israel, for the* Lord *fights for them'* (25). They learned too late that God fights for his people and they were destroyed as God brought the waters of the sea crashing down upon them (26-28). *Thus Israel saw the great work which the* Lord *had done in Egypt; so the people feared the* Lord*, and believed the* Lord *and his servant Moses* (31). **Are you feeling discouraged? Remember God's promises, rejoice in the Lord and take heart!** *If God is for us, who can be against us? ... In all these things we are more than conquerors through him who loved us* (Romans 8:31,37).

I will sing to the LORD

The song of Moses is the first song recorded in the Bible. Israel had seen the mighty hand of God at work in their deliverance and in the destruction of the Egyptians. They sang of:

- The easy victory of God over his enemies (1-12). One puff of God's wind destroyed the Egyptians!
- God's mercy, redemption and guidance (13).
- A confidence that the dread of God would seize those nations seeking to obstruct their pilgrimage to the promised land (14-16).
- God's purpose to bring them into the promised land (17).
- The everlasting sovereignty of God (18).

This great song of adoration and worship came from Moses, who had complained to the Lord that he was not an eloquent man (4:10). He could not remain silent following this marvellous deliverance of God and he exclaimed, *'I will sing to the LORD'* (1). When God works in the lives of his people, the silent lips burst into praise. God's victory over the Egyptians foreshadows his final victory over Satan, for the song of Moses and of the Lamb are linked (Revelation 15:1-4). **When did you last 'sing to the LORD' with all your heart?** Meditate on the words of Moses in this song and worship God with gladness. *'Who is like you, O LORD, among the gods? Who is like you, glorious in holiness, fearful in praises, doing wonders?'* (11).

The Israelites discovered that the pilgrim life is not easy and they became discouraged when they found the waters of Marah too bitter to drink (23-24). The Lord showed Moses a tree and the waters became sweet after he cast the tree into them (25). God promised his people, *'I am the LORD who heals you'* (26). We may have bitter trials or experiences which will be our 'Marah'. There is a tree where we find healing. Our blessed Saviour died on that tree at Calvary to heal the sinful and the broken heart. **He makes the bitter sweet for his people. Hallelujah!**

The LORD hears your complaints

The complaints of the people at Marah (15:24) were followed by a history of discontent against Moses and against God. The people complained that they would die of hunger in the wilderness and that it would have been better to have died at the hand of the Lord in Egypt (3). This was a terrible thing to say. That very hand of God had destroyed the Egyptians and had brought deliverance to Israel (15:6). Notice the times that the words 'complained' and 'complaints' are found in this chapter (verses 2,7,8,9 and 12). This complaining was evil in the sight of the Lord (Numbers 14:27) and would have been very hurtful to Moses (2-3).

Moses warned the people, '*The LORD hears your complaints*' (8,12; cp. 1 Corinthians 10:10). When we complain, we forget the priceless blessings that God has so freely bestowed upon us — forgiveness, cleansing, freedom from the dominion of Satan and of sin, belonging now to God's family, and eternal life. **When we complain, the Christian life becomes drudgery rather than a delight.** *Bless the LORD, O my soul, and forget not all his benefits* (Psalm 103:2).

The Lord was very gracious in providing his complaining people with food (12-15). He gave specific directions through Moses for the gathering of the manna. They were to gather according to each one's need (16). God said that he would not send manna on the Sabbath and he directed that they should gather double the amount of manna needed on the day before. The Sabbath principle had been given at Creation (Genesis 2:2-3) and was to be observed (this was before the Ten Commandments had been given). The Lord was showing an ignorant people the importance of the Sabbath in a practical way. The extra manna gathered for the Sabbath did not rot (23-25,29-30). Some gathered according to their greed and this angered Moses but they found that by the next day the manna had rotted (20). Others, as perverse as ever, went out to gather manna on the Sabbath, but they found nothing (27).

Is the LORD among us or not?

The sorry pattern of complaining continued when there was a shortage of water in the wilderness. The people asked, *'Is the LORD among us or not?'* (7). They had already experienced abundant evidence of God's goodness to them but God granted another miracle (1-7). Moses struck the rock and water gushed out before their eyes. The rock at Horeb speaks of Christ, smitten and wounded for us. Let us not tempt him by lusting after evil or by complaining (1 Corinthians 10:6-12). Moses called the name of the site of the rock *Massah* and *Meribah* which mean 'test' and 'quarrel'. The Israelites were never to forget their foolish and sinful behaviour at Massah and Meribah.

One problem was solved at Rephidim, but it was soon followed by another. The Amalekites attacked Israel where they were weak and vulnerable (8; cp. Deuteronomy 25:17-19). Moses told Joshua to assemble some men to fight the attackers and he led the Israelites to a great victory (9-13). Behind that victory was the work of Moses in holding up the rod of God in his hands, his weary arms being supported by Aaron and Hur. Though we are not explicitly told, it is almost certain that Moses was praying. Uplifted hands indicated prayer (Psalm 28:2; 1 Timothy 2:8). Joshua needed the prayers of Moses, who needed the fellowship of Aaron and Hur in his spiritual warfare. **If spiritual battles are to be won, and our churches are to grow and be strengthened, we must be faithful in prayer, both in private and at the prayer meetings.** We will not then ask: *'Is the LORD among us or not?'* but we will be rejoicing in the sure knowledge that he is.

> While Moses stood with arms spread wide,
> Success was found on Israel's side,
> But when through weariness they failed,
> That moment Amalek prevailed.
>
> Restraining prayer, we cease to fight;
> Prayer makes the Christian's armour bright;
> And Satan trembles when he sees
> The weakest saint upon his knees.   (William Cowper)

You shall be a special treasure to me above all people

Three months after they left Egypt, the Israelites arrived at a mountain in the desert called Sinai (1). God came down to the top of the mountain which was covered by a thick cloud. The thunder crashed, lightning flashed and the trumpet blast which summoned the people to the edge of the mountain grew louder and louder. The mountain shook at the awesome presence of God and the people trembled (16-19). God was showing the people that he is holy and that those who break his law are in great peril.

The return of Moses to Mount Sinai was a fulfilment of the promise which God gave him when he met him there at the burning bush (3:12). The Lord gave him some very reassuring words for the Israelites, reminding them of his care for them, like that of the eagle, which is so gentle in caring for its young, but will fiercely retaliate against any who threaten them (4-6). The Lord is awesome in his power, but, oh, so tender in his care for us.

God wanted Israel to be *'a special treasure'* to himself, obedient to his will and holy, a kingdom of priests. Their promise to obey God was short-lived, however (5-8). They should have been a shining light to the nations of the earth but they failed. The end result of repeated rebellion was the crucifixion of the Son of God (cp. Matthew 23:37-39).

Peter takes up the words of verses 5 and 6 to remind us that we are a special people (1 Peter 2:9). Christian, just stop and think for a moment. You are God's *'special treasure'*. God loves you so much that he gave his beloved Son to die a dreadful death to save you from your sin. You are a *'special treasure',* purchased at tremendous cost. The Lord will never let you go and you are never out of his sight as he lovingly watches over you. **As God's special treasure we not only have great privileges, but also awesome responsibilities.** We are to be holy people, obedient to his word. We are to proclaim the praises of God to a dark and needy world.

The LORD your God, who brought you out of ... bondage

The Lord's message for the Israelites was, '*I am the LORD your God, who brought you out of the land of Egypt, out of the house of bondage*' (2). The Israelites owed it to God to love him and to obey him. The Lord Jesus has brought us out of a bondage far worse than that of Egypt. We were once enslaved by sin and by Satan and we were released at great cost (John 8:34-36; 1 Corinthians 6:19-20; Ephesians 2:1-3; 1 Peter 1:18-19). We owe him our willing and joyful obedience. It is not legalism to obey God's commandments — it is life, liberty and peace.

God called Moses to the top of the mountain and gave him the Ten Commandments (19:24; 24:18). The first four of these commandments concern our relationship to God, and the remaining six our relationship to other people. They are summed up in the two greatest commandments: '*You shall love the LORD your God with all your heart, with all your soul, with all your mind, and with all your strength*' and '*You shall love your neighbour as yourself*' (Mark 12:29-31).

God will not tolerate any rival in our affections and worship. He commands: '*You shall have no other gods before me*' (3). He forbids us to make images of himself (4). We must worship God as he is revealed in the Bible. He is absolutely perfect, holy, powerful and good. Our own idea of God is not acceptable. God will punish those who speak to him or about him in a careless or irreverent manner (7). God commanded that one day in seven should be observed as a holy day of worship (8-11).

We are to honour our parents and respect human life because God made man in his own image (12-13; cp. Genesis 1:27). Murder is forbidden, but it is possible to commit murder in the heart (Matthew 5:21-22). We are to respect marriage — adultery is sin (14); and we must not steal (15). Lying is forbidden (16) and we must not covet what belongs to others (17). God will punish not only sinful outward actions but also sinful desires. **No one can truthfully say that they have always kept these commandments. That is why we need a Saviour!**

71

The blood of the covenant

God made a covenant with the Israelites at Mount Sinai. A covenant is a binding agreement between two or more people, bringing them into a special relationship and commitment to each other. The covenant brought great responsibilities as well as great privileges to the people of God. The Ten Commandments and the laws recorded in chapters 21 to 23 were written in *'the Book of the Covenant'* (4,7). The solemn promises made by the people that they would obey God's words (3,7) were soon to be broken (cp. 32:1-6). The Lord then called Moses to ascend the mountain to receive the tablets of stone containing the law and the commandments; he was accompanied by Joshua (12-13). Aaron and Hur were delegated to judge the people in his absence (14).

'The blood of the covenant' (8) was vital to the people of the covenant. It was through blood sacrifice that atonement was made for sin. *Without shedding of blood there is no remission* (or 'forgiveness of sin'; Leviticus 17:11; Hebrews 9:22). The covenant which God made with Israel is known as the old covenant. The Lord Jesus came to give us the new covenant which is a better covenant. The blood sacrifices of the Old Testament pointed forward to the great sacrifice of the Lord Jesus Christ on the cross (Hebrews 9:6-15).

What are the marks of true religion?

- The teaching that only the blood of Christ can atone for sin. He alone is the way to God the Father (John 14:6). When he instituted the Lord's Supper, Jesus took the cup of wine as a symbol of his blood shed to save sinners. He said, *'This cup is the new covenant in my blood, which is shed for you'* (Luke 22:20).
- Covenant people are also people of the Book (the Bible). We must know the Scriptures (2 Timothy 3:15-16; 1 Peter 2:2) and obey them (John 14:15). **A religion which denies the necessity of the blood of Christ for the pardon of sin, or which denies the supreme authority of Scripture and the need to submit to God's word is false; have nothing to do with it.**

Then Moses pleaded with the LORD his God

What a contrast we find in these verses between the disgraceful conduct of the Israelites and the self-effacing love of Moses as he interceded for them. Aaron had shown himself to be a weak, pathetic and compromising leader in the absence of Moses (1-5). He had no excuse for making the golden calf nor for encouraging the people to worship it as a symbol of God, under the guise of *'a feast to the LORD'*.

See the contempt of these rebels for one of the greatest leaders of men in history: *'As for this Moses'* (1). They also had contempt for God in worshipping a dumb idol (8). Little wonder that God was angry with them and would have blotted them out of existence (9-10). See Moses whom they so despised. The Lord offered him a new beginning, with a new nation descending from him (10). Moses had bemoaned his lack of eloquence (4:10), but he now prayed with fervour and a moving eloquence. *Then Moses pleaded with the LORD his God* that he would not destroy the people (11-13). He reasoned that if God destroyed Israel, the Egyptians would say that he had only brought his people out of Egypt to destroy them. Moreover, God had promised Abraham, Isaac and Jacob (Israel) that he would multiply their descendants and bring them into the promised land.

While Moses was in the mountain, God gave him instructions for the great ministry to be given to Aaron as high priest. At that very time Aaron was sinning in failing to stand for truth. Moses was also receiving details for the use of the gold in the furnishings of the tabernacle, but the people had used some of that gold to make an idol.

When Moses came down the mountain with Joshua, he heard the noisy singing and shouting of the people as they worshipped the golden calf. In his anger he broke the tablets of stone on which God had inscribed the Ten Commandments. He ground the calf to powder and made the people drink the gold dust with water (19-20). **That gold was gone for ever — unable to be used for God. If our energy and gifts are used for sinful pursuits, they are lost to the work of God.**

LUKE

The Gospel of Luke is the longest of the four Gospels, containing 1151 verses (Matthew, which has more chapters, contains 1071 verses). Luke *'the beloved physician'* (Colossians 4:14) was a faithful companion of the apostle Paul, joining him on his second missionary journey (cp. *'we'*, Acts 16:10 — *'they'* in previous verses). He remained with Paul until the end of his life (2 Timothy 4:11).

Luke was a careful historian giving the precise time for the setting of the births of John the Baptist and Jesus (1:5; 2:1-2). He wrote his Gospel to give Theophilus (whose name means 'loved by God') a history of the ministry of the Lord Jesus Christ. Theophilus was probably a high-ranking Roman official for he is addressed as *'most excellent'* (1:3), a title given to Roman governors (e.g. Acts 23:26; 24:3; 26:25). He may have been a new convert whom Luke wanted to encourage and build up in the faith (cp. 1:4).

Luke's good news is that Christ the Lord is the Saviour of sinners (2:11) and that he is full of compassion for the poor and the needy (e.g. 4:18-19; 7:13,39,43-50). *'The Son of Man has come to seek and to save that which was lost'* (19:10).

Palestine during the ministry of Christ

For with God nothing will be impossible

The Christian faith is based on facts, not on myths nor on the ideas of men. The events described in Luke's Gospel and the rest of Scripture really happened. Luke writes of *those things which are most surely believed among us* (1). The days of Herod (5) were evil and troubled times for Judea. The king was a tyrant and the land was under Roman occupation. Zacharias the priest and his wife Elizabeth were a godly couple but they were childless and Elizabeth was now past the age of child-bearing; this would have brought them much heartache, just as it does to those in a similar situation today. Zacharias could not believe the words of the angel Gabriel promising a son (5-19). He was to prove that *'with God nothing will be impossible'* (37).

During the sixth month of Elizabeth's pregnancy God sent the angel Gabriel to Mary. She was puzzled and troubled by his greeting which told her that she was highly favoured and that the Lord was with her (26-29). He then revealed that she would conceive and bear a Son whom she should call Jesus. Mary could not understand how this could be, since she was a virgin, but Gabriel told her that she would conceive by the Holy Spirit and that the child would be called *the Son of God* (30-35). Gabriel encouraged Mary with the news that her relative, Elizabeth, had conceived a son in her old age, *'For with God nothing will be impossible'* (36-37).

Mary's humble submission to God's will is lovely to consider (38). Betrothal in those times was more binding than engagement in the western world but it was not marriage. Mary would have to face the shame (in the eyes of the world) of conceiving out of wedlock (cp. Matthew 1:18-20). This passage clearly teaches that the Lord Jesus was born of a virgin. Those who refuse to believe this generally reject all other accounts of the supernatural in the Bible. **God is infinitely great and powerful; why should we consider anything to be too hard for him?** Let this encourage us as we come to the Lord with our prayers.

A decree went out from Caesar Augustus

And it came to pass in those days that a decree went out from Caesar Augustus that all the world should be registered (1). Everyone was obliged to register for this census in his own city and Joseph, a descendant of David, had to go to Bethlehem (3-4). The timing of this decree could hardly have been worse for Joseph and Mary. Travel in those times would have been very arduous for a pregnant woman and, to make matters worse, Bethlehem was overcrowded with visitors. The Lord Jesus was born in an outbuilding where the innkeeper kept his animals (5-7). We must look beyond the decree of Caesar Augustus to the eternal decree of God. **His purposes can never be thwarted** (Isaiah 14:27; 46:10; Ephesians 1:11; Hebrews 6:17) and he had purposed that Christ should be born in Bethlehem (Micah 5:2). **Caesar decreed because God had already decreed (cp. Proverbs 21:1).**

The shepherds were terrified when they saw the angel standing before them to announce the birth of Christ. He reassured them and told them that he was bringing them *'good tidings of great joy which will be to all people'*. The good news is the birth of a Saviour, the promised Christ (or 'Messiah'). **His title 'Lord' indicates that Jesus is no less than God.** *God was manifested in the flesh* (1 Timothy 3:16). The shepherds then hurried to Bethlehem to see the new-born King. Their account of the angelic visitation would have greatly encouraged Joseph and Mary. *Then the shepherds returned, glorifying and praising God for all the things that they had heard and seen* (20).

The Lord Jesus was circumcised the eighth day from his birth (21). According to the law of Moses a woman was unclean for forty days from the birth of her son. Her purification was completed with the sacrifice of a lamb as a burnt offering and a young pigeon or turtle dove as a sin offering. Those who were poor were able to substitute another of these birds in place of the lamb (Leviticus 12). Verse 24 indicates that Joseph and Mary were poor (they had not yet received the gifts from the wise men; Matthew 2:11).

The devil ... departed from him until an opportune time

Following his baptism the Lord Jesus was led by the Spirit into the wilderness to be tempted by Satan for forty days (1-2). He fasted throughout this time and he would have been weak in body through lack of food.

- Satan first tempted Christ to doubt. *'If you are the Son of God'* (3,9). God the Father had said at his baptism, *'You are my beloved Son; in you I am well pleased'* (3:22). The devil often assails us with doubts; remember how he questioned the word of God in Eden, *'Has God indeed said ... ?'* (Genesis 3:1).
- Satan then promised Christ the kingdoms of the world, *'Therefore, if you will worship before me, all will be yours'* (5-7). Jesus knew that the way to glory was through suffering and death (Philippians 2:5-11). Satan's promises are false. He promised Eve that if she took the forbidden fruit she would be like God (Genesis 3:5). She soon found this to be a lie.
- The devil's next tactic was to try to make Christ sinfully presume upon the care of God the Father by assuming that he would be rescued by angels if he threw himself from the top of the temple (9-12). Adam and Eve presumed that they would be able to eat the fruit and not die (Genesis 3:1-4). We must never tempt God by sinful presumption.

Satan misused Scripture when he tempted the Lord Jesus who responded by using the word of God (10-12). You will be stronger in the face of temptation if you know your Bible. You do not have to give in to temptation. You do not have to sin (Romans 6:14). *Now when the devil had ended every temptation, he departed from him until an opportune time* (13). **Satan is patient. He waits for the right moment to get us off our guard. Let us always be vigilant (1 Peter 5:8).**

The Lord Jesus returned in the power of the Spirit to Galilee but he was rejected in his own town of Nazareth (14-30)

He left all, rose up, and followed him

Peter readily allowed Jesus to teach the crowd from his boat. When Jesus finished, he told Peter to take his boat into deeper water and to let down his net for a catch. Peter protested that they had toiled all night without success but he said, *'Nevertheless at your word I will let down the net'* (5). They landed a huge catch and an astonished Peter learned that to trust in Jesus and to obey him brings blessing. He worshipped Jesus saying, *'Depart from me, for I am a sinful man, O Lord!'* (8-9). This was less a request for Jesus to go away but a recognition that he is God (*'Lord'* — cp. John 20:28; 2 Corinthians 4:5) and a confession of Peter's own sinfulness. Jesus reassured him, *'Do not be afraid. From now on you will catch men'* (10). Peter and his partners left their huge catch and their business interests to follow Jesus into full-time service (11). They would be used to bring many into God's kingdom.

The Lord Jesus had a very busy and tiring ministry but he was never too busy to pray (16; cp. 6:12; 9:28-29). If he needed to spend time in prayer, how much more should we recognize our need to pray. Many of us have prayer as a low priority in our lives and we are the poorer for it. The scribes and the Pharisees recognized that Jesus was asserting his deity when he told the paralytic that his sins were forgiven. They thought that Jesus was blaspheming because God alone can forgive sins. He knew their thoughts and rebuked them (20-23). The title *'Son of Man'* also speaks of deity (24; cp. Matthew 26:64-65).

Jesus called Levi, also known as Matthew (the Gospel writer), to follow him (27; cp. Matthew 9:9). Tax collectors were hated because they collected revenue for the Romans. They also had a reputation for being dishonest and corrupt. The scribes and Pharisees put them on the same level as the worst of sinners and wrote them off as far as salvation was concerned (30). No one is beyond the reach of God's mercy. Levi *left all, rose up, and followed him* (28). He did not become a secret believer but made a great feast to which he invited many other tax collectors whom he introduced to his Saviour (29). **Are you ashamed to own Jesus as your Lord? Are you following him?**

Blessed is he who is not offended because of me

When Jesus came to Capernaum, he was met with a desperate and urgent request from a Roman centurion. This man was highly regarded and loved by the Jews for his benevolence towards them (1-5). He was desperate to obtain help for his servant (Greek = 'slave') who was dying, *when he heard about Jesus* (3). He was a very humble man (6-7) and he had *'great faith'* (9). His message was, *'Say the word, and my servant will be healed'* (7). This man from a heathen background had greater faith than the Jews (9).

The compassion of the Lord Jesus was seen in the raising of the widow's son (11-17) and in his forgiveness of the sinful woman (36-50). The enemies of Jesus called him *'a friend of tax collectors and sinners'* (31-34). They were implying that Jesus was condoning sin but that was not true. He forgives the worst of sinners when they repent and trust in him (cp. 1 Timothy 1:15). His compassion was also seen in his dealings with John the Baptist (18-23). John had condemned Herod for his adultery and was thrown into prison (3:19-20; cp. Mark 6:17-18). He was troubled with doubt and sent two of his disciples to ask Jesus: *'Are you the Coming One, or do we look for another?'* (18-20).

John had been greatly used by God and his doubt was not the doubt of a scoffer but of a godly man puzzled at God's ways with him. Why had the Lord allowed his ministry to be cut short, leaving him to languish in prison, if Jesus were the Messiah he had proclaimed? He may also have expected Jesus to purge the nation of its wickedness and hypocrisy (cp. 3:7-9). Jesus told the two disciples to tell the depressed prophet about the things that they had heard and the miracles that they had seen (21-22). He said to them, *'Blessed is he who is not offended because of me'* (23). Are you stricken by dark doubt or despair because of some perplexing trial? Do not be offended at the Lord for his dealings with you. **You may not be able to trace the ways of God, but do trust him. He is wise and kind and he will never fail you.**

This man receives sinners

This is one of the best-known chapters in the Bible, containing the parables of the lost sheep (3-7), the lost coin (8-10) and the lost son (11-32). The Lord Jesus told these parables because of the complaining of the Pharisees and scribes (2). Tax collectors, who were infamous for their cheating, gladly heard Jesus and he accepted invitations to eat in their homes. He had also chosen a tax collector to be one of the twelve disciples (5:27-32). The Pharisees and scribes despised these people and did not believe that God would forgive them or receive them. They failed to recognize their own sins such as pride and hypocrisy.

We are all sinners because we have broken God's holy law and our condition without God is described as being *lost* (6,9,32). What a comfort it is to know that *this man* (Jesus) *receives sinners* (2) and that he seeks them and finds them, as the parables of the lost sheep and lost coin illustrate (19:10). The Lord Jesus receives sinners, seeks sinners and died to save sinners (Isaiah 53:6; John 10:11,15-18). This is a wonderful message.

The Lord Jesus was also accused of being *'a friend of sinners'* (7:34). Could we be accused of the same thing? The wicked lifestyle of some people may shock us and we cannot condone their wickedness. We will not win them by shunning them, however. Do we welcome those who are lost into our meetings, whatever their lifestyle? Do we seek to befriend them and win them to Christ? The lost sheep and lost coin were sought, found and restored, and there was great rejoicing.

The scribes and Pharisees should have been full of joy that sinners were being sought and converted. How different they were from the angels. Heaven is a place of indescribable joy but that joy is even greater whenever a sinner repents. There is *'joy in heaven over one sinner who repents'* (7) and *'joy in the presence of the angels of God over one sinner who repents'* (10). **The Lord delights in mercy (Micah 7:18). He loves to save sinners. That should encourage us in our prayers and in our evangelism.**

The things which are impossible with men are possible with God

The Lord Jesus told the parable of the persistent widow to encourage us to persevere in prayer (1). He said that *men always ought to pray and not lose heart.* The parable of the Pharisee and the tax collector (9-14) is a warning against pride. When we come to God, we must come as suppliants for mercy (13). Blind Bartimaeus had this attitude when he cried out to the Lord Jesus (38-39; cp. Mark 10:46-52). He also came to the Lord in faith (42). **Let us remember these vital elements in prayer — perseverance, humility and faith.**

The rich young ruler (18-23; cp. Matthew 19:16-22) found that his wealth and religion did not meet his deepest needs. Why was this? He wanted eternal life but he also wanted to hold on to his possessions. His wealth was his 'god'. No one can serve two masters. We cannot serve God and riches (16:13). *He became very sorrowful* (23) because he was not willing to face up to the cost of following the Lord Jesus. This involves getting rid of anything that has become a 'god' in our lives. Becoming a Christian is more than 'making a decision for Christ'. We must accept his lordship. **If he is not Lord of all, he is not Lord at all.**

The Lord Jesus said that *'it is easier for a camel to go through the eye of a needle than for a rich man to enter the kingdom of God'.* (The idea that the 'eye of a needle' was the name of a very narrow gate into Jerusalem is entirely without foundation.) The shocked disciples asked: *'Who then can be saved?'* Jesus reassured them with a glorious truth, *'The things which are impossible with men are possible with God'* (26-27). **No one is too hard for the Lord to save.** Jesus very soon demonstrated this truth to his disciples when he saved Zacchaeus, who was very rich (19:1-10). We must never lose heart when we encounter indifference to the gospel. The Lord is able to melt the hardest of hearts. He is able to save the vilest sinner and he can easily break the chains of sin which enslave people. We think, 'Impossible', but Scripture says, *'For with God nothing will be impossible'* (1:37). Let us persevere in prayer and in our evangelism.

The Son of man has come to seek and to save

The Lord Jesus passed through Jericho on his way to Jerusalem (1). This city was famous for its fragrant balm derived from the balsam tree and was an important trading centre which yielded high taxes for the Roman authorities. Zacchaeus held the influential post as chief tax collector for that region. His name means 'righteous' or 'pure' but he was probably a scoundrel who had lined his pockets to become rich through fraud (2,7-8). He was determined to see Jesus and he climbed up into a sycamore tree to see above the crowd (3-4).

The Lord Jesus knew all about Zacchaeus. You can imagine his surprise when Jesus called him by name and told him to be quick and to come down from the tree because he wished to stay at his house. The crowd murmured against Jesus for going into the house of such a sinner whom they considered to be far from God. Zacchaeus came to faith in Christ and his life was transformed. He promised to give away half of his possessions to the poor and to restore fourfold to those he had defrauded (8). What Jesus had told the disciples was demonstrated before their very eyes: *'The things which are impossible with men are possible with God'* (18:26-27). Jesus confirmed that salvation had come to Zacchaeus who was *'a son of Abraham; for the Son of Man has come to seek and to save that which was lost'* (9-10). **When the Lord is determined to save, nothing can stop him.**

Jesus was given a great welcome by the crowds gathering in Jerusalem for the Passover but he wept over the city that was to reject him and crucify him (28-44). He prophesied that Jerusalem would be laid waste: *'They will not leave in you one stone upon another, because you did not know the time of your visitation'* (41-44). This prophecy was literally fulfilled in AD 70 when the Roman army besieged the city, destroyed it and slaughtered its occupants after the Jews revolted against their rule. The holy Son of God had taught and worked miracles in their midst but they had rejected him. **When God's visitation of mercy is rejected a visitation of judgment is inevitable. How tragic not to know the time of God's visitation!**

Lord, remember me

The Jewish leaders had been plotting to kill Jesus (19:47; 20:19; 22:2, 47-71) and within a week of his arrival in Jerusalem, they arrested and tried him. They then led Jesus to Pontius Pilate and accused him of inciting the people to rebel against paying taxes to Caesar (a deliberate lie; 20:22-25) and of setting himself up as a King. This was another lie. Pilate found no fault in Jesus, but the chief priests insisted that he was guilty (4-5). When he discovered that Jesus was from Galilee, Pilate decided to pass the case over to Herod Antipas, the ruler of that region, who was visiting Jerusalem.

Herod wanted to see a miracle performed and he bombarded Jesus with questions; *but he answered him nothing.* Jesus had nothing to say to the murderer of John the Baptist (6-9)! **Herod had been given ample opportunity to repent of his sin (Mark 6:20) but it was now too late.** The chief priests and scribes were vehement in accusing Jesus, who was also mocked by Herod and his soldiers. We are not told why Herod and Pilate had been hostile to each other. They were reconciled that day, but they were enemies of God (10-12).

The Lord Jesus was led to Calvary and crucified with two criminals. The mocking crowds and the soldiers challenged him to save himself if he were the Christ. One of the criminals joined the mockers but the other became aware of the fear of God, of his own guilt, and of the power of Jesus to save him (35-42). He was wonderfully saved even as he was dying on a cross. He may never have prayed in his life, but his simple prayer was all that was needed: *'Lord, remember me when you come into your kingdom.'* Jesus assured him that he would be with him in heaven that very day (43; *paradise* = 'heaven'; cp. 2 Corinthians 12:2-4). **No one is beyond the reach of the grace of God, even when they are dying.** The Lord Jesus refused to save himself so that he could bear the punishment of sinners and conquer death. He showed his power to save even while he was dying. How wonderful is our great Saviour! Let us worship him and praise him.

It was necessary for the Christ to suffer and to rise from the dead

The women who followed the Lord Jesus were faithful to the very end (23:49,55-56). They returned to the tomb after the Jewish Sabbath. It was early Sunday morning and they found that the stone had been rolled away from the tomb and that the body of Jesus was missing (1-3). The two angels reminded the perplexed women that Jesus had said that he would be crucified and that he would rise the third day (4-7; cp. 18:31-34). They then remembered his words and hurried to tell the good news to the disciples but *their words seemed to them like idle tales, and they did not believe them* (8-11). Peter rushed to the tomb to check out the women's story and found the cloths that had been wrapped around the body of Jesus. He went away marvelling at what had happened (12).

The two on the Emmaus road were also *'slow of heart to believe in all that the prophets have spoken'*. Jesus opened up the Scriptures to prove that the Messiah had to suffer and to die before entering his glory (25-27). When he prayed before the meal at Emmaus, their eyes were opened to recognize him and he vanished from their sight. They then remembered how their hearts had burned within them when he opened up the Scriptures (28-32). The excited pair immediately returned to Jerusalem to share their good news.

They found a rejoicing company who told them that the Lord had appeared to Simon Peter. While they were speaking, Jesus appeared and stood among them. He proved his bodily resurrection by eating with them (36-43). **The resurrection of our Saviour is no idle tale.** He then told them that *'it was necessary for the Christ to suffer and to rise from the dead the third day, and that repentance and remission of sins should be preached in his name to all nations'* (46-47). It is just as important to preach the necessity of repentance as it is to preach the death and resurrection of Christ to save sinners, yet it is a neglected teaching among many professing Christians. Without repentance, there can be no remission of sins, no salvation.

LEVITICUS

The name 'Leviticus' comes from the Greek word '*Levitikon*' ('of the Levites') which is used for the title of the book in the Greek version of the Old Testament. The sacrifices and worship of ancient Israel are described in the book which also contains God's laws for a 'holy' people, set apart to him. Leviticus is one of the least read, least known and least understood of all the books of the Bible but its teaching is most important. The sacrifices it describes are no longer necessary for they point to the perfect sacrifice of our Lord Jesus Christ. This is demonstrated in the book of Hebrews which shows how our Saviour is a better high priest and a better sacrifice for sin.

Key words: Holy — holiness — blood — atonement.

NUMBERS

The title 'Numbers' is taken from the Greek translation of the Old Testament. This title is apt for chapters 1 to 3 (the record of the census taken at Sinai) and chapter 26 (the record of the census taken some thirty-eight years later in the plains of Moab). The Hebrew title of the book is 'In the Wilderness' (cp. 1:1). This is a more accurate description of the book as a whole, for it details the slow journey of the Israelites from Mount Sinai to the borders of Canaan (the promised land). The New Testament tells us that the events in the wilderness were recorded as an example to us for our admonition (1 Corinthians 10:1-11). The people were very slow to learn, and a sad saga of complaining and failure continued throughout their journey (12:1-2; 14:1-4; 16:1-3,41-42; 20:1-5; 21:4-5). The Lord judged them for their unbelief and constant complaining — not one of them who was over twenty years of age went into the promised land, except for Joshua and Caleb (14:26-30). The people wandered around in the wilderness because they went astray in their hearts (Psalm 95:8-11).

Atonement

The word *'atonement'* is mentioned a number of times in this chapter; it means 'a covering'. The Old Testament sacrifices atoned for sin, covering it from God's sight so that it no longer provoked his wrath. There can be no atonement or forgiveness of sin without blood sacrifice (17:11; cp. Hebrews 9:22). The Day of Atonement is the most solemn of all Jewish holy days. It was the only day of the year when:

- The high priest entered the Holy of Holies, which contained the ark of the covenant, the symbol of God's presence.
- Atonement was made for all the sins of all the congregation of Israel (16-17,21-22,30-34), who were to humble (*afflict*) themselves; this was an expression of sorrow for sin and repentance from it, accompanied by fasting (cp. Psalm 35:13; Isaiah 58:3).

The high priest first sacrificed a bullock as a sin offering for himself (3,6,11). He then entered the Holy of Holies (*the Holy Place*), burned incense, and sprinkled some of the blood on the mercy seat (the lid of the ark of the covenant) and on the ground in front of the ark (12-14). Two goats were taken and lots were cast to determine which should be killed as a sin offering for the people and which should be the *scapegoat* (7-10). The blood of the sacrificial goat was sprinkled in the Holy of Holies (*inside the veil*) in the same manner as the blood of the bullock (15). The high priest then laid his hands on the *scapegoat* (i.e. 'the escape-goat'), confessing over it the sins of Israel (20-21); it was then driven away into the desert, symbolizing the removal of their sins. After this he sacrificed burnt offerings for himself and for the people (3, 24).

The Day of Atonement foreshadowed the great sacrificial work of the Lord Jesus Christ (see Hebrews chapters 9-10). The Old Testament sacrifices brought outward cleansing (purifying of the flesh) but they could not bring inward cleansing to a guilty conscience (Hebrews 9:9,13-14; 10:4,11). All believers from the Old and New Testament eras are forgiven on the basis of Christ's death.

We are well able to overcome

The Lord directed Moses to send spies into the promised land, a leader being taken from each of the twelve tribes (1-16). They were to do a thorough job and bring back a report on the people, their cities, the fortifications, and the fertility of the soil. They were also to bring back some of the fruit of the land (17-20). Why did God want Moses to send the spies into Canaan when he knew exactly what lay ahead of them? We are not told, but a good report from the spies would have encouraged the people to persevere in the face of difficulties.

Ten of the spies were faint-hearted; they were very impressed by the richness of the countryside, but felt intimidated by the large fortified cities and by the descendants of Anak (27-28; the Anakim were giants who were about nine feet, or almost three metres, in height). Joshua and Caleb, the other two spies, took a positive stance in the face of this defeatism. They were persuaded that what God had promised, he is able to perform. God had promised them that he would give them the land (2; cp. Romans 4:20-21). Caleb said, *'Let us go up at once and take possession, for we are well able to overcome it'* (30).

Though there are difficulties in the Christian life, we must not have a defeatist attitude. Such thinking comes from unbelief and it will sap our strength, rob us of Christian joy and contentment, and will keep us from praising God as we ought. *We are more than conquerors through him who loved us* (Romans 8:37). Christian, are you being overcome by besetting sin, or by Satan's wiles and attacks? **Have you lost hope of conquest, or do you look to God to give you victory in your life and witness? Do you really believe the promises of God as you read them in the Bible?** *'We are well able to overcome.'*

> We go in faith, our own great weakness feeling,
> And needing more each day thy grace to know:
> Yet from our hearts a song of triumph pealing;
> We rest on thee, and in thy name we go.

(Edith G. Cherry)

He has a different spirit in him and has followed me fully

The people were more ready to believe the ten faithless spies than Joshua and Caleb. They cried and wept all night as they wallowed in self-pity. They murmured against Moses and Aaron but even worse, they reproached the Lord for bringing them out of Egypt (2-3). They wanted to appoint a leader to take them back to Egypt (4). Moses and Aaron were greatly distressed and they fell on their faces before the assembly (to call upon God). Joshua and Caleb urged the Israelites not to rebel against God and encouraged them, *'The LORD is with us. Do not fear them'* (6-9). Such was the revolt of the people that they would have stoned Joshua and Caleb, but for the intervention of God (10).

The Lord asked Moses how long the people would reject him and refuse to believe his word even though he had performed great signs among them (11). **Seeing signs and wonders does not necessarily strengthen faith.** Indeed, the Lord Jesus warns us against seeking signs (Luke 11:29; John 4:48). God told Moses that he would destroy the unbelieving people with pestilence and disinherit them. He would raise up a great and mighty nation from Moses (12).

Moses had great love for the people and prayed for them with much persuasion. He reminded God that the Egyptians and the other nations knew of his mighty acts and of his presence with them. Surely they would reproach the Lord if he now destroyed Israel and he pleaded with God to forgive the people according to the greatness of his mercy (11-19; cp. Exodus 32:9-13). The Lord told Moses that he had heard his prayer and had pardoned the people, but those who had rebelled would not see the promised land (20-23,29-31). God had heard their foolish complaint, *'If only we had died in this wilderness!'* and would do according to their words (2,28). The ten faithless spies were destroyed by a plague (36-37). Let us beware of an unbelieving and complaining attitude (27; cp. Hebrews 3:12-19) but rather be like Caleb of whom God said, *'He has a different spirit in him and has followed me fully'* (24). How do you follow God?

Everyone ... when he looks ... shall live

The Canaanite king of Arad attacked Israel and took prisoners. The people did not complain, but made a vow to God as they prayed for victory (1-2). *The LORD listened to the voice of Israel* (3). The change of attitude made a great difference. The Lord also listened when they started to complain again (4-6). The Lord Jesus referred to the incident found in verses 4 to 9 (John 3:14). These verses illustrate:

- The terrible plight of sinful man. *Sin is lawlessness* ('rebellion'; 1 John 3:4). Many of the rebels died from the poison of the snake bites (6). The poison of sin brings death (Romans 5:12; James 1:15).
- God's provision for needy sinners; a look at the serpent of bronze brought healing. God said, *'Everyone ... when he looks ... shall live'* (8). He gave his only begotten Son to save sinners (John 3:14-16).
- The need to know that we are sinners and to acknowledge our sin to God (7; cp. Psalm 51:2-4; 1 John 1:9).
- The need to obey God and to trust in the Lord Jesus Christ in order to be saved from our sins (cp. Romans 6:17-18; 10:9-13; Hebrews 5:9; 1 Peter 1:22). Only those who gazed at the bronze serpent in obedience to God, and who trusted him, were healed (9).
- The only way to forgiveness and cleansing from sin is God's way, through the Lord Jesus Christ (John 14:6; Acts 4:12). If a dying Israelite refused to look at the bronze serpent, he perished. The sinner who refuses to come to Christ will also perish (John 3:18).

Have you confessed to God that you are a sinner? Have you thanked him for giving the Lord Jesus Christ to save you? Have you called upon the Lord, asking him to save you? Do you joyfully obey God's word? Are you trusting the Lord Jesus day by day? If you cannot answer 'Yes' to these questions, I urge you to come to the Lord Jesus now. He will not turn you away.

NB. The people did not worship the bronze serpent. The second commandment forbids idolatry (Exodus 20:4-6). We must not venerate relics or images! Hundreds of years later, the people did venerate the bronze serpent and King Hezekiah smashed it in his purge of idolatry (2 Kings 18:4).

You shall not curse the people, for they are blessed

The Israelites camped in the plains of Moab after God had given them great victories over the kings of the Amorites and Bashan (1; cp. 21:21-35). The Lord had told Moses that he had given the Moabites their land and that Israel was not to fight with them or take that land (Deuteronomy 2:9). King Balak of Moab did not know of this restriction on Israel and he feared the worst (2-4). Knowing that he had little hope of defeating Israel, he hired Balaam the sorcerer to curse them (6). Balak was convinced that if Israel were cursed, they would then be defeated in battle (11).

Though Balaam was a sorcerer, he claimed that he was able to obtain direction from God (7-8; cp. 24:1). He was an evil man who, for money, would have willingly cursed God's people (7). The Lord warned Balaam not to go on this evil errand: *'You shall not curse the people, for they are blessed'* (12). Balaam, for all his psychic powers, was unable to say anything that would harm God's people (38). The next two chapters describe the frustration of King Balak as God turned the desired curse into blessing (23:11,20,25-27; 24:9-10). There is a reassuring comment on this incident in Deuteronomy 23:5: *'Nevertheless the Lord your God would not listen to Balaam, but the Lord your God turned the curse into a blessing for you, because the Lord your God loves you.'* Some Christians needlessly fear the curses of gypsies or occult practitioners. **God turns their curses into blessings and he will curse those who curse us (24:9).**

Balaam was a covetous man (cp. 2 Peter 2:14-16; Jude 11). He knew God's will, but wanted to change it for his own ends. He went back to the Lord hoping to obtain a different message from him (19). God used Balaam's donkey to rebuke him and to warn him of the folly of his perverse ways (22-35). **The Lord means what he says and we must not imagine that he will change his will to accommodate our disobedience.** The human heart is devious and we must never persuade ourselves that our will is God's will when his word indicates otherwise.

The Spirit of God came upon him

Balaam called for the usual sacrifices before he was to speak again but he abandoned any attempt at sorcery, seeing that it had failed to help him in his quest to curse Israel (23:29 - 24:1). His third prophecy gives a picture of Israel enjoying the abundance of God's blessing in the promised land (3-9). Can you imagine how the words, '*How lovely are your tents, O Jacob! Your dwellings, O Israel!*' (5), would have angered Balak? Balaam refers to Israel being ruled by a powerful king, *higher than Agag* (7). Amalekite kings were given the title '*Agag*' (cp. 1 Samuel 15:8).

The third prophecy ends with a warning which Balak ignored: '*Blessed is he who blesses you, and cursed is he who curses you*' (9). Balak would not accept this and he showed his anger by striking his hands together. He dismissed Balaam and did not pay him (10-14). He rightly said that the Lord had kept Balaam from being honoured by him (11). Balaam's fourth prophecy divides into four sections, each beginning with the words, *he took up his oracle* (15,20,21,23) and refers to the conquest of Moab, Edom, and other nations.

Balaam was a wicked man, yet *the Spirit of God came upon him* (2). He uttered beautiful and sublime prophecies, including a prophecy of the coming of the Lord Jesus Christ: '*A Star shall come out of Jacob; a Sceptre shall rise out of Israel*' (17; cp. Genesis 49:10; Psalm 45:6). **Balaam had a genuine experience of the Holy Spirit, but he was lost.** '*For whom is reserved the blackness of darkness for ever*' (2 Peter 2:15-17).

We must not allow ourselves to be deceived by those who claim that their ministries are marked by spectacular signs and wonders, or 'words of knowledge'. **We must look for the fruit of the Holy Spirit (Galatians 5:22-23) rather than claims of miraculous power which do not stand the test of careful scrutiny. Let us also remember the solemn warning of the Lord Jesus (Matthew 7:22-23).**

DEUTERONOMY

The word 'Deuteronomy' means 'second law' or 'repetition of the law'. It is taken from the title of the book in the Greek version of the Old Testament. The Hebrew title is 'These are the words' (see 1:1; 29:1). Most of the book is taken up with three addresses given by Moses to the people in the plains of Moab shortly before he died (1:5). Forty years had passed since the Israelites had left Egypt and they were to enter the promised land under a new leader. They would face fresh difficulties and temptations and Moses encouraged them. He also warned them against disobedience to God. There are over eighty quotations from Deuteronomy in the New Testament and the Lord Jesus quoted from it more than any other Old Testament book. His coming is foretold in chapter 18. The reading of Deuteronomy led to revival in Judah at a time of apostasy, wickedness and violence (2 Kings 22:8 - 23:25). The love of God is not directly spoken of between Genesis and Numbers, but it is referred to for the first time in Deuteronomy (4:37; 7:7-8; 10:15; 23:5; 33:3).

Key words: Do (over 100 times) — keep — observe — hear — remember.

JOSHUA

The Lord appointed Joshua to succeed Moses (Numbers 27:18-23). He had led the Israelites in battle soon after they began their journey from Egypt to Canaan (Exodus 17:8-13). His military training prepared him well for the task of leading the Israelites in their conquest of Canaan. More important by far was the spiritual training that he received at the side of Moses (Exodus 24:13; 33:11). He was one of the twelve spies who were sent to view Canaan and with Caleb he was faithful to God. They challenged and encouraged the people to trust in the Lord and to go in and possess the land (Numbers 14:6-10). 'Joshua' is the Hebrew form of the Greek 'Jesus'; his name means 'Jehovah saves' or 'Jehovah is salvation'.

Take heed to yourself, and diligently keep yourself

Moses reminded the people about the God to whom they belonged by covenant. God is near to us (7,37); he is invisible (15), holy (24), jealous (24) and merciful (31). He is our Creator (32), almighty in power (34,37) and in love (37). He is unique (the one and only God, 35,39). Theologians describe the character of God as 'the attributes of God'. To belong to such a wonderful God is a great privilege (32-38) and Moses gave a strong warning about forsaking him to worship idols and other gods (15-19,23-25,28). God cannot be seen (12,15-16) and we must not use carved images to represent him. He requires our wholehearted devotion and obedience. This is the pathway to blessing (39-40; *'that it may go well with you'*).

Moses urged each one: *'Take heed to yourself, and diligently keep yourself'* (9,15). We all need this timely reminder to watch ourselves (cp. 1 Timothy 4:16). Why is this so necessary? We are prone to forget what God has done for us, and the precious things of his word can soon depart from us (9). The Bible says, *'Keep your heart with all diligence, for out of it spring the issues of life'* (Proverbs 4:23). **We must be careful not to slip into a sloppy, careless lifestyle, lacking the discipline of prayer and obedience to God's word.**

Christian parents have the added responsibility of instructing their children and grandchildren in the things of God (9). It will require love, patience and, above all, example, to teach our children and grandchildren. Moses recalled the awesome occasion when the Lord spoke to Israel at Sinai (10-14). What an impression that must have left on the hearts of the young! Our children must be taught the fear of the Lord (10) and we must take them to worship with God's people each Lord's Day and to other meetings (cp. Acts 21:5; 2 Timothy 1:5; 3:15). The evil influences of society around them are like poison to their souls. We must expose them to godly influences.

'Take heed to yourself.' **When did you last think seriously about the state of your spiritual life?**

Beware, lest you forget the LORD

Jews throughout the world include verses 4 and 5 in their daily prayers; these verses are known as the 'Shema' (the Hebrew word for 'hear'). *'You shall love the* LORD *your God with all your heart, and with all your soul, and with all your strength'* (5). The Lord Jesus confirmed that this is the greatest commandment (Matthew 22:36-38). **Jehovah (Yahweh) alone is God. He will tolerate no rival — he demands first place in our lives and affections.**

The need for parents to instruct their children in the things of God is again stressed (7,20-25; cp. 4:9-10). We must spend time with our children and teach them God's word and talk about the things of God to them. We should encourage them to ask questions about Scripture (a child's natural curiosity will lead him to question us). We should be sure to pray with our children each day. Timothy owed much to the instruction of a godly mother and grandmother (2 Timothy 1:5; 3:15).

Prosperity has its perils! God warned his people of the danger of forgetting him after receiving from him *houses full of all good things* and stomachs full of good food. He said, *'Beware, lest you forget the* LORD*'* (11-12). This warning was important and necessary enough to be repeated in later chapters (8:10-12; 11:15-16; 31:19-20). Materialism has been a greater enemy of true religion than any other persecuting force. *'Houses full of all good things'* have ensnared many a Christian, leading to lukewarmness and a lack of zeal for God (cp. Revelation 3:15-19). Scripture warns us against desiring riches (Psalm 62:10; 1 Timothy 6:9-10). We may never worship carved images but our possessions may become our gods and cause us to forget the Lord. **Read Proverbs 30:8-9 and make it your prayer today.**

We must not only love God (5) but also fear him and serve him (13). These principles apply to God's people of all ages and not just to Israel of old (see Hebrews 12:28-29). God is jealous over us because he loves us (13-15). Do you want to know the blessing of God in your life? *'Do what is right and good in the sight of the* LORD*'* (18).

The faithful God who keeps covenant

Did God choose Israel because they were great in number? Not at all! They were very few (7). There was nothing in them at all to attract the love of God, yet he chose them to be *a holy people ... a special treasure* to himself (6). Why did God predestine (choose) us before the world was made (Ephesians 1:4-5; 2 Thessalonians 2:13)? Could it be that he foresaw some faith or goodness in us? Not at all! We are saved by grace, not works! (Ephesians 2:8-10). God's grace reaches the most unlikely people, humanly speaking. No wonder John Newton, saved from the depths of wickedness, could write the hymn beginning, 'Amazing grace! how sweet the sound that saved a wretch like me!' How wonderful that God should save hell-deserving sinners and make them his *'special treasure'* (cp. 1 Peter 2:9). God has chosen us to be holy (Ephesians 1:4). If our lives do not honour God in holy living, we should be asking ourselves if we are truly saved.

The LORD is *the faithful God who keeps covenant* (9). **He will never fail us nor forsake us, for we are his own special people in whom he delights.** Moses encouraged the people to trust and obey God who would then bless them in Canaan (13-14). *'He will love you and bless you ... you shall be blessed above all peoples'* (12-15). Christians are also *'blessed above all peoples'.* We have priceless spiritual blessings (Ephesians 1:3). Let us think about some of these blessings (all references here are from Ephesians):

- We were loved and chosen by God in eternity past (1:4; 2:4).
- We have been adopted into God's family (1:5).
- We have redemption through the blood of Christ and our sins are forgiven (1:7).
- We have eternal life and an inheritance in heaven (1:11,14,18).
- We have fellowship with Christ (2:6). We have access to God the Father through the Holy Spirit (2:18) who dwells within us (3:16).

We also have many more blessings in Christ. **Are you counting your blessings and rejoicing in God with a thankful heart?**

God will raise up for you a Prophet

The tribe of Levi was not to be given an inheritance of land when they entered Canaan. They were set aside to do the work of the Lord and Israel's responsibility to care for the Levites is again repeated (1-8). They were to be supported by the tithes and offerings of God's people. The same principle holds good today. Those who are set aside by the local church to work 'full time' in God's service must be adequately supported by the church (1 Corinthians 9:14; 1 Timothy 5:17-18). The Lord commanded that certain portions of animal sacrifices be given to the priest for himself as well as the first-fruits of grain, new wine and oil, and the first fleece sheared from the sheep (3-5).

There are two very stern warnings given in this chapter. The first concerns occult practices which are an abomination in the sight of God (9-14). Our nation is sinking into a cesspool of spiritism, astrology, fortune-telling and witchcraft. Occult books are prominently displayed in our bookshops and the 'stargazers' and spiritist mediums get plenty of television coverage. We must recognize that their practices are evil.

The other warning concerns false prophets (20-22). There are two types of false prophet, one claiming to speak in the name of the Lord, the other in the name of other gods (20; cp. 1 Kings 18:20-22). How can we discern between true and false prophets? Those who are false teach error and their predictions fail (20-22; cp. 13:1-5). Many today claim to have the prophetic gift, but their prophecies are generally trivial or false. Do not listen to counterfeits, whether they be spiritist mediums, fortune-tellers or so-called prophets. We have all that we need to know in the Bible (2 Timothy 3:16-17).

Moses told the people, *'The LORD your God will raise up for you a Prophet like me from your midst'* (15-18). **This prophecy points to the coming of the greatest prophet of all time, the Lord Jesus Christ (John 6:14; 7:40; Acts 3:19-23; Hebrews 1:1-4).** The holy Son of God not only brought the word of God to the people, he also died to save sinners and he conquered death.

A people for himself

In this his third address to the people Moses led Israel to renew the covenant which God had made with them (1,12-13). The older generation had died during the wilderness journey and it was important that those going into the promised land were fully aware of their privileges and responsibilities as God's covenant people. They had seen great signs and wonders from God (2-7), but they did not have spiritual perception. Spiritual perception is a gift from God (4) and we should rejoice much in the Lord if he has opened our eyes to the greatness of Christ and his work in dying to save us from our sins.

A covenant is a binding agreement (or treaty). In his covenants with men it is God who lays down the conditions and it is for us to obey him (9). Christians belong to the new covenant, sealed in the blood of the Lord Jesus (1 Corinthians 11:25; Hebrews 13:20). **This is a far better covenant than the one we are reading about in Deuteronomy (Hebrews 8:6).** What does it mean to be in covenant with God? It means that God has taken us to be 'a people for himself' (13). The word 'holy' applied to Christians means that we have been separated from this world to God, to be his special possession, a people for himself. The Lord blesses his covenant people as they love him and obey him (9). He expects a people for himself to be totally committed to him. The Israelites were again warned of the consequences of forsaking the covenant (18-28).

There is a false peace which is enjoyed by many people. Many bless themselves, saying, 'I shall have peace, even though I follow the dictates of my heart' (19). Many of the Israelites did just that (Jeremiah 11:7-8; 16:12). God has his secret things (29); we must not waste time speculating about the things that he chooses to conceal from us (e.g. the date of Christ's second coming).

A people for himself. The almighty, eternal, all-wise God is totally committed to all who belong to him. Christian, rejoice in him and be holy.

Choose life

Deuteronomy is full of warnings about the consequences of departing from God but it is also filled with promises of the compassion and grace of the Lord. Notice how many times the expression *'The LORD your God'* is found in this chapter. The Lord points to the time when the Israelites would be scattered and go into captivity because of their disobedience to him, but he promised that he would restore them and bless them if they returned to him (1-5). He would do for a repenting people what he had previously called on them to do for themselves: *'And the LORD your God will circumcise your heart ... '* (6; cp. 10:16; Romans 2:29). When God graciously works in a person's heart, they will then love him with all their heart and with all their soul (2,6,10).

God has his *'secret things'* which he does not reveal to us (29:29), but he has given us his word which is not hidden from us. His commands are not so distant or veiled in mystery that we cannot understand what he has to say to us. We must not spend our time speculating about the things that the Lord has not revealed, but get on and obey the things that he has plainly made known in the pages of holy Scripture (11-14).

Moses set before the people *life and good, death and evil* (15) and he challenged them to *choose life* (19). **The options are clear. Like Israel, we have to choose between blessing and cursing.** The challenge, *'choose life'*, is still sounded out in gospel preaching today. To *choose life* is to love God, to obey his voice and to cling to him (20). Is this too great a price to pay in choosing life? His love for us is such that he gave the One whom he loved most, even his own beloved Son, to die in agony to save us. His love for us is so great that he will hold on to us and never let us go (John 10:28-29; Romans 8:38-39). All that he asks of us is that we should love and obey him. When we truly love God, we want to please him; we want to cling to him so that nothing else will cause us to wander away from him. Lasting happiness is found only in loving God. **Are you rejoicing in the Lord because you have chosen life?**

Be strong and of good courage

Moses was now one hundred and twenty years old and he knew that he was soon to die. God had told him long before that he would not be allowed to cross the Jordan into Canaan. Though Israel would be without their aged leader, they had the promise that God would cross over Jordan before them, giving them victory over the Canaanite nations (1-5).

Moses urged Joshua and the people: *'Be strong and of good courage'* (6-7,23). They had no need to fear their enemies because the Lord was present with them and he would never leave them nor forsake them. Joshua and the Israelites had problems, trials, obstacles and battles ahead of them, but they had a great God with them. **Where does our strength lie?** Certainly not in ourselves — we are painfully aware of our weaknesses. **It lies in the same God whose presence is with us wherever we may go.** The Christian life is not easy and we sometimes ponder the future with apprehension. Our faith may well be severely tried, but we know that God will never leave us, nor forsake us, so that we may boldly say, *'The LORD is my helper; I will not fear. What can man do to me?'* (Hebrews 13:5-6). *'Be strong and of good courage.'*

The Lord summoned Moses and Joshua to the tabernacle where he appeared before them to commission Joshua as Israel's new leader (14-15). Joshua had no illusions about the difficulties facing him. As Moses' assistant he had witnessed the many acts of rebellion by the people. The Lord told Moses that after his death they would turn away to worship idols and bring his judgment upon themselves (14-18). God gave Moses a song which he was to teach the children of Israel (19). The Lord knows the inclination of men and women to rebel against him (21). The song reminded the people of God's goodness to them and warned them against backsliding from him (19-22,30; 32:1-43). Joshua was commissioned and the Lord promised him, *'Be strong and of good courage ... and I will be with you'* (23). We know that Joshua was a courageous leader who faithfully led Israel all his days, but the people did fall into a backslidden state following his death.

Ascribe greatness to our God

On the very day that Moses delivered his song to Israel God told him to go to Mount Nebo. From there he would be able to view the promised land before he died (48-52). The account of Moses' death is found in chapter 34. The song of Moses (31:30) is full of praises to God but it also contains warnings to the people against forsaking him. It rehearses God's unchanging faithfulness and contrasts it with the repeated failures of Israel.

Whenever we think of God we should remember his greatness. *Ascribe greatness to our God* (3).

- We see the greatness of God in his strength. He is called *'the Rock'* (4,15,18,30,31). He is almighty in his strength and power.
- We see the greatness of God in his work (4). *His work is perfect.*
- We see the greatness of God in his ways (4). *All his ways are justice.* He is righteous in all his dealings with us.
- We see the greatness of God in his truth (4). All the promises (and warnings) found in the Bible are true. God cannot lie (Titus 1:2).
- We see the greatness of God in his sovereignty. The Most High controls all the nations of the earth (8). There is no other God; he is in complete control of everything that happens (39).
- We see the greatness of God in his love for his people (9-10). He found Israel (*'Jacob'*) and encircled his people with his loving protection; he instructed them and kept them as the apple of his eye.
- We see the greatness of God in his compassion (36). Though the people of God were wayward, he had pity upon them.
- We see the greatness of God in his goodness (13-14). He had richly blessed and prospered his people.

Do not have small views of God. *Ascribe greatness to our God.* **Remember his greatness at all times — whenever you worship him, whenever you come to him with your needs, whenever you speak about him to others.** *O LORD, our Lord, how excellent is your name in all the earth!* (Psalm 8:1).

You shall meditate in it day and night

Moses had led the Israelites for forty years and God had appointed Joshua to succeed him as leader (Numbers 27:18-23). The death of Moses was not a signal for the Israelites to be paralysed by grief or inertia. *The LORD spoke to Joshua ... saying, 'Moses my servant is dead. Now therefore, arise, go over this Jordan, you and all this people, to the land which I am giving to them — the children of Israel'* (1-2).

The new leader faced the daunting task of leading the Israelites into the promised land. They had to cross the swollen River Jordan which was in flood, and on the other side they had to conquer fortified cities. Moses had encouraged Joshua before he succeeded him to the leadership of Israel (Deuteronomy 31:3-8) and now the Lord encouraged him. He gave Joshua some precious promises telling him that he would be invincible (2-9). God told him, *'Be strong and of good courage'* (6-7,9). What was the basis of Joshua's confidence? It was not his own military skills or strength but the promise of God's presence. *'As I was with Moses, so I will be with you. I will not leave you nor forsake you'* (5; cp. verses 9 and 17; 3:7,10; 23:10). This promise is applied to Christians in the book of Hebrews.

'This Book of the Law' (8) refers to the book of Deuteronomy (cp. Deuteronomy 31:9,11,24,26). God told Joshua, *'You shall meditate in it day and night.'* Those who are godly delight in God's word and meditate in it continually (Psalm 1:2). The Hebrew word used here for *'meditate'* means 'to mutter'. We see the connection in the beginning of verse 8: *'This Book of the Law shall not depart from your mouth, but you shall meditate in it day and night'* (i.e. 'mutter' or 'murmur' it). This meditation is not the vain, repetitive muttering of Hindu mantras and of letting the mind go blank. Christian meditation is the musing over God's word, having it in our hearts and upon our lips. We use our minds to think through the teaching of God's word; that word on our mouths will lead us to worship God and to witness for him. **Do you meditate on your Bible readings each day, repeating the verses, muttering them to yourself and thinking much about them?**

Especially Jericho

The spies were sent into Canaan before the Israelites prepared to cross the river. God had promised Joshua that he would give Israel the land of Canaan (1:2-5). Why then did he use these spies? Was he lacking in faith? Not at all! Their report would have been a great encouragement to Joshua (24), but there was another more important reason for their visit to Jericho. God had someone in that city, chosen in his eternal purpose, whom he was determined to save. *'Especially Jericho'* (1). It was there that the Lord wonderfully stepped into the dark and tragic life of Rahab, the prostitute.

There was nothing in Rahab's life to commend her to God or to man. She was cheap, even by the wicked standards of Jericho, but she was precious to God. A. W. Pink writes: 'By her choice, she was given up to the vilest of sins, but by the divine choice she was predestined to be delivered from the miry pit and washed whiter than snow by the precious blood of Christ, and given a place in his own family.'

Rahab did not have the privilege of Sabbath-day worship in Jericho and there was no instruction available from the word of God. She had, however, heard of the greatness of the Lord (9-11) and she was brought out of heathen darkness. Her faith is mentioned in the New Testament (Hebrews 11:31). **If God can save a Rahab, he can save anyone. His grace is such that it reaches the most unlikely people.** Let us be encouraged and persevere in prayer for those on our hearts, who are as yet lost. Let us rejoice in God's free and sovereign grace as we recall the way in which he brought the spies to the house of Rahab, and how he brought those into our lives who were able to point us to himself.

> On such love, my soul, still ponder, Love so great, so rich and free;
> Say while lost in holy wonder, Why, O Lord, such love to me?
> Hallelujah!
> Grace shall reign eternally.

(John Kent)

By this you shall know that the living God is among you

Joshua was an early riser (1; cp. 6:12; 7:16; 8:10)! He was eager to get on with God's work and not waste time lazing in bed. It is important to cultivate a habit of rising early enough to pray before we begin our day. We may fail in this respect if we keep late nights and do not have sufficient sleep. The Lord Jesus was also an early riser and disciplined in prayer (Mark 1:35).

The people set out to cross the Jordan after three days (1-3; cp. 1:11). They were led by the priests who were carrying the ark of the covenant and were separated from them by a gap of two thousand cubits (1000 yards or 900 metres). Joshua commanded the people to sanctify themselves because God would do wonders among them the next day (4-5). God promised Joshua: *'This day I will begin to exalt you in the sight of all Israel, that they may know that, as I was with Moses, so I will be with you'* (7). The Lord parted the Jordan as the priests who bore the ark stepped into its flooded waters, and the people walked over a dry river bed into the land of Canaan (15-17).

God gave this miracle as a confirmation of his promise to drive out the Canaanites. *'By this you shall know that the living God is among you'* (10-13). **We may not need God to part rivers for us, but he graciously gives tokens of his presence among us.** He answers prayer and transforms lives through his mighty power. As you now come to the Lord in prayer, remember that you are coming to *'the living God'*. Worship him and bring your requests to him with an expectant faith.

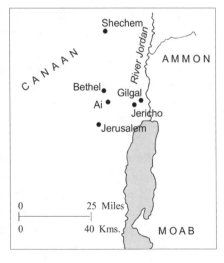

I have given Jericho into your hand

Jericho was a fortress city with massive walls some thirty feet in height and with houses built on top of them (cp. 2:15). Archaeologists have discovered that the city had an outer wall which was six feet thick; there was a gap of fifteen feet and then an inner wall which was twelve feet thick. Jericho overlooked the plain of Jordan and was at the entrance of a mountain pass which allowed entrance into Canaan. Its conquest was essential to Joshua's military campaign in Canaan.

How was Jericho to be taken? God instructed the Israelite army to march around the city once a day for six days (3). Soldiers headed the procession followed by seven priests with trumpets made from rams' horns. There were then four priests carrying the ark of the covenant and behind them the remaining soldiers. They marched in silence except for the trumpet blasts (3-14). They marched around Jericho seven times on the seventh day. On the seventh time round, at a given signal, they all shouted, and the huge walls collapsed! (15-16, 20). The slaughter of the people of Jericho may seem dreadful, but the Canaanite nations had sunk to the depths of depravity and evil. Rahab and her family were saved as she had been promised (25).

The strategy for taking Jericho would appear foolish to human reason, but *the foolishness of God is wiser than men* (1 Corinthians 1:25-29). Joshua believed God's promise, *'I have given Jericho into your hand'* (2). *By faith the walls of Jericho fell down* (Hebrews 11:30). We must not battle against Satan with worldly methods *for the weapons of our warfare are not carnal but mighty in God for pulling down strongholds* (2 Corinthians 10:4).

Some may consider preaching to be a foolish and outdated method of communicating the gospel but God uses this 'foolish method' to save souls (1 Corinthians 1:21-23). **Pray earnestly that the preaching of God's word at your church next Lord's Day will be in the power of the Holy Spirit. Pray for the triumph of the gospel in your neighbourhood so that the strongholds of Satan will collapse.**

I saw ... I coveted ... and took

There is a great contrast between Israel's experience at Jericho and their disarray and defeat at Ai. The defeat was all the more bitter for Joshua because the spies sent to Ai had suggested that the city would be easily conquered (2-5). Chapter 6 ends with the statement that *the LORD was with Joshua* but chapter 7 opens by informing us that *the anger of the LORD burned against the children of Israel.* The situation dramatically turned from the hearts of the Canaanites being melted to the hearts of the people of Israel melting (5; cp 5:1). A grief-stricken Joshua *tore his clothes, and fell to the earth on his face before the ark of the LORD* (6).

The reason for Israel's defeat was made plain. Achan had wilfully sinned in stealing things which were *'accursed'* or consecrated to the treasury of the Lord's house (1,11-12; cp. 6:18-19). The name 'Achan' means 'trouble' and this man certainly brought trouble to Israel. **There is a very solemn lesson here — sin is not a private matter!** If we are wilfully disobedient to the Lord, we will not only bring trouble upon ourselves, but also upon others, and we will also blight our church.

Achan was very foolish to imagine that he could hide his sin from God. How did Achan fall into sin? He confessed, *'I saw ... I coveted ... and took'* (21). Achan must have committed that sin many times in his mind before he ever *'took'* those things that belonged to God's treasury. The path of falling into temptation and sin is often similar to Achan's experience. Eve *saw ... that it was pleasant to the eyes, a tree desirable ... she took* (Genesis 3:6). We cannot always be blamed for what we see, but we sin when we turn what we see into an occasion for sinful thoughts (cp. Matthew 5:27-28).

Satan promises so much when he tempts us but sin brings only misery. Achan never did enjoy the benefit of his 'loot' and he forfeited his life (21,24-26). Eve's fall brought the most dreadful misery to her (Genesis 3:16). Sin is a very serious matter in the sight of God and it will certainly bring his judgment upon us (Romans 6:23; James 1:15).

Be very courageous to keep and to do all that is written in the Book of the Law

Joshua addressed the leaders of Israel before he died (chapter 23) and then he spoke to all the nation (chapter 24). He reminded the leaders of the nation of all that the Lord had done for them and he encouraged them to possess the inheritance which had not yet been taken (2-5). They had seen how God had fought for them (3) but they could not afford to relax. He urged them: *'Therefore be very courageous to keep and to do all that is written in the Book of the Law'* (6). The Lord had said the same thing to him when he began to lead Israel (1:7). **We do need courage to swim against the tide of unbelief and wickedness around us today and to obey God's word.**

Israel had to remain faithful to the Lord and to love him if they were to know his blessing (7-11). Idolatry and intermarriage with the heathen people around them would bring the anger and judgment of God upon them (7,12-16). These principles remain for every Christian. Idolatry has many subtle forms and we must keep ourselves from it (cp. Colossians 3:5). We must also keep ourselves from marriage to non-Christians (1 Corinthians 7:39; 2 Corinthians 6:14-18).

Joshua again reminded the people that God had kept all his promises (14; cp. 21:45). The Lord had fought for Israel and would continue to fight for them as long as they remained faithful to him (3,10). He will also fight for us if we love him and obey him (cp. Isaiah 54:17; Romans 8:37). He is worthy of all our devotion and praise. **Think about the greatness of God and worship him; remember his past faithfulness and praise him; look to the future, trusting in him.**

> When all thy mercies, O my God,
> My rising soul surveys,
> Transported with the view, I'm lost
> In wonder, love and praise.
>
> (Joseph Addison)

Choose for yourselves this day whom you will serve

It is significant that Joshua summoned the Israelites to Shechem to hear his farewell speech. It was there that the blessings were uttered for obedience from Mount Gerizim and the curses for disobedience from Mount Ebal (8:30-35). Joshua recounted their history from Abraham to the time in which they lived (1-13). Their history was a record of the grace and goodness of God to them. He challenged them to serve God (the words *'serve'* and *'served'* are found sixteen times in this chapter). *'Choose for yourselves this day whom you will serve'* (15). **What is involved in serving God?**

- We must *fear the* LORD (14). This is not a cringing, craven fear, but a sense of reverence and awe in the presence of a holy God (5:14; Isaiah 6:5; Hebrews 12:28-29). *The fear of the* LORD *is the beginning of wisdom* (Psalm 111:10).
- We are to *serve him in sincerity and truth* (14). The Hebrew word translated *'sincerity'* is also rendered as *'perfect'* (Genesis 6:9; Psalm 19:7); *'blameless'* (Genesis 17:1) and *'without blemish'* (Leviticus 1:3,10). God's service has no place for hypocrisy. Faithfulness is also implied in the meaning of the word *'truth'*. We must be faithful to God's truth and never compromise it by life or by lip.
- We must be wholly devoted to God (14). God has to be first; all other gods are to be put out of our lives, whether idols or riches (*'mammon'* — Matthew 6:24).
- We must obey God's word (24).

The people were very quick to say, *'We also will serve the* LORD*'* (18), bringing a caution from Joshua (19). Verse 31 contains a telling comment: *'Israel served the* LORD *all the days of Joshua, and all the days of the elders who outlived Joshua.'* Without good leadership they soon went astray (cp. Judges 2:7-12). Pray that the Lord will be pleased to raise up godly, discerning leaders in the church today. Be determined to follow the Lord with all your heart in these confusing and wicked times. **Have you chosen to serve God? Can you honestly say like Joshua, *'But as for me and my house, we will serve the* LORD*'* (15)?**

JUDGES AND RUTH

The tribes of Israel were governed by their elders for the ten years following the death of Joshua in 1390 BC. The period of the **Judges** extends from 1380 BC to the beginning of the reign of King Saul in 1043 BC (these dates are approximate). After the death of Joshua and his fellow-leaders the Israelites turned away from God to worship idols (2:7-13). The Lord punished them by bringing oppression from surrounding nations but when they repented, he had pity upon them and raised up judges to deliver them. When the judge died, the sorry pattern of apostasy and wickedness soon reappeared (2:14-19). The influence of the judge did not extend to the whole nation but was often confined to only part of the country. The function of the judges was:

- To act as magistrates applying God's law to the life of the nation and to keep sin in check (cp. Deuteronomy 16:18; 17:9; 19:17).
- To deliver the people from foreign oppression.

Key verse: *In those days there was no king in Israel; everyone did what was right in his own eyes* (17:6; 21:25).

The events recorded in the **Book of Ruth** occurred during the period of the Judges (1:1), probably between the years 1150 and 1120 BC. Ruth was David's great-grandmother (4:18-22) and David was born approximately 1040 BC. The book tells of the disaster that befell the family of Elimelech of Bethlehem who went to the land of Moab to escape famine in their own country. Elimelech and his two sons (who had married heathen women) died in Moab, and Naomi, his widow, returned to Bethlehem with Ruth, one of her daughters-in-law. Boaz, a near relative, willingly assumed the responsibility of kinsman-redeemer (Hebrew = '*goel*') by marrying Ruth, who is found in the family-tree of the Lord Jesus Christ (Matthew 1:5).

The story of Naomi and Ruth is one of bereavement, heartbreak, sorrow and disillusionment. In all these sad events, however, we see the wonderful purposes of God. How we all need to see this when everything seems to go wrong for us and when we face difficult times.

Yet they would not listen to their judges

The failure of Israel began while Joshua was still living. God had repeatedly warned the people not to make treaties (covenants) with the Canaanites and to tear down the altars used for idol worship. The situation became so serious that the *Angel of the LORD* came and rebuked the disobedient Israelites. They were to prove his words that the inhabitants of Canaan would be thorns in their side and that their gods would ensnare them (1-2). The people were so distressed that they wept (*'Bochim'* means 'weeping') and made sacrifices to the Lord (4-5). Events were to prove that their repentance was not lasting. True repentance brings a change in our lives and sin is loathed and forsaken.

After Joshua and his generation had died, *another generation arose after them who did not know the LORD* (10). God had warned Israel that the gods of Canaan would be a snare to them if they did not destroy their altars (2-3). We now see how these words were to prove true (11-13). Notice that it was God who delivered the Israelites into the hands of their enemies and that *the hand of the LORD was against them for calamity* (14-15). They received their just deserts, but God is great in mercy. *The LORD raised up judges for them, the LORD was with the judge and delivered them out of the hand of their enemies ... for the LORD was moved to pity by their groaning because of those who oppressed them* (18). After the death of the judge they reverted to their wicked and stubborn ways (19-20).

The Lord had allowed some of the Canaanites to remain in the land and to live alongside the Israelites for the following reasons:

- To punish the Israelites for their apostasy (3,20-21).
- To test Israel's faithfulness to himself (22; 3:4).

The people gladly accepted the role of the judges to lead them to victory, but they did not want to be instructed by them. *Yet they would not listen to their judges* (17). If we refuse to listen to God and to obey him, he will surely punish us. **Do you listen for God to speak to you as you hear his word preached or as you read your Bible?**

The LORD is with you, you mighty man of valour!

The Israelites were slow to learn the lesson which teaches us that God punishes sin. The Lord sent the Midianites, Amalekites and the people of the East to plunder Israel's livestock and harvests, reducing them to near starvation for seven years. When the people prayed to the Lord, he sent them a prophet to remind them that they were being punished because of their disobedience (7-10). God then raised up Gideon from the tribe of Manasseh to free them from their oppressors. *The Angel of the LORD* appeared to Gideon as he was threshing wheat in a wine press (to hide his meagre crop from the Midianites). Gideon was awestruck in the presence of the Angel of Lord (22-23).

Gideon was much aware of his own weakness and unworthiness (15). It is encouraging to read, however, that God saw Gideon as a *'mighty man of valour'* (12). **You may feel your own weakness and be discouraged, but who knows how the Lord may be pleased to use you if you trust in him and obey him?** God often chooses those who are weak to accomplish mighty deeds for himself (cp. 1 Corinthians 1:27). This principle is vividly illustrated in the next chapter.

Gideon's father was a leading idolater in the city and had an altar of the god Baal. God told Gideon to tear down this altar and to destroy the image of Baal. He was then to build an altar to the Lord and sacrifice his father's young bull. Gideon was afraid of the consequences of such an action and he acted by night. Obedience is often costly, but to his surprise, Gideon had the support of Joash, his father, against those who wanted to kill him for destroying the shrine of Baal (25-32). It appears that Gideon's brave action led to his father forsaking his idolatry. If we would be blessed and used by God, we must begin by honouring God in our homes! It was after Gideon had honoured God at home that *the Spirit of the LORD came upon him* (34). Gideon was still weak in faith and he put out a woollen fleece to prove God. The Lord soaked it with dew while leaving the surrounding ground completely dry and then reversed the miracle at Gideon's request (37-40). God is very patient with us, even when our faith is weak.

Lest Israel claim glory for itself

Gideon mustered an army of 32,000 to fight the Midianites and their allies, but God told him that he had too many! God's ways are different to ours (Isaiah 55:8)! All those who were afraid were told to return to their homes and Gideon was left with just 10,000 men. He may have felt discouraged to see his army so drastically reduced but God still said, *'too many'* (1-4). Gideon's army was further reduced to just 300 men (5-7). The Lord was determined to show Israel that their victory would come through him alone and not through their own military might, *'lest Israel claim glory for itself against me, saying, "My own hand has saved me"'* (2).

The Lord was mindful of Gideon's fears and told him to go with his servant to an outpost of the Midianite camp under cover of darkness. There, they heard an enemy soldier describing a dream which his companion interpreted as a sign that the Lord would give Gideon a great victory over them. When he heard these things, Gideon worshipped God and returned to encourage his three hundred men (9-15). He divided them into three companies. Each man had an empty pitcher with a lamp inside it in one hand, and a trumpet in the other. When Gideon blew his trumpet they were then to blow theirs and shatter the pitchers allowing the light to stream out from the lamps. This was to be done at the beginning of the middle watch (after 10.00pm) when most of the massive Midianite army would be asleep. This strategy caused panic, confusion and disorder among the Midianites so that they turned on each other. They were routed and fled in disarray, pursued by the Israelites who called on the tribe of Ephraim to guard the fords of the River Jordan and so cut off the fleeing Midianites.

What a mighty work the Lord wrought through Gideon and his small army! We are often aware of our own smallness and weakness as we serve God, but he is almighty and sovereign. **Let us be encouraged and always remember that any success that we enjoy in the Lord's work is not of our doing, but is of God alone. To him be all the glory.**

Then the Spirit of the LORD came upon him mightily

Samson was a man of immense physical strength, but his life was blighted by his great weakness regarding his inability to control his lust. His love affairs with Philistine women were to bring him sorrow and ruin. His godly parents pleaded with him in vain to seek a wife from among his own people rather than marry a Philistine (1-2). His words, *'Get her for me, for she pleases me well'* (3) show that he was more concerned to gratify himself than to please God. Intermarriage with the ungodly is a sin against the Lord (cp. Deuteronomy 7:1-4). **Many Christians live with bitter regret and remorse for their disobedience in marrying unbelievers. Let Samson be a warning to any who are contemplating such folly!**

When Samson was attacked by a lion, *the Spirit of the LORD came mightily upon him* and he was able, with his bare hands, to tear the beast apart. He visited his wife-to-be in Timnah and returned to see what had become of the carcass of the lion. He saw that it had become home to a colony of bees. He took honey from it which he shared with his parents (6-9). This incident gave him the idea for the riddle which he posed to the Philistine guests at his wedding. He challenged thirty of them to solve his riddle. The winner was to be provided with thirty linen garments and thirty changes of clothing at the expense of the loser (11-14). The Philistines threatened his bride and she relentlessly pestered him until he gave her the answer. They repeated the answer to Samson who now had to provide the prize.

Then the Spirit of the LORD came upon him mightily and he went to the Philistine city of Ashkelon where he killed thirty of their men to obtain the prize. An angry Samson deserted his bride who then married his best man (15-20)! **The fact that the Spirit of the LORD came upon Samson (6,19; 15:14) does not mean that God condoned his sin.** He overruled this sorry situation to use Samson's disobedience as an occasion to move against the Philistines who had been oppressing Israel for forty years (4-5; cp. 13:1). God is sovereign, but we must never use this wonderful truth as an excuse for our sin.

He cried out to the LORD

Samson later went to visit his wife and was furious to find that she had been given in marriage to another man. He caught three hundred foxes (Hebrew word can also mean 'jackals') and attached blazing torches to them. He loosed the terrified animals into the Philistine fields and so destroyed their harvest with fire. By way of reprisal, the Philistines burned to death Samson's wife and her father (1-6). This was the very thing that she had so feared (14:15). In an increasing cycle of violence, Samson brought havoc and slaughter to the Philistines (7-8).

The Philistines were determined to arrest Samson and came to attack Lehi in Judah. They demanded that Samson be handed over to them if the city were to avoid reprisals. The cowardly men of Judah preferred to accept Philistine oppression to fighting alongside Samson. **His patience and his gracious attitude to these faithless men is highly commendable.** He told the cowards that he would allow them to arrest him on behalf of the Philistines providing they did not attempt to kill him. *The Spirit of the LORD* again *came mightily upon him* and he snapped the ropes that bound him as the jubilant Philistines came to seize him. Single-handed he slaughtered one thousand of their soldiers using the jawbone of a donkey as a weapon (13-16). After this great exploit an exhausted and dehydrated Samson feared that he would die of thirst, *so he cried out to the LORD*. He acknowledged that God had given him a great deliverance and the Lord miraculously provided water from a spring (18-19).

In his faith and dependence upon God Samson was so different from the unbelieving men of Judah. **Let us learn from this. We must not sink into unbelief or apathy through discouragement.** Confusion grows in the professing church; false religion, occult and New Age practices increase in popularity; and wickedness abounds. Let us trust in God and have the courage to face the challenge. Spiritual victory is not to the faint-hearted, but to those who bravely persevere in serving God, trusting him alone.

But he did not know that the L{ORD} had departed from him

Samson's eyes were his downfall, and in the end he lost them! He went to the Philistine city of Gaza *and saw a harlot* [prostitute] *there, and went in to her* (1). Earlier in his life he had said to his parents, *'I have seen a woman ... get her for me'* (14:2). Those who live undisciplined lives live dangerously! Samson's entanglement with Delilah was his undoing. The fickle woman accepted a bribe from the Philistines to find out the secret of Samson's strength. She pestered him daily and wore down his resistance so that *he told her all his heart.* She discovered that his strength was linked to his Nazirite way of life (15-18; cp. 13:5). After lulling him to sleep, Delilah cut his hair and his strength left him. She then tormented him and the Philistines put him in shackles (19-21).

Samson lost more than his strength. *But he did not know that the L{ORD} had departed from him* (20). This is one of the saddest and most poignant verses in the Bible. The Philistines put out those eyes that had been the occasion of so much sin. Samson had lifted up the huge gates of Gaza on his shoulders (3). He was now back in Gaza as a prisoner grinding grain (21). Verse 22 points out that Samson's hair began to grow again. The Philistines organized a great celebration to sacrifice, and to praise their god, Dagon, for delivering Samson into their hands. He was taken from prison to the temple of Dagon which was packed with worshippers. The Philistines had stationed Samson between the supporting pillars of the temple (25). He cried out to the Lord for strength to strike the Philistines for the last time. God was gracious to his wayward servant and answered his prayer. With a mighty heave against the pillars Samson brought the temple crashing down, killing more Philistines in his death than in his entire life (23-30).

Let Samson's tragic life be a warning to us. Many a Christian has brought shame and misery to himself, his family and his church through lapses into sin. We must beware of Satan's wiles and resist every temptation that he puts in our path. **We must not allow our eyes to lead us into covetousness or lust (cp. 1 John 2:16). We dare not presume upon the presence of God if we walk in disobedience to his will.**

The Almighty has dealt very bitterly with me

Elimelech migrated to Moab with his family to escape the famine in Judah. They remained in Moab for about ten years (1-4). They should never have left the land which the Lord had given to them. While the people of Bethlehem survived the famine (6) Elimelech placed his family in a pagan environment in Moab where the people worshipped the fire-god Chemosh (Numbers 21:29; Deuteronomy 23:3-6; cp. 2 Kings 3:26-27). When his sons grew older, they married unbelieving women. Those of us who are parents have a solemn responsibility to bring up our children in a godly environment and under a sound biblical ministry. Many Christians have come to rue the day when, for the sake of material advancement, they have moved the family to an area which is spiritually barren.

Elimelech and his two sons died and after ten years in Moab Naomi decided to return to Bethlehem when she heard *that the LORD had visited his people by giving them bread* (6-7). Ruth was determined to stay with Naomi and she expressed her desire to go with her in a beautiful and tender manner. She said to Naomi, *'Your people shall be my people, and your God, my God'* (16-17).

Naomi returned to Bethlehem a broken woman. The years away from her home and her people had taken their toll. The people asked: *'Is this Naomi?'* (19). Naomi means 'pleasant' but she asked them to call her 'Mara' which means 'bitter' — *'for the Almighty has dealt very bitterly with me. I went out full, and the LORD has brought me home again empty'* (20-21).

The Lord is very gracious. When Naomi decided to return to her people and to her God she began to see the Lord's blessing in her life and that of Ruth. She proved the wonderful words of God written centuries later: *'I will heal their backsliding, I will love them freely'* (Hosea 14:4). **If you have backslidden from the Lord return to him now and repent of your sin. He will freely forgive you and he will restore your soul.**

She happened to come

God made provision for the poor in his law. Landowners were not to harvest the corners of their fields and forgotten sheaves were to be left for the needy to glean (Leviticus 19:9-10; Deuteronomy 24:19-23). Ruth took advantage of this law and went to glean at harvest time, to provide food for Naomi and herself. *She happened to come* (3). This verse reminds us that God wonderfully works in everyday events. *She happened to come* to the field of Boaz, a rich and near relative of Naomi. It may have been that Naomi had been too ashamed and broken in spirit to seek direct help from this relative.

Ruth discovered Boaz to be a most kind and godly man (8-15). Remember that these were the days of the judges when people were doing what was right in their own eyes (1:1; Judges 21:25). Boaz was a light in the prevailing darkness. He readily acknowledged the Lord; in his greeting to the reapers he said, *'The LORD be with you!'* (4). These were not empty words as subsequent events prove. Notice how Boaz encouraged Ruth in word (11-12) and in kind deeds (8-9,14-15). **Our churches need encouragers! Are you such a person, who is aware of other people's burdens, sorrows and struggles?** We need godly men and women who are thoughtful and understanding to fulfil this great ministry. Let us always seek to honour and glorify God by being kind (Ephesians 4:32; Philemon verse 7).

Naomi was surprised and delighted when Ruth returned well supplied with food. She praised God for his goodness, and for renewed contact with Boaz, a near relative of Elimelech (18-23). The Lord more than compensated Ruth for her sacrifice in leaving her family and country (11-12). Ruth *happened to come* but she discovered that there are no 'chance happenings' in her life because she belonged to God *under whose wings [she had] come for refuge* (12). **What a privilege to know that the Lord uses what we may perceive as ordinary and insignificant events in our lives to further his wise, kind and loving purposes (Romans 8:28).** Let us worship him for he is good! Let us thank him, for he so wonderfully directs our lives.

You are a virtuous woman

The customs described in this chapter and the next arise out of God's law for what is called 'levirate' marriage (Deuteronomy 25:5-10; cp. Genesis 38:8). When a married man died childless, his brother or nearest male relative was expected to marry his widow. The children of this union inherited the dead man's property and maintained the family line. The Sadducees referred to this law in their opposition to the teaching of the Lord Jesus (Luke 20:27-33). The near kinsman was also obliged to redeem (buy back) any property belonging to the dead relative, so as to keep it within the family (Leviticus 25:25-28).

Naomi explained God's law for 'levirate' marriage to Ruth. It appears that they had sold some land belonging to Elimelech before they left for Moab (4:3). Ruth, the childless widow of Mahlon, son of Elimelech, was entitled to call on a relative to be her kinsman-redeemer and to marry her. Naomi encouraged Ruth to propose to Boaz to fulfil this obligation (1-9).

Boaz was much older than Ruth who was probably in her late teens or early twenties. He had already been impressed by her love and loyalty to Naomi (2:11) and it had not escaped his attention that Ruth had gone into his field to work rather than to look for a husband (10). Ruth's godly conduct was already well known in Bethlehem; she was recognized as *a virtuous woman* (11). Boaz was attracted to Ruth but he was not prepared to dishonour God's law by depriving a nearer relative of his right as 'kinsman-redeemer' (12-13). The Lord was to honour him for his integrity.

Boaz and Ruth lived in days of moral decline but they were modest and chaste in their behaviour. Boaz was also concerned that Ruth's action would not be misunderstood (14). Our times are no different. **There must be no place in the Christian's life for unseemly talk, immodest behaviour or lack of integrity** (Ephesians 5:3-4). The Lord has chosen us and called us to be holy (Ephesians 1:4; 1 Peter 1:15). We must be different from those in the world (cp. Matthew 5:14-16).

I cannot redeem it ... lest I ruin my own inheritance

Boaz went the next day to the gate of the city, where in ancient times legal matters and disputes were settled (1). He found Naomi's nearest relative and called ten of the elders of the city to be witnesses. The man was more than happy to redeem the land for it would be a good investment. When he realized, however, that he would then be obliged to marry Ruth, he backed down (4-6). *'I will redeem it'* became *'I cannot redeem it for myself, lest I ruin my own inheritance.'*

The near relative took off his sandal as a token of his renunciation of the right to marry Ruth and to redeem the property that once belonged to Elimelech. Boaz was now free to redeem the property in question and to marry Ruth (7-10). The elders addressed Boaz and pronounced a beautiful blessing on him and on Ruth (11-12).

God gave Boaz and Ruth a son soon afterwards. The Lord turned Naomi's emptiness and misery into great blessing and much joy. What a contrast is found between the words of the women (14-15) and Naomi's outburst when she returned to Bethlehem (1:20-21). Things were no longer bitter ('Mara') for her but pleasant ('Naomi').

The book ends with a short genealogy which shows David to be the great-grandson of Ruth and Boaz (17-22). Ruth is also found in the royal line of the Lord Jesus Christ (Matthew 1:5). Boaz foreshadows our great Kinsman-Redeemer, the Lord Jesus, who redeemed us with his own blood (Ephesians 1:7; 1 Peter 1:18-19).

Ruth had left her family and country to follow the Lord (1:16-17) but he blessed her beyond her wildest dreams. **God honours and blesses those who follow him and obey him.**

JOHN

John, his brother James and Peter were the closest of the twelve disciples to the Lord Jesus Christ (Mark 5:37; 9:2; 14:33). In his Gospel, John does not refer to himself by name, but calls himself 'the disciple whom Jesus loved' (13:23; 21:7-20). He became a leader in the church at Jerusalem, being described as a 'pillar' in that church (Galatians 2:9). He spent his later years at Ephesus and was exiled to Patmos during the reign of the Roman emperor Domitian. It was there, while in the Spirit on the Lord's Day (Revelation 1:9-19), that he had his vision of the Lord Jesus in all his splendour and glory. John survived all the other disciples, dying approximately AD 98.

John was an eyewitness of the great miracles wrought by the Lord Jesus (21:24). He did not record as many of the miracles of Jesus as the other Gospel writers and none of the parables are found in his Gospel. He wrote his Gospel to introduce us, his readers, to the most wonderful Person who ever lived on this earth *that you may believe that Jesus is the Christ, the Son of God, and that believing you may have life in his name* (20:31).

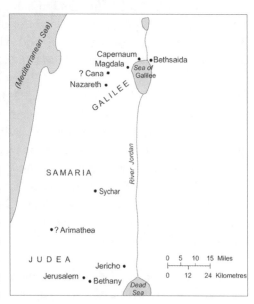

Sketch map of Judea, Galilee and Samaria

Key words: *Light — life — love*

119

In the beginning was the Word

John introduces us to the Lord Jesus Christ by describing him as 'the Word' (1,14). *In the beginning was the Word.* This title is given to Jesus because God the Father reveals himself through Christ and speaks through him (18; Hebrews 1:1-2). John leaves us in no doubt concerning the identity of the Lord Jesus. He was with God before the universe was made and he is God (1-2).

These verses not only inform us that the Lord Jesus is God, but also that he made all things. *All things were made through him* (3; cp. Colossians 1:16; Hebrews 1:10). Creation is the work of the Trinity: Father, Son and Holy Spirit (Genesis 1:1-2; notice the word *'us'* in Genesis 1:26). He is also the Giver of life who brings light to men who are in darkness because of sin (3-4). *'Life'* here and in much of this Gospel refers to spiritual life, and *'light'* is spiritual light or understanding (cp. 5:40; 9:39-41). John the Baptist was sent by God to bear witness of the Lord Jesus who is also described as *'the Light'* (6-9; 8:12; 9:5; 12:46).

The Word became flesh and dwelt among us (14). Just think about this for a moment. The Lord Jesus took human flesh with all of its limitations and weaknesses, except that he was and is sinless (cp. 2 Corinthians 5:21; Hebrews 4:15; 7:26). He knew hunger, thirst, weariness and pain. He is described as *a Man of sorrows and acquainted with grief* (Isaiah 53:3). The truth of the incarnation (Christ taking human flesh) is essential to the Christian faith (1 John 4:2-3), but we must always remember that the Lord Jesus did not cease to be God when he took human flesh. He is both God and man.

He came into the world that he had made, but the world did not recognize him (10). His own Jewish nation failed to acknowledge him (11) *but as many as received him, to them he gave the right to become children of God* (12). Man's will and nationality have no bearing on this new birth into the family of God; it is a supernatural, sovereign work of God himself (13). **Have you received the Lord Jesus Christ into your life as your Lord and Saviour and placed your trust in him?**

You must be born again

The work of the Trinity is displayed in the salvation of sinners. In John chapter 3 we see the love of God the Father (16-17), the sacrifice of God the Son (16) and the work of the Holy Spirit in bringing us to new birth (5,8; cp. Titus 3:5).

Nicodemus, a respected Jewish teacher, came to see the Lord Jesus at night to find out more about him. He discovered some very important truths that night. He learned that being religious does not guarantee a place in heaven and that to enter the kingdom of God a person had to be born again. There is good reason to believe that Nicodemus became a follower of Christ (7:50-52; 19:38-42). Why must we be born again?

- Because of our sinful human nature. We are *born of the flesh* (6) and we are all sinners by nature; *those who are in the flesh cannot please God* (Romans 3:23; 8:8).
- Because of our spiritual blindness. *Unless one is born again, he cannot see the kingdom of God'* (3).
- Because our eternal destiny depends upon it. *Unless one is born of water and the Spirit, he cannot enter the kingdom of God* (5). To be in the kingdom of God means to have eternal life and inexpressible joy. To be out of the kingdom means to perish, having the wrath of God upon us (16,36). On the day of judgment those who are not born again will wish that they had never been born at all.

Jesus reminded Nicodemus of the time when Israel rebelled against Moses and against God in the wilderness. The Lord punished them by sending poisonous serpents among the people and many died from the venom of these snakes. God told Moses to lift up a serpent of brass in the camp of Israel. All who obeyed and looked at the serpent were saved from death (Numbers 21). The Lord Jesus came down from heaven and had to be lifted up on the cross to save us. *For God so loved the world that he gave his only begotten Son, that whoever believes in him should not perish but have everlasting life* (16). **We would have no hope if Christ had not died in the place of sinners but we cannot be saved unless we are born again.**

Living water

The Lord Jesus left Judea to go to Galilee and *he needed to go through Samaria* (1-4). The most direct route to Galilee from Judea was through Samaria, but Jesus had another reason for going through Samaria. There was a sinful woman and others in her city to bring to faith in himself. Most Jews despised Samaritans who were a mixed race of Jew and Gentile. Their religion was mixed too, though they acknowledged the first five books of the Bible; they also looked for the Messiah (25). When the enemies of Jesus wanted to insult him, they called him 'a Samaritan' (8:48).

While the disciples were away buying food, the Lord Jesus was resting from his journey by Jacob's well. When a Samaritan woman came to draw water Jesus asked her for a drink (6-8). This surprised the woman, for no Jew would drink from a container used by Gentiles. Jesus then aroused her curiosity by speaking about the *gift of God* and *living water* (which the woman took to mean fresh spring water). She wondered how he could obtain such *living water* from such a deep well; could this stranger be greater than Jacob (9-12)? Jesus told the woman that the water from the well could only satisfy for a time, *'but whoever drinks of the water that I shall give him will never thirst'* (14). The woman misunderstood Jesus; she thought that he had some kind of water that, once taken, would quench her thirst for ever and do away with the need to draw and carry water (15).

Jesus went on to amaze the woman by revealing that he knew all about her immoral lifestyle (16-18). The astonished woman confessed that she knew that the coming Messiah would tell them all things (and Jesus had done this in her case). Jesus replied that he is that very Person (25-26). She forgot about water and on the arrival of the disciples, hurried back to Sychar, saying to the men, *'Come, see a man who told me all things that I ever did. Could this be the Christ?'* (27-30). Many Samaritans came to faith in Christ through the testimony of the woman (39-42). **She discovered the surpassing greatness of our Lord and Saviour. Have you?**

The one who comes to me I will by no means cast out

The feeding of the five thousand is the only miracle of Jesus which is recorded in all four Gospels. After Jesus had sent the crowds away, he told the disciples to cross the lake in the direction of Capernaum, while he went to a mountain to pray (15-17; Mark 6:45-46). A storm suddenly arose on the lake and the Lord Jesus came to the disciples walking on the water. They were terrified, believing that they had seen a ghost. He encouraged them, saying, *'It is I; do not be afraid'* and as he got into the boat the wind dropped and the storm was stilled (19-20; Mark 6:49-51). There are three miracles here that show the greatness of our Saviour:

- He walked on the water.
- He calmed the storm.
- The boat which was in the middle of the lake (Mark 6:47) was immediately at the shore after Jesus entered it (21).

The Greek for *'It is I'* (*ego eimi*) is literally 'I am' which is the covenant name of God (Exodus 3:14). The Jews recognized this when the Lord used the expression of himself on another occasion. They then attempted to stone him for blasphemy (John 8:58-59). **The disciples had no need to fear when their Lord and God was with them but they were unbelieving.** Why should we fear when we have such a Friend?

The multitude whom Jesus had fed wanted to make him their king but their faith was not genuine (15,26-30). Those who come to the Lord Jesus in true faith know spiritual satisfaction (35). They are given to Christ by God the Father (37,39; cp. 17:9-11), having been chosen in him before the world was made (Ephesians 1:4; 2 Thessalonians 2:13). We cannot come to Christ unless God the Father draws us to him (44) but we must never make this an excuse for rejecting Christ. He said, *'The one who comes to me I will by no means cast out'* (37). Have you come to the Lord Jesus? If not, what is holding you back? Come just as you are. He will accept you if you truly repent of your sin and trust in him.

One thing I know: that though I was blind, now I see

When the disciples saw the blind man they speculated on the cause of his blindness (2). The Lord Jesus saw him and had compassion on him (6-7). When the Pharisees saw him after he had received his sight, they were furious that Jesus had again been healing on the Sabbath. Some of them questioned how Jesus could do such miracles if he were a sinner (13-18). They asked the man his opinion of Jesus and he replied that Jesus was a prophet. This was too much for the Pharisees who refused to believe that the man had been blind and then healed, so they sent for his parents. They confirmed that their son had been born blind, but were fearful of saying any more. They knew that if they confessed Jesus to be the Christ (the Messiah), they would be excommunicated and made social outcasts (17-22).

The man was not intimidated by the enemies of Jesus, however. When these doubters again asked him how he had been healed, he answered, *'One thing I know: that though I was blind, now I see'* (25). The Pharisees had plenty of theories, but this man had experienced the power of God in his life. He responded to their persistent questioning by asking them, *'Do you also want to become his disciples?'* (27). The angry Pharisees were convinced that Jesus was a sinner and refused to acknowledge that he had been sent by the Father (29; cp. 5:36; 8:23). The brave man would not be silenced, however, and they excommunicated him (30-34).

Jesus sought, found and encouraged the man whom the Pharisees had cast out (34-35). The beggar received spiritual sight as he worshipped not just a man (11) nor a prophet (17), but the Son of God (35-38). He knew the loneliness of rejection, his own parents fearing to stand with him (20-22), but he discovered the surpassing worth and greatness of the Lord Jesus Christ. The Pharisees claimed to see but they were spiritually blind (39-42). **How dreadful to be blind to our own need of Christ to save us from our sins! How wonderful to receive spiritual sight from him who is 'the light of the world' (5; cp. 8:12)!**

I am the good shepherd

Those listening to the Lord Jesus were well acquainted with shepherds and sheep-folds. The sheep-fold was an area which was fenced off by a wall made of rocks. A gap in this wall served as a door which was guarded at night by the shepherd (or a door-keeper), who lay across the opening. It was common practice for several flocks to shelter in the same fold which was guarded by one of the shepherds. When the shepherds came the following morning, the door-keeper would admit them to the fold. They would then call their own sheep, each sheep recognizing his own shepherd's voice (2-5). The Jews did not understand what Jesus was teaching them in this illustration (6).

Jesus said, *'I am the good shepherd'* (10). The two main Greek adjectives translated 'good' in the New Testament are *'agathos'* and *'kalos'*. **The word used here is 'kalos' which means beautiful, noble, excellent and attractive. Jesus is all that to the believer.** He is *'the good shepherd'* of his sheep because:

- He loves them and gave his life to save them (11,15-18).
- He knows them and cares for them (13-14).
- He gives them abundant life, eternal life (10, 28).
- He keeps them secure for eternity (28-30).

Jesus is the door for the sheep to enter the sheep-fold (the kingdom of God). In this sheep-fold we are secure and have abundant life (7-10). The Lord's people (his *'sheep'*) are in constant peril from false shepherds (*'wolves'*) who care little for them, and who would scatter them and destroy them. A gospel minister has the solemn and awesome responsibility before God to guard the *'flock'* against false teachers (12-13; cp. Acts 20:28-30).

The blind beggar (chapter 9) had been cast out by false, uncaring shepherds (9:34), but was found by the good shepherd. He had heard his voice and had followed and worshipped him (9:37-38), finding abundant life (10). **Are you rejoicing in your good shepherd who loves you for ever?**

Lord, if ...

Lazarus and his two sisters were very close friends of Jesus who was a frequent guest in their home when he visited Jerusalem (just two miles away). When Lazarus was ill, they knew where to locate Jesus, though he was in Galilee. Their message was, *'Lord, behold, he whom you love is sick'* (3). We must always remember when we are ill or in trouble that God still loves us and tenderly watches over us.

Two days later Jesus told the disciples that they should return to Judea. Jesus said that the sickness of Lazarus would not lead to death, but was for the glory of God (4). They understood Jesus to mean that Lazarus would recover from his illness and that to return unnecessarily to Judea would invite further trouble from the Jews (6-8). The meaning of verses 9 and 10 is that the ministry of Jesus (the daytime, cp. 9:4-5) was fixed by God's eternal decree. No plot of the Jews could bring that ministry to a premature end. Jesus then told his disciples that Lazarus was asleep, but again they misunderstood him until he said plainly, *'Lazarus is dead'* (11-14).

Both Martha and Mary uttered the words, *'Lord, if...'* (21,32) but Martha also expressed her faith in the Lord Jesus (22). She knew that the prayers of Jesus are always answered and that Lazarus would be raised from the dead at the end of the world (22,24). She also stated her faith in Jesus as the Christ (the promised Messiah), the Son of God (27).

Jesus made a glorious statement concerning his power over death, *'I am the resurrection and the life. He who believes in me, though he may die, he shall live'* (25). Jesus has *'the keys of Hades and of death'* (Revelation 1:18). He raises sinners from spiritual death (cp. 5:25; Ephesians 2:1,5) and he will raise the bodies of all the dead when he comes again (5:28-29). Have you been thinking, praying or saying, *'Lord, if ...'*? **Think about the things that you know about the Lord Jesus in his greatness, in his love for you, in his wise and sovereign purpose over all of your circumstances, good or perplexing. He will never fail you nor forsake you. Take heart.**

As I have loved you ... you also love one another

The sandals worn by people in Palestine did not protect the feet from the dirt picked up when they walked on the dusty roads. In wealthy homes a slave washed the feet of guests. There was no slave at the Last Supper and none of the disciples volunteered to undertake this demeaning task. They were more interested in arguing about which one of them was the greatest than in doing the work of a slave (Luke 22:24-27). Jesus, who had all authority from the Father, rose up and put on the slave's apron and washed the feet of each of his disciples. We can be sure that Peter was not the only disciple to be embarrassed (3-6).

Why was Jesus so willing to wash his disciples' feet? He knew that he was about to go home to the Father who *had given all things into his hands* and *he loved them to the end* (1,3). He loved us so much that he humbled himself, taking the form of a servant (a slave). He was obedient to the Father's will, even to death (Philippians 2:7-8). If he has won our hearts, we will want to obey him (14:15). He has given us an example which he wants us to follow. He wants us to humbly serve one another (12-16). The Lord Jesus said, '*A new commandment I give to you, that you love one another; as I have loved you, that you also love one another*' (34). The New Testament repeats this commandment again and again (15:12,17; Ephesians 4:32 - 5:2; 1 John 2:9-11; 3:10-23; 4:7-11,20-21).

The word of God urges us, '*Love one another fervently with a pure heart*' (1 Peter 1:22). Love is patient and shows itself in practical deeds of kindness. Love in action means taking on the humble, the unnoticed, the self-sacrificing tasks. Jesus said, '*If you know these things, happy are you if you do them*' (17). 1 John 3:16 is as important as John 3:16. Ask the Lord to give you grace to love every believer known to you. Repent of any proud, awkward, selfish or thoughtless attitudes that make it difficult for other Christians to love you. **Love is the badge of Christian discipleship (35). Our religion is hypocritical if Christian love is absent from our lives.**

Peace I leave with you ... let not your heart be troubled

Judas Iscariot had departed from the Last Supper to go on his dark errand of betrayal (13:30). The eleven disciples were full of foreboding and fear, though Peter in a fit of bravado had indicated his willingness to lay down his life for his Master. Jesus warned Peter that he would deny him three times (13:36-38). Though Gethsemane and Calvary were only hours away, the Lord Jesus was more concerned for his troubled disciples than for himself. He reassured them, urging them to believe (trust) in him (1). He told them that he was going to prepare a place for them in his Father's house and that he would come again and receive them to himself so that they would be with him for ever (1-3). Jesus said to a puzzled Thomas, *'I am the way, the truth, and the life. No one comes to the Father except through me'* (6). Jesus is the only way to the Father, the only way to heaven. No other religion will do. There is no salvation apart from Jesus (Acts 4:12).

Jesus was going away but he promised that he would not leave the disciples as orphans. He would pray to the Father for them and he would give them another *'Helper'*, the Holy Spirit (16-18). Our obedience to the word of God is an evidence that we love him (21). There is a wonderful promise here, *'If anyone loves me, he will keep my word; and my Father will love him, and we will come to him and make our home with him.'* God, Father, Son and Holy Spirit dwell within all who love him and obey him (18,23). **How is your life before God? Are you doing everything to make him feel at home in your heart?**

Jesus again encouraged the disciples with a precious promise of peace, *'Peace I leave with you, my peace I give to you; not as the world gives do I give to you. Let not your heart be troubled, neither let it be afraid'* (27). We have peace with God *through the blood of his cross* (Colossians 1:20). Having peace with God (Romans 5:1) leads us to know the peace of God in our lives (Philippians 4:7; Colossians 3:15). **Are you troubled and fearful? Read Philippians 4:6-7 and trust in God. He will never fail you.**

Judas ... also stood with them ... Peter stood with them

After he had finished praying, the Lord Jesus and the eleven disciples left the house and went to the Garden of Gethsemane. The Kidron valley lay between the eastern wall of Jerusalem and the Mount of Olives (1). Judas had often been with Jesus in Gethsemane and he went there with a detachment of soldiers and officers from the chief priests and Pharisees (2-3). Jesus was not taken by surprise. He knew that he would be betrayed by Judas in Gethsemane and he went forward to meet his enemies (4). He asked them whom it was they were seeking and when they replied, *'Jesus of Nazareth,'* he said, *'I am he.'* They fell back to the ground and he again asked them whom they were seeking and told them that he was Jesus and that they should allow the disciples to go their way. He lovingly protected them to the end (5-8).

Imagine the anguish of the Lord Jesus as he was betrayed in Gethsemane. *Judas ... also stood with them* (5). The traitor had been a constant companion and friend for over three years but he was now standing with those who hated Jesus. What can be more heart-rending than seeing one, who once seemed so genuine in his faith, now standing with the enemies of Christ (cp. Philippians 3:18)?

Later that evening, the same words are said of Peter. *And Peter stood with them* (18). His motives were very different from those of Judas; he was standing there out of deep concern for his Master and wanted to know what these evil people were planning to do with his Lord. Peter's courage gave way as he was challenged about his relationship to Jesus. He had been so presumptuous in his protests that he would never deny the Lord (Matthew 26:33-35). However sincere his motives, Peter should never have *'stood with them'*. He thought that he was strong, when really he was weak, and he denied the Lord Jesus three times (17,25-27).

Judas is a frightening example of sham religion. Peter is a warning against self-confidence (cp. 1 Corinthians 10:11-12). Where are you standing?

Behold your King!

The Roman scourge was a whip which had several thongs, with pieces of bone or lumps of lead knotted into them, which tore open the victim's flesh. Pilate had Jesus scourged, though he acknowledged that he was innocent. He brought Jesus back to the Jews saying, *'Behold the Man!'* (1-5). He may have thought that no one would have considered this man a threat to Caesar as they looked at him. He was dressed in mock royal robes, his head torn by the crown of thorns, his face swollen and bruised from many blows, his body bleeding from the scourging.

The words of our reading today should fill us with a sense of awe and of wonder. Pilate said to the Jews, *'Behold your King!'* (14). The lonely, bleeding, disfigured man standing before Pilate was more than *'the King of the Jews'*. He is the King of kings (Revelation 19:13-16)!

- *'Behold your King!'* — His crown woven from long thorns which ripped his scalp and his brow.
- *'Behold your King!* — His face pummelled beyond recognition (cp. Isaiah 52:14) and his back torn apart by scourging.
- *'Behold your King!'* — Mocked, humiliated, nailed to the cross, dying in terrible agony.
- *'Behold your King!'* — Dying for his people. What a glorious King! What matchless love!

John was the only disciple of the twelve to be an eyewitness of the crucifixion (26,35). He emphasizes that the events at Calvary were a fulfilment of Old Testament prophecy (24,28,36-37). The Lord Jesus was in terrible pain and anguish but he tenderly commended his mother into the care of John. The loyal disciple took Mary to his own home — probably the house or rooms rented for the Passover; his real home was in Galilee.

We should meditate much on the suffering of our Saviour. We will then hate the very thought of sinning and we will welcome his reign over us. Let us worship him and praise him for his great love.

My Lord and my God

Mary Magdalene went to the tomb of Jesus very early in the morning hoping to anoint the body of Jesus with spices. The notion that Mary had previously been an immoral woman is without any foundation. She had good reason to love the Lord Jesus. Her life had been ruined by demon-possession until he had delivered her. She was very puzzled to find the stone rolled away and ran to tell Peter and John. They hurried to the tomb to find things just as Mary had described them (1-10). The Lord Jesus is King over death. He rose from the grave and on the first day of his resurrection he appeared to Mary Magdalene and to his troubled disciples (11-20).

Thomas was not with the disciples when the Lord Jesus first appeared to them. He wanted to see and feel the nailprints in his hands and the spear-wound in his side before he would believe (25). **We must be careful to distinguish between the doubts of those who rebel against God and mock, and the doubts suffered by the Christian.** We are sometimes tormented by doubt when Satan hurls his fiery darts at us (Ephesians 6:16); he plants doubts about God — his existence, his love and care for us, doubts about assurance of our own salvation. Such doubts bring darkness and despair, but we can emerge from these dark struggles with greater faith and devotion to the Lord.

The Lord Jesus knew all about Thomas, his doubts and struggles. He knew what he had said to his fellow-disciples. He appeared to the disciples a week later and Thomas was with them. Jesus called on him to look on his pierced hands and to place his finger there, to put his hand in his pierced side (27). He encouraged him, saying, *'Do not be unbelieving but believing.'* Thomas exclaimed, *'My Lord and my God!'* (28; yet another verse which shows that Jesus is God). Jesus said to him, *'Thomas, because you have seen me, you believe. Blessed are those who have not seen and yet have believed'* (29). **We have not yet seen the Lord Jesus; we walk by faith, not by sight (2 Corinthians 5:7), but he blesses us when we trust in him.** Do you joyfully worship and praise Jesus as your Lord and as your God?

Do you love me?

Peter and six other disciples went fishing on the Sea of Tiberias (Galilee). Peter said to them, *'I am going fishing'* and they went with him, but a night's fishing failed to produce a catch (1-3). They did not recognize Jesus when he stood on the shore early that morning. We are not told why this was so; it could be that they may have been supernaturally kept from recognizing him (cp. Luke 24:16); it may have been because of an early morning mist that blurred their view of him. Hearing that they had not caught any fish, he told them to cast the net on the right side of the boat. The catch was so great that they could not draw the net into the boat. John said to Peter, *'It is the Lord!'* Peter plunged into the water to reach Jesus ahead of the boat (4-7). The others followed, dragging the net full of fish behind the boat. Jesus had a charcoal fire prepared with fish cooking and also bread for breakfast. He told them to bring some of the fish which they had caught and they ate breakfast together (8-13).

After they had eaten breakfast, Jesus spoke to Peter who had denied him three times. The Lord challenged him three times, *'Do you love me?'* (15-17). On the first two occasions Jesus used the verb *'agapao'*, the greatest of the Greek words for 'love', meaning 'to have whole-hearted, self-sacrificing devotion'. Peter, in response, used the Greek verb *'phileo'* which means 'to have affection'. 'Peter, do you love me with all your heart and soul?' 'Yes, Lord, you know that I am fond of you.' The third time Jesus asked, 'Peter, are you fond [*'phileo'*] of me?' and he was grieved as his Master gently probed his heart.

He wants us to follow him with total devotion and obedience, even if it means laying down our lives for him (18-19,22). Why should we love the Lord Jesus? We should love him because he is perfect in all his ways. He loves us and willingly laid down his life on the cross to save us. He has had mercy on us and he cares for us. He is preparing a place in heaven for us. **We often sing of our love for Jesus and of our willingness to do whatever he asks of us but actions speak louder than words. Do you really love him?**

ACTS

Luke, *'the beloved physician'* (Colossians 4:14), wrote his Gospel and the Acts of the Apostles to give to Theophilus a history of the ministry of the Lord Jesus Christ and the apostles (1:1). This man was probably a person of some importance, for he is addressed as *'most excellent'*, a title given to Roman governors (Luke 1:3; cp. Acts 23:26; 24:3; 26:25). Luke continues in Acts where he left off in his Gospel (*'the former account'*, 1:1). The events in the book cover a period of some thirty-three years from AD 30 to AD 62.

The Acts of the Apostles has often been called 'the Acts of the Holy Spirit' because of its record of the mighty working of the Spirit of God through the apostles, particularly Peter and Paul (there are seventy references to the Holy Spirit in Acts). The words *'witness'* and *'witnesses'* are found throughout the book (1:8,22; 2:32; 3:15; 4:33; 5:32; 10:39,41; 13:31; 22:15; 23:11; 26:16,22). The gospel is for *'all nations'* (Luke 24:47). The Lord Jesus told the apostles that the Holy Spirit would come upon them and they would be witnesses to him *in Jerusalem, and in all Judea and Samaria, and to the end of the earth* (1:8). This promise and command are reflected in the three sections of the book:

1. Witness in Jerusalem (chapters 1 to 7) — AD 30-32
2. Witness in Judea and Samaria (chapters 8 to 12) — AD 32-43
3. Witness to the end of the earth (chapters 13 to 28) — AD 47-62

The dates shown above are approximate.

May God be pleased to challenge us and to enthuse us by the example of the early church. Let us work and witness for the same risen Lord.

You shall be witnesses to me

Luke makes a brief reference to his Gospel (*'the former account'*). He then reminds Theophilus that the Lord Jesus often appeared to the disciples during the forty days between his resurrection and ascension. He showed himself to be alive *by many infallible proofs* (3). They knew without a shadow of doubt that Jesus, who had been put to death by crucifixion, had risen from the dead. **Christianity is based on facts!** The Lord Jesus had opened their understanding that they might comprehend the Scriptures and spoke *of the things pertaining to the kingdom of God* (3; cp. Luke 24:45). These things included the necessity *for the Christ to suffer and to rise from the dead the third day, and that repentance and remission of sins should be preached in his name to all nations* (Luke 24:46-47).

Before he ascended into heaven (9-12), the Lord Jesus told the disciples to wait in Jerusalem for *the promise of the Father,* the outpouring of the Holy Spirit (4-8). They were at the beginning of a new dispensation when the Holy Spirit would dwell in every believer (Ezekiel 36:26-27; Acts 2:38; Romans 8:9-11,15-16; 1 Corinthians 12:13; Galatians 4:6). Jesus said, *'You shall receive power when the Holy Spirit has come upon you; and you shall be witnesses to me ... '* (8). **We too have the Holy Spirit but are we witnessing?** We are to tell men and women of the liberating power of the gospel which can rescue them from the tyranny of Satan and sin, and that they need to repent of their sin and to trust in Christ to save them.

There are discouragements in the work of the gospel and our message is often scorned and rejected. The half-brothers of the Lord Jesus Christ (sons of Joseph and Mary) did not at first believe in him (John 7:5). They were now praying with the eleven disciples and other believers (13-14). James and Jude became leaders in the church (12:17; cp. Galatians 1:19; Jude 1:1). **Let us persevere in praying for those we love and in witnessing to them.** This company waited on God in prayer before appointing Matthias to take the place of Judas Iscariot among the twelve apostles (15-26).

One accord

The Feast of Pentecost was celebrated seven weeks after the Passover (Leviticus 23:15-21). God chose this time to pour out his Holy Spirit on the first Christians who were expectantly praying in the upper room of a house in Jerusalem (cp. 1:12-14). They were enabled to speak the wonderful works of God in recognizable languages (1-11). Peter was then able to preach mightily in the power of the Spirit. He freely quoted from the Old Testament to show that the coming of the Holy Spirit was prophesied in Joel and that Jesus is the promised Messiah who would die and rise from the grave (17-21,25-28,34). The death of Jesus was planned by God but this did not excuse those who crucified him (23). Three thousand people were saved after Peter's sermon. The Holy Spirit worked in their hearts to bring them under conviction of sin, and to repentance and faith in God (37-41). They gladly received the word and were baptized in obedience to God's command (41). *And they continued steadfastly in the apostles' doctrine and fellowship, in the breaking of bread, and in prayers* (42).

Notice the unity of those early Christians. '*One accord*' (1,46) is translated from the Greek word meaning 'to be of the same mind'. This unity of mind is also found elsewhere in Acts (4:24; 5:12; 15:25; cp. Romans 15:6 — '*one mind*'). The Holy Spirit came in power to a united fellowship which prayed with unity of heart and purpose (1; cp. 1:14). This oneness of mind was also seen in the mutual love and trust found among those early disciples as they cared for each other (44-46). Oneness of mind includes oneness in truth. Biblical unity is not gained by compromising truth. Those first Christians *continued steadfastly in the apostles' doctrine* (42). Their unity enhanced their joy and their praise (46-47).

Unity in the local church is priceless. It is a foretaste of heaven on earth! Let us do everything in our power *to keep the unity of the Spirit in the bond of peace* (Ephesians 4:1-6; cp. Psalm 133). **How united are you with the believers in your local church? Do you show genuine love and practical concern for them?**

Men of good reputation, full of the Holy Spirit and wisdom

The disciples were *'multiplying'* (1) and a growing church is bound to have 'growing pains'. Satan is always on the lookout for ways to destroy the unity of a church. The apostles had such a great workload that they failed to notice that the Christian widows of the Hellenists (Greek-speaking Jews) were being neglected. This situation was not brought about by malice but it could have easily destroyed the unity of the Jerusalem church. It led to misunderstanding and then *murmuring against the Hebrews* (Aramaic-speaking Jews; 1).

The apostles were sensitive to this grievance and acted to maintain the unity and fellowship of the church. Those in the church were to seek out from among themselves *seven men of good reputation, full of the Holy Spirit and wisdom* to be responsible for the care of the widows (3). The apostles gave themselves *continually to prayer and to the ministry of the word... And the word of God spread, and the number of the disciples multiplied greatly in Jerusalem, and a great many of the priests were obedient to the faith* (4,7). A situation which could have blighted the church was turned into great blessing. The humble task of serving tables was important enough to need *men of good reputation, full of the Holy Spirit and wisdom.* What is the evidence of being *full of the Holy Spirit?* There is a beauty and attractiveness about such a life because it bears the precious fruit of the Holy Spirit (Galatians 5:22-23).

Stephen is described as being *full of faith and the Holy Spirit* (5) and *full of faith and power* (8). He was an outstanding Christian who was humble enough to *'serve tables'.* He faithfully, powerfully and boldly preached the gospel. All Christians have the gift of the Holy Spirit (2:38), but not all are equally godly or Christlike. Stephen's enemies disputed with him, but *they were not able to resist the wisdom and the Spirit by which he spoke* (10). His sermon in the next chapter shows that he had an excellent knowledge of Scripture. **We cannot have spiritual wisdom without a knowledge and love of God's word.** *Let the word of Christ dwell in you richly in all wisdom* (Colossians 3:16).

Everywhere preaching the word

A young man named Saul was involved in the killing of Stephen. He also *made havoc of the church,* persecuting Christians with great zeal (1-3). The outlook appeared to be very bleak for the church at Jerusalem as its members were imprisoned or scattered throughout Judea and Samaria. **God overruled this great persecution, however. The scattering of the Christians led to the spread of the gospel.** *Therefore those who were scattered went everywhere preaching the word* (4). The enemies of Christ may have silenced Stephen but God used his fellow-deacon Philip to proclaim the gospel. Philip's ministry made a great impact on a Samaritan city and the apostles sent Peter and John to see this work of God among the Samaritans (5-8,14). They also preached in many Samaritan villages (25).

This chapter also draws our attention to two individuals, Simon and the Ethiopian eunuch. Simon's faith was spurious though he was baptized and continued with Philip (13). His heart was not right in the sight of God (21) and his profession of faith deceived Philip. It is possible to deceive godly Christian leaders but all hypocrisy will be exposed on the day of judgment. The Lord directed Philip to leave the rejoicing city of Samaria to go to a desert region between Jerusalem and Gaza where he met the Ethiopian court official (26). The man was reading Isaiah chapter 53 which prophesies the death of Christ in great detail. Philip preached Jesus to the man, beginning with this passage of Scripture. The Ethiopian was saved and baptized and went on his way rejoicing (36-39).

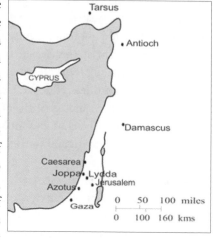

Witness in Judea, Samaria and Syria —places mentioned in Acts 8 to 12

He is a chosen vessel of mine

Saul of Tarsus was relentless in his mission to destroy the church (1-2; cp. 7:58 - 8:3). He was, however, kicking against a guilty conscience (5). He had evil intentions in visiting Damascus but he reckoned without God's sovereign and gracious purposes. God humbled him and blinded him with a dazzling light from heaven, and the risen Lord Jesus spoke to him (3-6). Ananias, a disciple at Damascus, could hardly believe that the man who had so relentlessly hunted Christians was praying (10-14). Saul was *'a chosen vessel of Christ'* (15) and was himself to suffer much for his Saviour (16). He was to be used more than any other man in the history of the church to proclaim the gospel and to plant churches. **No one is too hard for God to save. He may have many chosen vessels among those who presently appear to be indifferent or opposed to the gospel.** Let us pray with faith and expectation and persevere in our work for the Lord.

The Jews at Damascus were amazed to find Saul preaching in their synagogues that Jesus is the Son of God. They turned on him and plotted to kill him but the Christians at Damascus helped him to escape over the city wall at night (20-25). When he returned to Jerusalem, he was treated with great suspicion by the Christians in that city. They could not bring themselves to believe that he had really come to faith in Christ, but Barnabas took him, brought him to the apostles and spoke on his behalf (26-28). Saul began to speak boldly in the name of the Lord Jesus but the Hellenists (Greek-speaking Jews) attempted to kill him and he was sent to his home in Tarsus for his own safety (29-30). The churches multiplied as they experienced the comfort of the Holy Spirit and walked in the fear of the Lord (31).

Barnabas was a great encouragement to Saul (his name means 'son of encouragement'). He was prepared to trust Saul when others shunned him because of fear. Barnabas encouraged the new convert who was soon integrated into the life and witness of the church. **The ministry of encouragement is essential if a church is to be built up. Let us at all times seek to encourage one another.**

God shows no partiality

Cornelius, a Roman centurion, was a devout, God-fearing man, prayerful and generous (2). He was seeking God and the Lord sent an angel to him in a vision to tell him, *'Your prayers and alms have come up for a memorial before God'* (4). Cornelius was not yet a Christian but the Lord heard his prayers. He told the centurion to send messengers to Peter, who would tell him what he must do. God was already preparing the apostle through a vision to take the message of salvation to Cornelius (9-23). Peter went to Caesarea with the three messengers, accompanied by six of the Christians from Joppa (23; cp. 11:12). Cornelius was still spiritually ignorant and he tried to worship the apostle (24-26).

Peter and many early Jewish Christians still held to their old prejudices concerning Gentiles (non-Jews), considering them to be 'unclean'. God had told Peter in a vision to eat unclean animals. *'God has shown me that I should not call any man common or unclean'* (28). Before receiving his vision, he would not have entered the house of a Roman (28-29). Cornelius had invited his relatives and close friends to hear the apostle who told them, *'God shows no partiality'* (34). He saves all who believe (trust) in the Lord Jesus (43). Cornelius and those with him were saved as Peter was preaching (cp. 11:17-18). They received a similar experience to the apostles at Pentecost when the Holy Spirit was poured out upon them (44-48; cp. 11:15). The Jewish Christians who were with Peter *were astonished ... because the gift of the Holy Spirit had been poured out on the Gentiles also* (45).

Prejudice is a hindrance to the work of the gospel. We must never despise anyone because they are of a different race or station in life from ourselves. We are all sinners and we all need to be saved. The gospel is for all classes of people and for all races. *'God shows no partiality.'* Let us seek to reach all kinds of people. God may already be working in the lives of those who seem unlikely to be saved, preparing them to receive the message of the gospel.

They sent them away. So, being sent out by the Holy Spirit...

The church at Antioch was established by Christians who had been driven from Jerusalem by persecution (11:19-26). It became the base for the missionary activity of the early church.Their leaders were blessed in their evangelistic work (11:20-24) and diligent in their teaching (11:26). The people were also generous in their giving (11:27-30). After fasting and prayer, the leadership of the church set aside as missionaries two of their number, Barnabas and Saul (2-6). Fasting is a neglected discipline in the church today and we are the poorer for it. The church at Antioch was led by godly men who fasted and prayed (3; cp. 14:23). They earnestly sought the Lord and were led by the Holy Spirit in their decision-making. *They sent them away. So, being sent out by the Holy Spirit ...* (3-4).

There are some important principles for missionary work in these verses. Though Barnabas and Saul were called to their missionary work by God, it was their local church that recognized that call. They were also active in the leadership of the Antioch church. Unproven novices or those who are not already involved in serving the Lord in their local church should not be sent out as missionaries. If we disregard these biblical principles, we are asking for trouble.

The only conversion recorded in Cyprus was that of Sergius Paulus, the Roman proconsul. His friend, Elymas, an apostate Jew, a sorcerer and a false prophet, tried to turn him away from the faith. He was struck with blindness at the command of Saul (from now on called 'Paul') and the astonished proconsul believed (8-12). We must always remember that when God is at work, Satan is always active.

After they had arrived in Perga John Mark left them to return to Jerusalem (13). When they reached Antioch in Pisidia, Paul and Barnabas first went to the synagogue to preach the gospel but the following Sabbath almost the whole city came to hear the word of God (14,44). Again, there was opposition, this time from unbelieving Jews, but Paul and Barnabas left behind a rejoicing community of new believers.

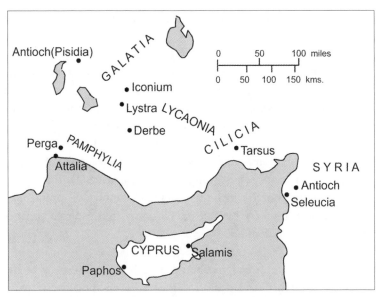

Paul's First Missionary Journey — Acts 13 & 14

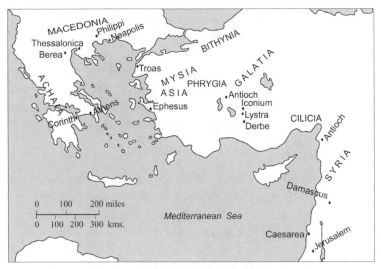

Paul's Second Missionary Journey — Acts 15:41 - 18:22

Some ... have troubled you ... unsettling your souls

We have already seen that Satan attacks the church from the outside with persecution (e.g. 8:1-3) and from within by seeking to destroy the unity of the church (e.g. 6:1). The devil will do all that he can to rob us of blessing. There is another instance here of an attack from within the church. Paul and Barnabas returned to the church at Antioch in Syria to report *all that God had done with them* (14:27) but trouble was not far away. Men came from Judea insisting that Gentile Christians submit to the rite of circumcision in order to be saved (1). This caused a dispute in the church which then decided to resolve the problem by sending a delegation, led by Paul and Barnabas, to consult the apostles and elders at Jerusalem (2).

News of Gentile conversions should have brought great joy to the Jerusalem church just as it did to other believers, but it resulted in the same dispute over circumcision that had taken place in Antioch (4-7). Happily, the matter was resolved when the apostles sent out a letter to the churches in which they stated that they did not endorse this false teaching (23-29). *Some who went out from us have troubled you with words, unsettling your souls ...* (24). **If you are a Christian, do not be surprised when you meet with professing believers who will trouble you with their words and who will unsettle your soul.** These people twist the meaning of Scripture and want everyone to follow their peculiar ideas. They are doing the work of Satan to unsettle your soul. If you have been troubled by such people, talk to your pastor or to a mature Christian whom you love and respect. They will be pleased to help you.

Even great and godly men have their differences or personality problems which Satan will seek to exploit. Paul and Barnabas were all set for their second missionary journey, but they parted from one another after a sharp dispute over John Mark. The church at Antioch supported Paul, who took Silas with him in the place of Barnabas (36-40). **Satan loves to divide us — let us learn to recognize his craftiness so that we will be on our guard.**

Come over to Macedonia and help us

Paul began his second missionary journey travelling north through Syria and then through Cilicia *strengthening the churches* (15:41). He had with him the letter from the apostles and elders at Jerusalem giving instructions for the Gentile Christians (4). Paul and Silas went to Galatia, and when they arrived in Lystra, Paul chose Timothy to join his missionary team. Timothy was to become one of Paul's closest and most trusted friends (cp. Philippians 2:19-23; 2 Timothy 1:2). They travelled north and then west but were forbidden by the Holy Spirit to preach the gospel in Asia and Bithynia. They were joined by Luke at Troas (notice how *'they'* in verse 8 becomes *'we'* in verse 10). It would appear that Luke remained at Philippi (17:1 — *'they'*) and rejoined Paul when he passed through Philippi on his third missionary journey (20:5-6).

While at the port of Troas Paul had a vision of a man pleading with him, *'Come over to Macedonia and help us'* (8-9). The people of Macedonia enjoyed the rich heritage of Greek culture, but all the learning and wisdom of the Greek philosophers had no answer to the desperate plight of mankind. One of these philosophers once said, 'The best thing of all is not to be born, and the next best thing is to die.' What wretched despair! Man without God is without hope (Ephesians 2:12). Has man's advance in science and technology changed things? Not at all! **Men and women are still sinners. They are lost and they need to be saved. We may not be privileged to have visions like Paul, but we have the same good news.** Are you taking the gospel to sinners around you? Are you willing to say, 'Lord, send me'?

This chapter records the triumphs of the gospel as Paul obeyed the Lord and went to Philippi in Europe:

- Lydia, whose heart the Lord opened (14-15).
- The demon-possessed slave-girl, delivered from the grip of Satan (16-19).
- The Philippian jailer and his family, who were saved through the witness of Paul and Silas (22-34).

The unknown God

Paul and his companions went from Philippi to Thessalonica and Berea. Paul's preaching in the synagogues of those two cities was followed by many conversions as well as persecution instigated by hostile Jews (4-6,12-13). He left Silas and Timothy behind in Berea while he travelled south to Athens (14-15). The city was renowned for its magnificent buildings and for its culture but Paul's spirit was provoked within him by its spiritual ignorance and idolatry (16; *'provoked'* means 'passionately moved'). They had shrines to all the gods known to them and they also had an altar inscribed *'TO THE UNKNOWN GOD'* to cover any other god of whom they were ignorant (23).

Paul proclaimed some essential truths that the Athenians needed to know about the God they did not know. He told them that:

- God made the world and everything in it (24).
- He is the Lord over all the universe (24).
- Temples cannot contain God, for he is everywhere (24,27).
- He sustains his creation (25).
- He is absolutely sovereign in all his purposes (26).
- Idolatry is a denial of God (29).
- God *'commands all men everywhere to repent'* (30).
- He will judge the world through the Lord Jesus whom he raised from the dead (31).

Some mocked Paul, some promised to hear him again, but others believed, including Dionysius, one of the philosophers of the Areopagus, and a woman named Damaris (34). **The true and living God is unknown to the people around us.** Some are sophisticated, cultured and articulate (like the philosophers of Athens), others boast no great education and many are poor and unemployed. They have one thing in common — they are lost, without God and without hope. We may be mocked when we witness to those around us, but there will also be encouragements. Let us persevere in prayer for the lost and look for every opportunity to make the gospel known to them. **We have the message that they need.**

I have many people in this city

Paul left Athens, the cultural capital of Greece, for Corinth, the commercial capital (1). The city had become a very important trading centre and at the time of Paul's visit had a population of half a million people. Athens was full of idols but Corinth was full of immorality, and was notorious throughout the ancient world for its debauched and sleazy way of life. The Roman emperor Claudius had driven the Jews from Rome shortly before Paul arrived in Corinth in AD 51/52. Aquila and his wife Priscilla had been among those expelled but the Lord used this adverse circumstance to bring them into contact with Paul at Corinth. The couple were to become very close and special friends of Paul (2-3; cp. Romans 16:3-5).

Despite the opposition of the Jews Crispus the ruler of the synagogue and many other Corinthians were saved (6-8). God spoke to Paul in a vision at night, reassuring him and urging him to persevere in the face of opposition. The Lord told him, *'I have many people in this city'* (9-10). Paul was encouraged and he remained in Corinth for eighteen months, teaching the word of God (11). God had choice vessels to pluck from Corinth's cesspool of wickedness (cp. 1 Corinthians 6:9-11: *'And such were some of you'*). **The fact that God predestined men and women to salvation before he made the world does not hinder the work of evangelism, but rather enhances it.** This truth has encouraged many thousands since Paul's day, among them great Christians such as John Calvin, David Brainerd, George Whitefield, William Carey and C. H. Spurgeon. We do not know who the elect are among those whom we meet day by day. Let us persevere in our evangelism, trusting that God has *'many people'* where we live, who are presently indifferent to the gospel.

Aquila and Priscilla travelled with Paul to Ephesus and remained there while the apostle continued his journey to Jerusalem (18-23). God used them to point Apollos to Christ. Apollos later went to Corinth where he greatly helped the believers and proved to the Jews that Jesus is the Christ (24-28).

Paul's Third Missionary Journey — Acts 18:23 - 21:17

1. Paul leaves Antioch for his third missionary journey, travelling to Galatia and Phrygia where he strengthens all the disciples (18:23).
2. He travels on to Ephesus, where he spends three years in evangelism and teaching (19:1-41; cp. 20:31).
3. Paul sends Timothy and Erastus into Macedonia (Acts 19:22).
4. Following the riot in Ephesus Paul leaves to go to Macedonia (20:1-3).
5. After staying three months in Greece, Paul travels from Philippi to Troas (20:4-5)
6. Paul and his companions spend seven days in Troas, before leaving for Miletus (20:5-16).
7. After meeting the Ephesian church elders in Miletus, Paul sails for Tyre (20:17 to 21:3).
8. The apostle and his companions spend seven days in Tyre before boarding their ship for the last leg of their journey. They travel on to Ptolemais and Caesarea, and then to Jerusalem (21:4-15).

So the word of the Lord grew mightily and prevailed

Paul went to Jerusalem and Antioch in Syria before setting out on his third missionary journey. He first travelled throughout Galatia and Phrygia, strengthening believers (18:21-23). He eventually arrived at Ephesus which was the most important city in the Roman province of Asia (now western Turkey). It was a great trading centre and place of pilgrimage to the shrine of the goddess Diana. In Ephesus he met twelve disciples of John the Baptist. They had not received the Holy Spirit when they believed the message of John because they had not heard about him and they did not know Jesus as their Saviour. They turned to Christ, were baptized, and received the Holy Spirit (1-6).

Paul went into the synagogue in Ephesus *and spoke boldly for three months, reasoning and persuading concerning the things of the kingdom of God* (8). Some believed but others were hardened and Paul withdrew from them. He then reasoned every day for two years in the school (the lecture-room) of Tyrannus (9). Notice the word *'reasoning'* in verses 8 and 9. **True Christian teaching does not bypass the human mind. True preaching and teaching not only stirs the heart but it persuades us and makes us think.**

The word of the Lord was heard throughout the province of Asia at this time (9-10). *So the word of the Lord grew mightily and prevailed* (20). The word of God prevailed over occult practices and idolatry (19,26-27) to such an extent that it threatened the livelihood of the Ephesian silversmiths who made and sold images of the goddess Diana (Artemis). They stirred up a riot against Paul but they were quieted by the town clerk and dispersed peacefully.

The early Christians were known as belonging to *'the Way'* (9,23; cp. 9:2; 24:22). They taught that there is only one way to God the Father — through the Lord Jesus Christ (4:12; cp. John 14:6; 1 Timothy 2:5). **All religions do not lead to God. To believe that they do is to be in spiritual darkness and great error.** It is another gospel (cp. Galatians 1:6-9). Let us always be faithful in pointing people to the Lord Jesus.

Therefore take heed to yourselves and to all the flock

Paul travelled from Ephesus to visit the churches in Macedonia where he *encouraged them with many words* (1-2). He then travelled south from Macedonia to Greece where he spent three months, mainly at Corinth. While there he wrote his letter to the Romans (cp. Romans 15:25-26). He changed his plan to sail from Corinth to Jerusalem because of a Jewish plot against him and returned through Macedonia to Troas (3-6). The early church met on the first day of the week to worship God and called it *'the Lord's Day'* (7; cp. 1 Corinthians 16:2; Revelation 1:10). Paul preached until midnight at Troas and a young man named Eutychus sank into a deep sleep during the meeting. He fell to his death from his precarious seat but Paul embraced his lifeless body and raised him from the dead (8-12).

When he arrived at Miletus, Paul sent for the elders of the Ephesian church and reminded them of his life and ministry among them (17-36). The Holy Spirit had warned Paul that imprisonment and trouble lay ahead of him but he did not count his own life dear to himself. **The most important thing for him was to remain faithful in his ministry,** *to testify to the gospel of the grace of God* (23-24). In his ministry at Ephesus Paul had declared *the whole counsel of God* (27). He urged the elders, *'Therefore, take heed to yourselves and to all the flock'* (27-28). He warned that *savage wolves* would come into the church to attack the flock (29). They must watch because some of their own number would depart from the truth and divide the church (30-31). Your pastor and church leaders are special targets for satanic attack. Pray that God will keep them pure in doctrine and life, that they will have God-given wisdom and discernment, and that they will stand firm in the face of discouragement and temptation to compromise.

Paul reminded the elders of his own example among them and told them that they must support the weak, for the Lord Jesus had said, *'It is more blessed to give than to receive'* (33-35). Paul knew that he would not see these people again and there were many tears as they parted (25,37-38).

The will of the Lord be done

The Holy Spirit again warned Paul both at Tyre and at Caesarea that he would be arrested and imprisoned if he went to Jerusalem (4,11). Was he disobeying God in his determination to go there? Such a thought is out of the question for Paul was always careful to obey the leading of the Holy Spirit (see 16:6-7; 20:22-23). The Christians at Caesarea wrongly interpreted the Spirit's warnings as a direction that he should not go to Jerusalem. He answered, *'What do you mean by weeping and breaking my heart?'* (12-13). He was sure that it was God's will for him to go there and this was later confirmed. God was leading him through Jerusalem to Rome (23:11). Paul and the Christians at Caesarea were submissive to the will of God and said, *'The will of the Lord be done'* (14). **There are times when we have to make costly choices in obedience to the Lord which may be painful to our closest friends as well as to ourselves.**

Paul gave the leaders of the Jerusalem church a detailed report of God's blessing upon his ministry among the Gentiles. They glorified the Lord but they had reservations. They had heard rumours that Paul was teaching Jewish Christians to forsake the law of Moses and all their cherished traditions (21). They feared that there could be problems with legalistic Jewish Christians. They devised a plan for Paul to prove that he followed the rules and kept the law (24). He was a most gracious man and agreed to comply with their plan. **The compromise led to the very situation that they had tried to avoid. Could it be that the Jerusalem church leaders were too sensitive to the Jews in their desire to avoid trouble?**

Paul was seen by some of his Jewish enemies from the province of Asia. They wrongly assumed that he had taken Trophimus, a Gentile Christian, into the temple (which was out of bounds to Gentiles). They stirred up the crowd and Paul was dragged out of the temple. The mob set upon him; he was rescued by the Romans and taken into custody (26-40). Paul was taken prisoner just as the Holy Spirit had warned but the Lord was working out his purposes through these events.

Felix was afraid

Paul was later sent to Caesarea to be tried by the Roman governor, Felix (23:26-35). The high priest used Tertullus, an orator, to give evidence against him. Felix was a cruel tyrant who would not have been convinced by the nauseating flattery of Tertullus (1-4). The orator accused Paul of being a troublemaker and of desecrating the temple (5-6). He even accused the Roman commander, Lysias, of *'great violence'* (7). Paul's sincerity in answering his accusers was quite apparent. The charges of troublemaking were quite untrue and he had come to the temple as a reverent worshipper (17-20). He did confess to worshipping God as a Christian, *according to the Way which they call a sect,* and to his belief in *a resurrection of the dead, both of the just and the unjust* (14-15).

Felix postponed making any decision about Paul until he had seen Lysias the commander, but he allowed the apostle to have visits from his friends (22-23). The Roman governor was living in an adulterous relationship with Drusilla, the daughter of Herod Agrippa I (whom an angel of God had struck down in judgment; 12:23). Felix later sent for Paul to hear more *concerning the faith in Chris*t (24). The apostle *reasoned about righteousness, self-control, and the judgment to come* with this wicked man. His powerful witness had such an effect that *Felix was afraid* (25). Though he was filled with fear, Felix was more interested in obtaining a bribe from Paul rather than in knowing peace with God (26). **Felix was uncomfortable with the challenge of the gospel. For those who repent of their sin, however, the gospel is the most wonderful news, offering free forgiveness, peace with God, eternal life and everlasting joy.**

Felix knew Paul to be innocent but left him in prison to avoid further problems with the Jews (27); this gesture did him no good at all. Secular historians inform us that Felix was recalled to Rome by the emperor Nero in AD 59 after the Jews had complained about Roman atrocities. He was disgraced and probably escaped execution through the influence of his brother Pallas, who was a favourite of Nero.

You almost persuade me to become a Christian

Herod Agrippa II was the son of Agrippa I, who had James, the brother of John, killed (12:1-2). He paid a courtesy visit to the new governor, accompanied by his sister Bernice (25:13). Paul's appeal to Caesar left Festus with a problem. He was required by Roman law to send a written account of the charges against Paul, but he did not possess any convincing evidence. He enlisted the help of Agrippa who had an intimate knowledge of the Jewish faith and culture (3). Festus may have had problems in understanding the Jews' case against Paul but he was left in no doubt concerning Paul's message about Christ — *Jesus, who had died, whom Paul affirmed to be alive* (19).

Paul spoke to a distinguished audience — the governor, King Agrippa and his sister, high-ranking army officers and the most prominent men of the city (23). Paul fearlessly challenged Agrippa as he testified and preached the word of God. He asked Agrippa, *'Why should it be thought incredible by you that God raises the dead?'* (8). The resurrection of the Lord Jesus should be our constant theme and a source of great rejoicing. Paul went on to relate to those present how the risen Christ had appeared to him and had completely transformed his life. He told them that Jews and Gentiles *should repent, turn to God, and do works befitting repentance* (20).

Paul was bound with chains at his trial (29) but this did not inhibit his preaching. Festus recognized that Paul was not a fool but a very learned man. He interrupted the apostle by crying out that *much learning* was driving him mad. Paul responded by stating that he spoke *the words of truth and reason* (24-25). The gospel is foolishness to the unbeliever, but the foolishness of God is wiser than men (1 Corinthians 1:23-25). Paul was not put off by the scorn of Festus and went on to challenge Agrippa (27). The king said, *'You almost persuade me to become a Christian'* (28). **It is not enough to be almost persuaded. We must be fully persuaded and committed to Christ. Where do you stand?**

Take heart, men, for I believe God

Paul had appealed to Caesar to obtain justice and so he had to go to Rome (25:11-12). He was accompanied by Luke (note the use of *'we'* in verse 1) and Aristarchus, a member of the church at Thessalonica (2). God has his ways of encouraging us and he even uses unbelievers to that end. The Roman centurion *Julius treated Paul kindly and gave him liberty to go to his friends* (at Sidon) *and receive care* (3). Though he was a prisoner, the apostle had a remarkable amount of liberty. The Lord encouraged Joseph in a similar manner when he was in prison. God was with him and *gave him favour in the sight of the keeper of the prison* (Genesis 39:21). There are priceless blessings for the believer who walks with God.

Paul knew that God wanted him to go to Rome (24) and so did Satan who did everything he could to frustrate God's purpose. The voyage was beset from the beginning by high winds and dangerous seas (4,7-10). The ship had left Fair Havens to sail to a sheltered port further along the coast of Crete (see map, p.154) and conditions appeared favourable at first (13). A terrifying storm arose soon afterwards, which became so severe and prolonged that any hope of survival was lost (20).

An angel visited Paul at night and reassured him, telling him that he must be brought before Caesar and that God would preserve the lives of all who were sailing with him. Paul told those aboard the ship of the angel's visit and of his message from God. He then said, *'Take heart, men, for I believe God.'* He told them that they would all survive when the ship ran aground (22-25).

Satan seemed to be winning and was bent on Paul's destruction even after he survived the shipwreck. The soldiers wanted to kill all the prisoners (including Paul), to prevent any attempt to escape. The centurion, wanting to save Paul, rejected their plan, and ordered that all who could swim should jump overboard to reach land (42-43). **Never forget that the devil can only do what God permits him to do.**

When Paul saw them, he thanked God and took courage

Paul was no stranger to shipwreck, and peril had been his constant companion. Over ten years earlier he had written to the Corinthians, *'Three times I was shipwrecked; a night and day I have been in the deep'* (2 Corinthians 11:25-26). In all these dangers he knew the presence, encouragement and help of God. The people of Malta showed *unusual kindness* to Paul and to those who were shipwrecked with him (2). The bedraggled survivors received more help than they could have dared expect. Satan again sought to kill Paul through the snake-bite but the amazed islanders thought he was a god when he *suffered no harm* (5-6). We can be sure that Paul not only healed the sick, but also preached the gospel during his three-month stay on the island (7-11). The people he met there would never be the same again.

When he arrived in Italy, Paul was allowed to stay seven days with Christians in Puteoli (14). When believers in Rome heard that Paul was heading for their city, some travelled the 43 miles to Appii Forum to meet him, others the 33 miles to the Three Inns. *When Paul saw them, he thanked God and took courage* (15). Though the Romans had good roads, they did not have the modern transport that we take so much for granted. Those Christians were eager to see Paul and thought nothing of making the journey to see him. This token of love and concern was a great encouragement to the apostle. **All Christians need to be encouraged, even leaders like Paul. A thoughtful and kind deed, an encouraging letter or phone-call may mean very much to a hard-pressed believer. In what way do you seek to encourage others?**

Three days after his arrival in Rome, Paul called the leaders of the Jews to meet him when he arranged another meeting at which he persuaded them *concerning Jesus ... from morning until evening* and some were convinced (23-24). Though Paul was under house-arrest, he continued to preach and to teach *the things which concern the Lord Jesus Christ* (31; cp. Philippians 1:12-14). He so loved Christ, he so loved people and wanted to win them to his Saviour, that he could not help but declare the gospel to sinners.

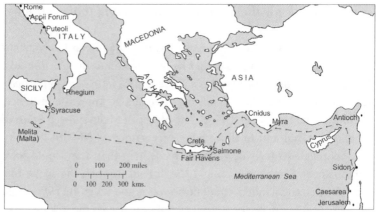
Paul's journey to Rome (Acts chapters 27 & 28)

After Acts chapter 28

Paul was imprisoned in his own rented house for two years (28:30). During this time (AD 60–62) he wrote his letters to the Ephesians, Colossians, Philemon and the Philippians. He was released from this imprisonment and was able to continue his missionary work for a year or two before being rearrested.

William Hendriksen suggests in his commentary on 1 & 2 Timothy and Titus (pages 39-40) that after his release Paul:

- Journeyed to Asia Minor, leaving Titus in Crete (Titus 1:5).
- He then went to Colosse as planned (Philemon 22) and then to Ephesus, where he was joined by Timothy who had been at Philippi (Philippians 2:19-23).
- Paul left Timothy at Ephesus to go to Philippi as previously planned (Philippians 2:24; though he was hoping to return to Ephesus; 1 Timothy 3:14-15). While in Philippi, Paul wrote his first letter to Timothy and also to Titus (approximately AD 63).
- He went from Philippi to Nicopolis to spend the winter and was joined there by Titus (Titus 3:12).
- He may have visited Asia Minor again and even Spain before his final imprisonment (cp. 2 Timothy 4:13; Romans 15:24). Paul wrote his second letter to Timothy from prison, shortly before he was executed.

1 & 2 SAMUEL, 1 CHRONICLES

The Hebrew Old Testament has only one book of Samuel; it was not divided into two books until the sixteenth century AD. This is an artificial division which breaks up the record of the reign of Saul and the end of his dynasty, as well as the history of David.

The first book of Samuel records the transition from the rule of the judges to that of the monarchy in Israel. Four characters dominate the record — Eli, Samuel, Saul and David. While Samuel was growing up in Shiloh, there were other judges beside Eli, who ruled different parts of Israel, e.g. Jephthah, Ibzan, Elon and Abdon (Judges 11 & 12). Samson was judge over Judah and Dan towards the end of Eli's life, overlapping into Samuel's period as judge at Shiloh. Samuel was a prophet as well as a judge (1 Samuel 3:20-21; 7:15).

We see in these books the contrast between the attitude of Saul and David. Saul rebelled against God's prophets and never came to true repentance but David heeded the prophets and repented of his sin. God promised David that his kingdom would last for ever. Our great Prophet, Priest and King, the Lord Jesus Christ, fulfilled this promise (2 Samuel 7:16; cp. Luke 1:32-33). Many of David's psalms contain prophecies concerning the Lord Jesus Christ (e.g. Psalms 18, 22 and 69). Some approximate dates may be useful:

1107 – 1067 BC	Eli is judge
1105 BC ?	Samuel born
1067 BC	Samuel is judge
1043 – 1010 BC	Saul's reign
1020 BC ?	Death of Samuel
1010 – 970 BC	David's reign

The first book of Chronicles covers the same period in Israel's history as the books of Samuel, some chapters being very similar (e.g. 2 Samuel 7; and 1 Chronicles 17). In Chronicles there is a greater emphasis on the religious life of the nation.

I ... have poured out my soul before the LORD

Elkanah faithfully took his family to Shiloh every year to worship and sacrifice to the Lord (3-4). All was not well in this religious family, however. Elkanah had two wives and one of them, Hannah, was desperately unhappy because she was childless and was despised by the other wife, Peninnah (6-7). Hannah described herself as *'a woman of sorrowful spirit'* (15). Though polygamy was common in Old Testament times, it was not the pattern for marriage ordained by God (Genesis 2:18,24; cp. 1 Timothy 3:2,12). It brought stress and trouble into many families (e.g. those of Abraham, David and Solomon).

Hannah's yearly visits to the tabernacle at Shiloh were never happy occasions (7-8) but the years of sorrow were soon to end. Following the family meal in Shiloh she went to the tabernacle to seek the Lord in prayer. Hannah was *in bitterness of soul* (10). It is a sad reflection on the state of religion in those times that Eli thought that Hannah was drunk in God's house as she fervently prayed (13-15). Hannah responded to Eli's accusation, *'No, my lord, I am a woman of sorrowful spirit. I have drunk neither wine nor intoxicating drink, but have poured out my soul before the LORD'* (15). **What a contrast to so much of our praying which is so dull and lifeless. When did you last pour out your soul before the Lord?**

Hannah came away from the tabernacle a different woman (17-18). She had called upon God to remember her and her prayer was answered (19). Hannah named her son Samuel, which means 'heard by God'. She had vowed that if God gave her a son, she would give him to the Lord, to serve him as a Nazirite throughout his life (11; cp. Numbers 6:1-5). She remained faithful to her vow and when Samuel was weaned, she brought him to Eli at Shiloh (22-28; in those days children were often three or four years old when weaned). Samuel grew up to be a great and godly man and the Lord gave Hannah three other sons and two daughters (2:20-21). **The Lord is no man nor woman's debtor; he richly repays those who are prepared to obey him and keep their vows.**

Those who honour me I will honour

This chapter paints a vivid contrast between two different parents: Hannah, a mother who honoured God; and Eli, who was a weak and pathetic father. Hannah kept her vow to lend Samuel to the Lord (1:11,28). He followed in her footsteps and was known for his prayer life (12:19,23; Jeremiah 15:1). Hannah's song is full of praise to God, expressing her joy and thanksgiving (1-10). It is also prophetical; the Lord's instrument to accomplish victory over Israel's enemies would be the king anointed by her son Samuel. This prophecy also points to Christ, the Anointed of God, the eternal King (10-11). Hannah honoured God and he blessed and visited her (21).

Eli failed to restrain his two wicked sons Hophni and Phinehas from their vile deeds (3:13). They committed sacrilege by taking sacrificial meat before the fat was burned, as laid down in the law (12-17,29; Leviticus 7:29-34). They also committed lewd, immoral acts in the tabernacle (22). Eli feebly pleaded with them but he should have removed them from the priesthood because they had violated their sacred office. He was the judge over Israel but he failed to punish his own sons (4:18). They had sunk to such depths of sin that *the LORD desired to kill them* (25). What solemn and terrifying words! A man of God warned Eli that the Lord would bring disaster to his family (27-36). He had honoured his sons more than he honoured God (29). There is a very important principle in these verses. God says, '*Those who honour me I will honour, and those who despise me shall be lightly esteemed*' (30). Hannah honoured God and he richly blessed her. **If you want to know the blessing of God on your life, you must seek to honour him in the way that you live.**

God never abdicates his sovereignty and he was quietly working out his purposes, beginning in the unhappy domestic life of a woman in the hill country of Ephraim. He wonderfully answered her prayer and she responded by faithfully honouring her promise to him. God was preparing young Samuel for great things.

Then the LORD appeared again in Shiloh

Worship had degenerated in Israel through the weakness of Eli and the wickedness of his sons Hophni and Phinehas. *The word of the LORD was rare in those days; there was no widespread revelation* (1). Another verse of Scripture is an apt comment on those dark days: *where there is no revelation, the people cast off restraint* (Proverbs 29:18). Things were soon to change following the call of Samuel. When he heard his name being called, he thought that he was hearing Eli. He did not recognize that God was speaking to him. He *'did not yet know the LORD'* (7) and this was his first encounter with the living God. Though Eli was wrong in so many ways he was still able to offer good spiritual advice to a puzzled Samuel (8-9).

The Lord told Samuel that Eli and his house had so often despised the Lord that no sacrifice would avail for them. Samuel was afraid to pass on to Eli the terrifying message of judgment that God had given to him (10-16). He told Eli everything when the old priest threatened to put him under a curse. Eli accepted the message, resigning himself to the Lord's will (16-18).

Samuel grew up *and the Lord was with him* (19). *Then the LORD appeared again in Shiloh. For the LORD revealed himself to Samuel in Shiloh by the word of the LORD* (21). What a contrast to the opening verse of the chapter. Through the ministry of Samuel the word of God was now spreading throughout the entire length of Israel from Dan in the far north to Beersheba in the deep south (20-21; 4:1). How did it all begin? God used the prayers of a humble, broken woman who poured out her soul before him.

We need to recover urgency in prayer and in the faithful preaching of God's word if we are to have any hope of blessing or of changing our nation. Pray that God will be pleased to raise up godly men and women in our land. Be fervent in prayer and ground yourself in God's word. The Lord will honour a faithful people.

That we may also be like all the nations

Though Samuel was a great and godly man, he made a terrible mistake in appointing his two sons as judges. Joel and Abijah were wicked men. They were dishonest and corrupt, accepting bribes and perverting the course of justice (1-3). We see a close resemblance to the story of Eli's two sons. The children of godly men and women sometimes rebel against the Lord, so bringing much heartache.

Israel's elders rightly wanted good judges but a more subtle reason lay behind their desire for a king (4-5). God told Samuel to warn the people that they would have cause to regret their clamour for a king (9-18). They were so determined to have a king, however, that they refused to listen to him. They responded by saying, *'No, but we will have a king over us, that we may also be like all the nations, and that our king may judge us and go out before us and fight our battles'* (19-20). They had forgotten that the Lord had miraculously helped them in the past (7:8-13). They were now looking for a king to fight their battles.

The Israelites wanted to be *'like all the nations'* (5,20) but God had chosen them to be different from all the nations (Exodus 19:5-6; Deuteronomy 7:6; 28:1). **The church has often made the mistake of becoming like the world in order to reach the world with the gospel. The world will never be won to Christ by worldly-minded Christians.** We are not to be conformed to this world but to be conformed to the image of Christ (Romans 8:29; 12:2; cp. 1 John 2:15-17). We must always trust in the Lord for his blessing on our Christian work, even when success seems to be far away.

The Lord allowed Israel to have their king. He did raise up good kings, notably David, but most of the kings of Israel led the people away from God, especially those of the northern kingdom after the death of Solomon. We read the words *'made Israel sin'* time and again (e.g. 1 Kings 15:30,34; 16:13,19,26). The words of Psalm 106:15 illustrate Israel's folly: *'He gave them their request, but sent leanness into their soul.'* **If God says 'No' to any of our prayers, it is for our good.**

I have looked upon my people,
because their cry has come to me

Saul came from an influential family in the tribe of Benjamin (1). He is described as being *a choice and handsome young man* (2). His father sent him and a servant to search for some missing donkeys. Their search was unsuccessful and they eventually came to the land of Zuph, birthplace of Samuel (cp. 1:1). The servant had heard that there was a man of God in the city who was a seer (or prophet). He would surely be able to give them direction; that seer was Samuel (1-14).

The Lord is sovereign over everything that happens, even over the loss of the donkeys, and in bringing Saul and his servant to Samuel. He told Samuel, *'Tomorrow, about this time I will send you a man from the land of Benjamin ... for I have looked upon my people, because their cry has come to me'* (15-17). Samuel was to anoint Saul as commander (prince) over Israel and he would deliver the Israelites from the Philistines. The history of Israel is marked by the rebellion and ingratitude of the Israelites toward God, and of his patience, compassion and love towards them. How good is the God to whom we belong and whom we worship.

The Israelites wanted a king so that they would be like all the other nations and Saul appeared to be the ideal man. He had everything going for him to be a godly and successful king. He had the prayers and the counsel of Samuel who was able to tell him all that was in his heart (19). He had the promise of God to help him and to give him victory against the Philistines (16).

The Lord often uses things in his purposes which may seem quite insignificant to us. The loss of his father's asses brought about a sequence of events that were to be life-changing for Saul and very important for Israel. One of the great joys of being a Christian is knowing that God is working all things together for good, even loss (Romans 8:28).

Valiant men ... whose hearts God had touched

Samuel instructed Saul to send his servant on ahead of them and he then brought to him the word of God (9:27). He anointed Saul and kissed him (1). The kiss here was a sign of respect and loyalty, not of affection (cp. Psalm 2:12). He promised Saul three signs which would confirm that he was God's anointed to lead Israel and that God was with him (7). Saul would meet:

1. Two men by Rachel's tomb, who would tell him that the lost donkeys were found (2).
2. Three men going to Bethel who would greet him and give him two loaves of bread (3-4).
3. A group of prophets with musical instruments at the hill of God (the mention of a Philistine garrison is an indication of the dominion of the Philistines over Israel). The prophets would be prophesying and the Spirit of the Lord would come upon him so that he too would prophesy with them and be turned into another man (5-6).

All these signs were fulfilled that day and God gave Saul another heart (9). Samuel again summoned the people to Mizpah where he reminded them of God's past dealings with Israel. He told them that by demanding a king, they had rejected God who had delivered their ancestors from the Egyptians and from their enemies (19). His words seemed to fall on deaf ears and they rejoiced when Saul was presented to them (24). Saul appeared to be a reluctant and humble king who hid himself but the Lord revealed his whereabouts. He was to become so different in later years when he would have killed David whom he perceived as a threat to his throne. He was brought from his hiding place and stood head and shoulders above the people (20-23).

Samuel proclaimed Saul as king and explained the rights and duties of the kingship (24-25). Saul had with him, *valiant men ... whose hearts God had touched* (26). **This is the great need in our churches today — men and women whose hearts have been touched by God.** Such people are loyal to God and his truth, faithful in service, courageous in the face of opposition, and ready to persevere in difficult times.

To obey is better than sacrifice

This chapter brings us to a much later date in Saul's reign and it records the reason for God's rejection of him as king of Israel. Saul was told to destroy the Amalekites, who were long-standing enemies of God's people (Exodus 17:8-16). This may appear harsh, but they were such a cruel, wicked and degraded people (cp. verse 33) that they were to be completely destroyed (3). Saul was victorious but he spared Agag, king of Amalek, and kept the best of the livestock (9). When God told Samuel of Saul's disobedience, the grief-stricken prophet *cried out to the LORD all night* (11). He heard that the king had gone to Carmel and then to Gilgal and that he had set up a monument for himself (12). That sums up Saul. He was a self-centred, self-willed man who sought his own honour rather than that of God.

Samuel went to Gilgal and Saul greeted him by saying that he had *performed the commandment of the LORD.* However, the bleating of the sheep and the lowing of the oxen gave the game away (13-14). We cannot hide sin; it cries out to God and he hears it (cp. Genesis 4:10). Saul tried to excuse himself by lying, saying that the animals were intended for sacrifice to God at Gilgal. Samuel told Saul that God had sent him on a mission to destroy the Amalekites, but he had failed to obey God. He had also done *evil in the sight of the LORD* by keeping the spoils of battle (15-19). Saul insisted that he had obeyed God, but that the people were responsible for taking the plunder and the animals (20-21). Samuel pointed out to Saul that rebellion and stubbornness are just as evil as witchcraft and idolatry in the sight of God. He had rejected the word of the Lord, and because of this God had rejected him from being king (22-23). Samuel executed King Agag and left. He mourned for Saul, whom he was never to see again (33-35).

God demands total obedience from us. Partial obedience is not good enough. *To obey is better than sacrifice* (22). The Lord Jesus became obedient to the point of death, even the death of the cross, in order to save us from our sin (Philippians 2:8). He said, '*If you love me, keep my commandments*' (John 14:15).

But the LORD *looks at the heart*

In the remaining chapters of 1 Samuel our attention is turned away from Saul to David. The Lord told Samuel that he had rejected Saul as Israel's king and had chosen one of Jesse's sons to replace him. Samuel was fearful because he knew that such a mission could provoke Saul to kill him (1-2; cp. 22:18-19). Samuel was to invite Jesse and his sons to a sacrificial ceremony; he would then anoint the new king (3-5).

Samuel made a common mistake as he looked for a king among Jesse's sons. Seven sons passed before Samuel but God indicated that he had not chosen any of them to be king though they were fine young men. God's choice was the youngest who had not been invited to the ceremony. David was a man after God's own heart and the Lord told Samuel to anoint him as king. The Spirit of the Lord then came upon David (6-13; cp. 13:14; Acts 13:22).

Samuel looked at outward appearances *but the* LORD *looks at the heart* (6-7). Never forget that *the* LORD *looks at the heart.* **He looks at your heart and my heart. He knows our motives and our desires. He sees our pretence when we try to impress others with our spirituality. Oh, let us be real and genuine. Let us get rid of all sham and pretence in our lives.** We may deceive our fellow-believers, we may even deceive ourselves, but we cannot deceive God. The Lord searches the heart (Jeremiah 17:10). Let us now examine our own hearts before the Lord.

Look at the contrast between Saul and David. *The Spirit of the* LORD *came upon David ... but the Spirit of the* LORD *departed from Saul* (13-14). The king had grieved away the Spirit of God through his persistent disobedience and he was now open to trouble from *a distressing spirit.* If we are walking with the Lord, we have no need to fear evil spirits, for they are subject to the sovereign will and power of God (14,23). Saul's servants suggested that a skilled musician be found, whose playing would soothe his troubled mind. The king readily agreed with this suggestion and so David was brought to the palace.

But I come to you in the name of the LORD

The ways of God are wonderful and surprising. David's errand to take food to his three eldest brothers serving in Saul's army was to lead to the defeat of the Philistines. Saul and his army faced the Philistines across the Valley of Elah (1-3). The awesome figure of Goliath, standing over nine feet (almost three metres) in height reduced Saul and his men to fear and trembling (11,24). Saul, now far from God, lacked any assurance that the Lord was with them. Goliath represented the Philistines and challenged Israel to produce a champion to fight him. The side whose champion was killed would then concede defeat (8-9, 23,51-52). Goliath bellowed out his challenge twice a day, for forty days, but Israel had no champion to meet him (16).

David's audacious offer to take on the challenge of Goliath angered Eliab, his eldest brother (28). David saw that the honour of the living God was at stake while Goliath was allowed to defy Israel (26,36). David's words were reported to the king who sent for him. Saul could hardly believe that this mere youth could defeat an experienced warrior like Goliath (32-33). David recalled the times when a lion and a bear had attacked his father's sheep, and God's help when he killed them (34-35). David was confident that God who had enabled him to kill the lion and the bear would give him victory over Goliath (36). He said to Saul, '*The* LORD, *who delivered me from the paw of the lion ... will deliver me from the hand of this Philistine*' (37).

Goliath was surprised and angered that the Israelites had sent a mere youth, apparently unarmed, to fight him (42-43). He cursed David by his gods but the young man was not intimidated by his curses or threats. **He knew that he was not meeting the giant in his own strength and he affirmed, 'But I come to you in the name of the LORD'S'** (45,47). Notice the boldness of David as he hastened and ran to meet Goliath before hurling a stone from his sling (48-50). Goliath crashed to the ground and David took the giant's sword and cut off his head. The Philistines fled from the Israelite army in disarray.

David behaved himself wisely in all his ways

Jonathan was a brave and accomplished soldier (14:1-23) who greatly admired David after his victory over Goliath and they became the closest of friends (1-4). There is no suggestion anywhere in Scripture that Jonathan's love for David was of a homosexual nature. Homosexual practices are wicked in the sight of God (Leviticus 20:13; Romans 1:27). Saul took David to live in the royal household and the young man became a commander in the Israelite army (2-5).

Saul's esteem for David turned to jealous, murderous hatred after he heard the women ascribing greater military prowess to David than to himself (6-12). Let us beware of envy. It is a sin that will tear us apart and bring much misery as it did in the life of Saul (see James 3:13-18). Jonathan was heir to the throne of Israel and had far more reason to feel threatened by David than his father. He remained a loyal and precious friend, however (cp. chapter 20; 23:16). *Saul prophesied when a distressing spirit from God came upon* him (10; cp. 19:23).

David behaved wisely in all his ways, and the LORD was with him (14; see also verses 5,15,30). He behaved wisely:

- When Saul tried to murder him (11).
- When Saul turned him out of his house to command a thousand soldiers (13).
- When Saul broke his promise to give him his daughter Merab, in marriage. David later married Saul's daughter Michal (17-21).
- When Saul sent him on a dangerous mission in the hope that he would be killed (25-27).

David behaved himself wisely despite the greatest provocation. God used these severe trials to strengthen and to bless him (30). **Are you being provoked by someone at home, at work, at school, or even at church? Remember David.** Be wise in your conduct; commit your way to God and trust him (Proverbs 3:5-6). He will honour and vindicate you and be with you as he was with David.

David inquired of the LORD

David was made king over Judah at Hebron after the death of Saul but it was another seven years before he ruled the whole of Israel (1-5; cp. 2:1-4). He wanted Jerusalem as his capital but it was still occupied by the Jebusites. They felt so secure in their well-fortified city that they vainly imagined that even the blind and the lame could successfully defend it (6). David conquered Jerusalem which also became known as 'Zion' and 'the City of David' (7). *So David went on and became great, and the LORD God of hosts was with him* (10). David owned his success to be of the Lord (12). We must remember to depend upon God and to trust in him always. When God is with us, what have we to fear (Hebrews 13:5-6)?

David had the help of Hiram king of Tyre in the construction of his palace (11). When the Philistines twice marched on Israel following the anointing of David as king (17-22), we read that *David inquired of the LORD* (19,23). God directed him and the Philistines were defeated on each occasion. David did not need to inquire of the Lord concerning his will for marriage. He would not have been ignorant of the Lord's command that kings must not multiply wives for themselves (Deuteronomy 17:17), yet he did just that. David appeared to have a 'blind spot' in this matter and the rivalries between the half-brothers born of these marriages were to bring great trouble and distress. We ignore God's word at our peril.

We do not need to pray for guidance in a situation where the Bible clearly directs us. For example, a believer must not marry an unbeliever and it is foolish and perverse for any professing Christian to engage in a courtship with someone who is not a Christian (2 Corinthians 6:14-18). We must shun any course of action which is questionable. God does not honour disobedience. Our motto should always be, 'If in doubt, don't.' If we love the Lord, we will seek to honour him in our lives.

The LORD tells you that he will make you a house

David had established his kingdom but he was concerned that God be worshipped in a proper building rather than in the tabernacle (a tent; 1-2). The prophet Nathan encouraged him to fulfil his God-honouring desire (3). However, the Lord had different plans, which he revealed to Nathan that night (4-17). God's will was not for David to build the temple, but for his son to do so (12-13).

Nathan came back to David and reminded David of God's grace toward him. The Lord had taken him from his humble work as a shepherd to rule over his people, Israel. He had been with David and given him victory over his enemies (8-9). Nathan then said to David, *'The LORD tells you that he will make you a house'* (11; cp. 27). This was not a building made of timber, stone, marble. It was a dynasty which would last for ever. God promised, *'Your house and your kingdom shall be established for ever'* (16). This promise speaks of the Lord Jesus Christ. When the angel Gabriel announced to Mary that she would be the mother of the promised Messiah, he said of Jesus, *'He will be great, and will be called the Son of the Highest; and the Lord God will give him the throne of his father David. And he will reign over the house of Jacob for ever, and of his kingdom there will be no end'* (Luke 1:32-33). When people called Jesus the Son of David, they were recognizing that he was the promised Saviour and King (Matthew 21:9; 22:41-45). **The glorious purposes of God in the salvation of sinners were centred in the holy Son of God whose human descent is traced from David.**

There are times when we may earnestly desire to serve God in a particular way but he blocks our plans (cp. Acts 16:6-7). We do not always know why God does this to us; it could be that we do not have the necessary gifts for the work we desire to do. Our faith is sorely tried when we suffer disappointment in God's work, but let us remember that the Lord's will is perfect and that he may have something better for us. **Remember, God is in control of all our disappointments. If we put the Lord first in our lives he will give us more than we could ever imagine (see Matthew 6:33).**

The thing that David had done displeased the Lord

This solemn chapter records the fall of David into the most dreadful sin. David had many wives and concubines (5:13) and he appears to be someone who could not control his lust. His undisciplined lifestyle made him very vulnerable to temptation, and sure enough, he fell. After defeating the Syrians, Joab led the Israelites against their Ammonite allies. David should also have been on the battlefield but he remained at the palace (1-2). **He was to learn that Satan strikes when we are off our guard. We are often safer when we feel the heat of the battle against evil than when we are at ease.**

David saw a woman bathing (2). The 'chance' glance was not enough for David. He looked again and again, feeding the lust that was rising up within him. *He saw ... sent and inquired ... and took her* (2-4). David schemed in every way possible to cover his adultery when he discovered that Bathsheba had become pregnant by him. He had hoped that if he gave Uriah home-leave from the battlefield, the man would believe that his wife had conceived at that time. Uriah was too honourable a person to be at ease while his fellow-soldiers were fighting and he did not go to his house as David had hoped (5-13). His loyalty stands in complete contrast to David's treachery.

David was very callous to use Uriah to carry a letter to Joab which contained his own death-warrant. The more he tried to cover his sin, the more he sinned. When he heard that Uriah had lost his life in battle, he sent a message to Joab, *'Do not let this thing displease you'* (19-25). The Hebrew is 'Do not let this thing be evil in your sight' (25). Sin cannot be lightly dismissed just like that. See the contrast in the statement of verse 27: *The thing that David had done displeased the* Lord ('was evil in the eyes of the Lord'). It may be hidden from men but it cannot be hidden from God. David's fall is a warning to each of us. Even the most spiritual person can fall into the most appalling sin. **Are you indulging in an unwholesome thought life? Is there anything in your life displeasing to God? Confess your sin and forsake it. If you cling to it, it will bring you misery and judgment.**

You are the man!

God was gracious to David in sending the prophet Nathan to him. Nathan's parable was simple but devastating in exposing David's sin. The king was very angry and vowed that the rich man who had stolen the pet lamb belonging to the poor man would die (1-5). David was passing judgment upon himself. Nathan said to him, *'You are the man!'* (7). David had not only taken Uriah's wife, but had also robbed him of his life (9). He had *despised the commandment of the LORD* (9; the sixth and seventh of the Ten Commandments — Exodus 20:13-14).

There are vital lessons to be learned from these verses:

- It is no light matter for a believer to sin. When we sin, we despise the Lord by a lack of appreciation for his goodness and by rebelling against his commandments (7-9).
- Though David truly repented (see Psalm 51 for his prayer) and found God's forgiveness (13), he had to live with the consequences of his sin for the rest of his life. He had killed Uriah with the sword of the Ammonites and the sword would not depart from his own house. God would raise up adversaries from his own house and his own wives would be taken from him and given to another (9-12). **Forgiveness does not cancel out the effects of our sin.** The immediate consequence of David's sin was that the child conceived in his adultery would die (14). The chapter ends with a record of the birth of Solomon to Bathsheba and of the fall of Rabbah, capital of Ammon (24-31).
- Another lesson to learn is that if a believer falls into public sin, it gives *great occasion to the enemies of the LORD to blaspheme* (14). The work and witness of many a church has been hindered by the bad testimony of professing Christians. Unbelievers blaspheme the name of God and understandably think to themselves, 'All talk and hypocrisy — so much for their religion and their God.' **Sin has terrible consequences for ourselves, for the church, and for the honour of God. Let us examine our hearts and repent of any unwholesome desires lurking within.**

I will not ... offer ... with that which costs me nothing

Satan moved David to take the census of Israel (1) but remember, Satan can only act with God's permission (cp. 1 Kings 22:19-23; Job 1:12; 2:6). Joab was not a spiritual man but he warned David against this futile exercise which had been conceived in the pride of his heart. The king would not listen to him and the census was taken but God was displeased with this thing and plagued the people (2-7). There was a provision for census-taking in Israel when a half-shekel ransom price had to be paid for each one numbered to avoid a plague (cp. Exodus 30:12-13).

David realized the folly of his actions and was convicted and in great distress (8, 13). The Lord sent Gad, the seer, with a message for David telling him that he would be punished for his sin. He must choose either three years of famine, three months of defeat by the sword of his enemies, or three days of plague in the land at the hand of the angel of the Lord. A very distressed David chose punishment at the hand of God, acknowledging that the mercies of the Lord are very great (9-13).

David witnessed the terrifying sight of the angel of the Lord standing by Ornan's threshing floor poised to destroy Jerusalem but there the Lord halted the plague in which seventy thousand men died (14-16). David's love for his people is shown in his acute anguish because Israel had suffered on account of his sin (17). The prophet Gad told him to erect an altar to the Lord on the threshing-floor (18). Ornan refused any payment for his threshing-floor and freely offered David wood and animals for the sacrifices (22-23). David insisted on paying him, saying, *'I will not take what is yours for the* LORD, *nor offer burnt offerings with that which costs me nothing'* (24).

There is a great challenge for us here. Our Saviour loves us and gave himself to save us from our sins. Surely we should be delighted to give generously to his work and to labour sacrificially for him. **Are we offering to God something that costs us nothing? Are we giving him only our second-best? Half-hearted service is not acceptable.**

Who then is willing to consecrate himself this day to the LORD?

David was near to the end of his life and he had gathered all the leaders of Israel together to tell them of his desire to build a house for the ark of the covenant. The Lord had told him, however, that he should not build the temple because he had been a man of war. Solomon his son should build the temple (28:1-6). Though David was not permitted to build the temple, he was lavish in his giving for it. He told the people, '*I have set my affection on the house of my God*' (1-3). He had challenged Solomon to serve God with a loyal heart and a willing mind (28:9) and he now challenged the people, '*Who then is willing to consecrate himself this day to the LORD?*' (5). The people would have associated consecration with the priests in their service for the Lord, but here they were all challenged to consecrate themselves to God. They responded by giving generously to the temple building fund and this greatly encouraged David (6-9). He then poured out his heart in worship and praise to God (10-19).

Let us think about consecration for a moment. We are easily influenced by the self-seeking, self-gratifying attitudes of the world around us, but we are not to be conformed to the world (Romans 12:1-2). There is far too much shallow Christianity around us but we must be different if we are to please God. **God's work is great (1) and it requires whole-hearted devotion. Consecration shows in our lives:**

- It is seen in our affections (3; cp. Colossians 3:1-5).
- It is seen in generous giving to God's work. It is God who prospers us and when we give to him, we are only returning to him what rightfully belongs to him (9,14). We should always remember that we are pilgrims here and that we cannot take our possessions with us into the next world (15).
- It leads to great joy and satisfaction (9).

How are things with you? Have you grown cold in your love to the Lord? Do not put off your response to the challenge of God's word. Now is the time to consecrate yourself to the Lord, not tomorrow.

ROMANS

Paul wrote his letter to the church at Rome towards the end of his third missionary journey, approximately AD 57 (15:25-27; cp. Acts 20:2-3; 1 Corinthians 16:1-4). He was in Corinth and planned to return to Jerusalem and afterwards visit Rome before going to preach the gospel in Spain (15:24-28). God had other plans for him, however; Paul did not go to Spain, but he did go to Rome as a prisoner (Acts 28).

Paul wanted to visit Rome:

- To impart to them *some spiritual gift* (1:11) in order to establish (strengthen) them. Most commentators do not see this as the impartation of supernatural spiritual gifts such as those listed in 1 Corinthians 12. Paul did not say 'some spiritual gifts', but used the singular 'gift'. His visit would be a gift to the church to establish them so that they would be encouraged together with him.

- To have some fruit among them (1:13). He may have been referring to his desire to see an increase of the fruit of the Holy Spirit in their lives as they were strengthened (cp. Galatians 5:22-23). I believe, however, that Paul was referring to his desire to see a harvest of souls won to Christ. He goes on to write that he was a debtor to these Gentiles (1:15).

Themes in Romans

- The righteousness of God is the main theme of the book (the words *'righteous'* and *'righteousness'* are found sixty-six times in Romans).
- The goodness of God (2:4; 5:8; 8:35-39; 11:22).
- The sovereignty of God (9:11-29; 11:1-36).
- The grace of God (3:24; 5:2,15-21; 6:1,14-15; 11:5-6; 12:3,6).
- The law of God (7:1 - 8:7).

I am not ashamed of the gospel of Christ

Paul wrote this letter while at Corinth, a city which was infamous for its vile, depraved and debauched way of life. The sins described in verses 21-32 were very much in evidence in Corinth. God is angry with sinners. *His wrath is revealed from heaven against all ungodliness and unrighteousness of men* (18; cp. John 3:36).

The word *'gospel'* is found four times in this chapter (1,9,15,16). Paul was ready and eager to preach the gospel because he gloried in its good news and in its power to save sinners. He declared, *'I am not ashamed of the gospel of Christ, for it is the power of God to salvation to everyone who believes'* (16).

Why is the gospel of Christ so wonderful? *In it the righteousness of God is revealed* (17). The gospel is God's answer to human sin. It is the good news of his great love in giving his Son to die for sinners (5:8); good news of forgiveness and reconciliation to God (4:7; 5:10-11); good news of peace with God (5:1); good news that sinful men can live a holy life when saved by Christ (6:2-6,13-14,22); good news of salvation from the wrath of God (5:9; 8:1); good news of eternal life (6:22-23).

Why is the gospel of Christ so glorious? *It is the power of God to salvation* (16). The Greek word translated 'power' is *'dunamis'* from which our English word 'dynamite' is derived. The gospel of Christ is dynamite. Many a dark and tragic life has been transformed by its power. We should expect to see God work in the lives of sinners when the gospel is preached. When we share the good news in personal witness to the unsaved, we are not just sharing a set of beliefs, but the power of God to salvation.

Sinners should be ashamed of their sin but Christians should never be ashamed of the gospel. Can we be ashamed that we are *beloved of God, called to be saints* (7)? Can we be ashamed of a gospel that saves sinners? *'I am not ashamed of the gospel of Christ, for it is the power of God to salvation to everyone who believes'* (16).

But now the righteousness of God ... is revealed

The Jews had the advantage of possessing the revelation of God through the Old Testament (*'the oracles of God'*, 2). They were sinners like the Gentiles (*'Greeks'*), however. *They are all under sin* (9,23). The terrible fruit of sin is described in verses 10 to 18. There are sins of omission as well as of commission. It is sin not to seek after God our Creator (11). The first section of Romans paints a very dark picture of man in his sin (1:18 - 3:20). Sin has left every man and woman: guilty and under God's condemnation (19); under the wrath of God (5-6); and enslaved, being under the power of sin (9).

We now come to God's answer which tells us what he has done to save us. Man is unrighteous, *but now the righteousness of God apart from the law is revealed* (21). That righteousness is revealed in the gospel (1:17). **Three words are used to show what God has provided to meet our desperate need:**

a. *Justification (being justified freely;* 24) deals with the problem of guilt and condemnation. To be justified is to be pronounced righteous by God resulting in the removal of condemnation (8:1). The source of our justification is the free grace of God.
b. *Propitiation* (25) deals with the problem of God's wrath. Propitiation is the turning away of wrath by an offering. The blood of Christ satisfies the demands of God's justice and thus his wrath is turned away from us. God the Father provided the propitiation in giving his only begotten Son (1 John 4:9-10).
c. *Redemption* (24) means release by payment of a price. The Christian has been freed from the bondage and tyranny of sin. Salvation is free, but it was purchased at tremendous cost, even the precious blood of Christ (1 Peter 1:18-19).

We have nothing to boast about (27) because our 'goodness' falls short of God's holy requirements (23) and our works cannot save us (27). Let us rejoice in our great Saviour who died and rose again to meet the requirements of God's law and to meet our deepest needs.

His faith is accounted for righteousness

The message of the gospel makes a person think. Paul poses question after question in Romans and then provides the answers. Some of his Jewish readers might have thought that he was saying that faith cancels God's law (3:31). He anticipates this question by referring to Abraham who is revered by every Jew (cp. John 8:39-40,53). Paul had written earlier that the law and the prophets witness to the truth of justification by faith (3:21). Abraham illustrates Paul's argument:

- Abraham was not justified by works, but by faith (2-3). The law had not been given when Abraham *believed God* but God imputed righteousness to him (i.e. put righteousness to his account) without works (3-6). The debt of sinful man can never be cancelled out by the works of the law because we have all broken God's law (3:20,23). We must trust in the holy Son of God who died and rose again to pay the debt (23-25). Such *faith is accounted for righteousness* (5).
- Abraham was not justified by circumcision (9-11). His faith was accounted to him for righteousness before he was circumcised (10; cp. Genesis 15:6; 17:24). Our sin has been imputed to the Lord Jesus Christ; it was put to his account; he was punished for it (Isaiah 53:6). His righteousness has been imputed to us (23-25; cp. 2 Corinthians 5:21). Those who know this imputation are blessed indeed (7-8).
- Abraham was not justified through the law (13-16). The Lord promised Abraham that he would have innumerable descendants and would be the father of many nations (17; cp. Genesis 15:5-6; 17:5). At that time the patriarch was childless and his wife past child-bearing age. Abraham believed the promise of God and was justified 430 years before the law was given. The promise was given without law-keeping as a condition for fulfilment (13; cp. Galatians 3:16-18).

Abraham's faith is a challenge to us all. *He did not waver at the promise of God through unbelief.* He was *fully convinced* that what God *had promised he was also able to perform* (20-21).We are justified through believing in God who delivered the Lord Jesus up to death at Calvary to save us from sin and who raised him from the dead (24-25).

But where sin abounded, grace abounded much more

This wonderful chapter describes some of the privileges and blessings that belong to those who are justified by faith.

- *We have peace with God through our Lord Jesus Christ* (1). As sinners we were the enemies of God, but now we are reconciled to him (10). We are no longer condemned for our **past.**
- *We have access by faith into this grace in which we stand* (2). We stand in *'this grace'* (justification) and have access to God the Father (Ephesians 2:18; 3:12) and to his throne of grace (Hebrews 4:16). This blessing is for the **present.** We have fellowship with God now.
- *We rejoice in hope of the glory of God* (2). The word 'hope' means 'confident expectation' of something yet to come. This hope does not disappoint because the love of God has been poured out in our hearts by the Holy Spirit who has been given to us (5). Our **future** is secure in Christ. We will see the glory of God in heaven.

We should never forget what we were without Christ. We were *without strength and ungodly* (6). The words *'without strength'* describe our helplessness as sinners. We were separated from God and unable to come to him. We were unable to deal with our guilt, with the power of sin or its result, death (*sin reigned in death,* 17,21). What amazing love that God should give his Son to die for such wretched sinners as ourselves! Now that we are *justified by his blood, we shall be saved from wrath through him* (9-11).

Adam brought ruin to mankind when he sinned. *Through one man sin entered the world, and death through sin.* Sin came into the world through his disobedience. His sin is imputed to all men and everyone born into the world is sinful (12-13,19). That sin brought death, judgment and condemnation into the world (16-18). The sinless Lord Jesus was obedient to the Father's will and he died to break the power of sin and death (18-21). *Where sin abounded, grace abounded much more* (20). **The reign of sin has been replaced in the life of the believer by the reign of grace, and that grace brings eternal life (21).**

Sin shall not have dominion over you

The grace of God is magnified in forgiveness and in the imputation of Christ's righteousness (his perfect obedience is put to our account). Grace abounds much more than sin (5:20). Paul now anticipates another question, *'Shall we continue in sin that grace may abound?'* (1). In other words, 'If the grace of God is magnified in his forgiveness of sinners, why not go on committing sin so that God's grace can abound in free forgiveness?' Paul's answer is emphatic: *'Certainly not!'* (2). **Christ's death secured our pardon and it also sealed our death to sin.** How can we continue to lead a sinful life now that we are dead to sin? We died to sin in the death of Christ — we *were baptized into his death ... buried with him ... united together in the likeness of his death* (3-5); *our old man* (nature) *was crucified with him ... has died with Christ* (6-8).

We also share Christ's resurrection life, being raised to lead a new life of obedience to God. Believer's baptism symbolizes our position — *buried with him* (Christ) *through baptism into death and raised with him to walk in newness of life* (3-4). Sin does remain in us (we will not be perfect until we reach heaven), but we must not allow sin to reign in us (6,12,14). **We do not need to be defeated by sin and we are to reckon ourselves to be dead to all its enticements** (11). We once used our minds and bodies (our *'members'*) in the service of sin, but now we must use them to please God (13). *'Do not let sin reign in your mortal body ... for sin shall not have dominion over you* (12,14).

Another question is now raised, *'Shall we sin because we are not under law but under grace?'* (15). Again, the response is the same, *'Certainly not!'* (15). **The Lord Jesus perfectly kept the law for us but that does not give us a licence to sin.** We have been saved to live holy lives. We are no longer slaves of sin or slaves of uncleanness (17,19), but we are now slaves of righteousness (18-19). Sin is a terrible and tyrannical master, bringing misery and death (21,23). Slavery to righteousness and to God results in holy living and eternal life (22-23). The more we love God, the more we will hate sin.

O wretched man that I am!

Paul has already shown that believers are no longer under the reign of sin because they *are not under law, but under grace* (6:14). He now explains how the Christian has been freed from the claims of the law by showing that when we are dead, we are no longer subject to the law (1; In civil law, a criminal cannot be brought to trial if he dies before the court sits). The *'law'* spoken of in Romans 7 is the law of Moses given at Sinai. The marriage relationship is used to illustrate the point. A woman is legally bound to her husband as long as he lives, but she is free to remarry if he dies (2-3). Every believer has *become dead to the law through the body of Christ* (4) to whom we are now united in his death and resurrection (6:3-4,8). We are now married to Christ *that we should bear fruit to God* (4). This blessed fruit is *fruit to holiness* (6:22; cp. John 15:8; Galatians 5:22-23) and is contrasted with *fruit to death* (5; cp. Galatians 5:19-21). The law exposes sin but this does not make it sinful; it is holy (7,12). Freedom from the law is not freedom to sin, but freedom to serve Christ in *the newness of the Spirit* (6).

We have already seen that sin no longer reigns over the Christian but it remains in him. **This remaining sin brings anguish to the life of every believer. Before he was saved, the Christian was at peace with sin, but now he is at war with it** (23). He has holy desires which are in conflict with remaining sin (15-25). This conflict will remain with us until we go to be with the Lord in heaven.

There is a teaching which suggests that through the Holy Spirit we are able to attain a state of Christian perfection in this life, the remains of sin being removed from our lives. We are told that we can know rest from our struggle with inward sin, our only warfare then being against the world and the devil. Don't believe such teaching! It is not true to Scripture or experience, and it takes a shallow view of the nature of sin. Though sin remains, it must not be allowed to reign! We are not under its bondage but when we do sin, we cry out, *'O wretched man that I am!'* (24). **If we can sin without a sense of grief and shame, we must ask ourselves whether we are truly saved.**

Children of God

Romans 8 is one of the most wonderful chapters in the Bible which cannot be adequately covered in one page of notes. All people are condemned in Adam (5:12,16,18; 6:23) but things are different for the Christian. *There is therefore now no condemnation to those who are in Christ Jesus* (1). There are two classes of people in the world — unbelievers *who live according to the flesh,* and Christians *who live according to the Spirit* (4-5). Those who teach that you can be a Christian and yet not have the Holy Spirit are in serious error. *If anyone does not have the Spirit of Christ, he is none of his* (9; cp. 11). We cannot live our Christian lives without the Holy Spirit. We lead our lives under his influence, not according to sinful flesh (1,4,5). With the help of the Holy Spirit, we put to death the sinful deeds of the body (13). Mortification (putting to death) of sin is necessary throughout the Christian life because of the remains of sin within us. The Holy Spirit leads us (14), he helps us in our weaknesses and he makes intercession for us (26). The Lord Jesus also prays for us (34).

Christians of all ages have found great comfort in verse 28. Since the Holy Spirit *makes intercession for the saints according to the will of God* (27), every adverse circumstance, every perplexing situation, every disappointment, and all fiery trial is in the will of God. We can have the same confidence as the apostle Paul. *And we know that all things work together for good to those who love God, to those who are the called according to his purpose* (28). **Suffering is not meaningless for the Christian though we may not be able to understand God's present dealings with us. God is making all things work together for good, even our suffering (see verse 18).** God will safely bring us to heaven. All those he has predestined, he calls, he justifies and he will glorify (30). God is for us and who dare condemn those whom God has justified? God loves us and nothing whatever can separate us from his wonderful love (35-39). Read this chapter again and bring your heartfelt praises to God who has done such great things for us.

Present your bodies a living sacrifice

The mercies of God so clearly described in the letter to the Romans demand a response! As those freed from the tyranny and bondage of sin, we owe it to the Lord to consecrate our lives to him. *Therefore ... present your bodies a living sacrifice, holy, acceptable to God, which is your reasonable service* (1). We express our personality through our bodies — it is through them that we sin or live in a manner which pleases God (cp. 6:12-13). **Dare we be half-hearted in our consecration when the Lord has done so much for us?** What is the will of God for your life, for my life? *Be not conformed to this world, but be transformed by the renewing of your mind, that you may prove what is that good and acceptable and perfect will of God* (2). The remaining chapters of Romans show how we should work this out in our lives.

Consecration to the Lord will mean that we will use the gifts that God has graciously given to us (3-8). There is a caution here for those who think that they are very gifted, especially if those gifts are not being recognized. Do not think of yourself more highly than you ought to think (3). Gifts must be accompanied by spiritual graces. We are reminded of some of the graces which should be evident in our lives if we truly love the Lord and our fellow-Christians (9-21). Our love for each other must be real and not sham. *Let love be without hypocrisy* (9). If we love the Lord, we will hate whatever is evil and we will cling to all that is good.

Many a Christian has been hurt by the careless behaviour of others within the church — some thoughtless or unkind word, lack of integrity, broken promises, lack of concern, and so on. We must *be kindly affectionate to one another with brotherly love, in honour giving preference to one another* (10). Saints have needs, but do we love them enough to meet their needs (13)? Are the graces described in verses 9 to 21 apparent in your life? Does Christian love determine your response to those who hurt you (17-21)? **This is your reasonable service (1). If you are not concerned to live as a Christian ought to live, you have no right to assume that your faith is genuine.**

Put on the armour of light ... Put on the Lord Jesus Christ

It is our *'reasonable service'* to be obedient, law-abiding citizens. God has provided rulers and leaders of state to maintain law and order and we must pray for them (1 Timothy 2:1-2). They are to punish evil-doers, even to the extent of using the death penalty for proven murder (4; cp. Genesis 9:6. God's covenant with Noah was for all mankind and it has not been cancelled). To resist authorities is to resist the will of God (2). We are only permitted to disobey them if obedience to them would cause us to disobey God (Acts 5:29). Christians must be model citizens and *render therefore to all their due* whether it be taxes, customs or honour (7). We must pray for the leaders of our nation and all in authority (1 Timothy 2:1-2). We must also be careful not to live beyond our means. Thousands are bringing misery to themselves and their families through debts that they could have avoided. There is a debt which is commendable — *owe no one anything except to love one another* (8).

We must live as those who expect the Lord's return. *Our salvation* (the coming again of the Lord Jesus Christ) is getting nearer and nearer. We must be watchful and prayerful and not caught up with the folly, the trivia and the sinful lifestyle of the world (11-12; cp. Luke 21:34-36; 1 Thessalonians 5:1-8). *Let us put on* [Greek word = 'clothe ourselves with'] *the armour of light* (12). Armour is the clothing for battle and we are faced with many battles in an increasingly godless society. Are you clothed with *'the armour of light'*? **You cannot wear this armour unless you have *cast off the works of darkness* which are described in verse 13.** Consecration to God will mean that we will shine in this dark world with its night life of drunken revelry, immoral behaviour, strife and envy.

Let us also *put on the Lord Jesus Christ* (14) so that we will not feed unwholesome desires. If Christ returned tonight, would you be ashamed because of unchecked sin in your life?

Disputes over doubtful things

The Bible gives many clear directives which must govern our conduct (e.g. the Ten Commandments, cp. 13:9). With some issues however, Scripture is silent or its teaching is not clear-cut. Christians have differing scruples of conscience which may lead to *disputes over doubtful things* (1). There were tensions in the early church. Jewish believers would not buy meat at the market because it was probably from animals that had been killed as an offering to idols. Their meat had to be 'kosher'. Moreover, they continued to keep Jewish holy days, as well as the Saturday Sabbath. They were offended at the apparent careless attitude of Gentile Christians in these matters, and the Gentiles treated them with contempt (10). The Gentile Christians rejoiced in their freedom in Christ and are called *'strong'* (15:1). Those with Jewish scruples are called *'weak'* (1-2) because they did not appreciate the liberty that we have in Christ.

Christians continue to be divided over issues where Scripture is silent or can be interpreted in more than one way. **Our personal behaviour is important! We must avoid any conduct that dishonours Christ. Remember, we belong to the Lord and serve him** (7-8). Christians can be very intolerant of their fellow-believers *over doubtful things.* We must *receive* the Christian who differs from us on matters of conscience (1-3). We must not *despise* him nor *judge* him (3-4,10). Beware of harsh, judgmental attitudes; your brother is God's servant and is answerable to him (4). *Let each be fully convinced in his own mind* (5).

We are answerable to God for our own behaviour. *We shall all stand before the judgment seat of Christ* (10) where *each of us shall give account of himself to God* (12). It is possible to become bogged down with petty rules and *neglect the weightier matters of the law* (Matthew 23:23). *The kingdom of God is not food and drink, but righteousness and peace and joy in the Holy Spirit* (17). We must not look for arguments over 'non-essentials', but rather *pursue the things which make for peace* (19).

The God of patience and comfort

Paul continues to write of the need for Christian love and unity (1-14) before mentioning his own plans and his desire to visit Rome (15-33). The Lord Jesus demands that we deny ourselves if we are to follow him (Matthew 16:24). One aspect of self-denial is shown in the way we treat one another. We *ought to bear with* the weakness of weaker believers, *and not to please ourselves* (1). We are to please our *neighbour for his good, leading to edification* (2). This will build him up as a Christian. Paul points us to the example of Christ who *did not please himself* (3). He was willing to bear the taunts of his enemies and the indescribable agony and shame of the cross to save us. Surely we should be able to sacrifice some of our liberty for the sake of our fellow-Christians. We also have *the patience and comfort* of the Scriptures (4) to help us cope with the niggling problems that can divide and destroy the unity of a local church. We need to learn the lessons of Scripture and apply them to our own life and circumstances.

See how Paul describes God in his prayer for the Romans:

- *May the God of patience and comfort grant you to be like-minded towards one another, according to Christ Jesus* (5). **God is very patient with us in all our failings and he also encourages us. We must treat our fellow-Christians as God treats us.** We must follow the example of the Lord Jesus (*'according to Christ'*). When we receive one another as Christ has received us and are of one mind, we will build up each other (2) and we will praise and glorify God (6-7).
- *May the God of hope fill you with all joy and peace in believing, that you may abound in hope* (i.e. 'confident expectation') *by the power of the Holy Spirit* (13). When our lives are flooded by joy and peace in believing, and are abounding in hope by the power of the Holy Spirit, we will not indulge in petty criticism and division.
- *Now the God of peace be with you all* (33). How precious is this peace in our lives and in our churches. **Pray for those who irritate you, and at all times seek to bring God's peace to troubled souls.**

1 & 2 KINGS, 2 CHRONICLES

The two books of the Kings cover a period of four hundred years in the history of Israel. They open with the death of King David and close with the people of Judah being carried off into captivity in Babylon. Solomon, who succeeded David, began well and built a magnificent temple for the worship of God. He was renowned for his God-given wisdom but was foolish in his personal life. He married many wives and succumbed to their heathen influence. He turned from the Lord and worshipped their gods, bringing divine displeasure and judgment upon himself (1 Kings 11). The lack of wisdom of Solomon's son, Rehoboam, brought about a great rebellion which divided the kingdom.

The turbulent history of the two nations is recorded in 1 Kings 12 to the end of 2 Kings. All the northern kings were evil but Judah was blessed with some good kings. Most of the prophets exercised their ministry during this period — Elijah, Elisha, Joel, Amos, Jonah, Hosea, Isaiah, Micah, Zephaniah, Nahum, Habakkuk and Jeremiah. Some of them prophesied to one kingdom, others to both. The Lord is merciful and slow to anger and he sent the prophets to warn his erring people. Persistent and repeated disobedience inevitably brought the judgment of God upon them and Israel went into Assyrian captivity in 722 BC, Judah to captivity in Babylon in 586 BC.

The second Book of Chronicles covers the same period of history as the books of the Kings but it concentrates on the kings of Judah. The kings of Israel in the north are only mentioned when involved in Judah's history (e.g. chapter 18). The reign of Solomon is covered and the subsequent history of Judah until the time of the captivity in Babylon. There were three great periods of reformation under godly kings:

- Jehoshaphat (19:4 - 20:30);
- Hezekiah (29:1 - 31:21);
- Josiah (34:1 - 35:19).

His father had not rebuked him at any time

1 Kings does not begin on a happy note. David was now elderly and frail; it was an unseemly and shameful thing for him to have the young woman, Abishag, as a bed companion to keep him warm. He had several wives and his servants were lacking godly wisdom in their advice to him (1-4). God had appointed Solomon to succeed David as king over Israel (1 Chronicles 22:9-10) though he was not the eldest son (cp. 2 Samuel 3:2-5). Amnon and Absalom, the first and third sons, were dead; Scripture is silent concerning Chileab, the second son, who may have died in battle. Adonijah, the fourth and eldest of David's surviving sons, knew that it was the Lord's will for Solomon to be king (2:15) but he planned to seize the throne. He was aided and abetted by Joab and the high priest Abiathar (5-10). He was very foolish to imagine that he could thwart God's purposes (cp. Psalm 2:1-4; Isaiah 14:27). The prophet Nathan informed Bathsheba, Solomon's mother, of the plot and counselled her regarding the action that they should take; she then informed David of the conspiracy (18).

David took immediate action to thwart Adonijah and his conspirators and Solomon was anointed king at Gihon, east of Jerusalem (28-39). When Adonijah and the guests at his feast heard the joyful and noisy celebration in Jerusalem and learned that Solomon had been anointed king, they dispersed in panic. Adonijah took refuge in the tabernacle, clinging to the horns of the altar (40-41,49-50). Solomon spared his brother and gave him a warning that if any further wickedness were found in him, he would be put to death (51-53).

Adonijah was very handsome like his half-brother Absalom; both were vain and proud (5-6; cp. 2 Samuel 14:25-26; 15:1). We read these telling words in verse 6, *And his father had not rebuked him at any time by saying, 'Why have you done so?'* David may have been frail, but he had the support of mighty men. A timely rebuke to his son would have spared David much heartache and trouble in his last days. **If we are cowardly and fail to deal with wrongdoing in our family or church for the sake of an easy life, we will reap a bitter harvest.**

Be strong, therefore, and prove yourself a man

The words of dying King David to Solomon are full of instruction and challenge. He urged his son, *'Be strong, therefore, and prove yourself a man'* (2). We must never confuse true manliness with the 'macho' image admired by so many in the world. 'Macho' man is aggressive in his masculinity, loves to charm young women, is full of himself, and is vain in his imagination. This is a far cry from the manliness that God requires of Christian men. **The church has a great need in these days for manly men!** The Christian man must:

- *'Be strong'* (2). He must refuse to compromise God's truth and be prepared, if necessary, to stand alone against error and wickedness.
- Be godly (3-4). He must maintain fellowship with God and keep his commandments.
- Be wise (6,9). He needs to exercise much wisdom in leadership at home and (where appropriate) in the church.
- Be kind (7). Strength does not exclude gentleness or kindness.

The perfect example of manliness is found in the Lord Jesus Christ. He burned with anger against the hypocrites and the wicked (Mark 3:5; John 2:13-17) but he was full of compassion for the needy. He was always noble and gentle in his dealings with women and he wept at the tomb of his friend (John 8:3-11; 11:34-36). *'Prove yourself a man.'* I wonder if Bishop Hugh Latimer had those words in mind when he encouraged his fellow Reformer, Nicholas Ridley, as they burned at the stake in 1555. 'Be of good comfort, Master Ridley, and play the man. We shall this day light such a candle, by God's grace, in England, as I trust shall never be put out.' **Christian men, take these words to heart and show Christlike manliness in your lives.**

The young king had to prove himself a man by taking decisive and firm action to deal with those who posed a threat to his throne. Adonijah had not learned his lesson and Solomon had him and his allies put to death, and Abiathar was removed from his position as high priest to be replaced by Zadok (13-35).

And Solomon loved the LORD *... except ...*

Solomon was foolish and disobedient to God in his marriage to the daughter of Pharaoh (1); this marriage, and his subsequent marriages to heathen women were to lead to spiritual declension in his own life and to trouble in Israel (see chapter 11). We read that *Solomon loved the* LORD *... except that he sacrificed and burned incense at the high places* (3). The people did not have a temple where they could make their sacrifices (2) but they did have the tabernacle. God had commanded that sacrifices were to be restricted to worship at the tabernacle which at this time was at Gibeon (Deuteronomy 12:5-6, 13-14; 2 Chronicles 1:3). The high places were associated with pagan worship and should have been destroyed rather than adapted for the worship of the Lord. Solomon ended his days building high places for the worship of false gods (11:6-10).

If God promised to give you anything you desired, for what would you ask? God made such an offer to Solomon when he went to worship at the tabernacle in Gibeon (5). The young king responded by acknowledging God's goodness to him but he was aware of his lack of experience to lead a great nation (6-7). He said, *'Therefore give your servant an understanding heart to judge your people, that I may discern between good and evil'* (9). He wanted to rule the nation with wisdom and justice. God was pleased with his unselfish request and gave him riches and honour as well as the wisdom for which he had asked (4-15). Are your prayers self-centred or do you honour God in your praying? The well-known story of the dispute between the two prostitutes over the baby is recounted in verses 16 to 28. The brilliant judgment given by Solomon was recognized by the people as God-given and gained him great respect.

The Lord Jesus loved us so much that he gave himself to die for our salvation. Dare we offer him less than our total devotion? Do not be like Solomon, who *loved the* LORD *... except.* **Is there something in your life that is spoiling your walk with God? Half-hearted devotion to the Lord is not acceptable (cp. Revelation 3:15-16).**

When each one knows the plague of his own heart

The ark of the covenant was brought from the tabernacle to the newly built temple (1-13), and after speaking to the people (14-21), Solomon came to God in prayer (22-54). He then blessed the congregation (55-61) and dedicated the temple (62-66). Solomon's prayer is one of the greatest recorded in the Bible. The glory of God filled the temple and though Solomon began his prayer standing (22), he was on his knees by the time he had finished (54). These verses point us to some of the essentials of prayer. How should we pray?

- We should begin with worship and adoration (23,27).
- We should praise God for answered prayer (24).
- The Bible has many precious promises for us which we should use in prayer. Solomon prayed that God would fulfil his promise to David (25-26).
- Solomon prayed for the people of God (28-53). We too should pray not only for those in our own church, but also for God's people and his work around the world. To do this, we need to be informed by reading missionary magazines and prayer letters.
- Solomon prayed for the Gentiles, that they too would come to a knowledge of God (41-43). We should pray for the progress of the gospel among those who are lost.
- We must confess our sin to the Lord (46-50).

We must never forget that we come as sinners into the presence of a holy God when we pray. Christians do have the remains of sin within. *'There is no one who does not sin'* (46; cp. 1 John 1:8-9). We must grieve over our sin and repent. *'When each one knows the plague of his own heart'* (38) there is no room for careless living; there is no light, flippant attitude in prayer as if God were our 'pal'. The Lord is awesome and full of majesty and in his holy presence we should know the plague of our own hearts (cp. Isaiah 6:1-5). **When we are conscious of this plague, we will not take victory over sin for granted; we will be watchful and prayerful at all times.**

I did not believe ... the half was not told me

This chapter describes the splendour of Solomon's court and the prosperity of Israel at that time. People came to Jerusalem from all parts of the world to hear the wisdom of Solomon, bringing costly gifts to the king (23-24). One such person was the queen of Sheba. She was so overwhelmed by Solomon's wisdom, the splendour of the temple and the opulence of the palace, that *there was no more spirit* ['breath'] *in her* (4-5). Sheba was probably the Yemen of today, which had rich gold mines in the north of its land. She probed Solomon with all manner of difficult questions, all of which Solomon answered (2-3). The queen confessed, '*I heard in my own land about your words and your wisdom. However, I did not believe the words until I came and saw it with my own eyes; and indeed the half was not told me*' (6-7).

There was a time when we did not believe in God as he is revealed in the Bible. We were ignorant, without God and without hope (Ephesians 2:12). Then the Lord opened our eyes to see the wonder of his greatness and his grace. We 'saw' that we were under condemnation, but also that the Lord Jesus died on the cross to save sinners. We were born again through the mighty working of the Holy Spirit in our lives. We found forgiveness and peace with God through the Lord Jesus Christ. Being a Christian is more wonderful than we had ever imagined. We are able to rejoice and echo the words of the queen of Sheba, '*I did not believe ... the half was not told me.*' Wonder of wonders, the best is yet to be! Heaven and glory await us!

Christian reader, ponder the greatness of your salvation and worship and praise God. Your Saviour and Friend is far, far greater than Solomon (8; cp. Matthew 12:42). **If you are not a Christian, I urge you to seek the Lord and his free forgiveness for your sin. Turn from your sin and trust in the Lord Jesus. You will not be disappointed, but will find that the half was not told you.**

The Lord God of Israel, who had appeared to him twice

These verses stand in stark contrast to all that we read in the previous chapter and they make very distressing reading. Solomon had defied God's command forbidding intermarriage between his people and those of other nations (2; cp. Deuteronomy 7:3-4). Through the influence of his pagan wives Solomon turned away from the Lord to serve false gods (1-6). The builder of the temple of the Lord became a builder of idol shrines (7-8). God was angry with him and told him that he would tear the greater part of his kingdom from his son and give it to his servant (9-13). The servant, Jeroboam, rebelled against Solomon who foolishly sought to kill him. He knew that God would give Jeroboam most of his kingdom and he should have realized that he could not thwart the Lord's sovereign purpose (11,40; Isaiah 14:27).

Does it not amaze you that Solomon could turn away from *the Lord God of Israel, who had appeared to him twice* (9)? On the first occasion the Lord answered his prayer for wisdom (3:4-15). The next time God specifically warned him against idolatry (10; cp. 9:1-9). Solomon had also witnessed fire falling from heaven to burn up the sacrifices as the glory of the Lord filled the temple (2 Chronicles 7:1). Does it not shock you that Solomon, who had prayed so eloquently for the heathen nations (8:41-43), should turn to worship their false gods? Does it not sadden you that Solomon, who built the temple, also built high places for idol worship (7-8)? Does it not astound you that Solomon, renowned for his wisdom, became such a fool?

Let Solomon be a warning to us all! Great spiritual experiences are no guarantee against backsliding. Satan is always looking for ways to entice us away from the Lord; he never gives up. Many a believer has disobeyed God to marry an unbeliever. Others have faithfully followed the Lord only to forsake him in their later years. It was *when Solomon was old, that his wives turned his heart after other gods* (4). Let us beware of complacency in our Christian lives. Let us be determined to *fully follow the Lord* (6). Let us repent of any backsliding before we drift away from God and from his people.

The turn of affairs was from the Lord

The nation of Israel was heavily taxed to pay for the extravagant lifestyle of Solomon in the latter part of his reign. After Solomon's death Jeroboam returned from exile in Egypt to lead a delegation to appeal to the new king for an easing of the tax burden (1-5). Rehoboam sent them away for three days so that he could seek counsel from those around him. He rejected the advice of the elders who counselled a sympathetic approach and listened to the hawkish young men. When Jeroboam and his delegation returned three days later, Rehoboam dealt with them in a rough and uncompromising manner. He told them that his regime would be far more severe than that of his father (6-15). Rehoboam soon had a major rebellion on his hands and his chief tax official was assassinated (16-19). The kingdom was divided (20) but Rehoboam wisely obeyed God's word through the prophet Shemaiah, that he should not go to war with the rebels (21-24).

Jeroboam knew that God had given him the northern kingdom (11:29-39) and he had no need to resort to devious plans to keep his kingdom intact. His two golden calves, one for the north of the kingdom in Dan, the other at Bethel in the south, and other idol shrines throughout the land were designed to keep his people from returning to worship at Jerusalem and so be influenced to serve Rehoboam (25-33). He set the northern kingdom on a path of rebellion against God from which it never recovered.

Why did Rehoboam (forty-one years old; 14:21) fail to take the more sensible advice of his elder statesmen (6-8)? Why did he refuse to listen with some sympathy to the complaints of the people? The answer is found in verse 15. *For the turn of affairs was from the* Lord, *that he might fulfil his word.* **God is in absolute control of all kings and of all political leaders (Proverbs 21:1). We must pray for kings and all** who are in authority (1 Timothy 2:2). Who would have thought that the gospel is now being preached in countries where Christians were once so vigorously persecuted? **The Lord reigns supreme. Let us be encouraged.**

Kings of the divided kingdom (after the death of Solomon)

Judah		Prophets	Israel	
930 — 913	Rehoboam		Jeroboam I	930 — 909
913 — 910	Abijam		Nadab	909 — 908
910 — 869	Asa		Baasha	908 — 886
			Elah	886 — 885
			Zimri	7 days
			Omri	885 — 874
872 — 869	Jehoshaphat		Tibni	885 — 881
(co-regency)			Ahab	874 — 853
872 — 848	Jehoshaphat	Elijah		
(total reign)				
853 — 848	Jehoram		Ahaziah	853 — 852
(co-regency)			Joram	852 — 841
853 — 841	Jehoram			
(total reign)				
841	Ahaziah	Elisha	Jehu	841 — 814
841 — 835	Queen Athaliah		Jehoahaz	814 — 798
835 — 796	Joash	Joel?	Jehoash	798 — 782
796 — 767	Amaziah		Jeroboam II	793 — 782
792 — 767	Azariah (Uzziah)		(co-regency)	
(overlap with Amaziah)		Amos, Jonah	Jeroboam II	793 — 753
792 — 740	Azariah		(total reign)	
(total reign)		Hosea	Zechariah	6 months
750 — 740	Jotham		Shallum	1 month
(co-regency)			Menahem	752 — 742
750 — 735	Jotham		Pekahiah	742 — 740
(official reign)		Isaiah	Pekah	752 — 740
750 — 732	Jotham		(in Gilead; overlapping years)	
			Pekah	740
735 — 732	Ahaz (overlap with Jotham)		(beginning of sole reign)	
732 — 715	Ahaz (official years)		Pekah	752 — 732
			(total reign)	
			Hoshea	732 — 723
			Captivity to Assyria	
715 — 686	Hezekiah	Micah		
697 — 686	Manasseh (co-regency)			
697 — 642	Manasseh (total reign)			
642 — 640	Amon			
640 — 609	Josiah	Zephaniah, Nahum, Habakkuk		
3 months	Jehoahaz			
609 — 598	Jehoiakim	Jeremiah		
3 months	Jehoiachin			
597 — 586	Zedekiah			
Captivity to Babylon				

Note on chart of kings and prophets

An accurate chronology for this period is very difficult to ascertain:

1. Some kings appointed their sons as co-rulers during their lifetime so that there is an overlap in some reigns.
2. In Israel years of kings were calculated from the month of Nisan (spring). In Judah years of kings were calculated from the month of Tishri (autumn).
3. Dates given here are based on Thiele's chronology (see Edwin R. Thiele — *A Chronology of the Hebrew Kings*, published by Zondervan).

Kingdoms of Israel and Judah after death of Solomon

The man of God who was disobedient to the word of the LORD

God was gracious to Jeroboam in sending a man of God from Judah to cry out against his altar at Bethel. The man prophesied that a king of Judah would one day defile that very altar. He named the king (Josiah) and this prophecy was fulfilled almost three hundred years later (2; cp. 2 Kings 23:15-20). He gave a sign to confirm his word from the Lord, saying that the altar would be split apart and its ashes poured out. An angry Jeroboam ordered the arrest of the man of God, but his outstretched hand was paralysed (*'withered'*; Hebrew = 'dried up' as in Authorised Version). The altar was split just as the man had indicated (1-5). Jeroboam was humbled by these two miracles and he pleaded with the man of God, *'Pray for me, that my hand may be restored to me'* (6). The Lord answered the prayer for Jeroboam's healing and the king offered the man hospitality and a reward. He refused this because God had told him not to eat or drink in that place (7-10).

The man of God was very courageous in denouncing Jeroboam in the presence of his subjects but his mission ended in personal disaster. He believed the lies of an old prophet who then denounced him for his disobedience (15-22). The man was killed by a lion after he left the house of the old prophet but it was a miracle that the lion did not eat his corpse or attack the donkey (23-28). The perverse old prophet lamented the death of the man of God (29-31) and described him as, *'The man of God who was disobedient to the word of the* LORD*'* (26).

What went wrong? The Lord had told him not to eat or drink in Bethel (7-10). He failed to discern that the old man was a false prophet who was contradicting the word of God. **However kind or convincing a person may appear, if they deny the teaching of God's revealed word, we must not listen to them.** The Lord Jesus warned, *'Beware of false prophets'* (Matthew 7:15). Satan is the master deceiver. We need to know the teaching of the Bible and to walk with the Lord. *Be sober, be vigilant; because your adversary the devil walks about like a roaring lion, seeking whom he may devour* (1 Peter 5:8).

The LORD God of Israel ... before whom I stand

Ahab became king of Israel some thirty-five years after the death of Jeroboam. His wife Jezebel, daughter of the king of Sidon, was an extremely wicked woman who massacred the prophets of the Lord while she zealously promoted the worship of the god Baal (16:31; 18:4). The Lord raised up a man to prophesy to Israel in those dark and tragic times — Elijah. The name 'Elijah' challenged all for which Ahab and Jezebel stood; it means 'Jehovah is God' or 'my God is Jehovah'. The public ministry of Elijah was dramatic and miraculous, but privately he was a mighty man of prayer. Through his prayers God sent a drought upon the land of Israel (1; cp. James 5:17-18). The people had to learn that Baal, who was supposed to provide rain and abundant harvests, was useless and powerless. The famine became severe and widespread after three years of drought (cp. 18:1-2) but the Lord used ravens to sustain Elijah at the brook Cherith. This was a miracle, for ravens naturally scavenge and gobble up every scrap of meat they find, but they brought bread and meat to Elijah both morning and evening (2-6).

The brook Cherith eventually dried up through lack of rain and the Lord sent Elijah to Sidon (Jezebel country) where there was also famine. Notice the sovereignty of God in these verses — *he commanded the ravens to feed Elijah* (4) and he *commanded a widow* to provide for him at Zarephath (9). The Lord miraculously provided for this widow, her son and Elijah throughout the famine (8-16). While Jezebel was busily promoting the religion of Baal in Israel, the Lord was bringing a widow and her son to faith in himself in Jezebel's own country. **No country is too dark and no land is able to close its doors to the gospel when God chooses to open them.**

Elijah was greatly used in prayer (cp. James 5:17). What was his secret? He was always aware of God's presence in his life. He confessed, *'As the LORD God of Israel lives, before whom I stand'* (1). He obeyed God's word without question, being confident that God is able to keep his promises (3-5, 8-10). **The world behaves as if God were dead. It is for us to proclaim him and show that he lives.**

How long will you falter between two opinions?

Ahab had searched his kingdom to have Elijah arrested and silenced. The fearless prophet obeyed the Lord without any question when told to present himself to the king (1-2,10). God had another servant, a secret believer, in the very palace of evil Ahab. Obadiah (not to be confused with the prophet of the same name) held very high office, being in charge of the royal household. *Now Obadiah feared the* LORD *greatly* (3,12). Through his inside knowledge Obadiah was able to save one hundred of God's prophets from massacre by Jezebel (4). God places some of his people in very unlikely places.

Elijah challenged the four hundred and fifty prophets of Baal to prove that Baal was able to answer prayer. Elijah wanted the great crowd present to be in no doubt that Jehovah ('*the* LORD') was the true and living God. They remained silent as he challenged them, '*How long will you falter* [limp] *between two opinions? If the* LORD *is God, follow him; but if Baal, then follow him*' (21). Elijah challenged the prophets of Baal to prepare a sacrifice to their god and he would also prepare a sacrifice to Jehovah. They should call on Baal to send fire to consume their sacrifice and he would pray that the Lord would send fire upon his sacrifice. '*And the God who answers by fire, he is God*' (24-25). Elijah taunted the prophets of Baal who prayed in vain for hours and shed their own blood in the hope of persuading their god to hear and to answer them (26-29).

The dignity and calm of Elijah as he prepared the altar for his sacrifice stand in marked contrast to the frenzied prophets of Baal (30-35). He told the people to saturate the sacrifice and the altar with water (no doubt obtained from the sea which was overlooked by Mount Carmel). His prayer is full of longing for the honour of God who sent fire from heaven to consume the sacrifice (36-38). The people then *fell on their faces; and they said, 'The* LORD, *he is God! The* LORD, *he is God!*' (38-39). The execution of the prophets of Baal may seem cruel (40), but they had doubtless played a major role in the massacre of the Lord's prophets (4) and were thus justly punished.

What are you doing here, Elijah?

Jezebel sent a messenger to Elijah stating that within twenty-four hours she would have him killed (1-2). *And when he saw* that, he arose and ran for his life* (3). He would have been bitterly disappointed that there was no evidence of national repentance following the defeat of Baal. We must not be surprised at the hardness of the human heart. The discouraged prophet wanted to die; he had had enough (4). He was physically, emotionally and spiritually drained. He keenly felt the loneliness and spiritual isolation often suffered by those who are godly (10). **It is a good thing that the Lord does not always answer our prayers as we desire.** We may pray foolishly when we are feeling discouraged or depressed. The prophet who prayed that he might die never did! He was one of two men in Scripture who went to be with the Lord without dying (2 Kings 2:11; cp. Genesis 5:24).

Notice how God cared for and encouraged his servant. Elijah rested and slept and the Lord sent an angel to feed him (5-8). He then *went in the strength of that food forty days and forty nights* until he reached Horeb (Sinai). The Lord twice asked him, *'What are you doing here, Elijah?'* (9,13). He had been ready to give up and he wanted to die but the Lord had more work for him. He was to anoint Hazael as king over Syria and Jehu as king over Israel. God would use both of these men as instruments of judgment against the wicked house of Ahab. He was to anoint Elisha to succeed him as a prophet. God had a faithful remnant in Israel who had not bowed the knee to Baal (15-18).

Dale Ralph Davis comments: 'Elijah has not been Yahweh's last broken servant. There are cases also in these new covenant days. It is hardly a state to be desired, and yet surely 1 Kings 19 teaches you that you needn't fear being a broken servant when you have such a kind and adequate God' (*The wisdom and the folly — an exposition of 1 Kings,* page 275, published by Christian Focus).

---

*   Dale Ralph Davis argues that this is a better rendering of the Hebrew than 'he was afraid' as found in some translations (e.g. English Standard Version).

So Ahaziah died according to the word of the LORD

Ahaziah was just as wicked as his father Ahab (1 Kings 22:52-53). He was seriously injured when he fell through the lattice of his upper room. He wanted to know if he would recover from his injury and sent messengers to go to the Philistine city of Ekron (forty-five miles or seventy-two kilometres from Samaria). There the priests of Baal-Zebub claimed to receive messages from their god (2). The messengers never reached Ekron. They were intercepted by Elijah who sent them back to Ahaziah with a message from the Lord. *'Is it because there is no God in Israel that you are going to enquire of Baal-Zebub, the god of Ekron?'* (3; this question is repeated in verses 6 and 16). The first commandment reminds us that the Lord hates idolatry and the worship of other gods provokes him to anger (Exodus 20:3; 1 Kings 22:53). Ahaziah would *surely die* because he had sought to obtain help from an idol rather than from the living God (3-6).

Elijah knew that Jehovah was the only true God who had sent drought, fire and rain in answer to his prayers. Ahaziah did not take kindly to Elijah's message from the Lord. He sent a band of fifty soldiers to arrest the prophet who called fire down from heaven to destroy them. He sent another band of soldiers to arrest the prophet, and the same fate befell them (11-12). He was again reminded that Jehovah was the true God, not Baal, but he persisted in his rebellion against God. Fire from heaven did not bring him to his senses and like his father he did not forsake his idolatry.

The third band of soldiers were spared when their captain pleaded with Elijah for their lives. The Lord assured Elijah that he would be safe in going with this man to repeat his message to Ahaziah. The king had become so hard in heart that he was insensitive to the voice of God. The Lord was merciful to the captain who humbled himself and pleaded for his life but *Ahaziah died according to the word of the LORD* (17). **If you close your ears to the voice of God, you do so at your own peril.**

You have asked a hard thing

Elijah was a mighty man of prayer but the Lord did not answer his request that he might die (1 Kings 19:4). The Lord had much work for him to do and a prophetic community was established at Bethel where Jeroboam, first ruler of the northern kingdom, had set up an idol altar (3; cp. 1 Kings 12:28-29). There was also a group of prophets at Jericho, another place where wicked men had defied God (5; cp. 1 Kings 16:33-34). Elijah was also able to prepare Elisha to succeed him. There are times when we do not pray aright because we feel low in spirit. It is a good thing that God does not always take us at our word. When he says to us, 'No', his reasons are always wise and good.

Elisha and the sons of the prophets knew that God was about to take up Elijah into heaven in a whirlwind, but they did not speak of it openly (3,5). Elisha would not leave Elijah, though urged three times to remain where he was (2,4,6). Elijah then asked him, *'What may I do for you, before I am taken away from you?'* Elisha requested a double portion of his spirit. Elisha knew that he needed the hand of God upon his life. Elijah told him, *'You have asked a hard thing'* (10). Subsequent events show that Elisha's request was granted. **Are you bold when you make your requests to God? Do you come to him in faith, expecting him to answer you?** *'Ah, Lord GOD! Behold, you have made the heavens and the earth by your great power and outstretched arm. There is nothing too hard for you'* (Jeremiah 32:17).

Elijah went up by a whirlwind into heaven (11) and Elisha was able to repeat the miracle of parting the Jordan river enabling him to cross over it (8,13-14). This was followed by two further miracles. The healing of the water at Jericho displayed the grace of God but divine judgment was seen in the incident outside of Bethel (19-25). The mob of youths who came out of Bethel to intimidate and mock Elisha received more than they had bargained for. The prophet cursed them *in the name of the LORD and two female bears came out of the woods and mauled forty-two of their company* (23-24). Those who despise God's servants are foolish indeed.

A notable woman

The miracles in this chapter demonstrate the way in which God cares for his people. The miraculous supply of oil enabled the widow to pay off her debts and to provide for the future (1-7). The Shunammite woman lost her son through death but he was restored in answer to Elisha's prayer (20-37). The poisoned stew was wonderfully purified (38-41) and one hundred men were fed from twenty loaves (42-44).

The Shunammite was not only notable (8) for her wealth but also for her godliness. Let us consider how practical she was in her religion:

- She gave regular hospitality to Elisha and she asked her husband to have their house extended to provide a room for this *'holy man of God'*. The prophet would have greatly appreciated this kindness as Shunem was some twenty-five miles from Carmel (a day's journey) where Elisha was living at that time (8-11,25).
- She appears to be more spiritual than her husband. She took the spiritual initiative in her home, but never usurped her husband's authority (9-10,22).
- She was contented (13; cp. 1 Timothy 6:6) and did not look for her kindness to be rewarded. The Lord honoured her beyond her wildest dreams and gave a son to the childless couple (14-17).
- From her husband's remarks (22-25) it is apparent that she regularly travelled to Carmel to worship God (a round trip of fifty miles). She was prepared to put up with a long uncomfortable journey by donkey in order to worship God in spirit and in truth. Far better travel some distance to worship and to be fed by faithful preaching than compromise by attending a non-evangelical church or a place where biblical teaching is despised.
- In great distress (27) at the death of her son she was convinced that the living God would meet with her, and he did (30-37).

The Shunammite was a notable woman who knew the smile of God upon her life, even in much distress. May her example challenge us to serve the Lord joyfully and to trust in him at all times.

Sketch map showing places mentioned in 2 Kings, chapters 4 to 9

201

Now I know

The grace of God is truly wonderful in reaching all kinds of people. Naaman, the commander of the Syrian army, had contracted leprosy but the Lord used this affliction as a means of bringing Naaman to himself. There is a contrast in these verses between the faith of *a young girl from the land of Israel* and the lack of faith in the king of Israel (Jehoram?). It appears that the young girl was treated very well in the home of Naaman. She showed no antagonism toward the Syrian whose army had brought such unhappiness to her. Had she been full of bitterness or self-pity, she would have been a poor witness to her faith in the Lord. She showed concern for her master and mistress in their difficult situation and they responded to that concern. She may not have possessed a great knowledge of the Scriptures but she was convinced that God was able to heal Naaman through the ministry of Elisha. We must show a genuine interest in people and concern for them if we are to be successful witnesses.

Naaman went to Israel laden with great riches in the hope of rewarding the prophet for curing him of his disease. The godless king concluded that Naaman's impossible request was an excuse for picking a quarrel with him (4-7). Though he was aware of the prophet Elisha, he did not trust in Elisha's God. Naaman had to learn a fundamental lesson about God — that his thoughts and ways are different from our thoughts and ways (cp. Isaiah 55:8-9). He was angry that Elisha did not come to speak to him personally. He wanted some dramatic display of God's power and was enraged at the prophet's instruction to dip seven times in the Jordan. Naaman's servant rightly pointed out that if Elisha had told him to do something great, he would have gladly complied. **When he was persuaded to do things God's way, he was healed (13-14).**

Naaman returned to Elisha saying, *'Indeed, now I know that there is no God in all the earth, except in Israel'* (15). He was also to find that God's grace is free and unmerited when the prophet refused his gift. He began to discover that we serve a wonderful and awesome God. **Do you know God? Is he real in your life and experience?**

Those who are with us

The sons of the prophets needed larger premises and one of them was felling a tree to obtain timber for the new building when the axe head fell into the Jordan (1-4). It would have been almost impossible to locate and recover it from the muddy river bed. The man was distressed because the axe was borrowed but it was miraculously recovered through Elisha's ministry (5-7).

The Syrian king was repeatedly thwarted in his battle plans against Israel because the Lord revealed them to Elisha who passed on the information to the king of Israel. A great army sent from Syria to capture the prophet surrounded him and his servant at Dothan (8-15). The young man was terrified when he saw the Syrians and their chariots surrounding the city. Elisha said to him, *'Do not fear, for those who are with us are more than those who are with them'* (16). The prophet prayed that the Lord would open his eyes and his prayer was answered. The young man saw the invincible army of God all around Elisha (17). The Syrian army was temporarily blinded through another prayer of the prophet and the helpless soldiers were led into the city of Samaria. The king of Israel wanted to kill them, but on Elisha's instructions he spared them and fed them. They returned to their own country to leave Israel in peace for a while (18-23). Samaria was later reduced to severe famine through a Syrian siege and the king blamed Elisha for this calamity and was determined to kill him (24-33).

How could Elisha remain calm in the face of such danger (15-16)? He knew that he was surrounded by God's army (17) and that no harm could befall him except by God's permission. Do you feel threatened? Are you fearful? If you belong to God, you have no need to fear. Take time to feast your soul on Psalm 91. Be encouraged, and worship and adore your great God. *For he shall give his angels charge over you, to keep you in all your ways* (Psalm 91:11). **Why are we often fearful? We do not spend enough time in the secret place of the Most High (Psalm 91:1) and we forget about** *'those who are with us'* **(16).**

21 JUNE   **2 Kings 7:1-20**

A day of good news and we remain silent

The siege of Samaria had brought such famine that some people had become cannibals to survive (6:28-30). Elisha had nothing good to say about wicked King Jehoram (6:32) but he had a great message of hope which promised an abundance of food within twenty-four hours. The king's officer refused to believe the prophet and said, *'Look, if the* Lord *would make windows in heaven, could this thing be?'* Elisha told the unbelieving royal equerry that he would see this provision with his own eyes but he would not eat of it (1-2).

Four leprous men, excluded from Samaria because of their disease, went to the Syrian camp in a desperate search for food (3-5). God had previously struck Israel's enemies with blindness (6:18) and he now worked to confuse their hearing. He caused them to hear the noise of a great army and they thought that the king of Israel had enlisted the help of powerful neighbouring states. *Therefore they arose and fled at twilight, and left the camp intact* (6-7). They fled from their camp just as the four lepers had set out for that camp. They left treasure and great stores of food and clothing (8). After they had feasted, the lepers realized that they had a great responsibility. They said to one another, *'We are not doing what is right. This day is a day of good news and we remain silent'* (9). They returned to Samaria with their news and the king sent men in the direction of the Syrian camp. They were able to confirm the good news but the unbelieving royal equerry was trampled in the rush of the people out of the city. Elisha's prophecy was fulfilled (17-20).

The leprous men would have been selfish and heartless if they had not taken their good news to the suffering, tragic, beleaguered city. They certainly expected God to judge them if they remained silent (9). **We have the most wonderful news in all the world.** News of a Saviour who died to save poor, needy sinners; who rose again to give pardon and eternal life to all who trust in him. People around us are perishing in their sin without our Saviour. **We know that we are not doing what is right if we remain silent. Can we, dare we, be ashamed of the gospel of Christ (Romans 1:16)?**

What confidence is this in which you trust?

Hezekiah was one of the best kings to reign over Judah. He had seen the dreadful effects of idolatry in the life of his father Ahaz (2 Chronicles 28:22-23) and he destroyed the idol shrines in the land. He also *broke in pieces the bronze serpent that Moses had made* (1-4). You may recall that God commanded Moses to make the serpent for the people to gaze upon and be healed of their serpent bites (Numbers 21:4-9). It had become venerated as a religious relic so that it was just as much an idol as any image of the god Baal. Hezekiah knew that it was only 'Nehushtan' (a piece of bronze) and he smashed it. Religious relics do not aid true worship; they offend God.

The northern kingdom had refused again and again to obey the voice of God and judgment was inevitable. During Hezekiah's reign they were overrun by the Assyrians (9-11). Sennacherib, the Assyrian king, afterwards turned his attention to the southern kingdom. He had accepted the tribute he had imposed on Hezekiah but he then came to attack Jerusalem (17-37). Sennacherib sent his army commander ('the Tartan') and two high-ranking officials ('the Rabsaris' and 'the Rabshakeh') to Jerusalem. They called for Hezekiah, but he sent his officials to meet them. The Assyrians spoke in Hebrew to make certain that everyone understood their threats (26-28) and demanded unconditional surrender (31-32). Sennacherib rightly scoffed at the futility of relying on Egypt for help, but he blasphemed God by scorning Hezekiah's counsel to trust in the Lord (19-24). He also misrepresented Hezekiah who had not destroyed God's altars but idol shrines (22). The Rabshakeh even claimed to have had a word from the Lord but this made no impression on Hezekiah who had cautioned his people not to argue with the Assyrians (25,36).

The words of the Rabshakeh about trust are very relevant. *'What confidence is this in which you trust?'* (19). Trusting in men and their schemes is futile, but it is not vain to trust in the Lord. **On what are you basing your confidence for salvation? On whom are you depending in difficult times?**

Hezekiah ... spread it before the LORD

What was the distraught king to do when his country was threatened with destruction and his own life was in danger? He went to the house of God and also sought the prayers of the prophet Isaiah who sent back a very reassuring message from the Lord (1-7). The Assyrian king again sent messengers to Hezekiah, bearing a letter for him which blasphemed God (8-13). *Hezekiah went up to the house of the LORD, and spread it before the LORD* (14). He then uttered a great prayer of confidence in God the sovereign Creator of heaven and earth. *'O LORD God of Israel, the One who dwells between the cherubim, you are God ... you made heaven and earth. Incline your ear, O LORD, and hear ...'* (15-16). He was realistic in his assessment of the military might of Assyria but the nations they had conquered were worshippers of useless idols which were powerless to save them. He knew that God could easily deliver Judah from the Assyrians and he prayed that the Lord would be glorified in their deliverance from their enemies (17-19).

The Lord sent Isaiah to Hezekiah, promising that he had heard his prayer and that he would punish the Assyrians for their blasphemy (21-31). The king of Assyria would not be able to conquer Jerusalem because the Lord was defending it (32-34). The angel of the Lord destroyed the Assyrian army in one night and Sennacherib was later assassinated while worshipping his useless god Nisroch (36-38). Those who mock God do so at their peril and they are very foolish. *He who sits in the heavens shall laugh; the LORD shall hold them in derision* (Psalm 2:4).

Think of the words of God concerning Hezekiah, *'Because you have prayed to me ... I have heard'* (20). Prayer makes all the difference. Are we encouraged by answers to our prayers because we have prayed? Or are we weak and discouraged because we have not prayed,? **Martin Luther rightly observed, 'Prayer is not overcoming God's reluctance, but laying hold of his willingness.' Let us be more faithful in prayer.**

I have heard your prayer, I have seen your tears

At the time of the Assyrian invasion (6) King Hezekiah was very ill, probably suffering from poisoning of his system which had gathered into a large boil (7). Isaiah brought him a message from God telling him that he was going to die from this illness. This was devastating news to the king who was also in a dire situation from the invading Assyrians (1). The distressed king was driven to seek the face of God in prayer (1-3). We can calculate, by comparing scriptures, that the king was thirty-nine years of age at this time and in the prime of his life (18:2,13; Isaiah 38:10). **Do you pray when you hear grim news?** God immediately responded to Hezekiah's prayer and told him, '*I have heard your prayer, I have seen your tears*', and promised that he would extend his life by fifteen years (5-7). **God does hear our prayers, he sees our tears, though he may not always answer us in the way we expect.**

God gave the king a miraculous sign to confirm his promise causing the shadow of the sun-dial to go back ten degrees (8-11). Isaiah instructed Hezekiah's servants to put a poultice of figs on the boil and he recovered (7). Those added years were a disaster for Hezekiah who fell into the sin of pride. *But Hezekiah did not repay according to the favour shown him, for his heart was lifted up* (2 Chronicles 32:25).

The Babylonians would have been delighted to hear of the destruction of the Assyrian army which had besieged Jerusalem. They sent ambassadors to Hezekiah to wish him well on his recovery from illness (12). *Hezekiah was attentive to them,* and showed them all his treasures (13). There isn't any evidence that he glorified God before the Babylonians for his recovery or for his deliverance from the Assyrian invaders. The Lord sent Isaiah to warn him that a day would come when all the treasures so proudly displayed would be plundered by the Babylonians and his descendants carried off captive. Selfish Hezekiah accepted the word of the Lord as good saying, '*Will there not be peace and truth at least in my days?*' (14-19). **He should have been very sorry that his folly would lead to trouble following his death.**

In affliction, he ... humbled himself greatly ... and prayed

Manasseh was only twelve years of age when he came to the throne and his reign was the longest in Judah's history. He plunged the land into the most appalling wickedness during a long reign of terror and he was a zealous idol worshipper. He rebuilt the high places his father had destroyed and desecrated the house of the Lord by placing pagan altars in its courts and an idol within its walls. He offered his children as sacrifices to the god Molech in the valley of the Son of Hinnom. He indulged in the occult, using witchcraft and consulting spiritist mediums (1-7). Manasseh seduced Judah to do more evil than the nations whom God had driven out of Canaan (9). He was a mass murderer who *shed very much innocent blood* (2 Kings 21:16).

Manasseh refused to listen to God and the Lord used the Assyrians to punish him. They took him off to Babylon (then under Assyrian rule) in chains and with a hook through his nose (10). The Lord worked in Manasseh's heart while he was imprisoned in Babylon. *In affliction, he implored the LORD his God, and humbled himself greatly ... and prayed to him* (12-13). You may be surprised that such a vile man was found seeking God. Even more amazing God heard him, and restored to him his kingdom. **The grace of God is very wonderful. No one is beyond the reach of his mercy and love.** Manasseh began to undo the evil that he had done, and commanded Judah to serve the Lord (15-16). Manasseh's regrets and repentance made little impact on his son Amon whose short, evil reign was brought to an end by assassination (21-25).

If you are praying for someone who shows no sign of turning to God, **remember Manasseh,** and persevere in your prayers. If you think that you are too sinful for God to save, **remember Manasseh,** humble yourself and seek God.

> Who is a pardoning God like thee?
> Or who has grace so rich and free?

> (Samuel Davies)

Because your heart was tender, and you humbled yourself

Josiah was the last good king to reign over Judah before the people were taken into Babylonian captivity. He came to the throne at eight years of age and *while he was still young he began to seek the God of his father David* (before he was sixteen years old; 1-3). He purged the land of idolatry and had the house of the Lord repaired (4-8). While the temple was being repaired, a copy of the Book of the Law (Deuteronomy) was discovered. Shaphan the scribe read the book before the king, and this had a profound effect upon Josiah. He realized that divine judgment was hanging over Judah because of the wickedness of its rulers and people in the past. He tore his clothes as a sign of sorrow and mourning over the sins of the nation (14-21; cp. Deuteronomy 28:15-68).

The Lord gave Josiah a reassuring message through Huldah the prophetess (22-28). He told him, *'Because your heart was tender, and you humbled yourself before God ... I also have heard you'* (27). The Lord promised Josiah that though he would bring calamity on Judah, it would not be during his lifetime. God hears the prayers of those who humble themselves before him. **What kind of effect does the reading or preaching of God's word have on you? Is your heart tender or hard? Do you obey the word or do you rebel against it? Have you ever humbled yourself before the Lord or wept over your sin?**

> O give me, Lord, the tender heart
> That trembles at the approach of sin;
> A godly fear of sin impart,
> Implant and root it deep within.

(Charles Wesley)

Josiah gathered the elders of Judah and the people of Jerusalem to hear the words of the Book of the Covenant. He *made a covenant before the* Lord, *to follow the* Lord *and to keep his commandments ... with all his heart and all his soul.* He led the nation in a godly manner throughout his life (29-33). Do you seek to obey God with all your heart and all your soul (31)?

No remedy

After Josiah's death three of his sons and a grandson reigned over Judah during a period of twenty-three years:

- Jehoahaz reigned only three months before the Egyptians removed him from the throne, replacing him with his brother Jehoiakim (1-4; cp. 2 Kings 23:32-34).
- Jehoiakim reigned for eleven years, and Jehoiachin his son for three months (5-10).
- The Babylonians besieged Jerusalem after the death of Jehoiakim. Jehoiachin surrendered and was taken captive to Babylon with the best craftsmen and soldiers of Judah (9-10; cp. 2 Kings 24:8-16). This captivity in 597 BC was the precursor of the captivity of Judah that was to follow eleven years later.
- The king of Babylon appointed Zedekiah, brother of Jehoiakim, to rule over Judah. His eleven-year reign was cut short when he rebelled against the Babylonians (11-20).

All these kings *did evil in the sight of the* LORD (1-14; cp. 2 Kings 23:32). Jeremiah prophesied through these reigns but he was much persecuted (e.g. Jeremiah 38:1-6). The Lord repeatedly warned the people and their leaders that they would be judged for their wickedness but they mocked his messengers and despised them *till there was no remedy* (16). God brought the Chaldeans (Babylonians) against Judah to judge the wicked nation (cp. 2 Kings 25:1-21). Jerusalem and its temple were destroyed and the nation was taken to Babylon, where they languished in captivity just as Jeremiah had prophesied (15-21).

No remedy. What fearsome words. A man or woman may become so stubborn in their rebellion against God, that he gives them up to their sin (Romans 1:24,26,28). **Those who despise God's word and mock the gospel do so at their peril!** *He who is often reproved and hardens his neck, will suddenly be destroyed, and that without remedy* (Proverbs 29:1). If you have not repented of your sin, do not despise the word of God, but *seek the* LORD *while he may be found* (Isaiah 55:6).

1 & 2 CORINTHIANS

The city of Corinth was conquered by the Romans in 196 BC. After a period of opposition the Romans destroyed the city in 146 BC and sold its citizens into slavery. Julius Caesar had the city rebuilt in 46 BC and by the time Paul arrived there on his second missionary journey (AD 51 or 52), the population had grown to 500,000. Corinth, a busy port and prosperous trading centre, was a religious city with twenty-six temples and shrines. Pagan religion does not demand a holy lifestyle! Corinth was infamous for its vile and depraved way of life.

Paul spent eighteen months preaching and teaching in Corinth and a church including both Jews and Gentiles was established (Acts 18:1-8). **He wrote his first letter** to them during his three years at Ephesus (AD 55-57; see Acts 19:1-41; 20:31; 1 Corinthians 16:5-8,19). Paul had heard alarming news of division and disorder in the church and he wrote to deal with this trouble (1:11; 5:1). He also answered a letter sent to him by the Corinthians themselves, in which they raised a number of problems (7:1). Paul began his answers to most of these problems with the words, *'Now concerning'* (7:1,25; 8:1; 12:1; 16:1,12).

The second letter to the Corinthians was sent within a year of the first, after he left Ephesus (Acts 20:1-6). He found Titus in Macedonia and from him heard of the reaction of the Corinthians to his first letter. Some of them had heeded Paul's instructions, but others still opposed his authority and his teaching (10:10-11; 11:5-15). In this letter the apostle defends his authority, his motives and his work. He also gives instructions about the collection for the poor Christians at Jerusalem (chapters 8 and 9; cp. 1 Corinthians 16:3).

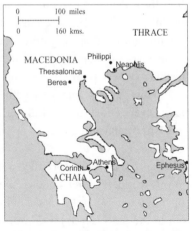

211

Called to be saints

Only a few, such as Paul, were called to be apostles (1), but all Christians are *called to be saints* (2). The Greek simply reads 'called saints.' A *'saint'* is someone who is *sanctified in Christ Jesus* (2; cp. 6:11). To be *'sanctified'* or *'holy'* means to be set apart to God, to glorify and to serve him. The Christians at Corinth were far from perfect, but they were all *called to be saints* and Paul thanked God for them (4). Those who are *called to be saints ... call on the name of Jesus Christ* (2; cp. Acts 7:59; 9:21).

Saints have wonderful privileges. The faithful God has called us into the fellowship of his Son (9). To know the Lord Jesus as our Saviour and as the Friend who never fails us is wonderful indeed! To be able to call on his name when we pray (2) assures us that he delights to hear us and to answer us. We have the grace and peace of God (3-4) and we are kept until the second coming of Christ (7-8). We cannot lose our salvation.

Saints have awesome responsibilities. We have to live holy lives. The great problem at Corinth was that many of the saints were not leading holy lives. Paul had to rebuke them because of their divisions and lack of unity (10-17). They were elevating some of the Christian leaders as cult figures, despising other men of God. Those who considered themselves most spiritual scorned the followers of Paul, Apollos and Cephas (Peter) pointing out that they themselves followed Christ (12). How pathetic they were with their petty arguments! **If we do not make every effort to maintain the unity of our local church, we deny our Christian calling (10).**

God has not chosen us or called us because of our wisdom or standing in this world. He often chooses the most unlikely people; we owe our salvation to God and saints should never boast (glory) in themselves but in the Lord (26-31). *Called to be saints.* **Let us examine our own lives. Let us repent of all that is unholy and ask the faithful God to give us the grace to live as we ought — as saints.**

The wisdom of God

The apostle reminds the Corinthians that his preaching methods were not patterned on worldly wisdom nor on fine oratory. He did not declare the testimony of God *with excellence of speech or wisdom* (1; cp. 1:26-31), but he had been with them *in weakness, in fear, and in much trembling* (3). Paul's preaching lacked the polished, persuasive words of human wisdom; it was *in demonstration of the Spirit and of power* (4). He wanted to see the Corinthians place their faith not *in the wisdom of men, but in the power of God* (5). Paul wrote, *'For I determined not to know anything among you except Jesus Christ and him crucified'* (2).

Those who are mature in Christ value spiritual wisdom more than *'the wisdom of this age'* (6). Paul wrote, *'But we speak the wisdom of God in a mystery, the hidden wisdom which God ordained before the ages for our glory'* (7). When the New Testament uses the word 'mystery' it does not mean something mysterious, beyond the reach of human understanding, but something which can only be known through the revelation of God by the Holy Spirit (10-13). *The natural man* [the unconverted man] *does not receive the things of the Spirit of God, for they are foolishness to him* (14; cp. verse 8).

This wisdom was ordained by God for our glory before he made the world (7). Just think of that! *The Lord of glory* was crucified *for our glory* (7-8). **He has prepared glorious things for those who love him** (9). Think of some of the things that God has given to us and prepared for us — forgiveness and cleansing from sin, reconciliation and peace with God through the blood of the cross, freedom from the power of Satan and sin, inexpressible joy, eternal life and heaven. **All these things are freely given to us by God (12).**

Brendan, one of Columba's evangelists during the sixth century AD, went to preach in the court of King Brude in Scotland. The king asked Brendan, 'If I accept the gospel and become Christ's man, what shall I find?' Brendan replied, 'Ah, sire, you will stumble on wonder upon wonder, and every wonder true!'

Do you not know that you are the temple of God?

Paul had earlier written, *'We speak wisdom among those who are mature'* (2:6-7) but he was not able to speak to the Corinthians *as to spiritual people, but as to carnal* (fleshly), *as to babes in Christ* (1-4). The envy, strife and petty divisions found among the Corinthians were typical of worldly behaviour; it was not Christian (3).

Corinth's pagan temples were places of wicked and lewd religious ritual, but the temple of God is totally different — it is holy. The Bible describes the church as *'a holy temple in the Lord ... a habitation of God in the Spirit'* (Ephesians 2:21-22). Paul reminded the Corinthians that as a church they were the temple of God. *'Do you not know that you are the temple of God and that the Spirit of God dwells in you?'* (16). The Holy Spirit dwells in the church and we must seek to maintain godliness and truth as our great priority. This will have a great bearing in all aspects of our church life such as our worship, our preaching, our teaching and our evangelism.

Paul gives a solemn warning. *'If any man defile the temple of God, him will God destroy'* (17). The words *'defile'* and *'destroy'* are translated from the same Greek word which means 'to corrupt'; cp. 2 Corinthians 11:3 — *'corrupted'* ('led astray', ESV). **If we spoil our church by embracing false teaching, by leading unholy lives or by promoting division, God will spoil our lives.** This grim warning should make us tremble.

We must beware of pride in our intellectual abilities and wisdom (18). The wisdom of this world is foolishness with God and we must reject it. Hero-worship of Christian leaders is not helpful and can easily encourage division as it did in Corinth (3-4,21-22; 1:12). We have a great inheritance in Christ and we belong to an almighty, precious Saviour (22-23). Let us boast only in him! Let us make every endeavour to keep our temple (the church to which we belong) holy and free from division. We are *'called to be saints'* (1:2).

You are not your own ... you were bought at a price

The division and strife were such at Corinth that believers battled
with each other in civil courts in disputes about money and property
(*'things that pertain to this life',* 3-4). Paul used the civil legal system
only as a last resort and never to obtain judgment against a professing
Christian (e.g. Acts 16:37-39; 25:10-11). This church prided itself in
its wisdom but Paul rebukes it for its ignorance. He asks them six
times, *'Do you not know?'* (2,3,9,15,16,19). If we parade our differences
before the world, we dishonour Christ. One day we will not only judge
the world, but also angels (2-3). How foolish to look to sinful men
to resolve problems between ourselves. A well-ordered church will
resolve disputes between its members but rather than dishonour God
it is better to suffer wrong (4-8).

The Lord had saved many of the Corinthians from very wicked and
depraved lifestyles (9-11). Some of them were misunderstanding
their liberty in Christ (*'Do not be deceived',* 9). **Christian liberty
means freedom from sin, not freedom to sin.** *Our bodies are not for
sexual immorality, but for the Lord* (13). Dare we become joined to a
prostitute or indulge in any other sexual sin? *'Certainly not!'* retorts
the apostle (15-16). We must *'flee sexual immorality'* (18). We must
not encourage sinful desires by reading pornographic literature or by
gazing at filth on television or the internet.

When we become Christians our bodies become members of Christ.
They belong to him (15). They are also temples of the Holy Spirit (19).
If our bodies are littered with sin they are not acceptable as dwelling
places for the Holy Spirit. We are not free to do just as we please. The
word of God challenges us, *'You are not your own ... you were bought
at a price; therefore glorify God in your body and in your spirit which
are God's'* (19-20). The Lord Jesus laid down his own life to redeem us
with his own precious blood (1 Peter 1:18-19). **We owe it to God to
glorify him in our bodies by keeping them from sin and by serving
him. Surely this is no hardship if we love him.**

The unbelieving husband is sanctified by the wife

Sex is a gift from God which is right and proper within marriage (1-5). Unfaithfulness to one's marriage partner violates that partner's exclusive rights (4). Husbands and wives must not deprive one another of their marriage rights except for a time given to fasting and prayer. Both single and married states are gifts from God — *but each one has his own gift from God* (7). **They are also recognized as a calling (17, 20, 24). Divorce between Christian couples should be unthinkable** but many professing Christians have yielded to the permissive attitudes of the world and have disregarded verses 10 and 11 (cp. Matthew 19:8-9). We rejoice, however, in the conversion of those who were divorced (and perhaps remarried) before they turned to Christ. They are not second-class Christians. Divorce is not the unpardonable sin.

A Christian must not marry an unbeliever (39). There is a problem, however, when someone is converted after marriage while their spouse remains an unbeliever. **That new believer will certainly face problems but this is no excuse for seeking a divorce** (12-13). Divorce is only permissible if the unbelieving partner refuses to live with the Christian spouse (15). *The unbelieving husband is sanctified by the wife* (14). This does not mean that they are saved by proxy, but they do have special privileges. They are under a Christian influence and they can see the gospel lived out in the Christian (cp. 1 Peter 3:1-2). Paul's encouragement to the Christian in such circumstances is, *'How do you know, O wife, whether you will save your husband? Or how do you know, O husband, whether you will save your wife?'* (16).

Verses 36 to 38 refer to the Christian father and the giving of his daughter in marriage bearing in mind *the present distress* at Corinth. Concerning those who are widowed, Paul lays down four principles:

- A wife is bound to her husband as long as he lives (39).
- Death severs the marriage bond (39; cp. Romans 7:2-3).
- Widows are free to remarry (39; cp. 1 Timothy 5:11,14).
- Christian widows may only be remarried to a believer (*only in the Lord;* 39).

I discipline my body

Paul had worked to support himself and his critics at Corinth had taken this as an indication that he was inferior to the other apostles. He defended himself and pointed out that they themselves were a proof of his apostleship (1-3). Paul did have the right to be married like the other apostles and to be supported financially but he had denied himself these liberties (4-6). He went on to show that Christians must support a full-time ministry (7-14). *Those who preach the gospel should live from the gospel* (14). Paul had a burning desire to reach sinners with the good news of his Saviour and he willingly gave up his rights *for the gospel's sake* (16-23).

The Isthmian Games held at Corinth every three years were ranked second to the Olympics. There was only one prize for each event in those ancient games and athletes subjected themselves to rigorous discipline in order to win a victor's laurel crown. The word *'competes'* (25) is the Greek word from which our English word 'agony' is derived. Think about the rigorous training of today's athletes in the hope of winning an Olympic medal. They subject their bodies to many hours of exercise and they maintain a healthy diet. The discipline continues day after day, year after year. They put to shame many of us who profess to love the Lord. Discipline involves self-control (*'temperate in all things'*, 25) and it is not aimless (26).

We do not compete for laurel crowns or earthly honours, but for *an imperishable crown* which will be given to us when we reach heaven (25). Are you running to obtain such a crown (24)? Paul writes, *'I discipline my body and bring it into subjection, lest, when I have preached to others, I myself should become disqualified'* (27). This verse does not teach that a Christian can lose his salvation, but he can lose his reward (cp. 3:13-15). The Bible makes it quite clear that a true believer is saved for eternity; he cannot be lost. Self-discipline is not easy but we are to exercise ourselves to godliness (1 Timothy 4:7). **Let us reject a lethargic way of life; it does not please our Lord and Saviour. We have a crown to win — let us go for it!**

'Concerning spiritual gifts'

One of the most controversial subjects among evangelicals today is that of spiritual gifts. Paul did not want the Corinthians to be ignorant *'concerning spiritual gifts'* (the Greek word *'pneumatika'* in verse 1 is 'spirituals' but it implies spiritual gifts, cp. verse 4). Ignorance concerning spiritual gifts has led to disaster in many a church today and in many a Christian life. Paul sets down some basic principles:

1. True worship is orderly (2).
2. The Holy Spirit exalts Jesus as Lord (3).
3. There are diverse gifts, ministries and activities of the Spirit (4-6).
4. Spiritual gifts are given for the profit of the church (7).
5. The Holy Spirit is sovereign in bestowing his gifts (11).
6. Every Christian is baptized by the Spirit into one body (that is the church, 13).
7. Though all members have differing functions, they belong to the one body of Christ and they need each other (14-24).
8. There must not be any schism (division) in the body and its members should care for each other (25-26).
9. God appointed apostles and prophets in the early church and gave miraculous gifts of the Holy Spirit (28-30).

Some people claim that they are apostles, prophets, or that they possess miraculous gifts of the Holy Spirit. These ministries and gifts passed away with the apostolic age (cp. Hebrews 2:3-4). The history of the church teaches us that over the centuries there have been bizarre practices and extravagant claims by people claiming to be specially endowed with the Holy Spirit. Those who make similar claims today deceive themselves. Their practices do not stand the test of Scripture. **We must seek the *'more excellent way'* of love (31) rather than chase after spectacular gifts.** When Christians love God and love each other they maintain the unity of the Spirit in the bond of peace (Ephesians 4:1-3). The divisions and disorders so apparent at Corinth can then find no place in the life of a local church.

The greatest of these is love

It is far more important to show the *more excellent way* of love in our lives than to display outstanding spiritual gifts. What is the gift of tongues without love? It is a hollow, metallic clanging that irritates rather than blesses (1). I may have the gift of prophecy and understand all mysteries that God has revealed; I may be able to utter a word of knowledge in any situation where it is required; I may have the faith to work wonders, but without love *I am nothing* (2). I may be self-sacrificing in giving even to the extent of laying down my own life, but if I do not have love, *it profits me nothing* (3).

Memorize verses 4 to 7 and meditate on the characteristics of love described in them. Think of the Lord Jesus Christ and how he showed the kind of love described in these verses. The Corinthian church would have been so different if they had been more loving to each other instead of being so divisive or disorderly. Examine your own heart. Are you patient and kind? Is the love of Christ seen in your life? Are you envious, boasting, proud, rude, selfish, easily provoked? Do you think evil, storing up grudges and bitterness against those who have hurt you? **If any of these unpleasant things (sins!) are present in your life, where is the love of Christ?**

Love bears all things, trusts, hopes and perseveres (7). *Love never fails* but it outlasts gifts of prophecy, tongues or knowledge (8). The Corinthians were *zealous for spiritual gifts* (14:12) but the apostle shows that the *more excellent way* of love is of greater importance. Prophecies will fail (be rendered useless), tongues will cease, knowledge (the gift of *the word of knowledge*) will vanish away, but *love never fails* (8). These gifts of direct revelation will pass away, but when? The answer lies in verse 10. *But when that which is perfect has come, then that which is in part* [words of knowledge, prophesying, 9] *will be done away.* Faith, hope and love are all vital, *but the greatest of these is love* (13). We must *pursue love* (14:1). **Why do we find this so difficult and unattractive? Because it costs us dearly to love, and so often, we are not willing to pay the price.**

In understanding be mature

Many of the Corinthians esteemed the gift of tongues above all other spiritual gifts, but it is inferior to prophesying. He who prophesies can be understood; he *speaks edification and exhortation and comfort to men* and he *edifies the church* (1-5). The apostle spoke in tongues more than any of the Corinthians who had a zeal for spiritual gifts. He urged them to have a greater zeal for the edification of the church. Paul preferred to speak five words with his understanding than ten thousand words in tongues so that he would be able to teach others (12-19).

Paul reminds us that tongues were a sign of judgment on Old Testament Israel (21-22; cp. Isaiah 28:9-14). They had refused the plain teaching of the prophets and would hear the stammering lips of foreign invaders. If our church services are chaotic and many are speaking in tongues, visiting enquirers and unbelievers will think that we are mad. We must not obscure the gospel by foolish behaviour or by speaking so that no one can understand us. We must be like children by lacking in malice *but in understanding be mature* (20). The prophetic gift is not available today because revelation is complete. **The preaching of God's word must be central in our worship and evangelism.** This is the way to understanding and maturity. *In understanding be mature.* How can we worship God if we do not understand who he is? How can the unbeliever respond to the gospel if it is not made clear to his understanding?

In what way are women to *keep silent in the churches* (34)? Does this mean that women cannot sing the praises of God and that they must remain in total silence? This view can hardly be correct because women prayed and prophesied in the Corinthian church (11:5). I believe that it means that women must not be given a leadership role in worship. They must not have a public teaching role nor have authority over men (cp. 1 Timothy 2:12). *Let all things be done for edification ... Let all things be done decently and in order* (26,40). **If we keep these two rules before us we will be spared many problems in our churches.**

If Christ is not risen

Some at Corinth denied the resurrection of the dead (12) and Paul now writes to correct their error. He directs our attention to the resurrection of Christ and of believers. The apostle reminded the Corinthians of *'the gospel which I preached to you, which also you received'* (1). What is the gospel? *That Christ died for our sins according to the Scriptures, and that he was buried, and that he rose again the third day according to the Scriptures* (3-4). If we deny these essential truths, we are not Christians and our faith is futile (2,14,17).

Paul stresses that the risen Christ was seen on different occasions by different people including a gathering of five hundred people (5-7). He then speaks of his own experience for he too had seen the risen Christ on the Damascus road (9; cp. Acts 9:1-6). *If there is no resurrection of the dead, then Christ is not risen* (13). *If Christ is not risen,* gospel preaching is pointless because it would no longer be good news; our faith is in vain and we are still in our sins (14,17). *If Christ is not risen,* there is no hope for the future; those who have died have perished and we are the most pitiable of all men (18-19).

How did death come into the world? It came through the sin of Adam which brought death upon all men (21-22; cp. Genesis 3; Romans 5:12). The Lord Jesus is described as *'the last Adam'* (45) and as the representative of all his people, he brings life and victory over death. *For as in Adam all die, even so in Christ all shall be made alive* (22). The Bible describes death as *'sleep'* for the believer (20,51). When a Christian dies, his soul (spirit) goes to be with Christ (Acts 7:59-60; 2 Corinthians 5:8; Philippians 1:23; Hebrews 12:23).

When the Lord Jesus returns, there will be a great blast of a trumpet and *the dead will be raised incorruptible.* The dust of those bodies will be transformed in a split second. Those who are alive will also be changed (51-52). Our new bodies will be like Christ's resurrection body. They will not suffer sickness, pain or death. Death will be swallowed up and its deadly poisonous sting removed. **Our labour is not in vain because Christ has risen (55-58).**

The Father of mercies and God of all comfort, who comforts us

Paul follows his opening greetings with a burst of praise to God for all the comfort that he and his companions had received from him. *Blessed be the God and Father of our Lord Jesus Christ, the Father of mercies and God of all comfort, who comforts us in all our tribulation* (3-4). The Greek noun and verb translated *'comfort'* and *'consolation'* are found ten times in verses 3 to 7. God is not remote from us nor is he unconcerned when we suffer. He promises, *'As one whom his mother comforts, so I will comfort you'* (Isaiah 66:13). He comforts the downcast believer (7:6) who trusts in him. **Are you laid low through trial or suffering? Be encouraged! Draw near to your heavenly Father now, though you may not feel like praying.** The *'God of all comfort'* will comfort you and you will soon be praising him.

Only those who have known suffering and the comfort of God are able to truly identify with others who suffer and to comfort them (4). God's holy word urges us to comfort each other (1 Thessalonians 4:18; 5:11; cp. 7:6). It is possible to be so full of our own troubles that we hardly notice that some brother or sister is going through a time of fiery trial. They may be assailed by the devil who is tormenting them with doubts. **Are you aware of the needs of others?**

Paul writes of some trouble that had come upon him and his companions in the province of Asia (probably in Ephesus) but he does not provide us with any details. It would appear that they were in great peril and in danger of losing their lives (9-10). Look at the way in which he describes his suffering here: *the sufferings of Christ abound in us ... we were burdened beyond measure, above strength, so that we despaired even of life. Yes, we had the sentence of death in ourselves* (5,8-9; cp. 6:4-10). Paul likened his enemies in Asia to *'beasts'* (8; cp. 1 Corinthians 15:32; Acts 19:23-41; 20:18-19). Though he had planted the church at Corinth, there was now opposition to him and to his ministry. He was hoping that by delaying his visit, they would have more time to deal with the serious problems in the church and so spare him the pain of having to discipline them (23; 2:1).

We do not lose heart

There are a number of things in the Christian ministry which may bring discouragement to the servant of God. Paul twice states in this chapter, '*We do not lose heart*' (1,16). Some of the things which could have disheartened the apostle are mentioned here:

- The hardness of gospel work because *the god of this age* (Satan) had blinded the minds of sinners so that they would not believe or receive his message (4). There is a veil over the minds of Gentiles as well as Jews (3-4; cp. 3:14-16).
- Physical weakness and danger (10,16-17).
- Opposition to his ministry (8-10). Paul had spent eighteen months in Corinth where he had suffered persecution (Acts 18:1-17). He had worked to keep himself and had endured much weariness and toil (11:9,27). The church was later infiltrated by false teachers who preached *another Jesus ... a different gospel* (11:3-4). A good work was being spoiled.

What encouraged Paul to persevere and not lose heart?

- He knew the mercy of God in his life (1).
- He was privileged to be a minister of the new covenant (1; cp. 3:6). This is a ministry of the Holy Spirit (3:8), of righteousness (3:9) and of reconciliation (5:18).
- He was privileged to preach the gospel of the glory of Christ (4).
- He trusted in the almighty, sovereign God *who commanded light to shine out of darkness* (Genesis 1:2-3). The same God is able to shine into the dark hearts of sinners to give *the light of the knowledge of the glory of God in the face of Jesus Christ* (6).
- Suffering does not last for ever, but glory and heaven do (16-18).

Have you been losing heart in your Christian life or in your work for the Lord? Oh, persevere! The Lord knows what he is doing with you and with his work.

Therefore we make it our aim ... to be well pleasing to him

This wonderful chapter is full of encouragement for the Christian. We may fear the process of dying and the parting from our loved ones, but death should hold no terror for the Christian. Notice Paul's certainty concerning the state of the Christian after death — *we know* (1). Our bodies, described as *our earthly house, this tent* (1) and *our outward man* (4:16), will be destroyed by death unless we are alive at the second coming of Christ (hence the *'if'* in verse 1). Our bodies are frail and subject to suffering; this should make us *groan* and desire to be with the Lord in heaven (2,4; cp. Romans 8:23). Never believe those who teach that a believer should never be ill. If this were the case, we would not *groan*. We also *groan because we* have remaining sin in our lives. God does heal according to his sovereign will and we must not let remaining sin reign over us (Romans 6:12-14) but there isn't any physical or spiritual perfection this side of heaven.

When we think of heaven and all that Christ has done for us, we should not only lift up our hearts in praise to God, but also seek to please him. Paul writes, *'Therefore we make it our aim ... to be well pleasing to him'* (9). **What is your ambition in your Christian life? Is it to be well pleasing to your Lord and Saviour?** Paul also gives another reason for living to please Christ. He knew that *we must all appear before the judgment seat of Christ* and give an account (10; cp. Romans 14:12). He did not fear condemnation (*there is ... no condemnation to those who are in Christ* — Romans 8:1), but evaluation. He did not fear loss of salvation (the true believer cannot be lost) but loss of commendation. You will have to give an account of your work (or lack of it) to Christ.

The apostle Paul was a great persuader (cp. Acts 24:24-25; 26:28). He writes, *'Knowing, therefore, the terror* [fear] *of the Lord, we persuade men'* (11). If you die without Christ, you will face judgment and hell unless you repent of your sin and ask the Lord Jesus to save you. If you come to him, he will accept you and make a new creation of you (17). *Be reconciled to God* (20).

See that you abound in this grace also

The Corinthians had been slow to respond to Paul's appeal for financial help for the poor Christians at Jerusalem (1 Corinthians 16:1-4; cp. Romans 15:25-27). He sought to encourage them by referring to the example of the churches in Macedonia (Philippi, Thessalonica and Berea were in Macedonia — see Acts 16:12 - 17:14). The Macedonian believers were suffering great persecution and were in *deep poverty* (2; cp. 1 Thessalonians 1:6; 2:14; 3:3), but they gave generously, though they could ill afford to do so. They saw that financial help was urgently needed and they begged the apostles to receive their gift (1-4).

What lay behind the generosity and sacrificial giving of the Macedonian churches?

* They *first gave themselves to the Lord* and then to the apostles (5). When we give ourselves to the Lord we will gladly help needy believers.
* The *grace of God* was bestowed on them (1). Generous, joyful Christian giving is a fruit of God's grace in our lives (1,6,7,9; 9:8,14; the same Greek word is translated *'gift'* in verse 19). The Corinthians rejoiced in their abundance of spiritual gifts (graces) and Paul urged them, *'See that you abound in this grace also'* (7).

Paul points to another example of grace. *For you know the grace of our Lord Jesus Christ, that though he was rich, yet for your sakes he became poor, that you through his poverty might become rich* (9). He was rich in his equality with God the Father, rich in his power and majesty as angels worshipped him, rich in his enjoyment of the perfection and glory of heaven, and rich in his possession of the universe. He became poor, taking human flesh to be born into a humble family, taking the form of a slave, being obedient to the Father's will, suffering humiliation, torture and death to save us from our sins and to make us heirs of heaven (Philippians 2:5-11; Romans 8:15-17; 1 Peter 1:4). The old saying is so true, 'When God touches a man's heart, he also touches his wallet.' **Has God touched your heart? Are you abounding *in this grace also*?**

My grace is sufficient for you

False teachers had impressed the Corinthians with their claims of visions and revelations from God. Paul now turns to that subject. He was almost certainly speaking of himself when describing the man caught up into heaven which he describes as *'the third heaven'* or *'Paradise'*. He made it appear that he was speaking of an acquaintance because of his reluctance to boast (1-4). He would prefer to boast of his own *infirmities* or weaknesses rather than of his exploits (5-6). He then writes of a very painful and perplexing experience.

Paul recognized that the abundance of revelations he had received could lead to pride. For this reason God had given him *a thorn in the flesh* to keep him from being *exalted above measure* (7). He does not explain the nature of this *thorn in the flesh* which he describes as *'a messenger of Satan'*; it may have been some physical weakness, a trial which was in his flesh (Galatians 4:15-16). He pleaded with God three times that it would be removed but the Lord replied, *'My grace is sufficient for you, for my strength is made perfect in weakness'* (8-9). **The Lord does not always say 'Yes' to our prayers, but he does give us grace and strength in all our trials.** He has wise and loving purposes in every trial and he tenderly watches over us. If you are passing through difficult times remember the sufficiency of God's grace. He will never let you down. He will never let you go. He will bring blessing out of your distress and you will emerge a stronger and more godly believer.

Paul was a great-hearted Christian. He had a great love for the wayward Corinthians, though they had shown little love for him. Verse 15 is magnificent! *And I will very gladly spend and be spent for your souls; though the more abundantly I love you, the less I am loved.* He was willing to give himself sacrificially for their benefit. He had never taken advantage of them and had done all things for their edification (17-19). Are you willing to spend and to be spent for those who behave badly towards you?

EZRA & NEHEMIAH

The books of Ezra and Nehemiah cover over one hundred years of Jewish history. Both men had their ministry during the reign of Persian king Artaxerxes I (464 to 424 BC).

Ezra was a priest and a skilled scribe in the law of Moses (7:6,12). He was a descendant of Seraiah the high priest who was slain by Nebuchadnezzar in 586 BC (7:1; cp. 2 Kings 25:18-21). God raised him up to teach the people his law and to lead the reformation some sixty years after the rebuilding of the temple. The book of Ezra deals with the history of the Jews after they returned to Jerusalem from Babylon in 538 BC. It is divided into two sections:

- Chapters 1 to 6 cover the return of the exiles from Babylon and the rebuilding of the temple by Zerubbabel. The prophets Haggai and Zechariah prophesied during this period (6:14). After a lapse in the building work because of opposition, the work was finally completed in 516 BC (seventy years after the destruction of the temple in 586 BC).
- Chapters 7 to 10 cover the return of Ezra from Babylon (458 BC) and his work of reformation.

Nehemiah was raised up by God to lead the people in rebuilding the wall of Jerusalem. The builders of ancient cities surrounded them with walls to give protection against their enemies. When the Babylonians conquered Judah in 586 BC Jerusalem, its temple and wall were destroyed.

Nehemiah was cup-bearer to the Persian king Artaxerxes I who appointed him to be governor of Judah (5:14). Nehemiah was a man of prayer (e.g. 1:4; 2:4; 4:9; 5:19; 13:31)! There was much opposition to the work of rebuilding the city wall just as there had been to the rebuilding of the temple in the previous century. Nehemiah was faithful and courageous in the face of this opposition. He persevered despite setbacks and discouragement, and the work was completed.

The Lord stirred up the spirit of Cyrus

Daniel had lived through the captivity of the Jews in Babylon and soon after the fall of that city the very aged servant of God set himself to pray. He called upon God for Jerusalem, for the rebuilding of the temple and for his own people, the Jews (Daniel 9:15-19). He had remembered the prophecy of Jeremiah concerning the seventy years of captivity and desolation, and that time was almost accomplished (Daniel 9:1). He confessed the sins of the people and called upon God, *'O Lord, hear! O Lord, forgive! O Lord, listen and act! Do not delay for your own sake, my God, for your own city and your people are called by your name'* (Daniel 9:19).

The Lord very soon honoured Daniel's fervent prayer when Cyrus, king of Persia, set in motion the return of the captives to Judah (1). At the end of 2 Chronicles we read that *the Lord stirred up the spirit of Cyrus king of Persia* (2 Chronicles 36:22-23). The same words are repeated in the first verse of Ezra. Cyrus encouraged the Jews to rebuild the temple (2-4) and the foundation was laid in 536 BC. He also returned to the Jews the treasures that had been taken from the temple (7-11).

It may seem amazing that a heathen king was so sympathetic to the Jews and to the work of God but Isaiah had predicted this almost two centuries earlier, even naming Cyrus (Isaiah 44:28 - 45:6). We must remember that God sovereignly controls the affairs of men (Daniel 4:34-35). *The Lord stirred up the spirit of Cyrus* (1) and he also moved upon the spirits of those who were to rebuild the temple (5). Daniel's prayer was answered. **We should feel a great sense of awe and privilege that our sovereign God answers prayer and that he moves upon people's hearts and lives.**Let us persevere in prayer (Luke 18:1), especially for those we have brought before the Lord for many years. Nothing is impossible with our almighty, sovereign God.

Praising and giving thanks to the LORD

The exiles who returned to Jerusalem are described as those *whose spirits God had moved* (1:5). When the Lord works in our hearts we become worshippers (cp. John 4:23). The returning Jews met with hostility from those who had occupied Judah during the captivity. Despite their fear because of their enemies, the leaders of the exiles built an altar for sacrifices to be made to God each day and the feasts were also observed (3-5).

We saw yesterday that when the Lord works in our hearts we will also give generously to his work (7; cp. 2:68-69). The priests and those associated with them (2:70) had to be supported, the workers who built the temple had to be paid, and materials for the building had to be purchased (7).

The building work began in 536 BC in the fourteenth month after the return from exile (8). The people were filled with joy when the foundation of the temple was laid. Some of the old men who had remembered the temple before its destruction were overcome with emotion and they wept (11-13). The priests and the Levites led the people in *praising and giving thanks to the* LORD (11).

The church is described as *'the temple of God'* (1 Corinthians 3:16-17); it is *built on the foundation of the apostles and prophets, Jesus Christ himself being the chief corner-stone* (Ephesians 2:20-21). The Lord Jesus has done so much for us and we who know the grace of God in our lives have greater reason than the returning exiles for *praising and giving thanks to the* LORD. **They were not silent in their praise (13). Are we?**

> Fill thou my life, O Lord my God,
> In every part with praise,
> That my whole being may proclaim
> Thy being and thy ways.

> (Horatius Bonar)

Let us build with you, for we seek God as you do

The enemies of the returned exiles tried many tactics to hinder the rebuilding of the temple. They began with the friendly approach and offered, *'Let us build with you, for we seek your God as you do'* (1-2). These people had been settled in the land by the Assyrians and they did have a form of religion that incorporated Jewish sacrifices but they did not seek God in the same manner as the Jews; theirs was a multi-faith religion. We read of them, *They feared the* LORD, *yet served their own gods* (2 Kings 17:33).

The people of God rightly refused their help, knowing that it is impossible to do the work of God in co-operation with those who deny the teaching contained in the word of God which had been given to them (the portions of the Old Testament Scriptures which they possessed). **The lesson for us today is quite obvious. We must not compromise the gospel by working with those who deny its essentials (see Galatians 1:6-9).** We cannot co-operate with those who deny the divine inspiration and authority of the Bible. We have nothing in common with those who deny that Jesus is God the Son who laid down his life and rose bodily from the grave to save sinners, or with those who teach that Christianity is one of many ways to heaven. The ecumenical movement does not represent true Christian unity; it is a confused company which shelters many heretics.

The enemies of the temple builders then harassed them in order to discourage them (4-5). Force was used to stop the building work and it was not recommenced until the second year of Darius, some fifteen years later in 520 BC (24; Darius I of Persia is not to be confused with Darius the Mede who conquered Babylon in partnership with the Persians in 539 BC). The letter sent to the king which slandered the Jews refers to a later period and was not about the temple, but referred to the rebuilding of the city walls (12-16). If we are faithful to God, we will be misunderstood, maligned and opposed, but he will vindicate us. Let us always look to him for he will never fail us.

The eye of their God was upon the elders of the Jews

The people became so discouraged by opposition that they made no attempt to restart their work of rebuilding the temple until stirred up to do so by the prophets Haggai and Zechariah (1-2). By this time the people had not only lost heart, but also lost interest in the challenge of rebuilding the temple (Haggai 1:7-11).

When they restarted the work, they were visited by Tattenai who was governor over all the provinces west of the River Euphrates (3-5). This visit may have been prompted by a complaint from the Samaritans and it seems that Tattenai was on a fact-finding visit. Zerubbabel, the governor of Jerusalem, whose Babylonian name was Sheshbazzar, (14,16), was answerable to him. Tattenai listened to what the Jews had to say before he sent a letter to King Darius. The elders told him how God had brought the Babylonians against Jerusalem to destroy the temple and to take the Jews into captivity. God did this because their ancestors had provoked God to wrath by their sin (11-12). It is interesting to see that Tattenai refers to the Lord as *'the great God'* (8). He mentioned the decree of Cyrus and asked the king if he would confirm that such a decree had been made (13-17).

Tattenai might have insisted that the building work cease until a reply was received from the king, *but the eye of their God was upon the elders of the Jews* (5). **Whenever you face opposition or trouble as you seek to obey God, remember that the eye of the Lord is on those who fear him (Psalm 33:18).** He lovingly watches over you and he is working all things together for good (Romans 8:28). He will never leave you nor forsake you (Hebrews 13:5-6).

> But saints are lovely in his sight;
> He views his children with delight;
> He sees their hope, he knows their fear;
> And looks, and loves his image there.
>
> (Isaac Watts)

The LORD *... turned the heart of the king of Assyria*

The decree of Cyrus was not found in Babylon but in the palace at Achmetha (Ecbatana), the ancient capital of Media (1-2). Darius confirmed that the decree should stand and he wrote to Tattenai and his Persian officials instructing that:

- The building work must not be hindered (6-7).
- The work was to be assisted from taxes paid to the king (8).
- Animals were to be supplied for sacrifices and prayers should be offered for the king and his sons (9-10).
- Any who changed this edict should be put to death (11).

Why was the king so favourable to the Jews? Was it because the decree of Cyrus had been found? That was an important discovery, but the real reason is found in verse 22. *For the* LORD *made them joyful, and turned the heart of the king of Assyria towards them, to strengthen their hands in the work of the house of God.* **The Lord is sovereign and he still moves upon the hearts of ungodly people,** either to save them, or to make them favour his people (cp. 1:1; Proverbs 21:1). There was great joy when the work was finished and the temple dedicated (15-16).

The work prospered through the prophesying of Haggai and Zechariah (14). The prophetic gift is not available today because Scripture is complete. God now speaks through the reading and preaching of his word. The motto of Glasgow which sat beneath the city coat of arms was, 'Let Glasgow flourish through the preaching of the Word.' In the twentieth century it was changed to 'Let Glasgow flourish.' That city has followed the way of those churches who no longer have time for the preaching of God's word. Is it any wonder that there is such confusion about religion in church and nation? We neglect preaching and teaching at our peril. **If we are to know God's blessing, we must also separate ourselves from all that displeases the Lord** (21). We are sanctified (separated) in Christ Jesus, called to be saints (1 Corinthians 1:2). Let us always seek to lead a life worthy of our calling (Ephesians 4:1).

I was fasting and praying before the God of heaven

Though Zerubbabel had completed the rebuilding of the temple in 516 BC, the wall of the city still lay in ruins seventy years later (the events in this chapter are dated at the end of 446 BC). Nehemiah, a Jewish exile, was a trusted servant of the Persian king, being his cup-bearer (11). His brother Hanani came from Jerusalem with disturbing news (2; cp. 7:2). God's people were in great distress, suffering reproach from their enemies and the wall had been destroyed; an attempt had been made to rebuild the city wall, but the work had been stopped through enemy opposition (cp. Ezra 4:12-13,23).

Nehemiah was much affected when he heard of the plight of the people in Jerusalem and its surrounding towns. He records, *'I sat down and wept, and mourned for many days; I was fasting and praying before the God of heaven'* (4). Nehemiah confessed his own sins and those of the people and called upon God to give him favour with the king (6-11). Nehemiah was a servant of a great earthly king but, first and foremost, he was the servant of the great and awesome God of heaven (4-6,11).

Nehemiah's sorrow for the plight of Jerusalem showed on his face. When the king asked him the reason for his sorrow, he was very fearful (2:2). The king's servants were not supposed to be unhappy in the presence of their sovereign (cp. Esther 4:2) and offenders could be severely punished, even by death. Nehemiah told his story to Artaxerxes, who then asked him, *'What do you request?'* Nehemiah turned his thoughts to God in prayer before making known his request (4). He had begun praying about the situation in Jerusalem in December 446 BC (Chislev, 1:1). It was in April 445 BC (Nisan) when he began to see the Lord answer his prayers (2:1). The king gave Nehemiah all that he asked for and also soldiers to escort him on his journey to Jerusalem (2:7-9). Why was this? Nehemiah acknowledged that it was *'according to the good hand of my God upon me'* (2:8; cp. 2:18). Nehemiah walked with God and found that the Lord had prepared the way for the king to honour his requests. **What blessing can compare with that of knowing the good hand of God upon us?**

Do not be afraid of them. Remember the Lord

We were introduced to the leaders of the opposition to God's people in chapter 2, verse 10. They were Satan's tools to hinder the work of God. They continued to pour scorn upon the Jews (1-3) but this drove Nehemiah and the people to seek God in prayer and to be on their guard (5-6,9). Scorn can be a very powerful and effective weapon in Satan's armoury. When Sanballat, Tobiah and their allies saw that scorn did not deter Nehemiah, they plotted to *attack Jerusalem and create confusion* (7-8). All this was too much for the builders from Judah who became weary, weak and discouraged (10).

The work prospered, however, because it was accompanied by prayer and by trust in God (9,20). Though the Jews were threatened by attacks upon them (13-23), they *had a mind to work* (6). We have seen repeatedly in our Bible readings that **God honours those who work. Lazy Christians dishonour God and accomplish little for him.** Nehemiah recognized that there was more at stake than the rebuilding of the wall; the fight was for the future of their children (14). We must always remember this in all that we seek to do for the Lord. We build for the future and faithful work is never in vain (1 Corinthians 15:58).

In the face of opposition Nehemiah encouraged the people, saying, *'Do not be afraid of them. Remember the Lord, great and awesome, and fight ...'* (14). Are you afraid of those who scorn and oppose the gospel? Do they intimidate you? **We serve the almighty God! Why should we be afraid when he is for us (Romans 8:31)?** *'Our God will fight for us'* (20); *'Remember the Lord, great and awesome, and fight!'* Be bold and persevere in your work and witness for the Lord. He will not fail you.

> Fear him, ye saints, and you will then
> Have nothing else to fear;
> Make but his service your delight;
> Your wants shall be his care.
>
> (Nahum Tate and Nicholas Brady)

Should you not walk in the fear of our God

Though Nehemiah faced many pressures from his enemies he was not lacking in problems from his own people. The men of Judah had grown discouraged (4:10) and now many of the people were starving through famine (2-3). The poor had been forced to mortgage their land and houses in order to buy food and to pay taxes levied by the Persian king. Some of their children had been taken into slavery because of unpaid debt (1-5). The rulers and nobles among the Jews were profiting from the distress of their poor neighbours by lending out money at what was then an extortionate rate (verse 11 indicates that it was interest at 1% per month, 12% per annum). They then seized the land and possessions of those who were unable to keep up the repayments. God had forbidden such practices (Leviticus 25:35-37).

Nehemiah was very angry with these heartless rulers and nobles, and after giving the matter serious thought, he rebuked them. He then called a great assembly against them (6-7). He showed great courage in admonishing those who were influential for he risked losing their support. Nehemiah challenged the rulers saying, *'What you are doing is not good. Should you not walk in the fear of our God because of the reproach of the nations, our enemies?'* (9). Sin brings reproach to the work of God and does great harm to the church. The nobles heeded the challenge and promised to restore all the land and the possessions that they had taken from the poor in usury (10-13).

Nehemiah showed a great example in his leadership. Power and authority did not corrupt him *because of the fear of God* (15). He was sensitive to a burdened people and did not exact from them taxes to support him as their governor (14-19). *The fear of the LORD is the beginning of wisdom* (Psalm 111:10). This godly fear produces a holy hatred of sin and a longing for greater holiness (2 Corinthians 7:1). It moves us to have compassion and practical concern for our needy brothers and sisters (Ephesians 4:32; 1 John 3:17-18). **Is it evident to those around you that you are walking in the fear of our God?**

I am doing a great work

The opposition to Nehemiah continued even though the wall had been rebuilt (1). His enemies tried the 'softly, softly' approach with a pretence of friendship but Nehemiah discerned their real intentions and refused to meet them. He sent this message to them, *'I am doing a great work ... Why should the work cease while I leave it and go down to you?'* (2-3). When their persistence failed, Sanballat sent his servant with an open letter which accused Nehemiah of planning a rebellion against the king of Persia. God's servant was well known to the king and he dismissed their lies as inventions (6-8). The devil used fear in an attempt to weaken Nehemiah's resolve but he was not deterred (9). He called upon the Lord to strengthen his hands.

The wall was completed in fifty-two days and Nehemiah's enemies became very disheartened *for they perceived that this work was done by our God* (15-16). There was a problem with some of the Jewish nobles, however; perhaps they bitterly resented Nehemiah for rebuking them and for his insistence that they restore the property of those who were in their debt (5:7-13). They acted in collusion with Tobiah who was quick to exploit the situation and sent letters to them. He also used his relationship (through marriage) with one of the wall-builders to gain influence (17-18; cp. 3:4,30).

The devil used fear in an attempt to weaken Nehemiah's resolve. *They all were trying to make us afraid ... Tobiah sent letters to frighten me* (9,19). Nehemiah knew that he was *doing a great work* (3). Jerusalem was the focal point for the worship of the living God and needed the wall for protection. All that we do for the Lord is *a great work*, be it preaching, teaching in Sunday School, raising our children in the fear of God, distributing tracts or speaking to others about the Lord. Even small and seemingly insignificant jobs in the church are *a great work* for God. **Let us be faithful and persevere in all that the Lord has given us to do and be determined never to give up through the fear of men.** *The fear of man brings a snare, but whoever trusts in the LORD shall be safe* (Proverbs 29:25).

The people ... rejoiced greatly, because they understood

The people gathered in Jerusalem and asked Ezra to read to them the Book of the Law of Moses. The reading was interspersed with explanation and continued from morning (sunrise) until midday (1-3). This was no dry reading exercise and the people were attentive. **Notice the emphasis on understanding (2-3,7-8,12-13).** The great need of the church in every age is for the powerful, clear preaching of God's word so that it is understood by all those who hear. *The people ... rejoiced greatly, because they understood the words that were declared to them* (12). Real joy as opposed to that which is worked up by emotionalism comes from understanding God's word, discovering in it the greatness of the Lord, the wonders of our salvation and our privileges and responsibilities as children of God.

The reading and exposition of the word of God also led the people to weep (9). **How often does the word of God move you to tears, tears of gratitude for all that the Lord has done for you, or tears of sorrow when it rebukes you for some sin in your life?** The first day of the seventh month was the Feast of Trumpets (1; cp. Leviticus 23:23-25) and Ezra told the people not to sorrow on this holy day — *for the joy of the LORD is your strength* (10). We must not only strive to understand God's word but also be ready to obey it. The people realized that they should be observing the Feast of Tabernacles in the seventh month and they obeyed God's word and set about keeping the feast (14-18; cp. Leviticus 23:33-43).

Do not despise preaching, for it is essential for the health and well-being of the church (2 Timothy 3:16 - 4:4). We need to understand the teaching of God's word if we are to avoid the deception being propagated by smooth-talking heretics, many of whom claim to be evangelical. Let us pray that the Lord will be pleased to raise up preachers and teachers of his word and that he will keep our pastors faithful to himself.

But you are God, ready to pardon, gracious and merciful

Two days after the end of the Feast of Tabernacles the Israelites separated themselves from all who were not God's people and gathered together to mourn over their sin, to confess it, and to worship God (1-3). The Book of the Law was read to them again for one fourth of the day (3; this is most likely a quarter of daylight hours, i.e. three hours; cp. John 11:9 where Jesus describes the Jewish day as lasting twelve hours). There were another three hours for the confession of sin and the worship of God. The Levites stood on stairs (raised platforms) and with a loud voice led the people in prayer. This beautiful prayer exalts the living God and gives us an inspired account of Old Testament history (5-38; cp. Psalms 105 and 106).

Here are some of the things that we learn from the prayer:

- There is only one God who created and sustains the universe (6).
- God sovereignly chooses men (e.g. Abraham) and deals with us by covenant (8,32).
- God is faithful: *You have performed your words, for you are righteous* (8; cp. verse 33).
- God is the God who works wonders (10-11).
- God is bountiful in his provision for his people. He gave Israel guidance (12); his law (13-14); food (15); and the Holy Spirit to instruct them (20). He met their every need (21); and gave them the land of Canaan (22-25).
- God is marvellous in his grace, mercy and kindness. Despite their many experiences of God's goodness, the Israelites still rebelled against him (16-18,26-30). *But you are God, ready to pardon, gracious and merciful, slow to anger, abundant in kindness* (17). How wonderful! God is ready to pardon. **If your heart is not right with God, confess your sin to him and repent of it. He is always ready to pardon. He is abundant in kindness.**

Who is a pardoning God like thee?
Or who has grace so rich and free?   (Samuel Davies)

GALATIANS

On his first missionary journey the apostle Paul established churches in southern Galatia at Antioch (in Pisidia), Iconium, Lystra and Derbe (Acts 13:13 - 14:23). He revisited these churches on his second missionary journey and may have established other churches further north (Acts 16:1-6). We cannot be certain just when Paul wrote his letter to the Galatian churches. Some (e.g. Calvin) believe that he wrote it after he had returned to Antioch in Syria from his first missionary journey, approximately AD 49. Others (e.g. William Hendriksen) think that Paul wrote the letter from Corinth during his second missionary journey, approximately AD 52.

The Galatian churches were being troubled by false teachers (Judaizers) who were insisting that Gentile converts be circumcised and observe Jewish feasts. These people were a menace and were causing much damage in the young churches. They also troubled the church at Antioch in Syria (Acts 15:1-5). Paul wrote to the Galatian churches out of very deep concern (1:6; 3:1; 4:15-20) to warn them against this pernicious teaching which brought bondage (4:9; 5:1-2). Any attempt to add to the work of Christ in salvation is *a different gospel*, a perverted gospel (1:6-7). A message of 'Christ plus' for salvation is a false gospel which denies the grace of God and the sufficiency of Christ's death to save sinners. Christ plus good works, plus baptism, plus penance, plus purgatory, plus anything else is a vain and useless gospel. We must guard our liberty and never compromise *the gospel of the grace of God'* (Acts 20:24).

239

A different gospel

False teachers had infiltrated the churches of Galatia. Their influence had undermined Paul's authority as an apostle as well as his message. He begins his letter by stressing that he was appointed an apostle, not by men, but by the risen Lord Jesus Christ and God the Father (1). This is the only letter of Paul in which there are no words of thanks to God for his readers (cp. Romans 1:8; 1 Corinthians 1:4, etc.). The apostle was so deeply distressed and dumbfounded at the news from Galatia that he wrote, '*I marvel that you are turning away so soon from him who called you in the grace of Christ, to a different gospel*' (6). Satan never rests and one of his wiles is to seek to deceive new Christians and new churches with false teaching.

We are called *in the grace of Christ* (6) but *a different gospel* is a perversion of the gospel of Christ (7). There is only one gospel, there is only one way to forgiveness and peace with God, and that is through the sacrifice of Christ for sins (4). Paul did not tolerate false teachers and he called down the curse of God upon them (8-9). False teachers may have pleasing personalities; some claim to perform miracles, but we must have nothing to do with them. Even if an angel from heaven came and preached a different gospel from that revealed in Scripture, we must shut our ears to him. **A different gospel leads in one direction only — to hell!**

The Judaizers may have represented Paul as a man-pleaser because he did not insist that Gentile Christians be circumcised, but the apostle emphatically denied this charge. He said that if he sought to please men, he would not be the servant of Christ (10). **We must never compromise the gospel to please men, or to accommodate ecumenical and inter-faith practices.** We may be slandered as isolationists or as bigots, but we must remain true to God. Let us remember, however, that we must always be gracious and courteous in our stand for truth. Our lives must commend our message!

Walk in the Spirit and you shall not fulfil the lust of the flesh

Paul urges the Galatians, *Stand fast therefore in the liberty by which Christ has made us free* (1) because they were children *of the free* (4:31). They had already been persuaded by the Judaizers to keep Jewish feasts (4:10) and they were now about to yield to them by being circumcised (2). Religious legalism, insisting on outward ceremonies and rites as essential to salvation, has dreadful consequences: Christ will profit us nothing (2). We become *a debtor to keep the whole law* (3) and we become *estranged from Christ* (4). We must not use our Christian liberty as an excuse for sinning, but rather to show the love of Christ in our lives (13-14)! *The works of the flesh* are dreadful and those who practise them are excluded from God's kingdom (19-21).

We often fail to do the things that we desire to do because there is a conflict between the Holy Spirit and the flesh (17; cp. Romans 7:15-23). We must *walk in the Spirit* (that is, live depending on his power and help) if we are to overcome sinful desires. *'Walk in the Spirit, and you shall not fulfill the lust of the flesh'* (16). *'The flesh'* is our fallen human nature which is sometimes referred to as our *'old man'* (Romans 6:6; Ephesians 4:22; Colossians 3:9). Christians can fall into terrible sin and the apostle found it necessary to name some of the works of the flesh (19-21).

Paul lays a great emphasis on the work of the Holy Spirit in the life of the believer: *we through the Spirit eagerly wait* (5); *walk in the Spirit* (16); *the Spirit against the flesh* (17); *led by the Spirit* (18); *the fruit of the Spirit* (22); *if we live in the Spirit, let us also walk in the Spirit* (25). The evidence of the Holy Spirit in our lives is not the ability to speak in tongues but in bearing fruit, and what precious fruit it is! *The fruit of the Spirit is love, joy, peace, longsuffering, kindness, goodness, faithfulness, gentleness, self-control. Against such there is no law* (22-23). **Let us think about this fruit and examine our own lives to see whether it is in evidence.** Do we radiate the beauty of the Lord Jesus? Let us be determined with God's help to *walk in the Spirit* and so please our Saviour. This is liberty and blessing indeed.

God forbid that I should glory except in the cross

Legalism may make us self-centred and proud (5:26), but to *walk in the Spirit*, and to be spiritual, is to be humble and concerned for others. What should we do when one of our fellow-believers in the church falls into sin? The expression *overtaken in any trespass* (1) suggests that the person was caught off guard and that he did not plan a deliberate course of rebellion against God. We must not be like the Pharisees and harshly condemn the fallen Christian. We should seek to *restore such a person in a spirit of gentleness* (1; cp. 5:23). We must remember that we too should be on our guard for we are not immune from falling. The law is fulfilled in loving our neighbour as we love ourselves (5:14). We are to *bear one another's burdens, and so fulfil the law of Christ* (2). This means helping one another to shoulder the difficulties, trials and weaknesses which beset us.

Some believe that Paul wrote with *'large letters'* (11) because he suffered from some disease of his eyes (cp. 4:15). Others believe that he signed off in large letters in order to emphasize his point that circumcision is of no avail. The Judaizers were trying to avoid persecution for the cross of Christ by boasting of the numbers that they had persuaded to submit to circumcision (12-13).

Paul indulged in a different kind of boasting from that of the Judaizers. He writes, *God forbid that I should glory except in the cross of our Lord Jesus Christ, by whom the world has been crucified to me, and I to the world* (14). The cross was to the world a symbol of shame (cp. 1 Corinthians 1:23) but we love the cross because without the death of Christ we would still be in our sins, lost and *having no hope and without God in the world* (Ephesians 2:12). Let us never boast of our good works or attainments but glory in the cross of our Lord Jesus. The crucifying work of the cross is again shown here. We are crucified to the world through the cross. The values, honours, pleasures and treasures of the world have lost their charm for those who love the Lord Jesus (cp. Philippians 3:7-8). **Have they lost their charm for you? Do you glory in the cross of Christ?**

ESTHER

The events recorded in the book of Esther took place some thirty-four years before the return of Nehemiah to Jerusalem. Ahasuerus is generally recognized as King Xerxes 1 who ruled over the Persian empire from 485 to 464 BC. Vashti was deposed in the third year of Ahasuerus (1:3-4) and Esther became queen in the seventh year of his reign (2:16). Shushan (or Susa) was one of three capitals of the Persian empire (the other two being Babylon and Ecbatana).

We do not know whom God used to write the book of Esther. Some believe it to be Mordecai who was an eyewitness to the things recorded here (cp. 9:20). There is not a single reference to the name of God in the book of Esther but his wonderful providence in preserving his people is clearly demonstrated. But for God's intervention the Jews would have been destroyed. There would have been no return to Jerusalem for Ezra in 458 BC or Nehemiah in 445 BC.

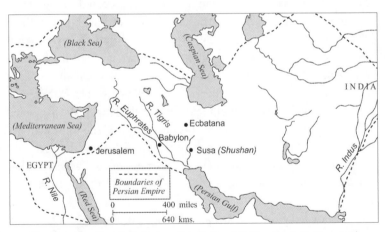

The Persian Empire during the time of Esther (see Esther 1:1)

I am grateful to Pastor Stephen Rees (of Grace Baptist Church, Stockport) for his Bible study notes on Esther. He brought out valuable lessons from this book, and with his permission I have incorporated them into these notes.

243

She obtained grace and favour in his sight

Ahasuerus reigned over a vast empire (1; see map). He held a great assembly for all his officials and servants; this lasted for six months and was followed by a feast where he proudly showed off his wealth (1-6). As the festivities came to an end, the king, merry with wine, decided to parade his beautiful queen before his guests but she *refused to come at the king's command* (10-12). The angry king acted swiftly — Vashti must be divorced and disgraced, and a successor found.

Ahasuerus commanded that the most beautiful women from all the provinces of the kingdom be brought to the palace; he would then chose a queen from their number. Esther, an orphan, was the adopted daughter of her cousin Mordecai (who was old enough to be her father). They must have been alarmed and fearful at the king's decree, for Esther was a very beautiful woman; *Esther also was taken to the king's palace* (2:8). We must be clear. Mordecai should never have allowed this to happen. He should have been prepared to die before handing his daughter over to Ahasuerus' harem (though in fact there is no suggestion in the passage that this round-up was anything but voluntary). God's law warned against intermarriage with the heathen (e.g. Deut. 7:3; cp. Ezra 9:10-12; Neh. 10:29-30). Not only that, but the terms of this 'marriage' were the most degrading possible. Esther must submit herself for a single night to the lust of the king. If she happened to please him, she might become his queen. If not, she must take her place among the rejected women of the royal harem, despised and lonely, never to know the joys of a true marriage or family life. In either case Mordecai was allowing her to enter an utterly ungodly society.

Esther *obtained grace and favour* in the eyes of the king and he took her as his queen (2:15-18). **A wicked king; a disobedient believer: can the Lord really be working out his purposes through the union of two such people as Ahasuerus and Esther? We know the answer.** The apparent chance discovery by Mordecai of a plot against the king's life was also part of God's plan, which is seen as the story of Esther unfolds (2:21-23; cp. 6:1-3).

For such a time as this

Haman was a very wealthy man (cp. 5:11) but he was evil. He wormed his way into the king's favour and was promoted to high office. By royal decree Haman had everyone bowing and scraping to him, except for one man, Mordecai (1-2). *Mordecai had told them that he was a Jew* (4). He refused to render homage to Haman, not out of disrespect, but because he was a Jew. It would appear that the act of homage involved some idolatrous act of worship. Haman was filled with rage at Mordecai's defiance. He was determined to destroy not only Mordecai, but every Jew throughout the whole kingdom (5-6).

Mordecai and the Jews throughout the empire were overwhelmed with anguish and distress when they heard the terrible news (4:1-3). Queen Esther, however, knew nothing of the king's decree. She was told of Mordecai's distress but she had no idea what had caused it. She had to send a messenger to find out from him what was happening (4:4-5). Mordecai sent another message to Esther, urging her not to remain silent, but to seek the deliverance of the Jews. He reminded her that God would deliver his people with or without her. Moreover, she would also perish if the king's decree were enforced (4:13-14). She knew that unless God intervened her situation was hopeless. In her desperation, she committed herself and her maids to fast for three days. She also called on the whole Jewish community to join her in this fast. Esther had earlier been joined with the princes of Persia in their feasting (2:18). She was now joined with the persecuted people of God in their fasting. **In God's great strategy Haman's plot has been used to bring God's people to repentance and to set them praying.**

Mordecai had challenged Esther with the question, '*Yet who knows whether you have come to the kingdom for such a time as this?*' (4:14). **We live in a time of great and urgent spiritual need.** We need to show great courage and determination to stand firm against all the evil pressures that we encounter. May God be pleased to raise up godly men and women for such a time as this. Christian, the Lord has a work for you to do, '*for such a time as this*'.

The king held out to Esther the golden sceptre

On the third day of the Jews' fast, Esther sought her audience with the king. *The king held out to Esther the golden sceptre that was in his hand* (2), signalling that her life was spared and that he was willing to receive her. Not only that, he was willing to lavish upon her whatever she requested, up to half his kingdom (3). Esther delayed making her petition but asked the king to attend a banquet later that day with Haman as guest. Ahasuerus readily agreed, and at the banquet asked her what it was that she desired. She asked for another banquet with Haman present at which she would make known her request (4-8).

Haman went from the banquet full of joy. He boasted to all his friends of his wealth and of the royal favours bestowed upon him. One man spoiled his happiness however; that man was Mordecai the Jew (9-13). Haman's wife, Zeresh, and his friends advised him to build a high gallows upon which to hang Mordecai (50 cubits = 75 feet or 23 metres). The gallows were built immediately. Haman was not prepared to wait for the day when the Jews were to be annihilated for his revenge upon Mordecai. He was going to seek the king's permission at the banquet for the execution of his enemy. He wanted him to hang high as a warning to any who would dare to defy the mighty Haman (14).

God gave Ahasuerus a sleepless night and so the restless king had the royal records read to him. The chronicles that were read contained the account of Mordecai's action which led to the king's life being saved. He learned that Mordecai had not been rewarded. When Haman later arrived at the palace the king asked him, *'What should be done for the man whom the king delights to honour?'* (6:1-6). Haman was sure that the king must be referring to him and suggested that such a man ride one of the king's horses in splendour through the city square. A herald should proclaim him as the man whom the king delights to honour (7-9). Haman had no time to request the execution of Mordecai. He was ordered to hasten and to lead the procession honouring Mordecai (6:10-11). **God's ways are truly amazing!**

So they hanged Haman on the gallows that he had prepared

When Esther revealed that her petition was to save her own life and the lives of her people, she said, '*We have been sold, my people, and I, to be destroyed, to be killed, and to be annihilated*' (1-4). The amazed king asked who could be responsible for such an evil plot (5). Esther informed him that Haman was the man. Ahasuerus discovered that Esther was a Jew and that Haman's gift (3:9) had been a bribe to persuade him to sanction the destruction of the Jews.

An angry king went into the palace garden. Haman discovered too late that the queen was one of those people he had plotted to destroy. He knew that he was doomed. He cast himself on Esther's couch to plead for his life. The king returned and wrongly concluded that Haman was assaulting his queen. One of the eunuchs pointed out that Haman had prepared gallows at his own house for Mordecai who had saved the king's life. Ahasuerus then ordered that the gallows be used for Haman (6-9). *So they hanged Haman on the gallows that he had prepared for Mordecai* (10). How true the words of the Bible: *Whatever a man sows, that he will also reap* (Galatians 6:7). **There is a saying that 'the devil looks after his own', and he may well do so until he has no further use for them.** Haman found to his great cost and too late that Satan is a terrible master and that the passing pleasures of sin bring a dreadful harvest.

Mordecai was honoured by the king but the Jews had many enemies and they were still in great danger (8:1-6). The king allowed Esther and Mordecai to issue a decree in his name which would cancel the effectiveness of the first decree. The Jews would be able to act in self-defence and kill all those who sought to destroy them. The decree was published throughout the kingdom (8:5-12). Mordecai was elevated to high office and *the Jews had light and gladness, joy and honour* (8:15-16). *Then many of the people of the land became Jews, because fear of the Jews fell upon them* (16-17). God moves in a mysterious way his wonders to perform!

The opposite occurred

Haman had determined by lot that the Jews would be slaughtered on the thirteenth day of the twelfth month and that all their possessions would be plundered (3:7,13). When the time came for the king's first decree to be enforced there was much bloodshed. The Jews (with the help of state officials) defended themselves from their enemies (1-5). There were probably a total of two million Jews scattered throughout the empire and these were saved from certain death and their enemies were destroyed (6-16). Their enemies had hoped to destroy them *but the opposite occurred* (1). **When we walk with God and delight in him, he works opposites on our behalf.** Remember the words of Joseph to his brothers, *'You meant evil against me; but God meant it for good'* (Genesis 50:20). *The opposite occurred.* Let this truth encourage you to persevere in any trial or opposition that you are facing.

Mordecai wrote to Jews throughout the empire and urged them to celebrate their great deliverance every year remembering *the month which was turned from sorrow to joy for them* (20-22). This is reflected in the two-day feast of Purim which is celebrated by Jews to remember their remarkable deliverance (26-28). Haman had cast lots to determine the day and the month of the slaughter of the Jews (3:7) — 'Purim' is named after casting Pur, the lot. The feast begins with fasting and lamentation (31) but gives way to feasting and joy, exchanging presents and making gifts to the poor (22). Mordecai went on to become very great and he used his influence to seek the good of his people (10:2-3).

Ahasuerus was a great king and the writer of the book is not afraid to admit it (10:1-2). Mordecai too became a great man, universally honoured. His greatness is recorded even in the annals of the Median and Persian kings. **But neither Ahasuerus nor Mordecai is the real hero of our story.** We have seen throughout the hand of God who in sovereign power protects his people and turns their sorrow into gladness. The feast of Purim was not instituted to celebrate the greatness of Ahasuerus but God's salvation.

JOB

Martin Luther considered the book of Job to be 'magnificent and sublime as no other book of Scripture.' It is the first of the poetic books of the Old Testament (the others are Psalms, Proverbs, Ecclesiastes, Song of Solomon and Lamentations). Job probably lived in the period of the patriarchs who had a greater life expectancy than later generations (Abraham died at one hundred and seventy-five and Job lived to a great age; 42:16; cp. Genesis 25:7). The Levitical sacrificial system had not been given at this time and righteous men acted as priests in sacrificing to God (1:5). Ezekiel 14:14,20 refers to the righteousness of Job and James 5:11 to his perseverance.

Job was blameless in the sight of God but the most terrible tragedy and suffering came upon him. His three friends were convinced that there was some secret sin in his life for which he was suffering divine chastisement but he strongly protested his innocence. We are reminded that there are no easy answers to the age-old problem of undeserved suffering. The main purpose of the book is to do with a man's relationship to God when all that he has is snatched from him.

We are encouraged to persevere in our trust in God even when we are baffled at his providence in our lives and when we cannot trace his ways. We are brought to see that 'God moves in a mysterious way his wonders to perform' and that for the righteous, 'Behind a frowning providence God hides a smiling face.' Job was prepared to trust God, even though God slay him (13:15), knowing that God was testing him to refine him (23:10). He was confident that he would see his Redeemer on the day of resurrection (19:25-26).

The greatness of God's power and majesty shine through the book. The title 'the Almighty' (Hebrew, 'Shaddai') is used of God forty-eight times in the Old Testament, thirty-one of them in the book of Job.

He fell to the ground and worshipped

Job was a man who *was blameless and upright, and one who feared God and shunned evil* (1). He was very, very rich — *the greatest of all the people of the East* (3). True greatness is not measured by what we possess, however, but by our relationship with God, and Job did not allow his wealth to spoil that relationship. The angels (the sons of God) and Satan came to present themselves before God. Satan told God that he had been roaming the earth and the Lord was able to point him to someone who shone as a bright light in the darkness around him. *'Have you considered my servant Job?'* (8).

Satan alleged that Job feared God only because the Lord had protected him and prospered him (9-10). Take away these blessings and Job would lose his faith and would curse God to his face. God accepted the challenge giving Satan permission to attack all that Job possessed but not to smite his person (11-12). It is important that we understand that though Satan is very active and very malicious, he can only act with God's permission. The scene was set for the dramatic and tragic events that befell Job and which led to the many questions and discussions that are found in this book.

Job was not aware of Satan's challenge to God nor of the fact that the devil was behind the tragic events that suddenly came upon him. Can you imagine how Job felt as one messenger and then another told him of disaster coming upon his flocks and herds? Worse was to come — his beloved children for whom he prayed much were all killed while feasting in the house of their eldest brother (13-19). In just a few minutes, Job had been reduced from a wealthy man to a pauper and his children were taken from him. Did Job curse God as Satan had suggested? *He fell to the ground and worshipped and he blessed the name of the LORD* (20-21). **If we murmur against God when small troubles befall us, we will not be able to worship him and bless him in the dark times.** We may lose everything in this world, but we will never lose our salvation and nothing can separate us from the love of God (Romans 8:35-39).

In all this Job did not sin with his lips

Satan had failed in his attempts to make Job curse God, but he works on the principle, 'If at first you don't succeed, try, try, and try again.' The Lord was again able to point out Job as a model of integrity and godliness (2-3) but Satan again challenged God, *'Stretch out your hand now, and touch his bone and his flesh, and he will surely curse you to your face!'* (4-5). He was suggesting that Job would curse God if he were made to suffer in his body. God gave him permission to smite Job, but not to take his life. The devil is only able to touch us with God's permission and he cannot possess a child of God (cp. Paul's thorn in the flesh, a messenger from Satan — 2 Corinthians 12:7).

There were no half-measures with the devil who then *struck Job with painful boils* from head to toe (7). He was such an appalling sight that his poor wife could take no more. She unknowingly became Satan's instrument to tempt her husband to curse God. She thought that he would be better out of his misery and urged him, *'Curse God and die!'* (9). Job rebuked her, pointing out that we must be prepared not only to accept good from God but also adversity (10).

Job's three friends had come to mourn with him and to comfort him, but such was his suffering, they did not recognize him. They were so shocked that they did not speak a word for seven days but they wept and mourned with him (11-13). It is better to remain silent than to speak when we cannot find the right words (13:5). When the friends did speak they were *miserable comforters* (16:2).

In all this Job did not sin with his lips (10). **He did not speak unwisely because he was ready to accept the dark providence of God as well as his blessings. This is far easier said than done.** We have so much to learn but God is patient with us. How we need to ponder our words before we speak lest we sin with our lips. Let us make Psalm 141:3 one of our prayers for today: *Set a guard, O LORD, over my mouth; keep watch over the door of my lips.*

But how can a man be righteous before God?

Job agreed with Bildad that God is absolutely just in all his ways. He said, *'Truly I know it is so, but how can a man be righteous before God?'* (2). Man is sinful hence Job's question here. How can a man prove his innocence before the God of unsearchable wisdom who may ask him a thousand questions none of which he would be able to answer (3)? Job acknowledged the greatness of God whose ways are beyond human understanding (4-12). He knew that even if he were righteous, he would not be able to answer God and his own mouth would condemn him. He could only beg for mercy from his judge (14-15,20).

In his dark despair Job could not bring himself to believe that God would answer him (16). He felt that it is of no advantage to be righteous because *God destroys the blameless and the wicked* (21-22). We know, of course, that that is not true. God does not destroy the righteous! In his distress Job was desperate to find a mediator to argue his case before God (33). We all need a mediator to plead our cause before God because we are sinners. The Lord Jesus Christ is our great Mediator (1 Timothy 2:5). He is God, but he took human flesh to live a perfect life on this earth. He suffered as a man and he knows us, understands us and pleads for us in the presence of the Father (Hebrews 4:14-16; 7:25). If you are feeling troubled or perplexed, remember that you do have a wonderful Mediator, and take heart!

'How can a man be righteous before God?' (2). **This is one of the most important questions a person can ask and it is essential that we know the right answer. On what basis can a man be accepted by God?** Some seek an answer in religious ritual, by good works, or by undertaking pilgrimages to holy places. None of these things can bring forgiveness of sins. The Bible says that everyone is guilty before God (Romans 3:19) but Job's question is answered in the gospel of Jesus Christ. We are justified through the blood of Christ (Romans 5:9). He bore the punishment for our sins that *we might become the righteousness of God in him* (2 Corinthians 5:21). There is no other way to righteousness. Are you right with God? Are you a true Christian?

Yet the righteous will hold to his way

Job was broken in spirit and in his despair he stated that his days were finished and that the grave was ready to receive him (1,11). His friends did not understand him because God had hidden from their heart the reason for his trial (2,4). He was not suffering because of some great sin in his life as they had alleged. He called upon God to lay down a pledge for him, to be his guarantor (3; this may refer to a custom by which a person going to trial gave a pledge to the other party that no advantage would be taken of them). Job fluctuated between despair and optimism in his answers to the three friends but there is a verse in this chapter which expresses great hope. *'Yet the righteous will hold to his way, and he who has clean hands will be stronger and stronger'* (9).

The believer may pass through periods of severe trial when his faith is sorely assailed, but he will never lose his salvation. Theologians call this great truth 'the perseverance of the saints'. We can be confident that God will complete the good work that he has begun in us (Philippians 1:6). We have eternal life through the Lord Jesus Christ and we cannot be lost (John 3:16; 10:27-28). God has chosen us to be saved and he will never lose us. Everyone whom he has predestined to salvation in eternity past, all who are called and justified, will be glorified (Romans 8:30). The Lord is able to keep us from stumbling and to present us *faultless before the presence of his glory with exceeding joy* (Jude 24). Let us encourage ourselves in the Lord and rejoice in him: *The righteous will hold to his way.*

> They may in the storms of temptation be tossed.
> Their sorrows may swell as the sea,
> But none of the ransomed shall ever be lost,
> The righteous shall hold on his way.
>
> Surrounded with sorrows, temptation and cares,
> This truth with delight we survey,
> And sing, as we pass through this valley of tears,
> The righteous shall hold on his way.

(Henry Fowler)

I know that my Redeemer lives

Roy Zuck writes: 'This chapter is a skyscraper among the forty-two chapters of Job that form the beautiful skyline of this poetic masterpiece. After decrying hostility from his accusers (1-6), from God (7-12), and from his relatives and friends (13-22), the suffering saint rose from the depths of his broken spirit to the heights of renewed confidence in his God (23-29)' (*Everyman's Bible Commentary*, Moody Press).

Job's friends had tormented him and wronged him (2-3) and in his despair he felt also that God had wronged him and was against him (6-12,21b). His close friends, his relatives and even his wife had shunned him (13-20) and he appealed to the three friends to have pity on him (21). **Let us learn to recognize the often silent cries of those who sorrow or suffer.** We need to be like the Lord Jesus Christ, who is gracious and full of compassion (cp. Matthew 9:36; Luke 4:18).

Though he was in terrible despair, Job here uttered one of the greatest affirmations of faith to be found in Scripture: *'I know that my Redeemer lives ... that in my flesh I shall see God'* (25-26). **Job was confident that even if he died, he would one day be raised to see his living Redeemer.** The disciples on the Emmaus road were very downcast because they thought that their Redeemer was dead (Luke 24:17-21). When they discovered that he was alive they were filled with great joy and excitement (Luke 24:32-33). We serve a risen Redeemer! Be glad and rejoice!

> I know that my Redeemer lives:
> What joy this blest assurance gives!
> He lives, he lives, who once was dead,
> And reigns, my everlasting Head.
>
> He lives to silence all my fears,
> To wipe away my falling tears,
> To soothe and calm my troubled heart,
> All needed blessings to impart.
>
> (Samuel Medley)

Surely God will never do wickedly

Elihu had heard the long discussion between Job and his three friends and he felt angry with all of them. He was angry with Job because he justified himself rather than God. He was angry with the three friends because they had failed to find anything helpful to say to Job except to condemn him (32:1-5). In this chapter he answers Job's complaint that God has wronged an innocent man (5). Elihu's approach was different from that of the three friends, though he too made false assumptions about Job (e.g. 7-8). He was saying something like this: 'I do not know why God is chastening you, but what is important is the way you react to your suffering. You add rebellion to your sin by your angry reaction to his dealings with you' (36-37).

Elihu reminds us that God is absolutely just and sovereign in all his ways. He said, *'Surely God will never do wickedly, nor will the Almighty pervert justice'* (12; cp. Genesis 18:25; Revelation 15:3). We must never *condemn him who is most just* (17). God is sovereign over all the earth and he sustains all creation (13-15). If it is not fitting to say to a king, *'You are worthless,'* how dare we accuse God of injustice? He is impartial in his dealings with rich and poor alike (18-20). God sees us all and he knows us all. He does not need to investigate us in judgment (before a court). He sees the deeds of the wicked and will punish them (21-30). God does not have to give us his reasons for the chastisement that we suffer (31-33).

Job's complaint that he had done nothing to deserve his suffering is one that is still heard today. Most of us have said at some time, or thought to ourselves, 'What have I done to deserve this?' **Life often appears to be unfair but it is not meaningless. We are not the helpless victims of fate! God is very wise, very gracious and very good. He has kind purposes for all who belong to him.** To remember these truths will equip us to face the trials and perplexities that befall us. *The sufferings of this present time are not worthy to be compared with the glory which shall be revealed in us* (Romans 8:18).

Then the LORD answered Job out of the whirlwind

Job and his friends had reasoned and disagreed but now the silence of heaven is broken. Job had said, *'I desire to reason with God'* and had prayed, *'Let me speak, then you respond to me'* (13:3,22), and *'Oh, that the Almighty would answer me'* (31:35). Here we read, *Then the LORD answered Job out of the whirlwind* (1). Notice that *the LORD answered Job* but he did not answer his questions. It is not for us to pry into the secret things of God even though we may find ourselves beset by perplexing questions (cp. Deuteronomy 29:29).

There had been too many *'words without knowledge'* (2) and God challenges Job, *'Now prepare yourself like a man'* (3; Hebrew = 'gird up your loins' — in other words, 'be prepared for combat'). Job had wanted to argue his case before God that he had been treated unfairly. He wanted answers but the Lord challenges him, *'I will question you, and you shall answer me'* (3). Instead of answering Job's questions, God asked him one question after another in which he pointed to the marvels of the inanimate world (4-38) and of the animal kingdom (38:39 - 39:30). Look at some of these questions (there are many more in chapters 39 - 41):

- *'Where were you when I laid the foundations of the earth?'* (4).
- *'Have you commanded the morning?'* (12).
- *'Have you entered the springs of the sea?'* (16).
- *'Have you comprehended the breadth of the earth?'* (18).
- *'Can you'* guide the great galaxies? (31-33).
- *'Can you'* control the weather? (34-38).

When we meet with God we see the questions that trouble us in a different light. We are overawed at the greatness and the majesty of the Almighty. We are painfully aware of our own weakness and ignorance. **We realize that God knows what he is doing with us, and though we cannot trace his ways, we will trust him!**

I know that you can do everything

Job was overwhelmed by the revelation of God's infinite power and he answered God, saying, *'I know that you can do everything, and that no purpose of yours can be withheld from you'* (2). God is absolutely sovereign and his purposes cannot be thwarted. What is the secret of confidence in prayer? It does not lie in ourselves or in an ability to pray eloquently. It comes from having confidence in God! — *'I know that you can do everything'* (2). How wonderful. Nothing is too hard for God. Nothing is impossible for him to do (Genesis 18:14; Luke 1:37; 18:27). Let us persevere in prayer. The Lord will never fail us.

Job realized that his understanding fell far short of the wisdom of the Almighty (3). He saw that he had sinned in the way he had reasoned about God and had been presumptuous to imagine that he could argue his case before God. He had such an experience of God that he was overcome by a sense of his own worthlessness. *'Therefore I abhor myself, and repent in dust and ashes'* (6). **When a man experiences God in his life, there is true repentance and humility.**

The Lord then spoke to Eliphaz and the other two friends. He was angry with them because they had not represented him correctly. They had uttered many wonderful truths about God but they had insisted that Job must have been guilty of some great sin to be suffering such calamity in his life. The Lord ordered them to offer up burnt offerings and told them to go to his *'servant Job'* who would pray for them (7-8). *The Lord restored Job's losses when Job prayed for his friends* and gave him *twice as much as he had before* (10). God gave him another ten children, seven sons and three daughters; his daughters were outstanding in their beauty (13-15). Is there someone who has hurt you? Pray for them. Do not harbour resentment or bitterness, for that will rob your life of blessing.

Now the LORD blessed the latter days of Job more than his beginning (12). **All ended well for Job (16-17) and it will end well for every child of God. Suffering does not last for ever and glory awaits us.**

EPHESIANS

Ephesus was the most important city in the Roman province of Asia (now the western coast of Turkey). It had a thriving port which has long since been silted up; the sea is now some six miles from the site of Ephesus. The city boasted the largest building in the Greek world, the massive temple of the goddess Diana (Artemis) which attracted thousands of pilgrims. Occult practices flourished and there was a great trade in making and selling Diana images, talismans, etc. which was threatened by the coming of the gospel (Acts 19:19,24-27). Paul paid a short visit to Ephesus on his second missionary journey, leaving Aquila and Priscilla there (Acts 18:19-21). He returned on his third missionary journey, staying for three years, two of which were spent in *reasoning daily in the school of Tyrannus* (Acts 19:1-41; 20:18-35). From Ephesus the gospel spread throughout the province of Asia and *the word of the Lord grew mightily and prevailed* (Acts 19:10-20).

Paul was in prison at Rome when he wrote his letter to the Ephesians between AD 61 to 63. He wrote to the Colossian church (also in Asia) at the same time. Tychicus, *a beloved brother and faithful minister in the*

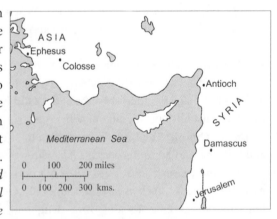

Lord, carried the letters to the churches (Ephesians 6:21; Colossians 4:7). There is a great emphasis on the church in this letter of Paul. The church is described as the *'Body'* (1:22-23; 4:4,16; 5:23,30); the *'Building'* (2:19-22); and the *'Bride'* (5:25-27,32) of Christ. The nature of the believer's life in Christ is described in chapters 1 - 3; chapters 4 - 6 show how that life is to be worked out in the church, the family, and the world.

Blessed be ... God ... who has blessed us

After his opening greetings Paul blesses God for all the spiritual blessings that he has bestowed upon us in the *'heavenly places'* (3). Christ sits at the right hand of God *'in the heavenly places'* (20) and though we are on earth we *sit together in the heavenly places* because we are *'in Christ'* (2:6). In this spiritual realm we not only enjoy God's blessings, but are also engaged in spiritual warfare (6:12).

Our English verb 'eulogize' comes from the Greek word used for *'blessed'* (3); it means 'to speak well of' or 'to praise'. **We have received so many blessings that our hearts should be filled with praise to the triune God.** We have been chosen by God the Father (3-6), redeemed by the Son (7-12) and sealed by the Holy Spirit (13-14). What are the spiritual blessings bestowed upon us? These are predestination (4,5,11), adoption into God's family (5), acceptance and forgiveness (6-7), redemption (7), knowledge of God's will (8-10) and a glorious inheritance (11,18). **What a wealth we have in Christ!** No wonder Paul rejoiced in *the riches of his grace* (7; 2:7) and in *the riches of the glory of his inheritance* (18). He described this wealth as *the unsearchable riches of Christ* (3:8).

Paul gave thanks for the Ephesians because of their faith in Christ and their love for **all** their fellow-believers (15-16). He prayed that God would give them *the spirit of wisdom and revelation in the knowledge of him,* and that they would know continued enlightenment that they might know *what is the hope of his calling; what are the riches of the glory of his inheritance in the saints; what is the exceeding greatness of his power towards us who believe* (17-19). Our glorious risen Saviour is head over all things to the church (20-23). All the blessings of salvation are in Christ (3,4,7,10,11,13). Let us think about our great privileges in Christ and praise God with all our heart. *Blessed be the God and Father of our Lord Jesus Christ, who has blessed us with every spiritual blessing in the heavenly places in Christ* (3).

The exceeding riches of his grace

We were in a terrible mess before Christ saved us. We were *dead in trespasses and sins* (1,5) and enslaved by Satan (*'the prince of the power of the air'*; 2). We were governed by the sinful desires of the flesh and of the mind and *were by nature children of wrath* (3). We *were without Christ ... having no hope and without God in the world* (12). We were helpless and hopeless in our sin, *but God, who is rich in mercy, because of his great love with which he loved us ... made us alive together with Christ* (4-5). Those words *'But God'* make all the difference. We fully deserved God's wrath, but in his mercy he gave his beloved Son to die for us. He freely forgave us and he has heaped marvellous blessings upon us. Paul almost runs out of superlatives to describe God's grace and he describes it as *'the exceeding riches of his grace in his kindness to us in Christ Jesus'* (7). James Denney describes grace as 'the love of God, spontaneous, beautiful, unearned, at work in Christ for the salvation of sinners'.

Salvation is the gift of God and we are saved by grace (8). The apostle states, *By grace you have been saved through faith, and that not of yourselves, it is the gift of God* (8). We owe everything to God. *We are his workmanship, created in Christ Jesus for good works* (9-10). We must never forget that there is a state of hostility between God and sinful men. We have offended God by our sin and we need to be reconciled to him if we are to be saved. God in his great mercy has provided the way of reconciliation in Christ (11-13). In Christ the racial barrier between Jew and Gentile is broken down (14-18), and we are members together of the church which is *the household of God* and *a holy temple in the Lord* (19,21).

Through the Lord Jesus Christ, we *have access by the Holy Spirit to the Father* (18). We are able to come into the presence of the sovereign King of the universe because of *the exceeding riches of his grace.* **Do you feel overwhelmed by such grace, kindness, mercy and love? Are you moved to worship, praise, love and obey such a glorious God?**

The mystery of Christ

Paul writes, *'For this reason ...'* (1) and then digresses from what he was going to say before returning to the subject in verse 14 where he uses the same expression. Notice how Paul views his imprisonment in Rome. He saw himself as *the prisoner of Jesus Christ* and not as the prisoner of Caesar (cp. 4:1). He was a prisoner because it was in God's purpose. What is *the mystery of Christ* (3-4,9; cp. Romans 16:25-26)? It is a secret which God has revealed; the *'mystery'* here is that salvation is not restricted to the Jews but that Gentiles are also included. Most Jews never grasped that the promises of the Old Testament point to the salvation of Gentiles (cp. Genesis 12:3; Isaiah 11:10; 49:6; 54:1-3; 60:1-3). *'In Christ'* Gentiles and Jews are *fellow heirs* [members] *of the same body, and partakers of his promise in Christ through the gospel* (6).

Paul rightly saw that his ministry to the Gentiles was *the gift of the grace of God* (7) and he was very humble despite his great success in planting churches. He goes on to write, *'To me, who am less than the least of all the saints, this grace was given, that I should preach among the Gentiles the unsearchable riches of Christ'* (8). Paul's purpose in preaching the unsearchable riches of Christ to the Gentiles was *that now the manifold wisdom of God might be known by the church to the principalities and powers* [angels] *in the heavenly places* (10). The word *'manifold'* basically means 'much varied' but F. F. Bruce suggests that it could be translated 'many-splendoured'. By whom is this many-splendoured wisdom of God made known? It is not made known by individuals but by the church. Paul again points us to the importance of the church in God's eternal purpose. We must never despise *'the church'* for which Christ gave his life (5:25). **The local church is the expression of the universal church and it is important that we are fully-committed members of a gospel church.**

Paul goes on to pray for the Ephesians and his benediction has a wonderful promise (20-21). To what end is it given? *To him be glory in the church by Christ Jesus* (21).

Be kind to one another, tenderhearted, forgiving one another

We bring glory to God in the church by leading holy lives, and details for Christian living are spelt out in Ephesians chapters 4 to 6. Having expressed his high view of the church, Paul urges us, '*Walk worthy of the calling with which you were called*' (1). Satan will do everything to destroy the unity of every true gospel church. He wants to divide us and thus to weaken us so that we pose no threat to his kingdom of darkness. He knows that a divided church does not bring glory to God.

Paul, *the prisoner of the Lord* (1), was bound by a chain (6:20). He pleads, *Keep the unity of the Spirit in the bond* [chain] *of peace* (3). We also must endeavour to maintain or *keep the unity of the Spirit in the bond of peace.* Look at the seven '*ones*' in verses 4 to 6. There is *one body* (the church), *one Spirit* and we share *one hope* of our calling, *one Lord, one faith, one baptism and one God.* If we are not at '*one*' with others in our church we are not walking worthy of our calling. Our lives must be marked by *lowliness, gentleness, with long-suffering, bearing* [putting up] *with one another in love* (2). Are you humble and gracious in your attitude to others?

The risen Christ has given us gifts according to his grace and these gifts are to be used for the building up of the church which is his body (7-16). If these gifts are neglected, or if we are immature (13-14), there will be problems in the church. We must also walk (lead our lives) in a different manner from unbelievers (17-32). In the church *we are members of one another* (25) and we must be careful that we do not grieve the Holy Spirit by sinning with our lips or our hands (25-30). Look carefully at verses 31 and 32. Is there any trace of bitterness, wrath, anger, clamour, evil speaking or malice in your life? If there is, I urge you to repent and put away all that is wrong in your life. If you do not, your life will be blighted, and you will bring disunity to your church. Let us show that we love Christ by being *kind to one another, tenderhearted, forgiving one another* (32) **for to do so is to walk worthy of our calling and to walk differently from those in the world.**

Be followers of God

Following on from the appeal that we should be kind to one another, forgiving one another (4:32), we are exhorted, *'Therefore, be followers of God as dear children'* (1). The Greek word translated *'followers'* means 'imitators'. Just as children imitate their parents, so we too must imitate God and show by our lifestyle that we belong to his family, walking in love (1-2), walking as children of light (3-14) and by walking circumspectly (i.e. carefully, wisely, 15-21). We must shun all forms of sexual immorality, covetousness, filthiness, foolish talk and coarse jesting. These things must have no place in the lives of those who belong to the kingdom of God (3-7). By leading godly lives and walking as children of light we will expose and shame *the unfruitful works of darkness* (8-14).

We must *walk circumspectly* making the best use of our time (15-16). As we are daily *filled with the Spirit* (18) we will give *thanks always for all things to God the Father in the name of our Lord Jesus Christ* (20); we will have psalms and hymns and spiritual songs welling up in our hearts and pouring from our lips (19). **What a blessed contrast to the way of the ungodly (4).** How can we give *thanks always for all things* (20)? How about the set-backs and the adverse circumstances of life? We should thank God that he is working all these things for his glory and for our good and that none of these things can separate us from his love in Christ Jesus (Romans 8:28,35-39).

Wives must submit to their husbands just as the church submits to Christ. This submission must be seen as part of their submission to the Lord who has appointed the husband as the head of the family (22-24). Husbands must love their wives *just as Christ also loved the church and gave himself for it* (22-26). This is not a picture of a wife in submission to a tyrant, but to one whom she greatly respects because he loves her, giving himself to her and for her. He must protect and care for his wife and love her as he loves himself (23,29,33). **Husbands and wives, be followers (imitators) of God.**

Be strong in the Lord

Our attention is now directed to the relationship between parents and children. Children must obey their parents because this is right; it is one of the ten commandments (1-2). One of the marks of an ungodly society is the disobedience of children to their parents (2 Timothy 3:2). Fathers have great responsibilities. They are not to provoke their children but rather *bring them up in the training and admonition of the Lord* (4). Fathers, notice that you must take the lead in the spiritual training of your children.

Christian employers must treat their employees with dignity and respect remembering that they are accountable to their own Master who is in heaven (5-9). However boring, irksome or tiring our work, we must do it *as to the Lord, and not to men* (7). When we see this as the will of God, we will be diligent at all times and not only work when we are being watched (6). Such an attitude banishes complaining and makes work enjoyable. **How is your testimony in your place of work? Does your conduct glorify God?** Let us strive to do all our work, whether at the factory, office, school, in the home or church *as to the Lord, and not to me*n.

We must seek with all our hearts to *be strong in the Lord and in the power of his might* because we have to contend with a powerful and cunning enemy (10-12). Satan and his wicked forces are always looking to take advantage of us and we must be on our guard by putting on *the whole armour of God* (11). Look at the Christian armour and be sure to equip yourself with each piece — truth, righteousness, the gospel of peace, faith, the word of God, and praying always in the Spirit (13-18). We are all in the fight and we need to pray for each other (*supplication for all the saints*; 18). Paul did not ask the Ephesians to pray for his release from prison but for boldness in proclaiming the mystery of the gospel (19-20). **There isn't a trace of self-pity in Paul. Why should there be? We can live the Christian life in the most difficult circumstances, even in prison, when we are strong in the Lord.**

PHILIPPIANS

Philippi was a Roman colony in the province of Macedonia (Acts 16:12). As a colony its government and customs were modelled on those of Rome. The Philippian church was the first church that Paul established in Europe (Acts 16:9-40).

Paul wrote this letter from prison in Rome between AD 61 and AD 63. He wrote to thank the Philippians for their generous financial support brought to him by one of their leaders, Epaphroditus (4:18). He wanted to reassure them that his imprisonment had *turned out for the furtherance of the gospel* (1:12-26). He also dealt with a threat to the unity of the church on account of friction between two of its women (1:27 - 2:4; 4:2). There is a great emphasis on Christian joy in the letter (in which the words *'joy'* and *'rejoice'* are found sixteen times).

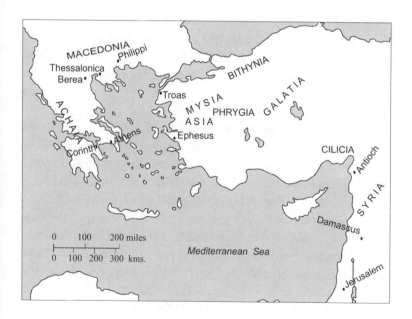

For to me to live is Christ, and to die is gain

The church at Philippi had its problems but Paul was able to pray for them with thankfulness and joy. He wrote, '*I thank my God upon every remembrance of you*' (3-4). Why was Paul so thankful to God for the Philippian church? It was for their *fellowship in the gospel* which had continued from the time that they had come to Christ (5). The Greek word translated '*fellowship*' means 'a sharing of the same things'; it is also translated '*communion*' (1 Corinthians 10:16; 2 Corinthians 6:14; 13:14). Christian fellowship is more than meeting together for worship, praise and prayer (though these are most important). It is having our fellow-believers in our heart (7). The Philippians had supported Paul with their prayers and gifts in the past and continued to do so now that he was in prison (4:14-18). Fellowship involves giving as well as taking — that is what sharing is about.

God will complete his work of salvation in us. *He who has begun a good work in you will complete it until the day of Jesus Christ* (6). We must always seek to lead lives that are *worthy of the gospel of Christ*, however, and be prepared to suffer for him (27-29). How should we pray for each other? Paul's prayer for the Philippians gives us the answer (9-11). Do you pray like that?

Paul saw the sovereign hand of God in all his circumstances. He assured the Philippians that his imprisonment had *turned out for the furtherance of the gospel* (12). His chains were '*in Christ*' and all of the palace guard heard the gospel as they took their turn to watch over him (13). Not only that, Paul's example had encouraged the Christian men in the church at Rome to be more bold in proclaiming the word of God (14). We must also remember that God is sovereign even when insincere men preach the gospel (16-18). Paul lived for Christ whether in prison or at liberty (20). He had no fear of death for to be with Christ *is far better* (23). He could sincerely assert, '*For to me, to live is Christ, and to die is gain*' (21). **Is the same thing true of you? Are you living for Christ, seeking to please him in all that you do?**

Let nothing be done through selfish ambition or conceit

Paul writes of his joy being completed, not by his release from prison, but to hear that his beloved Philippians were of one mind enjoying unity among themselves (1-2). Two women, Euodia and Syntyche, were quarrelling (4:2) and their dispute was threatening the unity of the church. Our conduct is only *worthy of the gospel of Christ* as we live in unity with our fellow-believers in our own local church. We must with one mind strive together for the faith of the gospel if we are to see the blessing of God on our work (1:27; cp. Ephesians 4:1-6).

Wrong motives in any work for Christ are a threat to Christian unity. It is possible to work for Christ for the wrong reasons (1:15-16). *Let nothing be done through selfish ambition or conceit, but in lowliness of mind let each esteem others better than himself* (3). Selfish ambition and pride in Christians have torn apart many a church. We may 'pride' ourselves on not being selfish but do we esteem others better than ourselves and seek their interests before our own? **If our Christianity is genuine we will have the attitude described in verses 3 and 4.**

Paul drives home his appeal for unity and humility with one of the most wonderful and moving passages in the whole of the Bible (5-11). How are we to deal with the sins of selfishness and pride in our lives? We must take to heart the example of the Lord Jesus. *Let this mind be in you which was also in Christ Jesus* (5). The Son of God is equal with the Father but he took *the form of a servant* (Greek '*doulos*' = 'a slave'), and was obedient to the Father's will, even to the point of submitting to torture and death on the cross (6-8; cp. Matthew 26:36-44). Let us ponder this. The Lord Jesus completely denied himself to pay the highest possible price to save us from our sin, from Satan and from eternal hell. He is now *highly exalted* in heavenly splendour and one day we will gaze on him, admire him, adore him and worship him in heaven. Do you love the Lord? Do you rejoice in awe and wonder at the greatness of his love for you? **Do you desire with all your heart to please him? Then you must have his mind and attitude and be Christlike in your life.**

Our citizenship is in heaven

Paul was about to close his letter, writing, *'Finally, my brethren, rejoice in the Lord'* (1) when he felt the need to warn them against false teachers, particularly Judaisers (2-11) and sensualists, who lived for their own lusts and who *set their mind on earthly things* (17-19). The church has always been under threat from false teaching and the apostle emphasizes the need for vigilance with a threefold *'Beware'*. He was not polite about those people who perverted the gospel of Christ. He wrote, *'Beware of dogs, beware of evil workers, beware of the mutilation!'* (2). We must never compromise with false teaching or welcome false teachers among us.

Paul could have boasted in his Jewish pedigree (4-6), but he counted these things as rubbish compared to *the excellence of the knowledge of Christ Jesus* (7-9). He was driven by an overwhelming desire to know Christ *and the power of his resurrection, and the fellowship of his sufferings, being conformed to his death* (10). Those who would know Christ's power in their lives must die to self, to all fleshly ambition and desires (cp. Galatians 5:24). **Are you willing to follow Christ on the pathway of suffering as well as of joy?**

Philippi was a Roman colony (Acts 16:12) and its people prided themselves in their Roman citizenship with all its privileges. Paul reminded the Philippian Christians that they had a more glorious citizenship. *'Our citizenship is in heaven'* (20). As citizens of heaven, we must not set our minds on earthly things (19) but rather *seek those things which are above* (Colossians 3:1) and remember that we are *strangers and pilgrims on the earth, desiring a heavenly country* (Hebrews 11:13-16). **Are you eagerly waiting for the return of Christ from heaven (20)?** What a wonderful day that will be! He will transform our poor, weak, decaying bodies and raise them to immortality (21; cp. 1 Corinthians 15:51-53; 1 John 3:2). Let us *rejoice in the Lord* (3:1) and *stand fast* in him (4:1) for *our citizenship is in heaven*.

The peace of God, which surpasses all understanding

Paul remembered the time when Euodia and Syntyche had laboured with him in the gospel and he tenderly appealed to them to be reconciled with each other (2-3). Paul urged his *true companion* (whose identity we do not know) to help these women resolve their differences. How can we *rejoice in the Lord always* when everything seems to be going wrong, when we are ill, when we are suffering? The Philippians knew that Paul was not telling them to do what he did not do himself. He had sung the praises of God from a filthy Philippian dungeon after being unjustly arrested and beaten (Acts 16:22-34). What do we have to rejoice about? We have a wonderful Saviour who has saved us from our sin at tremendous cost. We enjoy the blessings of our salvation such as forgiveness of sins and peace with God. We should rejoice that our Father in heaven is sovereign over every circumstance in our lives. We should rejoice in daily fellowship with the Lord and in his love and goodness to us each day.

Many of us fail to let our gentleness (big-heartedness) be known to all men (5) and we may be unnecessarily anxious because we fail to commit **everything** to God in prayer, bringing our requests to him with thanksgiving (6). If we will but trust him, he will give us his peace, always. *The peace of God, which surpasses all understanding, will guard your hearts and minds through Christ Jesus* (7). Many a saint of God, in the most distressing circumstances, has known the peace of the Lord possessing his heart in a remarkable way; this is alien to the world and beyond its comprehension. If we are to enjoy this wonderful peace of God in our lives we need to be disciplined in our thought life as well as in our prayer life. Look at the things upon which we should meditate every day (8). How are your prayer life and your thought life? Paul was not writing from theory; the Philippians had seen the evidence of these things in his life (9). No wonder he was content, even in prison (11). He had the surpassing peace of God (7), the invincible strength of Christ (13) and the unlimited riches of Christ to supply every need (19). **What do you really know about Christian contentment?**

COLOSSIANS

Colosse and Laodicea were cities in the Roman province of Asia, situated in the fertile valley of the River Lycus. Colosse was over 100 miles east of Ephesus and some fifteen miles south-east of Laodicea. The gospel was preached throughout Asia when Paul was based at Ephesus (Acts 19:10) though it appears that the apostle had not been to Colosse (1:3-4,7-8). It is possible that Epaphras, himself a Colossian (4:12-13), heard the gospel in Ephesus and after coming to faith in Christ took the good news to Colosse.

Paul wrote his letter to the Colossians between AD 61 and 63 at the same time as he wrote to Philemon and to the Ephesian church, the letters being carried by Tychicus (4:7; cp. Ephesians 6:21). The apostle, in prison in Rome, was concerned that false teachers were having an unsettling and disturbing influence upon the Colossian church. These teachers were saying that there is more to the Christian life than ordinary Christianity, and that a fuller experience and a greater freedom than those which they had thus far enjoyed were available to them (it seems much like the modern evangelical scene). Paul insisted that all God's fullness is to be found in Christ alone, warning against *'philosophy and empty deceit'* (2:8).

As with some of the other early churches there were Judaisers who taught that Gentile Christians must submit to the rite of circumcision, observe Jewish dietary laws and feast days (2:11-16). Moreover, some were worshipping angels (2:18) and practising a false asceticism (2:20-23). Paul combats these errors by showing that Christ is God and that his work in saving sinners is complete and sufficient (1:13-23). He also gives instruction on practical Christian living. There are many similarities in Colossians to the Ephesian letter, e.g:

- Colossians 1:14 and Ephesians 1:7.
- Colossians 1:18 and Ephesians 1:22-23.
- Colossians 3:16 and Ephesians 5:19.
- Colossians 3:18-25 and Ephesians 5:22 - 6:9.

That you may have a walk worthy of the LORD,
fully pleasing him

Paul was encouraged to hear of the progress of the Colossians and he thanked God for them. True faith in Christ is accompanied by love for God's people (*'saints'*) and it brings forth spiritual fruit in our lives (4-6; cp. Galatians 5:22-23). Paul prayed for the Colossians, that they might *be filled with the knowledge of his will in all wisdom and spiritual understanding.* We need wisdom and spiritual understanding so that we will be *grounded and steadfast* in the faith to keep us from being shaken or moved from God's truth by false teachers (23). Paul also prayed that they would lead a life *worthy of the Lord, fully pleasing him, being fruitful in every good work and increasing in the knowledge of God* (10) and that they would be *strengthened with all might, according to his glorious power.* The power that Paul desired for the Colossians was power to enable them to have endurance (*'patience'*), longsuffering and joy in trial (11; cp. James 1:2).

The Lord Jesus Christ is God (15-19; cp. 2:9). *'First-born'* (15) does not mean that there was a time when he did not exist and that he was the first to be born way back in eternity. *'First-born'* means that he is superior in position to everyone and everything (cp. Old Testament use, Exodus 4:22; Deuteronomy 21:16-17). Jesus is the great Creator of all things (16; cp. John 1:1-3). He is the eternal One (*'before all things'*; cp. Revelation 22:12-13) and *in him all things consist* (17). He holds the whole of the universe in his hands and he lovingly holds us and will always take care of us. He will never fail us. *He is the head of the body, the church, who is the beginning, the first-born from the dead, that in all things he may have the pre-eminence* (18).

God has done so much for us. He has given us forgiveness of sins through the blood of Christ and reconciled us to himself, *having made peace through the blood of his cross* (14,20). He has delivered us from the power of darkness and has brought us into the kingdom of his beloved Son (13). Let us now thank him with grateful hearts. **We owe God so much. Surely, we will want to lead a life worthy of the Lord, fully pleasing him.**

You are complete in him

Paul had never met the Christians in Colosse or Laodicea but he had a great concern for them (1). The noun *'conflict'* is similar to the verb *'striving'* in the previous verse (1:29). Our word 'agony' is derived from the Greek. Paul agonized in prayer for the Colossians (cp. 4:12-13, *'labouring'*, i.e. 'striving' *in prayers*). Paul prayed that their hearts might *be encouraged, being knit together in love* and that they would *attain to all riches of the full assurance of understanding, to the knowledge of the mystery of God* (2). He was concerned that they might be led astray by false teachers being deceived *with persuasive words* (4). False teaching has an attraction for the unwary and disguises error within truth, having *an appearance of wisdom* (23).

There was much at stake (and there still is). In God, Father and Son, *are hidden all the treasures of wisdom and knowledge* (2-3). *'The mystery of God'* is not some dark and mystical knowledge, but something that he reveals through the Holy Spirit. As we increase *in the knowledge of God* (1:10) we will discover more and more wonderful things from his *treasures of wisdom and knowledge* (cp. Romans 11:33-36; 1 Corinthians 2:6-16). As we have received Christ Jesus the Lord so we must live (*'walk'*) in him. We must not only be rooted in Christ but also *built up in him and established in the faith* as we have been taught, *abounding in it with thanksgiving* (6-7).

False teachers still deceive millions. *Beware lest anyone should cheat you through philosophy and empty deceit* which come from human tradition and worldly principles (8). The philosophy that Paul refers to here was not the thought of the Greek philosophers; it was a mixture of Christianity, Jewish ceremonialism, worship of angels and asceticism (see verses 11-23). The high-sounding talk of false teachers was nothing more than *empty words* (Ephesians 5:6). The Lord Jesus is God and he has supreme authority over spiritual powers. *For in him dwells all the fullness of the Godhead bodily and you are complete in him* (9-10). **We have a wonderful salvation. Don't let smooth-talking heretics shake your faith in Christ.**

Your life is hidden with Christ in God

The believer is frequently described in the New Testament as being *'in Christ'*. When we are born again through the mighty work of the Holy Spirit in our lives, we are united to Christ. *Your life is hidden with Christ in God* (3). There is no more condemnation and we shall never perish. Wonderful indeed! There is more than this involved in our union with Christ however. We are to put to death those evil things that once held sway in our lives (5,7). We must get rid of everything that is displeasing to him. We have *put off the old man with his deeds,* and have *put on the new man* (9-10). How do we put off the old man with his deeds? We must get rid of sinful attitudes, words and actions; we have no need to be under the dominion of sin (5,7; cp. Romans 6:14); we must not feed sinful desires.

Your life is hidden with Christ in God. We are not only united to Christ in his death but also in his risen life (1; cp. Romans 6:1-5). This means that we are to set our mind *on things above, not on things on the earth* (2). Heavenly-mindedness is quite a rare quality today. The old life is now finished and we must live to please God. Our new life in Christ should be seen in our lives. Paul goes on to set the standard for Christian behaviour in the local church (9-17), in the home (18-21), in the place of work (22 - 4:1) and among the unsaved (4:5-6). When we *put on the new man* (10) we clothe ourselves with wonderful Christian virtues. It is easy to opt out of church life if we do not get on with some people, but as *'the elect of God'* (12), we just have to get on with people and show the beauty and love of Christ in our lives (14).

We must let the peace of God rule in our hearts, be thankful and let the word of Christ dwell in us richly in all wisdom and have praising hearts (15-16). Whatever we do must be done in the name of the Lord Jesus, with thanksgiving, and what we do in the workplace must be done *heartily, as to the Lord* (17,23). **If we do not recognize that our life is hidden with Christ in God we will hide the Saviour from those around us and we will fail in our Christian witness.**

Let your speech always be with grace

The imprisoned apostle did not ask for prayer that he be released, but rather, that God would enable him to speak for Christ (3-4). We are to be wise in our behaviour to those outside of Christ and we must redeem the time (5). Time is too precious to waste and we must make good use of it. How much time do you fritter away in worthless activities when you could be learning so much from the word of God or could be using that time to work for him?

Let your speech always be with grace, seasoned with salt, that you may know how you ought to answer each one (6). Salt prevents corruption and the word of God commands, *Let no corrupt communication proceed out of your mouth* (Ephesians 4:29). Filthy, abusive, blasphemous, malicious language and lies must have no place in our conversation (3:8-9). How do we season our conversation with salt as we seek to answer the questions or the mocking of unbelievers? *Let the word of Christ dwell in you richly in all wisdom* (3:16). This will have a dramatic effect upon our speech as it is seen in our lives. The people *marvelled at the gracious words* spoken by the Lord Jesus Christ (Luke 4:22). **Do we seek to be like our great Saviour in the way in which we speak to those around us?** *Let your speech always be with grace.*

Paul's love and esteem for his fellow-workers are quite apparent in his closing greetings. These faithful men had *proved to be a comfort* to the imprisoned apostle (11). Epaphras, a Colossian who was with Paul at Rome (12-13; cp. 1:7-8), faithfully laboured in prayer for the church at Colosse. Paul was able to say, *'I bear him witness that he has a great zeal for you.'* This godly man had a great love for his people which drove him to toil in earnest prayer for them. Paul highly valued his Christian companions. **Can it be said that you have proved to be a comfort to your pastor or to any of your fellow-believers?** Paul closes his letter by asking for prayer. *Remember my chains* (18). Our prayers for God's servants are important.

PSALMS

The title 'The Book of Psalms' is used in the New Testament (Luke 20:42; Acts 1:20). The Greek word ('*Psalmos*') is a translation of the Hebrew title ('*Mizmor*') used in fifty-seven of the Psalms. '*Mizmor*' is a song which is accompanied by a stringed instrument. David wrote almost half of the Psalms; other writers include Moses (Psalm 90), Solomon (Psalms 72; 127) and Asaph (Psalms 50; 73 - 80).

The Psalms have always been a hymn book for the church as they were for Israel (cp. Ephesians 5:19). They are a rich devotional handbook which we should know well and continually use. They encourage us to worship God. They give us much insight into the blessings, struggles and moods of a saint of God in various circumstances — in joy and in sorrow; in trial and in rest; in danger and in peace; in defeat and in victory; in penitence and in praise; in doubt and in trust. The Psalms are a great antidote to the false teaching that gives the impression that the Christian should always be on the 'mountain-top' of rejoicing and blessing, living above struggles or sorrow.

Hebrew Poetry is not based on rhyme or metre as is usual with English verse, but uses a number of devices, the most common being parallelism. In parallelism, a similar or a contrasting thought is expressed:

Psalm 30:5: *Weeping may endure for a night,*
But joy comes in the morning.
Proverbs 15:20: *A wise son makes a father glad,*
But a foolish man despises his mother.

Another device is the use of acrostics, e.g. Psalm 119 which has twenty-two sets of eight verses, one set for each letter of the Hebrew alphabet. In each set, every verse starts with the same letter of the alphabet, e.g. verses 1-8 all begin with the same letter 'Aleph'.

I warmly commend C. H. Spurgeon's commentary on the Psalms, *The treasury of David.*

Blessed is the man who walks not in the counsel of the ungodly

This psalm presents us with a vivid contrast between the godly and the ungodly. There are two men, two ways and two destinies. *'Blessed is the man'* can be rendered 'Oh, the blessedness of the man' (cp. the Beatitudes in Matthew 5:3-12). Satan deceives millions with the lie that holiness kills happiness. What nonsense! The pleasures of sin do not last (cp. Hebrews 11:25). True happiness is only found in godly living. If we are always miserable there is something wrong with our walk with the Lord.

The godly person does **not** *walk in the counsel of the ungodly* (he does not think as they think, he has a different outlook on life); he does **not** stand in the path of sinners (he keeps himself from sinful behaviour). He does **not** sit *in the seat of the scornful*; the *'seat'* is the place of instruction (cp. Matthew 23:2). *The seat of the scornful* is where sin is taught to others.

The godly man shuns evil-doing and does not delight in the company of the wicked. He delights in God's word (*'the law of the LORD'*) and meditates in it (2). How often do you meditate upon God's word, apart from the brief time when you read your Bible each day? The godly man is like a strong, fruitful tree (3). He is a picture of stability and he bears precious fruit (cp. Galatians 5:22-23). **The Lord will prosper your way as you count your blessings, delight yourself in his word and meditate upon it.**

The psalmist goes on to contrast the ungodly with the righteous. The ungodly are unstable (4). They will be condemned on the day of judgment and will not be able to enter heaven to be *in the congregation of the righteous* (5). Their way shall perish, but the way of the godly is blessed by the smile of the Lord (6). The psalm begins with the word *'blessed'* and ends with the word *'perish'*. Two ways and two destinies. Are you *in the congregation of the righteous*? If you are not, come to the Lord Jesus and ask him to forgive your sins and save you. As you trust in him and obey him you will know God's blessing upon your life.

Blessed are all those who put their trust in him

Dale Ralph Davis observes: 'Psalm 1 deals with the most urgent individual matter; you must know where you are going and must be sure you belong to the congregation of the righteous. Psalm 2 says that you must know where history is going' (*The way of the righteous in the muck of life*, pages 27-28). Spurgeon called this psalm 'the Psalm of Messiah the Prince'. It divides into four sections:

Verses 1-3:   The nations raging and speaking.
Verses 4-6:   The Lord in heaven laughing and speaking in his wrath.
Verses 7-9:   The Son of God ('*his Anointed*' or 'Messiah') speaking.
Verses 10-12:   The psalmist speaks, appealing to the rulers to humble themselves before God.

The psalm opens with a question, *Why do the heathen rage ... ?* How futile for them to oppose the Lord and *his Anointed* (Jesus). This refrain was taken up by the church at Jerusalem when persecuted by the Sanhedrin (Acts 4:25-26). The puny opposition of men against God and his people brings laughs of derision from the Almighty. *He who sits in the heavens shall laugh* (4). God is quite undisturbed by the raging of the wicked and he has set his King on his holy hill of Zion (6). He cannot be toppled from his throne.

We can take great encouragement from the fact that Christ is King and that no weapon formed against the child of God shall prosper (Isaiah 54:17). He will come again to severely punish all who oppose him (Revelation 2:27; 6:12-17; 19:11-16). Verse 7 is quoted in Acts 13:33 and Hebrews 1:5. The wrath of God will come upon all who reject Christ. If you are not a Christian, take to your own heart the psalmist's words to the kings of the earth: *Be wise ... serve the* LORD *with fear ... Kiss* [a sign of obeisance and humility] *the Son, lest he be angry . ... Blessed are all those who put their trust in him* (10-12). **Are you reverently serving the Lord? Have you put your trust in him?**

The law of the LORD is perfect, converting the soul

Psalm 19 is divided into two parts which deal with two different ways in which God reveals himself to men. Two great truths about revelation are set before us:

- Natural Revelation: In nature — in the works of God (1-6). The universe and the earth with their beauty and wonders reveal to man that there is a God. There is no excuse for atheism which is folly (Psalm 14:1), nor for agnosticism which believes that we cannot know whether or not there is a God. *The heavens declare the glory of God* (1; cp. Romans 1:20). God's handiwork is there for all to see; it is a universal language which even the most primitive man can understand (3-4).

- Special Revelation: In the Bible which is the word of God (7-14). The world around us tells us that there is a Creator, that there is a God, but it cannot tell us how to get right with God or how we can know God. The Lord has not left us to grope in ignorance, however. He has given us the Bible. Look at the descriptions of the word of God: *the law of the LORD ... the testimony of the LORD, etc.* (7-9). It is through God's word that the soul is converted, is made wise, is enlightened (7-8). God's word is *perfect ... sure ... right ... pure ... clean ... true and righteous.* God's word is more precious than pure gold (10). How much do you desire to know it and to obey it?

God's word reveals to us the sin in our lives, sending rays of light into the darkest recesses of our hearts. It will lead us to pray, *Cleanse me from secret faults. Keep back your servant also from presumptuous sins* (12-13). As we begin the day, let us meditate upon this lovely psalm and rejoice in its truths.

Let the words of my mouth and the meditation of my heart be acceptable in your sight, O LORD, my strength and my Redeemer (14).

The Lord is my Shepherd; I shall not want

Are you able to recite Psalm 23 by heart? If not, be determined to memorize this psalm which has been a source of comfort for God's people throughout the ages. Never let its familiarity rob you of its richness. I want particularly to direct your thoughts to the significance of the opening words, *The Lord is my shepherd; I shall not want.* This wonderful promise is for every believer! There is no want (lack) for those who fear the Lord and seek him (Psalm 34:9-10). Consider what this means to us:

- He provides for us, supplying all our spiritual and material needs (2; cp. Philippians 4:19).
- He leads us (2-3).
- He restores us when we stray from him (3).
- He comforts us in the dark valley experiences (4).
- He protects us (5).
- He causes our *'cup'* to overflow with blessings (5-6).
- He has secured our future in heaven (6).

The Lord Jesus Christ, our good shepherd, purchased these blessings for us at tremendous cost. He laid down his life for his sheep (John 10:11,15,17; cp. Romans 8:32). Are you one of the Lord's sheep? His sheep hear his voice and they follow him in joyful obedience (John 10:3-4). **Have you lost your Christian joy through coldness of heart, through backsliding? Return to your shepherd who will lovingly restore your soul.**

If you are not a Christian, come to the Lord Jesus Christ, repenting of your sin, trusting only in him to save you. You will then be able to say, *'The Lord is my shepherd; I shall not want.'*

> He is my refuge in each deep distress;
> The Lord my strength and glorious righteousness;
> Through floods and flames he leads me safely on,
> And daily makes his sovereign goodness known.
>
> (William Gadsby)

Do not fret

This is an acrostic psalm which tells us three times, *'Do not fret'* (1,7,8). To fret is to worry, to be agitated within, to be vexed. It is right that we should be deeply concerned at the rising tide of wickedness around us, but it is possible to become so obsessed with wicked people and their deeds that we turn our eyes away from the Lord. We will then fret and become depressed. What is the antidote to keep us from fretting?

1. We must enjoy daily fellowship with God:
    *   *Trust in the* L ORD *... and do good; ... and feed on his faithfulness* (3). Look to the faithful God and you will not fret.
    *   *Delight yourself also in the* L ORD *and he shall give you the desires of your heart* (4). This is a wonderful promise, but it is important to note that when we delight ourselves in the Lord, our desires will be God-centred rather than self-centred.
    *   *Commit your way to the* L ORD (5). The Hebrew says, 'Roll your way upon the L ORD.' Your cares may be too heavy to carry; roll all of them upon God and trust in him.
    *   *Rest in the* L ORD *and wait patiently for him* (7). Be calm, be patient. God's time is the best time.
    *   *Cease from anger and forsake wrath; do not fret — it only causes harm* (8).

2. We should also consider the end of the wicked. *They shall soon be cut down* and *cut off* by God, the righteous Judge (2,9,28). Do not fret at the wicked. They have no future (38).

3. Consider the blessings of the righteous:
    *   Past blessings (25).
    *   Present blessings (16,23-24).
    *   Future blessings (11,18-19,22,28-29,34,37,39-40).

Are you agitated within? Are you fretting? Oh, let the precious words of this psalm be impressed on your mind! Let them sink into your heart. Meditate on them, rejoice in them, and you will soon find that fretting will give way to praise.

The sacrifices of God are a broken spirit

The title of this psalm indicates that David wrote it after he had been confronted by the prophet Nathan following his adultery with Bathsheba (2 Samuel 12:1-15). He was under great conviction for his sin and he truly repented. What is the evidence of true repentance?

- A plea for mercy based on the fact of the *loving-kindness* of God and according to the multitude of his *tender mercies* (1). Think of that! God's mercy is so great that there is a multitude of tender mercies to deal with a multitude of sins.
- A desire for forgiveness and for a thorough cleansing from sin (2, 7,9-10).
- A frank confession of sin with no excuses (3).
- A sense of the enormity of sin. It is not only against those we have wronged, but also against God (4).
- A recognition that we sin because it is our nature to sin. We were *'brought forth in iniquity'* (5).

We should be deeply troubled when we sin. Sin will destroy our testimony and it will silence our lips. When God restores the joy of our salvation our mouths are opened to teach transgressors the ways of God and to praise him (12-15). Have you lost the joy of your salvation (12)? Is it because of sin? Oh, confess that sin to God, and repent of it.

The blood of Christ cleanses us from all sin (1 John 1:7,9) but there are sacrifices that God wants from you. *The sacrifices of God are a broken spirit, a broken and a contrite heart — these, O God, you will not despise* (17). There is a false gospel which is influencing many evangelicals today; it is the gospel of self-esteem. The answer to the needs of sinners is not self-esteem, but a broken heart for sin. **When our sin breaks our heart, we will not lightly sin again.** The previous psalm, Psalm 50, refers to the sacrifice of praise (Psalm 50:14,23), but there is also the sacrifice of a contrite heart. Such sacrifices God will not despise, but will accept according to the multitude of his tender mercies.

Blessed be the LORD God ... who only does wondrous things

Spurgeon suggests that David, near to his end, prayed for Solomon his son who committed these words to writing: 'It is, we conjecture, the Prayer of David, but the Psalm of Solomon' (see title and also verse 20). The psalm begins with a prayer for God to give his *judgments* ('justice') to the king and his righteousness to the king's son (1). Our attention is directed to a greater King, however. Verses 2 to 17 foretell the coming of David's greater Son, the Messiah, the Lord Jesus Christ. Isaac Watts based his hymn, 'Jesus shall reign where'er the sun doth his successive journeys run' on this passage of Scripture. Let us think about the reign of Christ:

- He will bring justice to God's people and save them from oppression (2-4,12-14).
- The righteous will flourish and enjoy peace under his rule (5-7).
- He will reign over the whole world; rulers will bring tribute to him *and all nations shall serve him* (8-11).
- Prayer will be made for him and people will praise him (15).
- He will remove the curse from the earth so that an abundant harvest will be gathered from mountain-tops (16; cp. Genesis 3:17-19).
- His reign will continue for ever and people of all nations will be blessed in him and will call him blessed (17). This is a fulfilment of the promise given by God to Abraham (Genesis 12:1-3).

The psalm ends on a great note of praise to God: *Blessed be the LORD God, the God of Israel, who only does wondrous things! And blessed be his glorious name for ever! And let the whole earth be filled with his glory. Amen and Amen* (18-19).

The Lord Jesus will come again in great power and majesty and he will destroy all his enemies. He will then rule for ever over a world from which the curse has been removed, when there will be everlasting peace and joy (cp. Revelation 21:3-4; 22:3). **The thought of this filled the psalmist with praise. Does it thrill you? Are you looking forward to the coming of the Lord Jesus?**

Let the beauty of the LORD our God be upon us

The hymn, 'Our God our help in ages past', is based on this psalm whose title states that it is 'a prayer of Moses the man of God'. A man of God is certain to be a man of prayer and Moses was known for his life of intercessory prayer (Exodus 32:9-14,30-32; Jeremiah 15:1).

How does Moses pray? He begins with worship, remembering that God is eternal. He has always been, he is, and he will always be. *Before the mountains were brought forth, or ever you had formed the earth and the world, even from everlasting to everlasting, you are God* (2; cp. Revelation 4:8). We often comment that 'time flies', but to the eternal God a thousand years pass like a day (4; cp. 2 Peter 3:8). By way of contrast man's life is so short and God returns our body to destruction in the grave, to dust (3); 'God resolves and man dissolves' (Spurgeon). We may live seventy or eighty years (10) but we soon pass away (5-6) like:

A flood — flowing, growing, going. *Grass* — sown, grown, mown.

Moses also remembers that God is holy and that he is angry with sinners. We cannot hide our sins from him (7-8). Time is short and precious and we should often take up the prayer, *'So teach us to number our days, that we may gain a heart of wisdom'* (12). We need always to make the best use of our time (Ephesians 5:16) in living to please God and to work for him.

Moses calls upon God for mercy and asks that he will let his work appear to his servants and that his glory will be seen by their children (16). The beauty of God must be seen in our lives if we wish to see him establish our work (17). The Hebrew word translated beauty means 'pleasantness' or 'delightfulness' (cp. Psalm 27:4). **Biblical holiness is attractive and delightful, never a miserable thing. May our lives radiate the beauty of the Lord Jesus.** *Let the beauty of the LORD our God be upon us* (17).

I will be with him in trouble

Psalm 90 begins by reminding us that the everlasting God is our *dwelling place* (1; cp. verse 9) In this psalm we are reminded of the priceless privilege of the child of God who dwells in the secret place of the Most High (1). He overshadows us with his almighty love and though he does not promise to keep us from illness or danger, we know that he is in control of all our circumstances. He does promise to be with us in our deepest troubles, though we do not necessarily feel his presence (15). The Most High God is our habitation (9) and whoever attacks us attacks God. Dare Satan and his wicked demons attack us? The Lord has charged his angels to care for us and to keep us in all our ways (11; cp. Psalm 34:7; Hebrews 1:13-14). Those who have set their love on God are given precious promises in verses 14 to 16. He promises to deliver and honour, to answer prayer, to be with them in trouble, to give them satisfaction and salvation.

Christian, are you anxious and troubled? Take heart, the Most High God is with you. He lovingly and tenderly watches over you and says of you, *'I will be with him in trouble'* (15). Trust in him, he cannot fail. In his comments on verses 9 and 10 Spurgeon writes, 'It is impossible that any ill should happen to the man who is beloved of the Lord; the most crushing calamities can only shorten his journey and hasten him to his reward. Ill to him is no ill, but only good in a mysterious form. Losses enrich him, sickness is his medicine, reproach is his honour, death is his gain. No evil in the strict sense of the word can happen to him, for everything is overruled for good. Happy is he who is in such a case. He is secure where others are in peril, he lives where others die' (*The treasury of David*).

My volumes of *The treasury of David* were signed and presented by Spurgeon to a friend in 1887. These words must have been a great blessing to the man twenty-two years later. He pencilled in the margin, 'My heart says, "Amen" with 10,000 "Hallelujahs". This is my experience, 13-10-1909.' **God's promises are still the same for you. *I will be with him in trouble.***

Serve the LORD with gladness

We sing this well-known psalm with the words, 'All people that on earth do dwell, sing to the Lord with cheerful voice ... ' It is a great little psalm which tells us how we should praise God and why we should praise him:

- Let us be joyful in our praise (1). Worshippers were encouraged to go to the temple with *a joyful shout* and to serve him with gladness (cp. Psalms 95:1-6; 98:4-6). It is a sad reflection on many of us that the dirge-like singing and the miserable looks on some of our faces as we praise God are more suited to a funeral lament than the worship of the living God. Matthew Henry comments, 'Gospel worshippers should be joyful worshippers.'
- Let us be thoughtful in our worship (3). *Know that the LORD, he is God; it is he who has made us.* Any form of worship that discourages thoughtfulness or the use of the mind is spurious. 'Knowledge is the mother of devotion, and of all obedience ... Know it; consider and apply it, and then you will be more close and constant, more inward and serious, in the worship of him' (Matthew Henry).
- Let us be thankful in our praise (4). *Enter into his gates with thanksgiving ... Be thankful to him.*

Why should we praise God? The Lord is worthy of our adoration and praise because:

- He *is good.*
- Because *his mercy is everlasting.* It will never be exhausted.
- Because *his truth endures to all generations* (5). It does not change and it will not fail us.

How do you worship the Lord? Is your heart overflowing with joyful praise to him? *Serve the LORD with gladness; come before his presence with singing* (2; cp. Psalm 95:2).

Bless the Lord, O my soul!

This psalm begins and ends with *'Bless the Lord, O my soul!'* There is all the difference in the world between God's blessing men and men's blessing God. When God blesses men, he bestows favour and mercies upon them. When men bless God, they speak well of him, adoring him for his greatness, praising him for all his blessings. In this latter sense, blessing is the opposite of cursing. Psalm 103 is a call for us to bless God for all that he is and for all that he does for us. The hymn,'Praise, my soul, the King of heaven' is based on this psalm.

Are your prayers just 'shopping lists' comprising 'Lord, bless so-and-so and please bless me'? Your prayer life would be much richer if you started to *'bless the Lord'* and to open your heart to worship him with all your being (1).

- *Bless the Lord* because he has forgiven all your sins, healing you, redeeming you, and what a crown he places upon your head (3-4, 12)! His blessings are far more precious than the Crown Jewels.
- *Bless the Lord* because he has made us his children even though we are dust, and he lovingly cares for us (13-14).
- *Bless the Lord* because he is righteous and just, because he is a merciful and gracious God, and he reigns supreme (6-19).

If all the angels and the heavenly hosts are called upon to bless the Lord (20-21) how much more we poor sinners, saved by his matchless grace and so abundantly blessed.

Bless the Lord, O my soul!

Some years ago, I visited a member of our church, who was dying. This dear lady had not spoken all day and I read the first fourteen verses of this psalm to her. In her weakness, she struggled to speak and she then exclaimed, *'Bless the Lord, O my soul!'* She departed peacefully to be with her Lord a couple of hours later.

The LORD is your keeper

We live in a very uncertain world and millions of people consult horoscopes. Some claim that it is 'just for fun', but they open themselves to occult influences. Many really do believe that the position of the stars and planets at a given time holds the key to their future. What nonsense! How can the stars guide us or determine our 'fate'? Psalm 121 is our answer to horoscopes.

The psalmist looked out at the hills around Jerusalem (1), knowing that *as the mountains surround Jerusalem, so the LORD surrounds his people* (Psalm 125:2). How can we be confident in the face of an unknown future? This psalm tells us: *'The LORD is your keeper'* (5). The words *'keep'*, *'keeper'*, and *'preserve'* come from the same Hebrew word and are found in every verse, except verses 1 and 6. Let us think about the One who keeps us:

- Our help *comes from the LORD, who made heaven and earth* (2). We do not trust in the stars, but in the One who made them (Psalm 8:3; Isaiah 40:25-26).
- Our help *comes from the LORD*, who keeps our feet steady in the dangerous and difficult paths of life (3). A traveller in the mountainous regions of Israel would need to be sure-footed, lest he tumble to his death. The moving or slipping of the foot indicates being in a situation of great danger (cp. Psalm 38:16; Psalm 73:2).
- Our help *comes from the LORD, who* never slumbers nor sleeps (3-4). In distressing times we may feel that God is distant and perhaps unaware of our trials. Not so! *He who keeps you will not slumber* (3).
- The Lord will protect us day and night (5-6). He will preserve us from all evil and keep us in all our ways for evermore (7-8).

The Lord will never let us go nor let us down. **Christian, are you being sorely tested and tried? Lift up your eyes to the Lord. He will never fail you. Your sovereign Protector lovingly cares for you. Come to him and cast** *all your care upon him, for he cares for you* **(1 Peter 5:7). Hallelujah!**

The LORD has done great things for us, whereof we are glad

We do not know when this lovely psalm was written but many commentators believe that it was after the return of the exiles from Babylon. The collapse of the Babylonian empire and the release from captivity brought great joy. The laughter and singing of the returning exiles was observed by the Gentiles who acknowledged the hand of God upon them saying. *'The LORD has done great things for them'* (1-2). The joyful Israelites took up the same refrain, *'The LORD has done great things for us, whereof we are glad'* (3). Spurgeon comments, 'The Lord who alone turns our captivity does nothing by halves: those whom he saves from hell he brings to heaven. He turns exile into ecstasy, and banishment into bliss' (*The treasury of David*).

The returning exiles soon encountered opposition when they began rebuilding the temple and the walls of Jerusalem. They discovered that God's work brings Satanic-inspired opposition (see the books of Ezra and Nehemiah). How true this is of the Christian life. At conversion we have the experience of forgiveness and acceptance by God, of deliverance from the power and pollution of sin. We have the joy of new-found fellowship with God and with his people. This may seem too good to be true and cause us to wonder whether we are dreaming or not (see verse 1). We then face the battles of the Christian life and Satanic attacks and know discouragement and disappointment, but if we *sow in tears we shall reap in joy* (5).

If we love the Lord we cannot be indifferent to the plight of the lost. We will want to win souls for Christ. We can read all the best books on personal evangelism and soul-winning and seek to put what we learn into practice and still lack success. If that is so, could it be that we rarely weep? Spurgeon comments, 'Winners of souls are first weepers for souls.' **When did you last weep before the Lord over the plight of the lost?** Have you been discouraged in your work for God? Do not give up. Remember what the Lord has done in the past and be encouraged. *The LORD has done great things for us, whereof we are glad.*

Great is the LORD, and greatly to be praised

This is an acrostic psalm, the verses beginning with successive letters of the Hebrew alphabet except for the letter 'nun'. The verse with the missing letter is supplied in the Septuagint and in the Dead Sea Scroll manuscripts; it is included in the English Standard Version of the Bible, being added to verse 13. In this psalm David extols and blesses God. He blesses God for:

- His greatness (1-6). How sad that many extremely intelligent people worship useless idols or venerate images. The only true God is the triune God, Father, Son and Holy Spirit, whom we worship. *Great is the LORD, and greatly to be praised; and his greatness is unsearchable* (3; cp. Psalm 48:1). God is awesome in his person and in his mighty acts. How good it is to meditate on the *glorious splendour* of his majesty (4-6).
- His goodness (7-10). God is not only great in all his majesty and works, but also in his goodness. He *is gracious and full of compassion, slow to anger and great in mercy. The LORD is good to all* and yet most people do not acknowledge his goodness.
- The *glorious majesty of his kingdom* (11-13). What a marvellous kingdom it is and what a privilege it is to belong to this everlasting, righteous kingdom. We owe so much to our King who loved us and died on the cross to save us from our sins.
- His gracious works (14-21). He upholds those who fall (14) and he meets our needs (15-16). *He is near to all who call upon him* and he hears them (17-18). *He will fulfil the desire of those who fear him* (19) and he *preserves all who love him* (20). Dear believer, think about these precious promises. They are for you if you are walking with God.

When we think about these things, our hearts should overflow with praise. Let us declare his greatness and sing of his righteousness (6-7). *Great is the LORD, and greatly to be praised.*

PROVERBS

Most of the proverbs in the Book of Proverbs came from King Solomon (1:1). No doubt they were among the three thousand proverbs spoken by him (1 Kings 4:32). The Hebrew word translated 'proverb' ('*mashal*') 'indicates a brief, pithy saying which expresses wisdom' (E. J. Young). They are 'short sentences drawn from long experiences'. The Book of Proverbs has been described as 'Laws from heaven for life on earth' (William Arnot). This is the third of the poetical books, with parallelism being used many times (e.g. 1:7-8; see introduction to the Psalms). Many commentators believe that Proverbs 8:22-31 speaks of Christ who is *the wisdom of God* (1 Corinthians 1:24,30), *in whom are hidden all the treasures of wisdom and knowledge* (Colossians 2:3).

The purpose of the book is *to know wisdom and instruction* (1:2). Paul wrote, *Do not be unwise, but understand what the will of the Lord is* (Ephesians 5:17). The Book of Proverbs will help us to be wise.

Some themes from Proverbs

P ride and its dangers:	6:16-17; 8:13; 11:2; 13:10; 16:18; 20:6; 27:2; 29:23.
R ecognizing a fool:	1:7; 12:15-16,23; 13:20; 14:9; 17:24; 18:2-7; 19:1; 20:3; 23:9.
O pen-handedness:	3:9-10; 11:24-25; 13:7; 19:6,17; 22:9; 28:27.
V irtuous wife:	12:4; 18:22; 19:14; 31:10-31.
E vil woman:	2:16-19; 5:3-20; 6:24-26; 7:5-27; 22:14; 30:20.
R espect for parents:	1:8-9; 6:20-21; 13:1; 15:20; 19:26; 30:17.
B ad company:	1:10-19; 4:14-19; 13:20; 24:1-2; 29:24.
S loth or idleness:	6:6-11; 10:4-5; 13:4; 18:9; 20:4; 21:25; 24:30-34.

The fear of the LORD is the beginning of knowledge

If you are a Christian, you should desire to be wise. The Book of Proverbs will point you in the right direction. We obtain wisdom through receiving *'instruction'* (3). The word *'instruction'* (2-3,7) is also translated *'chastening'* (3:11) and it carries the idea of discipline and training. We all need spiritual wisdom because it has a vital bearing on our behaviour and character (3; cp. James 3:17-18). *'Justice'* (3) means 'rightness', *'judgment'* is the same as discernment, and *'equity'* is fairness. We all need to do what is right, to have discernment and to be fair in our attitude to others if we are to have *'prudence'* (the ability to act wisely and sensibly, 4).

Discipline alone is not enough, however. We must know the fear of God in our lives — *The fear of the LORD is the beginning of knowledge* (7; cp. 9:10). In his *Commentary on Proverbs* (published by The Banner of Truth Trust), Charles Bridges describes *'the fear of the LORD'* as 'that affectionate reverence, by which the child of God bends himself humbly and carefully to his Father's law'. If you know the fear and instruction of the Lord in your life you will acquire more wisdom than the man with the brightest intellect who despises God.

The training of children is the responsibility of both parents (8). Fathers must not opt out but must take the lead. I write to Christian men. Are you leading family worship in your home, teaching God's word and instructing your family in Christian living? What kind of example are you to your children? We must warn our children against the enticement of sinners (10). We must teach them that the godless materialism found around us is not pleasing to the Lord (19).

Wisdom is personified in verses 20 to 33. She cries out to be heard and warns us not to be foolish by despising wisdom and instruction (7) or by hating knowledge (22). To refuse wisdom is to travel on a road which leads to terror and destruction (24-32). Wisdom promises, *'Whoever listens to me will dwell safely, and will be secure without fear of evil'* (33).

Trust in the Lord with all your heart

Notice the tender appeal of father to son throughout the Book of Proverbs (*'My son'* — 1:8,10,15; 2:1; 3:1,11,21, etc.). God speaks to us through his word as a loving father speaking to his son (1). There are some very basic lessons about practical Christian living in this chapter.

- Obey God's word. *But let your heart keep my commands* (1). We need to read God's word, meditate on it and obey it.
- Hold fast to *mercy and truth* and do not allow them to forsake you. *Write them on the tablet of your heart* (3). They are inseparable twins (see Psalms 25:10; 85:10; 89:14; 100:5; 117:2; Micah 7:20). We must love mercy as much as we love truth. We are merciful when we have compassion on needy fellow-Christians and help those in need (Colossians 3:12-14; 1 John 3:16-17).
- *Trust in the Lord with all your heart, and lean not on your own understanding* (5). This does not contradict the command to seek the understanding linked with wisdom and the fear of God (2:2-4,11). It is trusting in God when we are bewildered and can find no rational answer to God's dealings with us. If we lean on our own understanding and are wise in our own eyes (7) at such times, we will sink in despair.
- *In all your ways acknowledge him, and he shall direct your paths* (6). The Hebrew word translated *'acknowledge'* is usually translated *'know'* (e.g. 4:1,19; 27:1). We must know God in the home, at work, in serving him, in suffering, in grief or in prosperity.
- *Fear the Lord and depart from evil* (7).
- *Honour the Lord with your possessions.* We must be generous in our giving if we would know God's blessing (9-10; 27-28).
- *My son, do not despise the chastening of the Lord* (11). Remember that the Lord corrects us because he loves us and delights in us (12; cp. Hebrews 12:5-11).

Notice the stress on *'heart'* religion (1,3,5). **If we are right in heart, we will know the enjoyment and blessing of God in our lives. We will be content and a blessing to others.**

Keep your heart with all diligence

We are again reminded of the need for parents to instruct their children from the word of God and to set them a godly example (1,11). We must give our children *good doctrine,* teaching them to obey the word of God (2-4). This is vital for their spiritual well-being. Solomon remembered how his father David had taught him the value of wisdom and understanding (4-9). *Wisdom is the principal thing; therefore get wisdom, and in all your getting, get understanding* (7). We live in confusing and evil times and strange doctrines and practices are found in many churches that profess to be evangelical. We obtain wisdom and understanding from knowing and obeying the Word of God.

The way of the righteous is contrasted with the way of the wicked (10-19). We must not enter the path of the wicked which is a way of evildoing, of darkness and ignorance (16-17,19). *But the path of the just is like the shining sun, that shines ever brighter unto the perfect day* (18). We know the presence, care and direction of God when we walk this blessed path. It is a path which leads us to love, honour and enjoy God. **The path of the just is a clean and wholesome path that leads to heaven. Are you on it?**

We must watch our hearts, our lips, our eyes and our feet (24-27). *Keep your heart with all diligence* (23). Charles Bridges describes the heart as 'the citadel of man — the seat of his dearest treasure. It is fearful to think of its many watchful and subtle assailants ... here Satan keeps — here therefore must we keep special watch. If the citadel is taken, the whole town must surrender. If the heart be seized, the whole man — the affections, desires, motives, pursuits — all will be yielded up' (*Commentary on Proverbs*). The heart is a spring out of which spring both sin and holiness (Matthew 12:34-35). The unregenerate heart is a fountain of poison, the purified heart a well of living water (Matthew 15:19; John 4:14). **We are prone to wander from God and to grow cold towards the Lord Jesus Christ.** *Keep your heart with all diligence, for out of it spring the issues of life* (23).

Things the LORD hates

The Book of Proverbs warns us against pledging ourselves as a surety for others who borrow money, whether they are friends or strangers (1-5; cp. 11:15; 17:18; 22:26). Many people have lived to regret taking on such a liability and have brought financial ruin upon themselves and their family. There are those who readily borrow and who rashly spend, even among professing Christians. Let these verses also be a warning against taking on excessive financial commitments for ourselves. We are encouraged in our 'consumer society' to load ourselves with debt. We should ask ourselves, 'Do I really need whatever it is I want to purchase and cannot presently afford? Do I have the means to pay off the loan? Will my Christian life suffer because I will have to work excessive hours of overtime to pay off the loan? Will God's work suffer because my giving will be reduced?' We must live within our means, not beyond them.

Ants are a nuisance when they invade our homes but they are a great example to us in their prudent, hard-working way of life. *Go to the ant, you sluggard!* (6-11). There are a number of warnings against the sin of laziness in Proverbs. If you are unemployed, you can still find plenty of voluntary work to do. The church needs workers.

Look at the *things the LORD hates* and which are *an abomination to him* (16-19). He not only hates the sin of murder but also pride, lying and trouble-making. **If we sow discord among our brothers and sisters in the church (19), we will reap a terrible harvest of bitter strife and division. Be determined to shun these things that God hates.**

There are many warnings against adultery and immorality in Proverbs, some of them being found in verses 20 to 35. This wicked world would seek to persuade us that sex outside of marriage and adultery are quite acceptable. They are not. Adultery begins in the heart (25; cp. Matthew 5:27-28). If we entertain sexually immoral thoughts, we play with fire. A sure antidote to the sins of the heart is to hide God's word there (21-24; cp. Psalm 119:11). Let us always order our lives by his word.

10 SEPTEMBER   **Proverbs 8:1-36**

Whoever finds me finds life

There are many voices that seek to entice us away from God but their way is the way of death and hell. In this chapter wisdom is personalized. She cries out to be heard, especially by the simple who are so easily seduced by sinners (1-5). We have already seen that true wisdom is obtained through knowing God's word and through diligently applying it to our lives. The translators of the New King James Version have entitled this chapter 'The Excellence of Wisdom'. This excellence is seen in:

• Wisdom's words (6-8). Wisdom speaks of excellent things, of right things, and of truth and righteousness. If we have spiritual wisdom, we will shun all wicked or perverse talk, and be gracious and kind in our speech.
• Wisdom's worth (10-11,17-21). Many people spend all their time and energy in the pursuit of money or possessions but very few seek after wisdom. If we diligently seek wisdom, we will find it (17) and its blessings are priceless (cp. 3:13-18). To find spiritual wisdom is to obtain *favour from the LORD* (35).
• Wisdom's ways (12-17). Wisdom, prudence and the fear of the Lord go together. To have wisdom is to hate pride, arrogance and every wicked way.
• Wisdom's warning (33,36). Those who hate wisdom love death. If we despise and scorn the wisdom of God, we will harm our own soul and choose death. It is not only folly to reject God's word, it is death (36; cp. John 5:40). If you are not a Christian, I urge you, *'Forsake foolishness and live'* (9:6). Come to Christ who says, *'Whoever finds me finds life'* (35).

It is difficult to avoid the conclusion that verses 22 to 36 speak of the Lord Jesus Christ. He is called the wisdom of God (1 Corinthians 1:24,30; cp. Colossians 2:3). He is the eternal Son of God, begotten by the Father (23-25). He is the master craftsman by whom the worlds were made and in whom God the Father delights (30; cp. John 1:1-3; Colossians 1:16; Matthew 3:17; 17:5).

295

11 SEPTEMBER

Proverbs 10:1-32

The desire of the righteous will be granted

A new section of the book, called 'The Proverbs of Solomon', begins with this chapter and runs through to chapter 22, verse 16. This chapter, like others in Proverbs, has a number of contrasts between the righteous and the wicked. Notice the number of times the word *'righteous'* is found in this chapter. The Lord has chosen us and called us to be holy (Ephesians 1:4; 1 Peter 1:15-16). Let us think of some of the blessings of the righteous:

- His righteousness delivers from death (2).
- He knows the smile of God upon his life. *Blessings are on the head of the righteous* (6) and the Lord lovingly provides for him (3).
- He leaves his mark long after he dies. *The memory of the righteous is blessed* (7). Most of us remember with great affection and thankfulness godly Christians, now with the Lord, who led us to the Saviour, or who helped us to grow in our knowledge of Christ.
- His work *leads to life* and is not in vain (16; cp. 1 Corinthians 15:58).
- *The desire of the righteous will be granted* (24; cp. Psalm 37:4). Mind you, he is not taken up with selfish desires, but he seeks the honour of God and he is submissive to God's will (1 John 5:14-15).
- *The hope of the righteous will be gladness* (28). Godly living brings lasting joy and contentment in this life and in the world to come! Where are you looking for your satisfaction? **Are you seeking first the kingdom of God and his righteousness (Matthew 6:33)?**

The righteous man has a teachable spirit (8,17). He is not a know-all who refuses to listen to the counsel of others (Psalm 32:8-9). He is gracious in his speech (32) and he brings blessing through his words (11,20-21,31). He has an everlasting foundation (9,25,30; cp. Matthew 7:25) which gives him stability in his life. The godly person is not easily shaken by false teaching or by times of trial when his faith may be sorely tested.

296

A wholesome tongue is a tree of life

God sees all things and nothing escapes his eyes (3,11). It is a great encouragement to the Christian that we are never out of the sight of the Lord who lovingly watches over us.

God also hears all things. We were reminded yesterday that our words have much power for good or for evil and we need to control our tongues. The soft answer is far more effective than the fierce words of a lashing tongue (1). *A wholesome* [healing] *tongue is a tree of life* (4) that speaks a word *in due season* (23). The Hebrew word translated *'wholesome'* (4) means 'healing'; it is elsewhere translated *'healing'* (Malachi 4:2) and *'health'* (4:22; 12:18; 13:17; 16:24). Do your words bring healing and encouragement to some needy soul or do they hurt and wound? Before we speak about others, we should ask ourselves, 'Is it true? Is it helpful? Is it necessary? Is it kind?' God hears all that we say and we will be judged for our words (Luke 12:3). Let us at all times seek to have healing tongues.

Religion without righteousness is useless. *The sacrifice of the wicked is an abomination to the Lord, but the prayer of the upright is his delight* (8). God will hear the prayer of the repenting sinner, but not the prayers of those who have no intention of obeying his word. The Lord delights in the prayers of his children and he loves the person who follows after righteousness (8-9). If you are a Christian, that should give you great encouragement and incentive to pray. God wants us to seek him in prayer and to come to his throne of grace with our thanksgiving and requests. *He hears the prayer of the righteous* (29).

The fear of the Lord brings contentment, even in times of poverty (16-17). A contented heart is a priceless possession! Paul could write of his contentment though he was in prison (Philippians 4:11). *Godliness with contentment is great gain* (1 Timothy 6:6). **If you are restless and discontented, examine your life. Are you lacking in godliness?**

Buy the truth, and do not sell it

This chapter begins with a call for moderation in eating (1-3) and a warning against covetousness and miserliness (4-8). Scripture teaches us to have respect for the property of others. Ancient landmarks marked the boundaries of fields and evil men would often seek to remove such landmarks in order to seize land for themselves. Orphans and widows were particularly vulnerable to such predators. Landmarks were to be left intact and to remove them invited the curse of God (10-11; cp. 22:28; Deuteronomy 19:14; 27:17). The value of the 'rod' is again taught in verses 13 and 14 (cp. 13:24; 22:15; 29:15,17). The old saying, 'Spare the rod and spoil the child' still holds true! We must remember, however, that it is sinful to smack a child in a fit of anger. We must also recognize that there are other effective forms of punishment (e.g. depriving a wayward child of privileges).

We come under many pressures to compromise Christian truth. Verse 23 should be impressed on our hearts and fixed in our minds! — *Buy the truth, and do not sell it.* It is wicked to exchange the truth of God for a lie (Romans 1:25). Truth is not cheap! We may have to buy it at the expense of friends, job, reputation or even life. Though costly, it is a bargain because it never loses its value. It is the knowledge of the truth that brings freedom to sinners (John 8:32). Bridges observes, 'Those who sell the truth, sell their own souls with it.' **We must not sell the truth in order to obtain unity with those who deny the gospel or to gain acceptance with men.** *Buy the truth, and do not sell it.* Let us be bold and gracious, *speaking the truth in love* (Ephesians 4:15).

There are more warnings in this chapter against the misuse of strong drink. The person who is intoxicated with drink is in physical and moral danger (29-35). Drunkenness is sin (1 Corinthians 6:10; Galatians 5:21; Ephesians 5:18). It blocks the exercise of self-control (a fruit of the Holy Spirit — Galatians 5:23). We should not seek the company of drunkards or gluttons (20). We should seek the fellowship of God's people which is precious and delightful (Acts 2:41-42).

A woman who fears the LORD, *she shall be praised*

Most Bible commentators believe that King Lemuel is used as a pen name for King Solomon. He recalls the advice given to him by his mother (2). She warned him against loose-living and drunkenness (3-4) and taught him to speak up for the poor and needy who cannot speak for themselves (8-9).

Hebrew poetry sometimes uses acrostics, e.g. Psalm 119 which has twenty-two sets of eight verses, one set for each letter of the Hebrew alphabet. Proverbs closes with an acrostic poem which praises the virtues of a wise and godly wife (10-31). Matthew Henry comments, 'This description of the virtuous woman is designed to show what wives the women should make, and what wives the men should choose.' Physical beauty eventually fades, but the beauty of a godly life endures. Physical attraction does play a large part in our choice of spouse, but surely we must look first for the beauty of godliness (cp. 1 Peter 3:4).

The virtuous wife is a priceless treasure and rare. Such a wife is from the Lord (19:14) and her husband *safely trusts her* (11). She stands in beautiful contrast to the evil woman (e.g. 30:20,23). She does her husband good (12), she does her household good (13-15,21,27) and she does the poor and needy good (20). She is hard-working (13-19, 22,24,27), wise and kind (26). Her beauty is more than skin-deep (30) and her husband and family praise her (28-29). A good husband does not take his wife for granted and children should not be thoughtless but show their appreciation for their mother.

What is the secret of a godly and beautiful personality? We are directed to where we began in Proverbs — *the fear of the* LORD (30; cp. 1:7). *A woman who fears the* LORD, *she shall be praised* (30). Those who fear the Lord are blessed indeed (Psalm 112:1). As we leave the book of Proverbs, let us remind ourselves of Charles Bridges' definition of *the fear of the* LORD: 'It is that affectionate reverence, by which the child of God bends himself humbly and carefully to his Father's law.' **Do you have this kind of** *fear of the* LORD?

ECCLESIASTES

The Hebrew title of Ecclesiastes, 'Qoheleth', means one who addresses an assembly and is translated 'the Preacher'. The authorship of the book is disputed. Many (e.g. Charles Bridges, Stuart Olyott) believe that there are strong reasons to indicate that Solomon is the author (cp. 1:1,12; 2:7,9; 12:9). Those who would disagree (e.g. Derek Kidner) point out that Solomon's name is absent from the book, whereas he is named in Proverbs and in the Song of Solomon. Ecclesiastes is often misunderstood because it appears to be very pessimistic. The word 'vanity' ('meaningless', NIV) appears more than thirty times throughout the book.

Purpose of Ecclesiastes

The preacher looks at life 'under the sun' (1:3,9,14; 2:11,17-22, etc.) and demonstrates that life without God is utterly futile and meaningless. Human wisdom, science, achievements, possessions and pleasures do not satisfy man's deepest needs. 'All is vanity and grasping for the wind' (1:14; 2:11,17,26; 4:4,16; 6:9). Many years after Ecclesiastes was written, Augustine prayed, 'You have made us for yourself, and our hearts cannot find their rest until they find their rest in you' (*Confessions of Augustine*). Having demonstrated that man in his sin is lost, *having no hope and without God in the world* (Ephesians 2:12), the preacher directs our attention to our Creator (12:1). Our duty is to *fear God and keep his commandments* (12:13). This alone brings meaning to life and leads to lasting joy.

Vanity and grasping for the wind

The answer to the first question of the *Westminster Shorter Catechism* tells us we were made 'to glorify God, and to enjoy him for ever'. Life without God can prove to be very frustrating. Where can we find lasting satisfaction? Fun, laughter and wine (1-3), building fine houses and beautiful gardens with pools and orchards (4-6), acquiring many servants, having great herds and flocks (7) cannot satisfy our greatest need, which is spiritual. The possession of wealth and pleasure does not satisfy the deepest yearning of the heart. It is *vanity and grasping for the wind* (11). The British actor George Sanders took an overdose in April 1972. In his suicide note, he wrote, 'Dear world, I am leaving you because I am bored. I feel I have lived long enough. I am leaving you with your worries in this sweet cesspool — good luck!' He found that life had become meaningless to him and he could stand it no longer. How tragic!

The harsh facts of life can be very depressing — the wise man is not kept from dying any more than the fool; death reduces them to the same level (13-17). The Preacher considers work from the standpoint of a godless man and he exclaims, *'Therefore I hated life ... then I hated all my labour'* (17-18). A man may accumulate wealth by hard toil, but he cannot take it with him and who knows whether he may leave all to a son who is lazy and foolish or to someone who has not had to work to inherit his wealth (18-21)? Life without God is *'vanity and grasping for the wind'* (26).

Thank God that we know better! The Lord has provided the way of salvation for guilty, undeserving sinners through the death and resurrection of Christ. He gives us reconciliation to himself and lasting joy and peace (Ephesians 2:1-22; 1 Peter 1:8).

> Fading is the worldling's pleasure,
> All his boasted pomp and show;
> Solid joys and lasting treasure
> None but Zion's children know.   (John Newton)

Remember now your Creator

We must remember God now. The Book of Ecclesiastes shows that it is folly to forget God. The sooner we follow Christ and love and obey God, the better. *Remember now your Creator in the days of your youth, before the difficult days come* (1). The difficult days of old age are vividly described in picture language (2-7). Remember God while your mind is clear and receptive to light (*while the sun and the light, the moon and the stars, are not darkened*). Remember God before you have weak arms and trembling hands (*the keepers of the house*). Remember God before your legs (*the strong men*) become weak and before your teeth (*the grinders*) drop out. Remember God before your eyes (*windows*) grow dim, and before your ears (*doors*) shut with deafness. Remember God before the restless nights come, before the fear of *terrors in the way* come upon you. Remember God before you return to your eternal home when your body (*the dust*) will return to the earth and your soul meets God (7).

One of the heartaches of preaching regularly in an old people's home is to encounter those who have been hardened by years of living without God. They are on the brink of eternity but their minds are closed to, or unable to take in, the message of the gospel. Remember God now, before it is too late, or you will not be prepared for the day of judgment (14; cp. 11:9). How should we remember our Creator? *Fear God and keep his commandments, for this is the whole duty of man* (13). *For what is your life? It is even a vapour that appears for a little time and then vanishes away* (James 4:14). **Remember now your Creator ... before the difficult days come.**

> When as a child I laughed and wept, Time crept.
> When as a youth I waxed more bold, Time rolled.
> When I became a full-grown man, Time ran.
> When older still I daily grew, Time flew.
> Soon I shall find in passing on, Time gone.
> Will Christ have saved my soul by then? Amen.
>
> (Verse on the old clock in Chester Cathedral)

1 & 2 THESSALONIANS

After planting the church at Philippi, Paul and his companions went to Thessalonica. Paul preached in the synagogue and many were converted to Christ, both Jew and Gentile (Acts 17:1-9). Jewish opponents raised a mob to attack the apostles, but Paul and Silas escaped by night, going to the town of Berea. These events probably took place in the early summer of AD 50 and Paul wrote his first letter to the Thessalonians some nine to twelve months later.

Paul had been very concerned for the infant church which was suffering persecution. He had sent Timothy back to Thessalonica to encourage them, to establish them and to bring news of them to him (3:1-5). Timothy came to Paul (who by this time was in Corinth — Acts 18:5) with the good news that the Thessalonians were standing firm and making the gospel known despite persecution. He reported that some were needing further instruction concerning the second coming of Christ. Paul wrote to them as soon as he had received Timothy's report to encourage them and to deal with their problems.

Paul wrote his **second letter to the Thessalonians** soon after the first. They had not resolved their problems concerning the return of Christ. Some of them had understood the teaching that Christ would return suddenly (1 Thessalonians 5:2-3) to mean that he was to come back immediately. They had given up work and had become idle busybodies, living on the generosity of others (3:6, 11-12). Paul urged the Thessalonians to stand fast and hold the traditions (2:15) taught them by word and letter (there is nothing wrong with tradition firmly based upon God's word). He pointed out that certain events must precede the second coming of Christ (2:1-12) and he exhorted them to deal with the disorderly (3:6-15).

In God

The opening greetings in this letter are from Paul, Silvanus (Silas), and Timothy. Paul describes the Thessalonian church as being *in God the Father and the Lord Jesus Christ* (1; cp. 2 Thessalonians 1:1). Christians are also known as those who are *in Christ* (e.g. 2 Corinthians 5:17; Philippians 1:1). *Your life is hidden with Christ in God* (Colossians 3:3). Being 'in God' means that we are surrounded by the love and care of the Almighty. We can say with Moses, 'LORD, *you have been our dwelling place in all generations*' (Psalm 90:1).

The Christian is 'in God' because of his election by God (4). To realize that God graciously chose us in Christ before he created the world should cause us to worship him with much gratitude and praise (cp. Ephesians 1:3-6; 1 Peter 1:2-5). We must never think that God chose us because we deserved to be saved, nor because he foresaw that we would choose him. Such a view is not biblical and fails to understand the meaning of the word 'foreknowledge'. An evidence of being 'in God' is that we have turned to God from our sinful ways (9).

The Thessalonian church had been born in persecution and suffering (6; 2:14; 3:3-4; 2 Thessalonians 1:4-7; Acts 17:5-9) but they were 'in God' who is greater than any foe who dared oppose them. Undaunted by persecution they *sounded forth the word of the Lord* (8). **Being 'in God' makes all the difference in the world to our lives. Are you fearful? Are you facing problems and difficulties? Are you suffering ridicule, scorn and opposition as a Christian? Remember that you are 'in God' and take heart!**

> In heavenly love abiding,
> No change my heart shall fear;
> And safe is such confiding,
> For nothing changes here:
> The storm may roar without me,
> My heart may low be laid;
> But God is round about me,
> And can I be dismayed?
>
> (Anna L. Waring)

We were gentle among you

Paul now reminds the Thessalonians of the ministry of Silas, Timothy and himself among them. They had been witnesses of the high standards set by Paul and his fellow-workers (10; see also the expression *'as you know'* — verses 1,2,5,11; cp. 1:5).

The gospel is mentioned four times in these verses (2,4,8,9). They had enjoyed great success in their evangelism. What was their secret?

- They were bold to preach the gospel despite opposition, conflict, and persecution (2).
- They did not compromise their message to please men. *But as we have been approved by God to be entrusted with the gospel, even so we speak, not as pleasing men, but God who tests our hearts* (4).
- Their behaviour had always been beyond reproach (3,5-6). *You are witnesses, and God also, how devoutly and justly and blamelessly we behaved ourselves among you* (10).
- They were so zealous to make Christ known that they laboured and toiled night and day to pay for their own support as well as serving in the work of the gospel (9).
- They had a great love for those to whom they preached. This was seen in their attitude to the Thessalonians. They did not only share the gospel with them, but also their own lives (8). They were like loving parents. *We were gentle among you, just as a nursing mother cherishes her own children* (7). They had also *exhorted and comforted* every one of them *as a father does his own children* (11). Such an example is a great challenge to us in serving Christ. **We must be firm and unyielding in the face of error, but always gracious and gentle. Let us always seek to honour God by being approachable, kind and understanding to Christians and to unbelievers.**

Paul's aim in his ministry among the Thessalonians was that they *would have a walk worthy of God* (11-12). He calls us *into his own kingdom and glory* (12; cp. Romans 14:17). This is a call to holy living (4:7) and if we do not obey God, we are not walking worthy of him. Let us remember that we represent the Lord in all that we say and do.

We are appointed to this

Paul went on to Athens, leaving Silas and Timothy in Berea (Acts 17:14-15). When they joined him in Athens it was decided that Timothy should return to Thessalonica. They were very concerned for the infant church and they could *no longer endure* the suspense of not knowing how they were doing in the face of suffering (1,5). Timothy's mission was *to establish* the infant church, to *encourage* them concerning their faith, and to ascertain the state of their faith (2,5).

The Thessalonian church had been born in the face of persecution (cp. 1:6; 2:14). The apostles had warned them that they would suffer tribulation and they did not want this to disturb their faith (3-4). Some false teachers tell us that the Christian should be able to live above suffering and trouble but the Bible tells us, *'We are appointed to this'* (3; cp. John 15:20; 16:33; Acts 14:22; 2 Timothy 3:12; 1 Peter 4:12-13).

Some sects (e.g. Christadelphians) deny the existence of the devil as a person but this is a denial of the teaching of Scripture. The tempter (Satan) is always active! (cp. Matthew 4:1-11). If he cannot shake our faith by persecution, he will seek to entice us from God and into sin through temptation (5). **We are appointed to suffer with Christ, but we shall also reign with him (2 Timothy 2:12). When we understand this, we will not sink under suffering, but rather glory in it and be stronger for it (Romans 5:3-5).**

Timothy brought good news to Paul of the faith and love of the Thessalonians which greatly encouraged the apostle who was enduring affliction and distress through opposition at Corinth (6-7). He prayed that God would soon direct his way to them and that they would increase and abound in their love for each other (10-12) and in their sanctification (*'holiness'* — 13). The coming again of the Lord Jesus Christ is a great incentive for us to be holy (13; cp. 2 Peter 3:11-13; 1 John 3:2–3). Are you progressing in faith, love and holiness? Could your pastor write of you, *'We were comforted ... by your faith'* (7)?

We ... shall be caught up ... to meet the Lord in the air

Paul now returns to the theme of walking (living) to please God (1; cp. 2:12). How are we to please him? By obeying the commandments of the Lord Jesus (2).

- We must shun all forms of sexual immorality (3-8). This is a very timely warning as we live in a corrupt society where sexual immorality is tolerated and rarely condemned. Each of us must exercise control over his own body (*'vessel'*, cp. 2 Corinthians 4:7). We must not feed our minds on unclean things. The Lord has called us to holiness and if we reject this commandment, we reject God who has also given us his Holy Spirit (7-8).
- We must love each other (9).
- We must aim to lead quiet lives, not being lazy or busybodies, but rather getting on with our own work. This is essential if we are to have a good testimony before those who are not believers (11-12).

Some in the Thessalonian church were grief-stricken over loved ones who had died as believers. They were confused as to what would happen to them when Christ returned. Would they miss out on the great day of resurrection? The second coming of Christ will be wonderful for all Christians, past and present. It will be a day of resurrection for God's people. The Lord will come from heaven with a great shout and a trumpet blast (16; 1 Corinthians 15:51-55). When we die, our souls are immediately brought into the presence of God in heaven (2 Corinthians 5:8; Philippians 1:23), but our bodies will not be raised until the return of Christ. When Jesus comes again, every eye will see him. He will not come in secret (Revelation 1:7). *The dead in Christ will rise first* and believers who are alive at that time will also be given new bodies and shall be *caught up together with them in the clouds to meet the Lord in the air. And thus we shall always be with the Lord* (16-17). **We will see our Lord in all his breathtaking splendour and glory (2 Thessalonians 1:10) and we will admire, adore and worship him! We do not sorrow as others who have no hope (13). Let us comfort one another with this glorious truth.**

Let us watch and be sober

The Lord Jesus will return unexpectedly *as a thief in the night* (2; cp. 2 Peter 3:10). Though it will be wonderful for the Christian, it will be dreadful for the ungodly, who will not be able to escape divine judgment (3; 2 Thessalonians 1:7-9). The unbeliever is lulled by Satan into a false sense of security and he sleeps a deadly slumber so that he is unaware of coming judgment. We are *sons of light and sons of the day* (5) and we must be ready for Christ's return by being watchful and sober (5-6; Mark 14:38; Colossians 4:2; 1 Peter 4:7).

Let us watch and be sober (6). To be sober is to be serious and clear-minded. The drunkard sees the world through glazed eyes and from a swirling head. The sober person sees things as they really are. The Christian who is *'sober'* can be relied upon for his spiritual judgment and common sense. He is not carried away with the latest religious novelties. We must not only be on our guard by being vigilant and serious-minded, but also by *putting on the breastplate of faith and love, and as a helmet the hope of salvation because God did not appoint us to wrath, but to obtain salvation through our Lord Jesus Christ* (8-9). To *watch and be sober* is not to be miserable but enables us to comfort and build up one another (11).

Paul exhorts the Thessalonians concerning their attitude towards:

*   Their pastors (12-13).
*   Their fellow-believers (14-15).
*   God (16-18).
*   The Holy Spirit and his gifts (19-22).

There are two lovely descriptions of God in verses 23 and 24:

*   He is *the God of peace* (23; cp. Romans 16:20; 2 Thessalonians 3:16) who gives us his precious peace (John 14:27).
*   *He ... is faithful* (24). Paul was confident that God would answer his prayer for the Thessalonians. God is faithful, *who also will do it.* How wonderful! **We too are able to pray with confidence because God is faithful. He cannot and he will not fail us.**

When the Lord Jesus is revealed from heaven

In giving thanks for the Thessalonians (3), Paul was thanking God for answered prayer. He had prayed that he would be able to visit them to perfect what was lacking in their faith and that the Lord would make them increase and abound in love to each other (1 Thessalonians 3:10-12). God had answered these prayers without the necessity of a visit from Paul (3). **The Lord does not always answer our prayers in the precise way that we may expect, but he is wise and good in all his ways. Let us praise his name.**

Paul was also encouraged to hear of their perseverance (*'patience'*) and faith in persecution (4-5). We should always remember that persecution for the sake of Christ brings blessing (Matthew 5:10-12; Acts 5:41; Romans 5:3-4) and that God will punish our persecutors. *It is a righteous thing with God to repay with tribulation those who trouble you* (6). Many refuse to believe that God will punish sinners having the mistaken notion that such an action would deny his love. This idea fails to take into account the justice of God. *It is a righteous thing with God* to punish sinners. *When the Lord Jesus is revealed from heaven with his mighty angels* it will be a terrifying day for those who do not know God and for those who refuse to obey the gospel of Christ (7-8). They will *be punished with everlasting destruction from the presence of the Lord* (9). The word *'destruction'* means ruin rather than annihilation. Eternal ruin involves banishment from the presence of God and from the glory of his power; it means an eternity of conscious existence in hell (cp. Matthew 7:23; 25:41; Revelation 14:11).

The coming of the Lord Jesus will be a glorious day for Christians (*'saints'*, verse 10) however! We will be given eternal rest from trouble, suffering and sin (7). **We will not be so much concerned with our own glorified state as with the surpassing beauty, radiance and majesty of our Saviour.** We will gaze and gaze upon him with great admiration (10). We will worship and adore him, and we will praise him for ever for his great grace in saving poor sinners such as us. We have a marvellous calling; let us live worthy of it (11)!

The man of sin

There was some confusion in the Thessalonian church *concerning the coming of our Lord Jesus Christ.* Some were teaching that Christ's coming was already upon them. It would appear that some claimed to have a revelation from the Spirit of God that this was so (*either by spirit*). Others claimed that Paul had communicated this to them by word of mouth or by letter (1-2). Paul warns the church not to be deceived. There will be a *falling away* from the Christian faith before the return of Christ (3; cp. Matthew 24:10-13) and increasing lawlessness (6-7). Before Christ comes, wickedness will be unleashed on a great scale and men will *take pleasure in unrighteousness* (12). There will be a similarity to the days of Noah (Genesis 6:5,12-13; Matthew 24:37-39) and then *the man of sin* will be revealed (3).

The man of sin is also called 'the son of perdition' (3), 'the lawless one' (8) and 'the antichrist' (1 John 2:18,22). There have been many 'antichrists' who have deceived millions of people (2 John 7) but there will be a leader behind the great deception and lawlessness which shall precede the return of Christ. He will oppose God and his church, claiming to be divine and demanding that men worship him (4). He will have Satanic power enabling him to work amazing miracles which will deceive many into following him. These miracles are *signs, and lying wonders* (9). The Reformers believed that the Pope is the antichrist. Antichrists have risen up from within the ranks of the church (1 John 2:18-19). It is likely that the final antichrist will be a religious leader who will deny that Jesus is the Christ, the Son of God (1 John 2:22-23; 4:1-3). He will be destroyed by the Lord Jesus at his coming (8).

We must beware of smooth-tongued deceivers (3). If we refuse to *receive the love of the truth,* we invite the judgment of God who will give us over to delusion (10-11; cp. Romans 1:24-25). Every Christian has been chosen by God from the beginning for salvation (13). **We must stand fast and hold to the traditions based on Scripture (15). We will never compromise the truth if we love it. Do you love the truth and obey it?**

Do not grow weary in doing good

Paul wrote both of his letters to the Thessalonians while he was labouring in the wicked city of Corinth. There was much opposition to the gospel and he draws to the end of his letter with a request, *'Finally, brethren, pray for us'* (1-2; cp. Acts 18:1-18). Do you feel weak and vulnerable when there is opposition to your witness? Rejoice in the wonderful promise of verse 3: *But the Lord is faithful, who will establish you and guard you from the evil one.*

The Thessalonian church was flourishing, but it was not without problems. *We hear that there are some who walk among you in a disorderly manner* (11). These people were unsettling the church with extravagant claims concerning Christ's return (2:2-3). They were lazy, *not working at all* and they expected others to provide for them (11-12). They were also *'busybodies'* making a nuisance of themselves and causing mischief by interfering in other people's affairs (cp. 1 Thessalonians 4:11). If they did not obey God's word and work for their living, they were to be excluded from fellowship until they repented (6-15). Brotherly love does not mean that we should tolerate those who are disorderly. The Greek word translated *'disorderly'* (or *'unruly'* — 1 Thessalonians 5:14) was used in military circles to describe a soldier who was out of step with everyone else as the soldiers marched. The problem with *'disorderly'* people is that they generally insist that they are the only ones who are right, and that everyone else is wrong.

We must be busy workers rather than busybodies. Many evangelical churches owe their survival to the 'faithful few' who toil, giving much time and money to support the work of God. Those who do little and give little can easily discourage those who are faithful. Paul encouraged the Thessalonians to follow his own example (7-9). **Do not measure your spirituality against the weakest Christian in the church, but aim to be like the most godly person that you know.** *'Do not grow weary in doing good'* (13). Paul closes by praying that the Lord would bless the Thessalonians with his peace, presence and grace.

SONG OF SOLOMON

Solomon composed 1,005 songs (1 Kings 4:32). The title *'The song of songs'* (1:1) means 'the best of songs' (cp. *'vanity of vanities'* — Ecclesiastes 1:2). This song is about the love of a man and a woman committed to one another in marriage. It has a powerful message for our permissive society where lust is often confused with love. True love is tender (2:2-4), passionate (8:6), enduring and priceless (8:7), and it is totally committed to the beloved (5:9-10).

Interpretation of the Song of Solomon

Christians differ in the way that they interpret the book and there are three ways of looking at the Song of Solomon:

- The Naturalistic Interpretation takes the book as it stands, viewing it as describing pure, marital love, without any spiritual meaning. The problem with this view is that the Lord Jesus says that the Old Testament Scriptures speak of him (Luke 24:27,44-48), but the naturalistic view denies this.
- The Allegorical Interpretation takes the book as entirely figurative. This has been the most accepted view among Jews and Christians. The former see the poem as an allegory of God's love to Israel. Many Christians interpret the book as an allegory of Christ's love for his church and of their love for him (e.g. Matthew Henry, George Burrowes, C.H. Spurgeon, Dr Peter Masters). The language of Psalm 45 which speaks of Christ (Psalm 45:6-7; Hebrews 1:8-9) is similar to that found in parts of the Song of Solomon.
- The Typical Interpretation. Stuart Olyott takes this view, seeing 'the characters and events of the Song of Solomon as suggestive of spiritual truths, without there being an exact equivalence, as in an allegory'. He outlines each of the three interpretations and highlights the problems that we encounter in them (*A life worth living and a Lord worth loving* — commentary on Ecclesiastes and the Song of Solomon, published by Evangelical Press).

My beloved is mine, and I am his

The bridegroom compares himself and the Shulamite to flowers (1-2). He likens himself to *'the rose of Sharon'* (this may refer to the fragrant narcissus found in the fertile plain of Sharon, on the Mediterranean coast). He then speaks of the attractiveness of his bride, who for him surpasses all other women, just as a lily is more beautiful than thorns. The couple who love each other want to be together and cannot bear to be apart. They admire each other and delight in one another (2-3,8-14). Human love is very wonderful but Satan seeks to debase it. Sex is a God-given gift to be enjoyed within marriage (Hebrews 13:4). We must resist the permissive attitude of the world around us. Those of us who are married must always have 'eyes' only for our spouse (14). Whether single or married, we must all *abstain from sexual immorality* (1 Thessalonians 4:3-8).

When we are 'lovesick' (5) for the Lord Jesus, we cannot 'see' enough of him. We seek him in prayer, listen to his voice through the Bible and give him the adoration and worship of our hearts. We admire him for his worth, his beauty and his love to us. We trust in him and we want to please him. We reflect on his love for us with awe and wonder as we ponder how he poured out his soul to death to save us from our sin. The Lord Jesus will one day call us to himself: *'Rise up, my love, my fair one, and come away. For lo, the winter is past'* (10-11). The winter of bodily weakness, suffering, trial and sin will then be no more. We will be made perfect (Hebrews 12:23) and we will worship him and enjoy him as never before. Presently we rejoice in him saying, *'My beloved is mine, and I am his'* (16).

I lift my heart to thee, Saviour divine;
For thou art all to me, And I am thine.
Is there on earth a closer bond than this,
That my Belovèd's mine and I am his?

(Charles E. Mudie)

ISAIAH

Isaiah's ministry stretched over a period of some sixty years. He prophesied from before the death of King Uzziah (740 BC) and he recorded the death of King Sennacherib of Assyria (681 BC) — see Isaiah 1:1; 6:1; 37:38. His name means 'The LORD [Yahweh] is salvation'. His wife is called *'the prophetess'* (8:3) and there was prophetic significance in the names of his two sons (7:3; 8:3-4). Jewish tradition holds that he was a cousin of King Uzziah.

Historical background (see 2 Kings chapters 15 - 21; 2 Chronicles chapters 26 - 32). Uzziah (also known as Azariah) was a good king who enjoyed a long and prosperous reign of fifty-two years. During his reign, however, Judah drifted into spiritual decline which continued through the reign of his son Jotham. Ahaz, son of Jotham, was a wicked idol worshipper who sought the help of the Assyrians rather than trust in the Lord when Syria and Israel came to attack Judah (chapter 7; cp. 2 Kings 16). The Assyrians had conquered the northern kingdom of Israel in 722 BC taking the people off into captivity. They repopulated the land with people from other parts of their empire (2 Kings 17). Hezekiah, son of Ahaz, was a godly man who led Judah in spiritual reformation. When the mighty army of Assyria threatened Jerusalem, God brought a miraculous deliverance (chapters 36 and 37; cp. 2 Kings 19; 2 Chronicles 32). Hezekiah's son, Manasseh, was the most wicked king ever to rule over Judah. According to Jewish tradition, he had Isaiah sawn in half (cp. Hebrews 11:37 which may refer to this).

Contemporary prophets. Micah also prophesied to Judah during Isaiah's lifetime. Hosea prophesied to the northern kingdom of Israel.

Isaiah's message. He repeatedly warned Judah about the folly of their sin and of trusting in political alliances for their security. Looking ahead of his own lifetime to the Babylonian exile, he had a great message of consolation for the exiles. He prophesied of the coming of the Lord Jesus Christ and of his sufferings and death, more than any of the Old Testament prophets.

I saw the Lord sitting on a throne

King Uzziah intruded into the priestly ministry by burning incense to God who struck him with leprosy on account of his presumption; a long reign of fifty-two years years ended in disgrace (2 Chronicles 26:16-23). In the year that Uzziah died, Isaiah had a vision of God in the temple that transformed his life. He writes, *'I saw the Lord sitting on a throne, high and lifted up'* (1). Judah was in spiritual decline and there was apprehension among the people as Assyria become increasingly powerful and belligerent, but the prophet was reminded that God is absolutely sovereign. He cannot be toppled from his throne!

Isaiah saw the glory of the Lord Jesus Christ, who is God (John 12:41; cp. Hebrews 1:3,8). He was overwhelmed by the majesty and dazzling splendour of the exalted God. He was gripped by the truth of God's holiness, for he repeatedly used the title *'the Holy One of Israel'* when speaking of the Lord (e.g. 1:4; 5:19,24; 10:17,20). The seraphim (winged angelic beings) are sinless, yet they covered their faces in the presence of God (2). Isaiah keenly felt his own sinfulness in the presence of the Lord (5). **An appreciation of God's holiness brings a sense of our own sin and unworthiness.** Though we are God's children, the only acceptable way to serve God is *with reverence and godly fear* (Hebrews 12:28). God had a work for Isaiah who needed not only to confess his sin, but also to be cleansed from it (7). If we are to serve God acceptably, we must know the cleansing work of the blood of Christ in our lives (1 John 1:7) and be holy (1 Peter 1:15-16). We must witness with clean lips (7).

Isaiah's commission from God was tough! He would not see great success, but rather experience the heartache of ministering to a people who were dull, lethargic and indifferent to his message (9-11). In the difficult days that were to follow, he would remember that he was serving the eternal King of glory and he would be encouraged to persevere. **Christian, are you discouraged? Remember that you serve the King of all creation. He is in control of all things, and his purposes cannot fail nor be frustrated.**

His name will be called Wonderful, Counsellor, Mighty God

Deuteronomy chapter 18 warns against spiritism and other occult practices and goes on to promise the coming of Christ (verses 9 to 18). We have the same here in Isaiah. The warning at the end of chapter 8 is followed by wonderful verses which prophesy the coming of the Lord Jesus (9:1-7). Zebulun and Naphtali suffered the ravages of Assyrian invasion in 734 BC. They were oppressed and in darkness but they were to be privileged in the future by having the Messiah, *the Light of the World,* to live among them in Galilee (1-2; Matthew 4:12-16).

How foolish it is to grope in the darkness of the occult when we can walk in the glorious light of Christ (2). Why trust in spiritist mediums and fortune tellers when the Son of God has the government of the world upon his shoulder (6)? Why seek the counsel of occult practitioners when you can know the Lord Jesus who is called *'Wonderful, Counsellor, Mighty God, Everlasting Father, Prince of Peace'* (6)? Some translations do not have the comma after *'Wonderful'* so that the title is *'Wonderful Counsellor'*; this is perhaps the best way of rendering the verse.

Verses 6 and 7 clearly show that the promised Messiah is God. He is the *'Wonderful Counsellor'*. He is wonderful in his Person and in his work of creation and redemption. He is the source of all wisdom and knowledge and he needs no counsel (25:1; cp. Proverbs 8:14; Romans 11:33-34). He wisely guides his people (28:29). Jesus is *'Mighty God'* sitting on the throne of David (7; cp. Psalm 89:19-37). His reign is eternal (*'Everlasting Father'* = 'Father of Eternity'). Lasting peace only comes through the *'Prince of Peace'* who gives us peace with God *through the blood of his cross* (Ephesians 2:14; Colossians 1:20).

Have you discovered the loveliness and preciousness of the Lord Jesus in your own life? To reject Christ will bring everlasting darkness into your soul. To embrace him as your Lord and Saviour will bring inexpressible joy, light and wonderful peace.

The Spirit of wisdom and understanding

Isaiah's prophecy contains many warnings of judgment, but it also has many wonderful and encouraging passages and chapter 11 is one of these great passages which prophesy:

- The coming of Christ (1-5). Christ's first coming is prophesied (1-3) and then his second coming as King and Judge of all the world (4-5). We are again reminded of his human descent from the house of Jesse (King David's father). The Spirit of the LORD was upon Christ (2; cp. 61:1-2; Luke 4:16-22). *The Spirit of wisdom and understanding, the Spirit of counsel and might, the Spirit of knowledge and of the fear of the LORD* (2). *Wisdom and understanding ... knowledge.* The Holy Spirit does not bypass our minds as some people would have us believe. His presence in our lives produces reverence and godly fear.

- His kingdom (6-9). I do not believe that these verses are to be taken literally. John Calvin and Matthew Henry understand them as a picture of violent opposers of the gospel being subdued and won to Christ. **When Jesus comes again, there will not only be a miraculous change in us (Romans 8:23; Philippians 3:20-21; 1 John 3:1-3) but also in creation.** This is known as *the regeneration* (Matthew 19:28) or *the restoration of all things* (Acts 3:21). We look forward to a new heaven and a new earth (2 Peter 3:10-13; Revelation 20:11; 21:1-5). *For the earth shall be full of the knowledge of the LORD as the waters cover the sea* (9; cp. Habakkuk 2:14).

- The gathering of the remnant (10-16). A remnant returned to Israel after the captivity in Babylon (cp. Ezra 1), but I believe that the ultimate fulfilment of these verses lies in the salvation of a remnant of Jews throughout the gospel age, where they are gathered into the church of Christ (cp. Romans 11:5).

Behold your God!

Isaiah looked ahead to the captivity of the people in Babylon (cp. Psalm 137) and he had a message of comfort for them (1-2). The Jews were faced with two perils in Babylon where idolatry and occult practices were rife. They were in danger of losing their faith in God and there was also the peril of believing that God was so angry with them that he had cast them off. This problem is addressed in verses 27 to 31.

Isaiah's message to the people was, *'Behold your God!'* (9). He asks question upon question in order to direct their eyes (and ours) to the living God (12-31). We too live in evil days when occult and pagan teaching have become widespread and influential. We must stand firm and always fix our gaze upon God who is supreme in power:

- See his greatness compared with the world he created (12).
- See his greatness compared with the wisdom of men (13-14).
- See his greatness compared with the nations of the world (15-17). They are like a drop of water in a bucket, like the finest grains of dust left on the scales. *All nations before him are as nothing.*
- See his greatness compared with idols (18-20). Foolish men worship idols which they made, but we worship God who made us.
- See his greatness compared with the rulers of the world (21-24).
- See God's greatness compared with the stars (25-26). The Babylonians were expert astrologers but God's people have no need of horoscopes. The Lord created the vast galaxies and he controls all the stars. He wisely and lovingly cares for all who trust in him and obey him (11). *'Lift up your eyes on high, and see who has created these things'* (26). Let us worship and adore him.

We often languish in fear and doubt because we do not wait upon God. *Those who wait on the Lord shall renew their strength* (31). To wait on the Lord means to depend on him, to be patient and submissive to his will, to look to him. Have you been taking your eyes away from the Lord? Encourage yourself in him, *looking unto Jesus, the author and finisher of our faith* (Hebrews 12:2-3). ***Behold your God!***

Behold my Servant whom I uphold, my Elect One

Our reading today is the first 'Servant Song' found in Isaiah (the others are in 49:1-9; 50:4-9; 52:13 - 53:12). Israel is described as God's chosen servant (41:8), but these songs do not refer primarily to Israel, but to the Lord Jesus Christ (see Matthew 12:15-21 which confirms this). We were earlier encouraged, *'Behold your God!'* (40:9) but our eyes are now directed to the Son of God, *'Behold! my Servant whom I uphold, my Elect One in whom my soul delights!'* (1). Let us think about the Lord Jesus Christ as he is described in these verses:

- God the Father chose the Lord Jesus (*'my Elect'*) for a special task and he delights in him (1; cp. Matthew 3:17; 17:5).
- Jesus came as a servant to do the Father's will in order to save us from our sins (1; cp. John 4:34; Romans 5:19; Hebrews 10:7).
- The Holy Spirit was upon him (1; cp. Luke 4:17-22; Acts 10:38).
- He came to *bring forth justice to the Gentiles* (1), to *bring forth justice for truth* (3). People must admit the truth that they have wronged God by their sin if they want to be saved.
- He will not fail nor be discouraged in his mission to bring justice and truth throughout the earth (4). He will come again in great power and glory, when he will judge the world in righteousness (Acts 17:31).
- He is gentle in his dealings with us (2-3). Bruised reeds are useless and smouldering wicks, which do not give light, are of no worth. Our wonderful Saviour patiently and tenderly works in our lives, healing and restoring.

God, the almighty Creator and Sustainer of the universe, gives reassuring promises to his Servant (6-7). He has called him and will hold his hand and keep him until his work is completed. He will be given *as a covenant* to be *a light to the Gentiles,* to open blind eyes, to release prisoners from the prison house of sin, to make light shine into their hearts (2 Corinthians 4:6). God will not share his glory with graven images or any other god (8). **Are you trying to serve two masters, or robbing God of his glory (cp. 1 Corinthians 6:19-20)?**

I will preserve you and give you as a covenant to the people

Today's reading contains the second 'Servant Song'. In verses 1 to 6 the Servant speaks, and in verses 7 to 9a, the Lord speaks to his Servant.

The Servant (Jesus) calls on the people to listen to him. God the Father had called him from the womb. He says to him, *'You are my servant, O Israel, in whom I will be glorified'* (1-3). God had also called the nation of Israel from the womb to glorify him, to be his witnesses, but Israel had failed to honour and obey the Lord (3; cp. 44:2; 43:10-24). The Lord Jesus came to do what Israel had failed to do.

The ministry of the Lord Jesus Christ was marked by suffering. He knew discouragement (4; cp. John 6:66-67) and he was despised by men and rejected by his own nation (7; cp. 53:3; John 1:11). God the Father speaks words of encouragement to his despised Servant. Kings and princes shall worship him (7). He has *heard* him, *helped* him and *preserved* him. He has given him *as a covenant to the people* (8; cp. 42:6). His mission was not a failure. He saves Jews and Gentiles (6) and he draws people to himself from all over the world (12; there is no clear evidence that 'Sinim' refers to China as some believe).

How is Christ *'a covenant'* to us (8)? God gave him to die for sinners, sealing the new covenant with his own precious blood (John 3:16; Matthew 26:28; Hebrews 9:14-15). God preserved him from wicked men until the appointed time came for him to die at Calvary (cp. John 7:30; 8:20). Some of his covenant blessings are described in these verses. He gives us light (6) and sets us free from sin's dark prison (9). He provides for us and guides us (9-10). **What a wonderful covenant! What a wonderful Saviour! He says, 'Listen to me' (1). Are you listening?**

> God of the covenant — changeless, eternal
> Father, Son, Spirit in blessing agree,
> Thine be the glory, our weakness confessing,
> Triune Jehovah, we rest upon thee.

(Jessie F. Webb)

A word in season to him who is weary

The third 'Servant Song' found in verses 4 to 9 gives us a threefold picture of the Lord Jesus:

- The One who graciously speaks (4). His speech was earlier likened to *'a sharp sword'* (49:2; cp. Revelation 1:16) but he also knows *how to speak a word in season to him who is weary.* In the synagogue at Nazareth, all bore witness to him, and marvelled at the gracious words which proceeded out of his mouth (Luke 4:22). Let us always aim to imitate Christ in this respect. Our tongues are unruly. An evidence of godliness is a bridled tongue and gracious speech (James 3:2-8). We will then be able *to speak a word in season to him who is weary.*

- The One who obediently suffers (5-6). He had an ear open to the voice of the Father and did not rebel against his will (cp. Matthew 26:38-44; Philippians 2:8). We are here given a preview of the suffering of the Lord Jesus before he was crucified — the scourging, the beating about the face and the humiliation as he was spat upon (Matthew 26:67; 27:26-31).

- The One who trusted in God to help him (7). He was taunted, as he hung on the cross, *'He trusted in God; let him deliver him now if he will have him; for he said, "I am the Son of God"'* (Matthew 27:42-43). He set his face like a flint and endured the most appalling suffering to save us from our sin. He was sure that God the Father would help him and vindicate him (8-9).

Believers sometimes walk in the darkness, knowing severe trials and perplexity but there is a word of encouragement for those who fear the Lord and obey his Servant: *'Let him trust in the name of the LORD and rely upon his God'* (10). **His love for us is very great. He will never let us down, he will never let us go.** There is a warning for those who reject the Servant of the consequences of their rebellion: *'You shall lie down in torment'* (11).

Yet it pleased the LORD to bruise him

The fourth 'Servant Song' is probably the best known and most loved passage in the Book of Isaiah. The prophet wrote these words some seven hundred years before the Lord Jesus died at Calvary. His description of Christ's suffering is so accurate, however, that it would seem that he is actually standing at the cross reporting the death of Jesus. The passage begins with the statement, *'He shall be exalted and extolled and be very high'* (52:13) but Isaiah did not see a vision of awe-inspiring majesty, but of the most appalling suffering. The face and body of Christ were mutilated beyond recognition (14). *He shall sprinkle* (or 'startle') *many nations* (15). Kings shall see him and bow before him when he is highly exalted (Philippians 2:9-11). They will shut their mouths in wonder as they see his wounds.

The Son of God was born in obscurity and poverty *as a root out of dry ground* (2). His divine glory was veiled by his humble human roots and he was *despised and rejected* (3). His suffering was so intense that he is described as a Man of sorrows (3) who travailed in soul (11) and who *poured out his soul unto death* (12). He died with the wicked (the two robbers) and he was buried in a rich man's tomb (9). He suffered without complaining. *He opened not his mouth* (7).

It is important that we understand that the death of Christ was no accident. *Yet it pleased the LORD to bruise him* (10; cp. Acts 2:23; 4:27,28). Why did Jesus die on the cross? *He was wounded for our transgressions, he was bruised for our iniquities* (5). He died for God's people (the elect). *For the transgression of my people he was stricken* (8; cp. Matthew 1:21). The sinless Saviour was *numbered with the transgressors* (12) and punished by God the Father. *The LORD has laid on him the iniquity of us all* (6). **Do you really love God? Have you responded to his love by forsaking your sin? Do you seek to please him with all your heart?**

> Amazing love! how can it be
> That thou, my God, shouldst die for me?   (Charles Wesley)

Ho! Everyone who thirsts, come to the waters

The appeal in this chapter was initially to the exiles in Babylon who were probably seeking satisfaction in material things, but it has a far wider application. The first two verses of the chapter picture men and women thirsting and hungering for satisfaction. The chapter ends with a picture of great joy and freedom.

God is gracious and he invites sinners to himself (1-3). '*Ho!* [i.e. 'pay attention'] *Everyone who thirsts, come to the waters.*' He offers salvation freely, '*without money and without price*', to all who will come to him. This gracious invitation is repeated in the closing verses of the Bible, '*Let him who thirsts come. And whoever desires, let him take the water of life freely*' (Revelation 22:17). Thousands of people spend all that they have in the quest for satisfaction. They look for personal fulfilment in seeking for wealth, pleasure and all kinds of earthly comforts (cp. Ecclesiastes 2:1-11). Others turn to drug-induced experiences which lead them to disaster and misery. How terribly sad! There can be no lasting joy and peace apart from God (2).

God invites us, '*Come to me, hear, and your soul shall live*' (3). If you are not a Christian, I urge you, '*Seek the LORD while he may be found*' (6). Tomorrow may be too late! **What is involved in seeking God and coming to him?** You must call upon him, asking him to forgive your sin and to save you (6). You must forsake your sinful ways and thoughts and then God '*will have mercy*' and '*he will abundantly pardon*' (7).

God's thoughts and ways are far higher than those of men (8-9). We must remember this truth in every aspect of our Christian work. **The Lord gives us a lesson from nature to encourage us to persevere in our work for him.** He gives rain and snow to water the earth so that seed will germinate, grow and produce a harvest (10). When he sends forth his word, it will bring forth spiritual fruit. '*So shall my word be that goes forth from my mouth; it shall not return to me void, but it shall accomplish what I please and it shall prosper in the thing for which I sent it*' (11).

He has clothed me with the garments of salvation

One Sabbath day, the Lord Jesus read the first two verses of Isaiah 61 to the congregation in the synagogue at Nazareth. He told them that this prophecy was being fulfilled among them (Luke 4:16-22). He came (1-2):

- To preach good news *to the poor;* this includes not only those who have no money, but those who are poor in spirit, who know that they cannot save themselves. They recognize their spiritual poverty and their need of God's help (cp. Matthew 5:3).
- *To heal the broken-hearted,* giving them comfort and peace.
- *To proclaim liberty to the captives.* He sets free those who are imprisoned by the evil one and who are gripped by guilt.
- *To proclaim the acceptable year of the* LORD. He saves and accepts sinners. The gospel is the most wonderful news in the world.
- To proclaim *the day of vengeance of our God.* The Lord Jesus often spoke of the day of judgment (e.g. Matthew 13:40-42; 25:31-46).

When the Lord Jesus saves us, he not only forgives us and frees us from the power of Satan and sin, but also clothes us *with the garments of salvation* (10). These garments are *the garment of praise* (3) and *the robe of righteousness* (10). He clothes us with his righteousness and with praise for all that he has done for us (10-11). **What do you know about being joyful in God? Does your life display his righteousness? Are you full of praise to him?** *The garments of salvation* are righteousness and praise to our most wonderful God and Saviour. Are your garments of salvation seen by those around you?

> Jesus, thy blood and righteousness
> My beauty are, my glorious dress;
> Midst flaming worlds, in these arrayed,
> With joy shall I lift up my head.

> This spotless robe the same appears,
> When ruined nature sinks in years!
> No age can change its glorious hue;
> The robe of Christ is ever new.   (N. L. Von Zinzendorf)

JEREMIAH & LAMENTATIONS

Jeremiah was the son of a priest. His ministry covered a period of more than forty years, from the thirteenth year of Josiah's reign over Judah until after the fall of Jerusalem (1:1-2; 43:1 - 44:30). This period is recorded in 2 Kings chapters 22 - 25 and in 2 Chronicles chapters 35 & 36. Josiah, a godly king, purged the land of idolatry (2 Chronicles 34:3-8) but his reformation did not remove idolatry from the hearts of the people. Josiah's sons were wicked and the religious leadership was corrupt. After Josiah's death idolatry again flourished.

Jeremiah pleaded with the people to forsake their wicked ways and to return to the Lord. He warned them that God would punish them by delivering them into the hands of the Babylonians but his message was rejected. He was hated and considered a traitor for bringing such a message and he was persecuted, imprisoned and threatened with death (20:2; 21:1-10; 26:8-11; 37:1 - 38:13). After the fall of Jerusalem the Babylonians treated him kindly (39:11-12; 40:2-5). The Jews who were left in the land fled to Egypt after the murder of Gedaliah, the governor appointed by the Babylonians. They took Jeremiah with them against his will and they rejected his message (chapters 42 - 44). He suffered much loneliness and heartache in his ministry and is known as 'the weeping prophet' (cp. 9:1; 13:17). He spoke not only of judgment, but also of a gracious God who has mercy on repenting sinners (e.g. 3:12-15,22; 4:1-2). He also looked beyond the return of the Jews from Babylon to the coming of Christ, the *Branch of Righteousness* (23:5-6; 33:14-17), and to the new covenant (31:31-33; 32:40).

Lamentations is a poetical book which according to Jewish and Christian tradition was written by the prophet Jeremiah (though his name does not appear in the book). Each of the five chapters in the book contains a lament over the destruction of Jerusalem by the Babylonians. The prophet acknowledges that Jerusalem was destroyed as an act of righteous judgment (1:18). God used the Babylonians to punish his sinning people (1:5,12-15; 2:1-8,17). There is a moving affirmation of the mercy and faithfulness of God in chapter 3:19-39.

Before I formed you in the womb I knew you

Jeremiah was the son of Hilkiah, a priest in the town of Anathoth, some three miles north-east of Jerusalem (1). The priests of Anathoth were probably descended from Abiathar who was disgraced during the reign of King Solomon (1 Kings 2:26). Jeremiah would have been born during the reign of Manasseh, the most wicked king ever to reign over Judah. Josiah came to the throne two years after the death of Manasseh. *'A prophet to the nations'* (5) was born when circumstances were very difficult for those who loved God.

The Lord told Jeremiah when he called him, *'Before I formed you in the womb I knew you'* (5; cp. Galatians 1:15). God had set Jeremiah apart (*'sanctified'*) for his work before he was born. The Lord had sovereignly chosen Jeremiah and had reassured him with this truth. God the Father has also chosen every believer in Christ *according to the good pleasure of his will.* This choice was made before the creation of the world (Ephesians 1:4-5; 2 Timothy 1:9). Let us think back as far as we can in our imagination — before the great galaxies were created and placed in the vastness that we call 'the universe'. God set his love upon us and chose us in Christ before time began. If God is for us and has purposes of good for us, what have we to fear? (see Romans 8:28-31).

Jeremiah was painfully aware of his own youthful shortcomings (6) but the Lord encouraged him, putting his words in his mouth and promising to deliver him from his enemies (8-9). Jeremiah had a tough, heartbreaking ministry, but God was always with him. Do you feel inadequate to serve God? That is not a bad thing because, like Jeremiah, you are inadequate in your own strength. Remember, when God calls us to work for him, he also equips us. Are you full of foreboding or fear? God is with you to deliver you. **He does not promise us an easy Christian life, but he will safely bring us through trials, through suffering and through death, if we will but trust him (Romans 8:35-39).**

They have also healed the hurt of my people slightly

God calls upon the tribe of Benjamin who lived in the Jerusalem area to blow the trumpet (a horn); this signalled grave danger (1; cp. 4:5,19,21). The invaders would come and destroy the land, as sheep devour lush pasture (3-5). The day of peace was running out, giving way to the long shadows of evening (4). Jerusalem was rotten to the core, being likened to an underground reservoir which supplied only polluted water. The wicked city was ripe for judgment (6-8). The whole nation was corrupt and to make matters worse, prophet and priest were lulling the people into complacency by smooth talk with promises of peace. *They have also healed the hurt of my people slightly, saying, 'Peace, peace!' when there is no peace* (14). Sin is like a tumour that needs to be removed by thorough surgery. The ointment of soothing platitudes is useless.

The parallel for us today is obvious. False 'Christianity' with its men-pleasing leaders has forsaken God's word, except for its comforting passages. They do not warn of judgment or hell; they do not preach biblical repentance and faith in God; they deny the necessity of atonement for sin through the death of Christ. Thousands are enchanted and deceived by these false teachers.

The Lord appealed to his people, *'Stand in the ways and see, and ask for the old paths, where the good way is, and walk in it; then you will find rest for your souls.'* Stubborn Judah refused to walk in the good way and would not listen to the word of God (16-17). Their sacrifices were useless because they refused to heed God's word (19-20). God would reject his people because they had rejected his law (19,30). Judah would be invaded from the north and plundered (21-26). We live in very confusing times when strange teachings and practices have been introduced into many evangelical churches. **We must remain faithful to 'the old paths' which rely on God's word alone for doctrine and practice. These old paths have stood the test of time and they will never fail us.** Let us beware of seemingly attractive new paths — in reality, they are a slippery road to hell.

THE LORD OUR RIGHTEOUSNESS

False shepherds (wicked kings) had neglected God's flock and had scattered them. The Lord promised that he would set good shepherds over the remnant of those whom he would gather from exile (1-4). There follows a wonderful prophecy concerning the Lord Jesus Christ (5-6; cp. 33:15-16). He is described as a *'Branch of righteousness'* (cp. Isaiah 11:1-2; Zechariah 3:8; 6:12). The Hebrew translated *'Branch'* is not the usual word but one which describes a shoot sprouting up from the roots of a tree which had fallen down. The royal house of David had become like a fallen tree but from its roots would spring a tiny shoot which would grow into a mighty tree (cp. Romans 15:12). The Lord Jesus came to this earth and was born into a humble family from David's line, but he is the almighty King. One of his titles is *'THE LORD OUR RIGHTEOUSNESS'* (Hebrew = *'Jehovah Tsidkenu'*). **Jesus is more than a man, much more than a prophet, and greater than any angel. He is Jehovah God.**

The Lord Jesus is our righteousness (cp. 1 Corinthians 1:30). We do not have to work for our salvation and if we did, we would not succeed. The perfect obedience and righteousness of Christ are put to our account (*'imputed to us'*, Romans 4:22-25). He bore our sin, being made sin for us, that we might become the righteousness of God in him (2 Corinthians 5:21). How wonderful! We are *justified freely by his grace* (Romans 3:24).

Just before he became a Christian, the poet William Cowper was in great despair on account of his sin. He then read Romans 3:24-25 and wrote, 'Immediately I received strength to believe it, and the full beams of the Sun of Righteousness shone upon me. I saw the sufficiency of the atonement he had made, my pardon sealed in his blood, and all the fulness of his justification. Unless the Almighty arm had been under me, I think I should have died with gratitude and joy.'

Grace in the wilderness

The Lord had words of encouragement as well as of judgment for the people. Northern Israel (Ephraim) would be rebuilt and its land cultivated. The people would again worship God in Jerusalem (1-6). Verse 2 speaks of something yet to take place as if it had already happened. *'The people who survived the sword found grace* [favour which they did not deserve] *in the wilderness.'*

What God says about the Jews in these verses is also true of every Christian: *'Yes, I have loved you with an everlasting love; therefore with lovingkindness I have drawn you'* (3). Christian, before God created the world and the stars, he loved you. He loves you now and he will love you for ever (Ephesians 1:4; Romans 8:28-39; 1 John 4:19)! When you were in the 'wilderness' of sin and alienated from God, you found grace. The Lord has drawn you to himself with lovingkindness. He gives you grace in the wilderness of suffering, heartache and trial; grace in the wilderness of disappointment. There is grace in the wilderness of backsliding. The Lord chastises us because he loves us and yearns over us (18-22; cp. Hebrews 12:5-11). **He gives grace in every 'wilderness' experience.**

The Lord would ransom a remnant from the might of their enemies (7-11). Jacob's wife Rachel was buried at Ramah which is about five miles north of Jerusalem (Genesis 35:16-20). She is seen weeping over the exile of her sons Joseph and Benjamin (15). This prophecy also points to the sorrow of Bethlehem at the slaughter of its infants by Herod (Matthew 2:17-18). The Lord promised restoration and hope in the future to a sorrowing, despairing people (16-17). The wonderful promises in this chapter were given during dark days of judgment upon Judah. There are prophecies here which relate to the return of the remnant of the Jews to their land (23-30; 38-40) and beyond that time to the new covenant in which Jewish and Gentile believers are united in Christ (31-37). Some of the promises here are applied to Christians in the New Testament (33-34; cp. Hebrews 8:8-12; 10:16-17).

Great is your faithfulness

The prophet identifies himself with the sinning people of Jerusalem and Judah (40,48-51). He keenly feels the hand of God against them in judgment and cries out, *'I am the man who has seen affliction by the rod of his wrath'* (1). The Lord uses affliction to bring us back to himself when we backslide (Psalm 119:67). How does God afflict us?

- He leads us in paths of darkness and bitterness (2-6).
- He hedges us in, trapping us like a prisoner (7).
- He shuts out our prayer so that he appears to ignore us (8,44).
- He thwarts our plans (9).
- He makes us miserable (11).
- He takes away our peace (17).

The prophet now moves from a position of no hope (18) to an attitude full of hope (21,24,26,29). He called to mind great truths about the character of God (21). *Through the Lord's mercies we are not consumed, because his compassions fail not. They are new every morning; great is your faithfulness* (22-23). He declared, *'The Lord is my portion,' says my soul. 'Therefore I hope in him!'* (24). When God is our portion we have every reason to hope in him. We should also remember whenever Satan or the world seeks to dangle before us the passing pleasures of sin, whenever we are tempted to trust in material things, that nothing can compare with the priceless privilege of having God as our portion.

His great faithfulness is also a source of comfort to the perplexed child of God who is passing through very trying times. **Let us not sink into despair in our 'valley' experiences but trust in God who is faithful and who will not fail us.** We do become impatient in difficult and testing times, sometimes wondering whether there will be an end of our particular trial. Let us take verses 25 and 26 to heart: *The Lord is good to those who wait for him, to the soul who seeks him. It is good that one should hope and wait quietly for the salvation of the Lord.* To wait upon God means to depend upon him, patiently submitting to his will. Never forget that God is faithful — *Great is your faithfulness.*

EZEKIEL & DANIEL

The Babylonians besieged Jerusalem in 597 BC and took King Jehoiachin captive to Babylon with the princes and mighty men of Judah. **Ezekiel** the priest was among these captives (1:1). Zedekiah was installed as puppet king over Judah (2 Kings 24:10-17) and reigned for eleven years. He rebelled against the Babylonians who besieged Jerusalem for eighteen months (588 BC — Jeremiah 52:1-11). Jerusalem was destroyed in 586 BC and Zedekiah and the people, except for the poor, were transported to Babylon (Jeremiah 39:9-10).

In the fifth year of his captivity (593 BC) Ezekiel was called by God to prophesy to the captives in Babylon and to those remaining in Jerusalem. He reminded his fellow-captives that the catastrophic events of 597 BC were a result of God's righteous judgment on a rebellious people. Many of his prophecies are precisely dated and his ministry continued for at least twenty-two years (29:17). The later chapters of Ezekiel look forward to the restoration from exile and to spiritual renewal. There is much use of parable and symbolism in the book.

In the third year of the reign of King Jehoiakim of Judah (605 BC) many young Jews of noble descent were taken captive into Babylon. **Daniel** and his three friends were among these captives (1:1-7). Daniel held influential positions for over sixty years in the empires of Babylon and Persia. The Lord Jesus called him 'Daniel the prophet' (Matthew 24:15). He prophesied of the fall of the Babylonian empire and of subsequent Middle East events until the coming of Christ, of the rise of the Antichrist, and of the second coming of Christ. Though Daniel served great earthly kings, the truth emphasized in his book is that the Lord God is absolutely sovereign over all the nations of the world (e.g. 4:34-37). We will not understand the book of Daniel if we fail to see God's sovereign hand at work throughout its pages. What was the secret of Daniel's great spiritual strength? He was a man of prayer (2:17-23; 6:10-11; 9:20-21) and one who knew his Scriptures (9:2,11,13). He knew God. His life testified to the truth of the words, 'The people who know their God shall be strong, and carry out great exploits' (11:32).

The hand of the LORD was upon him there

The book opens with Ezekiel in his thirtieth year and in exile by the River Chebar. The Chebar was a great canal to the south of Babylon which linked the Euphrates and Tigris Rivers. The Babylonians had removed Ezekiel far from his home and 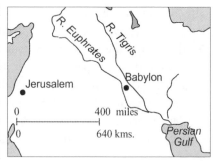 country but they could not remove him out of the reach of God. *The hand of the LORD was upon him there* (3; cp. 3:14,22). The Lord gave him a strange but awesome vision of four creatures coming out of a whirlwind (4). Each creature had four faces and four wings (6,10). The faces represented God's creation: man, the apex of creation; the lion, king of the wild beasts; the ox, representing domestic animals; the eagle, chief of the birds. Beside each living creature was a wheel (15). The four wheels rotated in harmony with each other as the living creatures moved (16-21). There was a *firmament* (ESV = 'an expanse') *like the colour of an awesome crystal* above the creatures (22) and above it was a throne (26). High above the throne was the likeness of a man surrounded by burning splendour (26-27). What Ezekiel saw in his vision was the form of God's Son. He saw *the glory of the LORD* (28).

Ezekiel fell on his face in awe and reverence (28). Isaiah and the apostle John were similarly overwhelmed by the glory of God (Isaiah 6:5; Revelation 1:13-17). Ezekiel's work for God would not be easy for he was to minister to rebellious Israel (2:3-8). He was surrounded by the military might, the idolatry and superstition of Babylon but above all the difficulties was the Almighty, awesome in his majesty and sovereignty, enthroned over all the world (24,26). *The hand of the LORD was upon him there* in captivity. **Let us remember that even in the darkest times or in the most bleak and hopeless of situations, if God's hand is upon us, we have no need to fear.** *If God is for us, who can be against us?* (Romans 8:31).

The soul who sins shall die

The proverb in verse 2 was very common in Ezekiel's day (cp. Jeremiah 31:29): *The fathers have eaten sour grapes, and the children's teeth are set on edge.* It was used by the people in their belief that the disasters that had befallen them were a punishment for the sins of previous generations. They refused to accept that they themselves had any responsibility for the judgment that God had visited upon them. The Lord did say that he would visit the sin of the fathers on the children (Exodus 20:5), but the verse was being misapplied by Ezekiel's contemporaries. The prophet takes the case of three generations — grandfather (5), son (10) and grandson (14). The grandfather, a righteous man, has a wicked son; he in turn has a son who leads a righteous life. The wicked will die for his own sin, the righteous will surely live because he faithfully kept God's judgments (4-18).

Ezekiel showed the people that they had no excuse for their wickedness. *The soul who sins shall die* (4). In Romans 1 the apostle Paul records a similar list of sins to those found in these verses. God's word through the apostle is that *those who practise such things are worthy of death* (Romans 1:32). Death came into the world through sin — *the wages of sin is death* (Romans 5:12; 6:23). Death is separation, not extinction. The soul is separated from the body at death (2 Corinthians 5:8), but the ultimate horror for the unrepentant sinner is the separation of the soul from God for ever in hell (Matthew 25:41; 2 Thessalonians 1:9).

God does not delight in the death of the wicked. *He delights in mercy* (Micah 7:18). This message is repeated in our reading today (23,32; see also 33:11-20). *'I have no pleasure in the death of one who dies,' says the Lord GOD.'Therefore turn and live!'* (32). Notice that God repeats his calls for repentance and a turning away from sin (21,23,27,28,30, 32). Conversion involves obtaining for ourselves *a new heart and a new spirit* (31) and only God can give these. **Have you asked God to give you a new heart and to change your life? Have you repented of your sin?**

I will give you a new heart

The Lord here rehearses the reasons for the judgment that he had brought upon Israel (16-23). The people had defiled the land by their wickedness and idolatry and they had dishonoured the name of God. The Lord said, *'But I had concern for my holy name, which the house of Israel had profaned'* (21). God's name is bound up with his holy and glorious character. Jesus taught us to pray, *'Hallowed be your name'* (Luke 11:2). We must live godly lives if our witness is to have any effect on those with whom we have to do. God says, *'The nations shall know that I am the* Lord *... when I am hallowed in you before their eyes'* (23). So much that passes for Christianity today is very man-centred, but if we are to hallow the name of the Lord, we must be God-centred in our worship, in our preaching and in our witness. May the Lord sanctify his *great name* (23) so that the unbelievers around us will know that he is the Lord.

God promised the restoration of the Jews to their land for his *holy name's sake* (24-38), but how much more important the promises that God would cleanse the Jews from their wickedness and idolatry. This he promised to do by changing their lives: *'I will cleanse you ... I will give you a new heart ... I will put my Spirit within you'* (25-27; cp. 37:14). Blessing follows cleansing from sin (23) and if our hearts are not right we will not enjoy God's blessing. **How is your heart? Is it hard (***'a heart of stone'***)?** Oh, turn from your sin to Christ and call upon him to save you. He will then give you a new heart and he will put his Holy Spirit within you.

Notice that the Jews were to pray for the fulfilment of these promises. *I will also let the house of Israel inquire of me to do this for them* (37). Daniel in his old age remembered the promises God had given through the prophet Jeremiah and he prayed earnestly for their fulfilment (Daniel 9:1-19). These verses look further ahead than the return of the Jews to their land following the captivity in Babylon. They also look ahead to the new covenant which was sealed with the blood of Christ.

Can these bones live?

Ezekiel was transported by the Spirit of God to a valley where a great army had encountered a sudden disaster and had been wiped out. All that remained of this army were the bones which had been dried out in the heat of the sun. God asked the prophet, *'Can these bones live?'* and he replied, *'O Lord God, you know'* (1-3). God then told him to prophesy to them saying, *'O dry bones, hear the word of the Lord!'* (3-4). When Ezekiel did this, there was a noise and the bones came together but they were still lifeless (7-8). God then told him to prophesy to the breath (that is, the breath of God), *'Breathe on these slain, that they may live.'* Life came into the corpses and there was a very great army (9-10).

What was the meaning of this vision? The bones represented the whole house of Israel. The Jews were in captivity in Babylon and they were full of despair. They were saying, *'Our bones are dry, our hope is lost, and we ourselves are cut off!'* (11; cp. Psalm 137). The Lord told them that just as the bones were brought to life, they would be restored to their land and Israel would again live as a nation (12-14). This restoration is also promised in verses 15 to 28. The Lord told Ezekiel to take two sticks and to write on them the names of Judah and Joseph, the chief tribes of the southern and northern kingdoms. He was then to join them together, as a symbol of their return to their land when they would again be one nation with one king from the house of David. These prophecies look beyond the return of the Jews from Babylon. Their complete fulfilment is in the Lord Jesus Christ who is the promised king and shepherd (24-25; cp. 34:23-25; John 7:42; 10:11-16; Acts 13:22-23). They speak of the new covenant of which he is the mediator (26; Hebrews 9:15; 12:24).

There are encouraging lessons for us in the raising of the dry bones. We seem to make little impact in our gospel witness and we long for God to show his great power by saving many sinners. *Can these bones live?* (3). The dry bones became a mighty army after hearing the *word of the Lord* (4,10). **The preaching of the word of God and the work of the Holy Spirit are essential for the success of the gospel (14).**

But Daniel purposed in his heart that he would not defile himself

King Nebuchadnezzar of Babylon invaded and defeated Judah in the first year of his reign (605 BC). He plundered Jerusalem of its treasures and took many captives to Babylon including Daniel and his three friends. Jehoiakim continued to reign over Judah as a puppet king for the next eight years. **Daniel chapter 1 shows that God is absolutely sovereign.** *The Lord gave Jehoiakim king of Judah into his* [Nebuchadnezzar's] *hand* (2). The Hebrew verb '*nathan*' meaning 'to give', is used three times in relation to the activity of God (2,9,17).

The Babylonians handpicked certain Hebrews to be trained with a view to oversee Jewish affairs in their administration. Daniel and his three friends were among those chosen to undergo three years of special training so that they could serve the king of Babylon (5). Nebuchadnezzar even changed their Jewish names which included in them the name of God ('*El*' and '*Iah*' or '*Jah*', the latter two being shortened forms of 'Jehovah'). Daniel became 'Belteshazzar' (7) which means 'Keeper of the hidden treasures of Bel' (one of Babylon's gods; cp. Isaiah 46:1). **Nebuchadnezzar removed God from their names, but he could not remove God from their hearts.**

The trainees were privileged to enjoy delicacies from the royal kitchen, but such food and drink was dedicated to the gods of Babylon. To eat that food was to be identified with pagan worship *but Daniel purposed in his heart that he would not defile himself with the portion of the king's delicacies* (8). The stand taken by Daniel and his friends took tremendous courage (commentators suggest that Daniel was only about fourteen years of age at that time). God is absolutely sovereign. He brought about Daniel's captivity (2) and he also gave him favour with the high court official (9). He gave Daniel and his friends knowledge and wisdom which far surpassed anything that Babylon could offer (17-20). They were determined to make their stand for God and he honoured them (cp. 1 Samuel 2:30). Have you purposed in your heart not to defile yourself with the dreadful enticements of our permissive society? **Don't just admire Daniel — follow his example!**

But there is a God in heaven

Nebuchadnezzar was lying on his bed thinking about the future when he fell asleep and had a strange dream (29). He was greatly troubled and decided to put his magicians, astrologers, sorcerers and wise men to the test. They were not only to interpret the dream, but also to describe details of the dream itself. They protested that they would need to be told the dream if the king wanted an interpretation. The angry king, realizing that their claims were fraudulent, ordered their execution (5-13). Daniel and his three friends were numbered among the wise men (1:20) and they were in grave danger. Daniel requested that the king give him time so that he would be able to tell him the interpretation (14-16). Daniel and his friends then sought God in prayer, confident that he would hear and answer them (17-18).

The Lord revealed the dream and its interpretation to Daniel, who then worshipped and praised him (19-23). We are encouraged to pray because God is infinitely wise and powerful (20). **We are again reminded that he is sovereign over the affairs of nations.** *He removes kings and raises up kings* (21). Nebuchadnezzar asked Daniel if he were able to make known to him the dream and its interpretation. He reminded Nebuchadnezzar that the occult diviners had been helpless to rise to his challenge, *'but there is a God in heaven who reveals secrets'* (26-28). Daniel was careful to point out that it was God who had given the dream to the king and that it was God who had revealed its meaning. The image in the dream represented Babylon and the empires that were to follow. The stone represents Christ, whose kingdom will never be destroyed (35,44).

An amazed Nebuchadnezzar *fell on his face, prostrate before Daniel* (46). **Think of that! The great despot, the powerful ruler, bowing before the servant of God. He was now convinced that there was no one like Daniel's God (47).** Millions follow the advice of astrologers and occult practitioners. Their advice is useless (cp. 1:20) and they are instruments of Satan to deceive and lead many to hell *but there is a God in heaven* whom they can know through Jesus Christ.

Our God whom we serve is able to deliver us

The experience of Shadrach, Meshach and Abed-Nego illustrates the truth of 2 Timothy 3:12 — *all who desire to live godly in Christ Jesus will suffer persecution.* It was common practice for Assyrian and Babylonian kings to erect great statues of themselves. The image of Nebuchadnezzar stood ninety feet high and nine feet wide (a cubit is eighteen inches or just under half a metre). Daniel's three friends were among the important people summoned to the dedication of the image (2,12). Nebuchadnezzar had already acknowledged the greatness of God (2:47) but he was still a proud idolater. He ordered that all those present at the dedication should bow and worship the image when the orchestra played (4-6). Shadrach, Meshach and Abed-Nego were different, however (12). They would not eat food offered to idols (1:7-8) and they would certainly not bow to one. They considered that it was more important to please God than to please the powerful king of Babylon (cp. Acts 5:29). When everyone bowed down, they remained standing.

The three friends were not intimidated by the threats of the king who challenged them, *'Who is the god who will deliver you from my hands?'* (15). Their brave reply was, *'Our God whom we serve is able to deliver us from the burning fiery furnace, and he will deliver us from your hand, O king'* (17). The years of 're-education' in Babylon had not destroyed their faith in God. The heat of the furnace was so intense that those who threw the friends into it were themselves killed by the flames (22). **The three were not delivered from the fiery furnace, but they were preserved in it.** An astonished Nebuchadnezzar saw four men walking unharmed in the flames and he recognized that one of them was the Son of God (25). The Lord Jesus was with them and he brought them through in triumph. **They proved the promise of Isaiah 43:2.**

Nebuchadnezzar admitted: *'There is no other God who can deliver like this'* and he promoted the three brave men (29-30). Is your faith being tested? Remember that God is in complete control of all your circumstances, however trying they may be, and that he is faithful (1 Corinthians 10:13).

The signs and wonders that ... God has worked for me

We can be greatly encouraged by reading or listening to testimonies of Christian conversion. This chapter records the testimony of King Nebuchadnezzar (1-2). He states, *'I thought it good to declare the signs and wonders that the Most High God has worked for me.'* We have already seen that the king had failed to indoctrinate Daniel and his three friends, even though he had given Daniel the name of his god (8; cp. 1:7). Nebuchadnezzar had been forced to acknowledge the greatness of God (2:47; 3:28-29), but he had not yet humbled himself before the Lord nor had he turned from his sin, especially the sin of pride.

Nebuchadnezzar had a dream in which he saw a great tree which was felled at divine command and reduced to a stump (10-15). He had good reason to be troubled because kings were often represented as trees in Babylonian literature (4-5). The magicians, astrologers and soothsayers were not able to interpret the dream but the king knew that God would enable Daniel to give him its interpretation (5-9,18). Daniel was afraid to make known its meaning to the king, but did so at his insistence (19). God would humble Nebuchadnezzar and Daniel urged him to repent of his sin (27).

It appears that Nebuchadnezzar did not repent of his sin. One year later he was admiring his great building achievements and was full of pride (he had built the Hanging Gardens of Babylon, one of the seven wonders of the ancient world). Suddenly, a voice from heaven thundered words of judgment (31-33). Nebuchadnezzar became like an animal and lost his reason. God humbled the proud tyrant and when his reason returned he was a changed man. Nebuchadnezzar declared one of the greatest affirmations of God's sovereignty to be found in Scripture (34-35). He recognized that God *does according to his will* in heaven and on earth. His sovereign reign will never end (3,17,26,32,34-35,37). Be encouraged by Nebuchadnezzar's testimony. Be faithful in your witness, however difficult your circumstances. Persevere in your prayers for those who are lost. **No one is beyond the reach of God. He can save the worst sinner!**

Weighed in the balances, and found wanting

Belshazzar was probably the grandson of Nebuchadnezzar (*'father'* in verse 2 can mean 'ancestor' or 'grandfather'). We know from historical records that his father, Nabonidus, entrusted the throne to him while he was away waging war in central Arabia. While Nabonidus was away fighting, Belshazzar was feasting. He had the holy vessels, which had been taken from the temple in Jerusalem, brought to the feast. He and his guests used them as wine-cups. *They drank wine, and praised the gods of gold and silver, bronze and iron, wood and stone* (2-4). Belshazzar's drunken orgy at his great feast was a defiant rebellion against almighty God. Enough was enough. The party had to stop!

The merrymakers were dumbfounded as fingers of a man's hand appeared and wrote a strange message on the wall. The king was terrified (5-6)! The wise men, astrologers and their fellow occult practitioners were at a loss to give the meaning of the message (7-8). The queen (probably the wife of Nabonidus) came into the banquet hall and suggested that Belshazzar consult Daniel (9-12). Belshazzar sent for Daniel (the prophet was now an old man) offering him great honour and gifts if he would interpret the writing on the wall. Daniel was not interested in royal gifts however; he was more concerned to deliver God's word to Belshazzar (13-17).

Daniel reminded him of Nebuchadnezzar's testimony and told him that he had no excuse for his wickedness and defiance of God. He had not humbled himself before God (13-22). The message on the wall spelled out his doom (24-28). He had been *weighed in the balances, and found wanting* (27). Belshazzar was slain that night as the armies of the Medes and Persians diverted the waters of the River Euphrates, draining the water that ran under the city walls. The army entered Babylon under the walls and took the city. Darius the Mede received the kingdom from Cyrus (31). **Belshazzar had seen proof upon proof of God's power in his early years. He had seen the change wrought by God in the life of Nebuchadnezzar, but he hardened his heart. Those who despise God will be punished.**

He believed in his God

Darius, the new king of Babylon, appointed 120 satraps (provincial governors) to govern the kingdom of Babylon. They were accountable to three governors (one of whom was Daniel) for all their revenues. Though Daniel was now old, he excelled the other two governors and Darius recognized his honesty and integrity. The king had plans to set Daniel over the whole realm (1-3). The other governors and the satraps were very jealous of Daniel and this drove them to plot his downfall.

They sought to find some accusation against Daniel so that the king would remove him from office. They failed because Daniel was so transparently honest and faithful (3-4). Their words in verse 5 are very significant: '*We shall not find any charge against this Daniel unless we find it against him concerning the law of his God.*' They plotted to make Daniel choose between his God and the king knowing that Daniel would never compromise his loyalty to the Lord.

They succeeded in deceiving the king with their flattery and lies. He did not realize that '*all the governors*' (7) did not include Daniel. He signed the decree forbidding prayer to any god or man apart from himself for thirty days. Daniel did not panic when he heard of the king's decree (7-9). He prayed to God as was his custom (10) and his enemies reported his action to the king (11-13). They knew that Darius could not change his decree and he reluctantly gave the order for Daniel to be thrown to the lions (14-16). He was convinced that God was able to deliver Daniel but he had a sleepless night (16-18).

The king was overjoyed to find the man of God unharmed in the morning. Daniel told the king that God had sent his angel to shut the mouths of the lions (18-23). He was unharmed *because he believed in his God* (23). Darius made a decree in which he acknowledged the greatness of God and ordered that God should be feared (25-27). **We serve the living God! We do not trust him in vain!**

Then I set my face toward the Lord God

Daniel was taken captive to Babylon in 605 BC and he lived to see the collapse of the Babylonian Empire in 538 BC. He remained faithful to God throughout his long life. He was not only a great man of prayer but also one who searched the Scriptures. Though much of the Bible had not been written in those days, Daniel searched what Scriptures were available. In the first year of the reign of Darius (537 BC) Daniel was reading the book of Jeremiah (1). He realized that Jeremiah's prophecy that the Babylonian captivity would be for seventy years was about to be fulfilled (see Jeremiah 25:8-11; 29:10-14). Daniel had prayed throughout his exile in Babylon facing Jerusalem (6:14) but he now knew that the Jews would soon be allowed to return to his beloved city.

The promises of God's word stirred Daniel to pray. He wrote, *'Then I set my face toward the Lord God to make request by prayer and supplications, with fasting, sackcloth, and ashes'* (3). Daniel came before God with reverent prayer as he confessed his own sins and those of the nation (5-19). He reminded God of his righteousness (7,14-18) and of his mercy (3). The Lord heard his prayer, sending the angel Gabriel to tell him that he was *greatly beloved* (23; cp. 10:11). Many Jews returned from exile soon afterwards to rebuild Jerusalem and the temple. **Without prayer we are very weak. With prayer and God's word to feed us, we will be strong.**

The seventy weeks (literally 'seventy sevens', 24) has been the subject of much disagreement between Christians since the time of the early church fathers. We must beware of trying to calculate dates by manipulating these 'seventy sevens'. What is beyond doubt is the prophecy of the coming of the Lord Jesus who would *be cut off, but not for himself* (26). Isaiah prophesied, *'For he was cut off from the land of the living; for the transgression of my people he was stricken'* (Isaiah 53:8). His perfect sacrifice brought an end to animal sacrifices for sins (27; cp. Hebrews 10:11-18). The Jews rejected their Messiah and the Romans destroyed Jerusalem and the sanctuary in AD 70 (26).

HOSEA

Israel was divided after the death of Solomon (approximately 930 BC) following a rebellion by Jeroboam I who became king over the ten northern tribes. Solomon's son Rehoboam was left to rule over the remaining two tribes of Judah and Benjamin. The two separate kingdoms were known as Israel in the north (capital — Samaria) and Judah in the south (capital — Jerusalem). The turbulent history of the two nations is described in 1 Kings chapters 12 - 22 and 2 Chronicles chapters 10 - 36.

Hosea prophesied during the reign of Jeroboam II of Israel and four kings of Judah, the last of them being Hezekiah (1:1). His ministry (mainly to the northern kingdom) stretched over a period of at least forty years. Jeroboam died in 753 BC and Hezekiah began his reign over Judah in 715 BC. Hosea probably ended his days in Judah after the northern kingdom went into Assyrian captivity in 722 BC.

When Hosea began his ministry, Israel was enjoying great prosperity, but wickedness and corruption were rife. The nation had forsaken the Lord to serve Baal, the god of the Canaanites, and the goddess Ashtoreth. These idols were supposed to give fertility, bumper harvests and prosperity to those who served them (cp. 2:8). The worship of these gods had been a cause of unfaithfulness to the Lord for many generations (cp. Judges 2:13; 1 Kings 11:5).

Hosea's wife Gomer was unfaithful to him and drifted into prostitution, eventually becoming a slave. Hosea bought her out of slavery, restoring her to himself as his wife (3:1-5). God used Hosea's heartbreaking circumstances to show Israel her unfaithfulness in leaving him to serve idols and to show his steadfast love to the backsliding nation. Amos, the prophet of the broken law, sets forth the righteousness of God. Hosea, the prophet of the broken home, sets forth the grace of God.

A door of hope

Gomer was a selfish and fickle woman, forsaking her husband and family to indulge in sinful pleasures. Israel was no better. She was unfaithful to God who is pictured as calling upon individuals to plead with their mother, the nation of Israel (1-2). The Baals are described as Israel's lovers, but she did not know that it was the Lord who had prospered her (5,8). How would God respond to such unfaithfulness?

- He would chastise his people (6-7). *'Therefore, behold, I will hedge up your way with thorns, and wall her in.'* When we stray from the Lord, he will also chastise us and bring frustration, difficulties and darkness across our paths. He does this to restore us to himself, so that we will be able to say, *'For then it was better for me than now.'*
- God would *'therefore'* take away Israel's prosperity which she thought that Baal had given to her (this happened soon after the death of Jeroboam II) and he would punish her (9-13). This punishment was to be seen in Assyrian oppression and then captivity.

The first two *'therefores'* in this chapter bring a warning of chastisement and of punishment (6,9). The third *'therefore'* (14) introduces a message of hope and of restoration. This is a wonderful passage of Scripture which shows the grace of God to an undeserving, unfaithful people. Look at the *'I wills'* in verses 14 to 23 as blessing after blessing is promised. God, who had been slighted by unfaithful Israel, would *'allure her'* (14). The nation's treachery had brought terrible trouble upon her people but the Lord promised that *the Valley of Achor* ('trouble', Joshua 7:26) would become *a door of hope* (15). God would restore his people so that Israel would call God *'my husband'* rather than *'my master'* (16; Baal means 'master').

The Hebrew word translated *'loving-kindness'* (19) is also translated mercy (e.g. 4:1). We too are like Israel, being prone to wander from God. Have you been growing cold in heart and unfaithful to the Lord? Return to him now! He will turn your dark valley of trouble into *a door of hope.* Are you discouraged? God's promises are fulfilled in Christ for you. **There is hope for you in the valley of trouble. Take heart!**

I will heal their backsliding, I will love them freely

Chapter 13 contains sombre warnings of judgment but this chapter is full of consolation and hope. How could there be hope for a nation which was to be destroyed and its people transported to exile in Assyria? There was a remnant whom God graciously kept, just as there was in Judah, which later went into captivity in Babylon. This remnant came to worship God in Judah early in the reign of Hezekiah (2 Chronicles 30). These were probably those who heeded the passionate plea of the Lord recorded here, *'O Israel, return to the LORD your God'* (1).

How should a backslider pray? He should say, *'Take away all iniquity; receive us graciously'* (2). Repentance for sin and a renunciation of trust in anyone but the Lord is essential. Israel had been looking to political alliances either with Assyria or with Egypt, which had superb horses for riding into battle, to guarantee her survival (3). Restoration to God brings grateful praise to him (*'the sacrifices of our lips'*). He is so wonderful and gracious and he gives here a glorious promise to any repenting backslider, *'I will heal their backsliding, I will love them freely'* (4). The Lord also promises spiritual refreshment (*like the dew,* 5), beauty and fragrance (*like the lily,* 5-6), and stability (*roots like Lebanon,* 6). The Christian should enjoy stability and show the beauty of the Lord Jesus in his life.

When a backslider returns to the Lord, he discards those 'idols' that enticed him away from God. Like Ephraim, he says, *'What have I to do any more with idols? I have heard and observed him'* (8). **Is there someone or something in your life which has caused you to backslide? Turn from these 'idols' now and return to the Lord your God.** *The ways of the LORD are right* (9). Walk in them.

> The dearest idol I have known,
> Whate'er that idol be,
> Help me to tear it from thy throne,
> And worship only thee.
>
> (William Cowper)

1 & 2 TIMOTHY

Paul's letters to Timothy and Titus are known as 'the Pastoral Epistles'. It appears that Paul was released from imprisonment in Rome as he had anticipated (Acts 28:30; Philippians 1:25; 2:24; Philemon 22). He was not in prison when he wrote his **first letter to Timothy** and the letter to Titus. After his release from prison Paul was able to continue his missionary work for a year or two before being rearrested.

Timothy was probably converted during Paul's first visit to Lystra (Acts 14:6-7) and is described as his *'true son in the faith'* (1:2). He joined the apostle on his second missionary journey (Acts 16:1-3) and became a very close and trusted friend (Philippians 2:19-23; 1 Thessalonians 3:2). Timothy was a reserved and timid man who did not enjoy good health (1 Corinthians 16:10; 2 Timothy 1:6-7; 5:23). He was overseeing the church at Ephesus where some were teaching false doctrine (1:3-4; cp. Acts 20:29-31) and Paul urged him to deal with this problem and gave him directions for ordering the life of the church. He impressed upon Timothy the need for personal discipline and godliness (3:12-16; 6:6-14).

Rome was devastated by fire in AD 64 (said to have been started by the wicked emperor Nero for his own entertainment). Nero blamed the Christians for this and unleashed terrible persecution on the church. Thousands of Christians were tortured and killed. It was probably during this persecution that Paul was again imprisoned and put to death. His **second letter to Timothy** is the last of all his letters in the New Testament. It was possibly written within a few months of his death and Paul was most anxious for Timothy to come to Rome to see him before he died (cp. 4:6,9). He faced death with a calm dignity and with an expectation of the Lord's reward for faithful service (4:6-8). As a man who knew that he was nearing death, he urged Timothy to persevere *as a good soldier of Jesus Christ* (2:3) and to shun false teaching (2:16-18; 3:1-9). The great antidote to false teaching is sound doctrine and Hendriksen points out that the apostle urges Timothy to: hold on to it (1:13-14), teach it (2:2,24), abide in it (3:14) and preach it (4:2).

Love from a pure heart, from a good conscience

Paul had warned the Ephesian elders that savage wolves would come into their church, not sparing the flock (Acts 20:29). Those fears had been realized when he wrote to Timothy six or seven years later. Some at Ephesus had forsaken the simplicity of the gospel by posing as teachers of the law (7). They had become obsessed with myths centred around Old Testament family trees and were spending their time in vain speculation. This divided the church with worthless disputes which failed to bring godly edification (3-6). Never waste your time on any teaching which cannot be established from Scripture. Paul urged Timothy, *'Remain in Ephesus'* (3). He was not to run away from the problems facing him but to remain and deal with those who were spreading error in the church. The purpose of the *'commandment'* (same root in the Greek as the verb *'charge'* in verse 3) that Timothy was to give to the church at Ephesus was *love from a pure heart, from a good conscience, and from sincere faith* (5).

The law of God used rightly will strike at the conscience of sinners (8-10). Unless people know and feel their guilt before God, they will never repent of their sin. Paul considered himself the chief of sinners but he was full of praise to God for saving him and entrusting him with the ministry of the gospel (13-15). Verse 15 contains the first of the 'faithful sayings' in 1 Timothy. *This is a faithful saying and worthy of all acceptance, that Christ Jesus came into the world to save sinners.*

Hymenaeus and Alexander were false teachers who had strayed from the truth. They had rejected *faith and a good conscience* and had made shipwreck of their faith, blaspheming the Lord Jesus by denying his resurrection (19-20; cp. 2 Timothy 2:17-18). To be *'delivered to Satan'* means to lose God's protection from the devil (20); it probably involved excommunication (cp. 1 Corinthians 5:5). We are involved in a warfare against the powers of darkness (Ephesians 6:11-12). **Let us seek always to have that love in our lives which comes** *from a pure heart, from a good conscience, and from sincere faith* so that we may be able to *wage the good warfare* (18).

347

Lifting up holy hands

We are to pray for all kinds of men, especially those in authority that they will govern us wisely so that we will be able to lead quiet, peaceable, godly and reverent lives (1-3). Many people believe that verses 4 and 6 deny the doctrine that Christ died only for his elect (known as 'particular redemption' or 'limited atonement'). That is not so! William Hendriksen writes, 'Does Titus 2:11 really teach that the saving grace of God has appeared to every member of the human race without exception? Of course not! ... Again, does Romans 5:18 really teach that every member of the human race is justified? Does 1 Corinthians 15:22 really intend to tell us that every member of the human race is made alive in Christ? ... The expression "all men" as here used means "all men without distinction of race, nationality, or social position," not "all men individually, one by one"' (pages 93 and 94, *Commentary on 1 & 2 Timothy and Titus*).

A mediator is someone who stands between two opposing parties. Our sin has alienated us from God. Christ took human flesh and gave his life a ransom to bridge the gulf between a holy God and sinful men. *There is one God and one mediator between God and men, the man Christ Jesus* (5). Our salvation is based on the merit and the death of Christ alone. There is no other mediator who is able to save us or help us.

Men are to lead the congregation in prayer in public worship (8). The Greek word used here and in verse 12 ('*aner*') means a male and is different from '*anthropos*', translated '*men*' in verses 1 and 4. There is much controversy concerning the ministry of women but the word of God is quite explicit — women are not to teach or to have authority over men in the church (11-12). The apostle is not suggesting for a moment that women are inferior to men; in relation to Christ he stresses their equality (Galatians 3:28). What he does state here is that there is a difference in function. *Lifting up holy hands* in prayer is common in Scripture (e.g. Exodus 9:29; 17:11-12; 1 Kings 8:22). **Praying hands must be holy hands (cp. Psalm 24:3-4). God will not hear our prayers if we are entertaining sin in our lives (Psalm 66:18).**

He must have a good testimony

The word *'bishop'* (1-2) means 'an overseer' (as translated in the English Standard Version). There can be several *'bishops'* in the same church (Philippians 1:1). The New Testament is quite clear in its teaching that the *bishop* is the same office as that of an elder who shepherds (pastors) and oversees the church (Acts 20:17,28; 1 Peter 5:1-2). Verse 1 seems to indicate that it is good for a man to desire to be an overseer in the church. Motive is of great importance. Any man who is seeking personal standing or gain must be excluded (3,6). Selfish ambition has no place in God's service. The pastor leads the church as one who is a servant of God and of his people. He is responsible to give an account to God for the spiritual well-being of the flock (Hebrews 13:17). This is an awesome responsibility which is not to be undertaken thoughtlessly or prayerlessly.

The Lord requires the highest standards in the lives of those who would shepherd his people. A man who aspires to eldership *must be blameless, the husband of one wife, temperate* [self-controlled], *sober-minded, of good behaviour, hospitable, able to teach* (2-5; Titus 1:6-9). He must be *one who rules his own house well* (4). He must not be a recent convert (*'not a novice'*) and *he must have a good testimony* among the ungodly (6-7). The vices listed in verse 3 must be absent from his life. The vital importance of godliness in elders is seen in the word *'must'* (2,7). Many men have been appointed as elders who are seriously lacking in the necessary qualifications for that office. This has been disastrous and left churches weak and confused.

The word translated *'deacon'* (*'diakonos'*) means 'a servant' or 'one who serves at a table' (cp. Acts 6:2); it is sometimes translated *'minister'* (e.g. Colossians 1:7). All Christians should serve one another but there is a distinct office of deacon in the local church (Philippians 1:1). This is a spiritual work which requires spiritual men who have a pure conscience and a proven godly character (8-13; cp. 1:5,19). The church is *the pillar and ground* [or foundation] *of the truth* (15). **It is important that it has godly leaders.**

A good minister of Jesus Christ

The church is *the pillar and ground of the truth* (3:15). Satan works tirelessly to infiltrate it with false teachers because he wants to destroy it. We must not tolerate false teaching because error is demonic (1). Slaves and animals were branded with the seal of their owner. False teachers have their conscience seared (branded) so that they cannot tolerate truth (2); this indicates Satan's ownership. False teaching is often laced with many man-made rules (3-4). God *gives us richly all things to enjoy* (6:17) and that includes marriage and food.

The word *'minister'* is translated from the Greek word *'diakonos'* ('servant') but it is not restricted to the office of deacon. In verse 6 it refers to Timothy, an apostolic delegate and teacher in the church. What is expected of *a good minister of Jesus Christ*? He must proclaim the truth and warn against error. He must be *nourished in the words of faith and of the good doctrine* taught by the apostles. He exercises himself in godliness and rejects superstitious fables (6-7).

Another *'faithful saying'* is that *bodily exercise profits a little, but godliness is profitable for all things ...* (8-9). Godliness brings the promise of life. What is this spiritual life? It is the enjoyment of fellowship with God in Christ; it is the love of God *poured out in our hearts by the Holy Spirit*; it is *the peace of God which surpasses all understanding* (John 14:23; 1 John 1:3; Romans 5:5; Philippians 4:7) as well as glory to come in heaven. A good minister is *an example to the believers in word, in conduct, in love, in spirit, in faith, in purity* (11-12). He will give attention to the reading of Scripture, to exhortation and to teaching (13). **These things are most important in the life of the church!**

Verse 10 does not teach universalism (that all will be saved). The Bible overwhelmingly rejects such a notion. This verse clearly demonstrates that the gospel is for all people whatever their race or standing but only those who believe (trust) in Christ enjoy the benefits of salvation. **Are you exercising yourself to godliness?**

A reputation for good works

Timothy's relationship to people in the church was most important. He was to be like a son in exhorting older men and women, and as a brother in the way he dealt with younger men and women. This indicates that love and respect are essential in pastoral work. Pastors must be pure and beyond reproach in their dealings with women (1-2). The remainder of the chapter deals with the honouring of widows (3-16) and elders (17-25).

The early church undertook to provide for those of its widows who had no children or grandchildren to support them (4,16). If a Christian shows no concern to provide for his own parents or grandparents, he denies the faith (8). Some elderly people are neglected by their families. They may or may not need financial help but there are jobs we can do for them which they are unable to do for themselves; they need frequent visits and encouragement. Widows who were supported had to have *a reputation for good works* (9-10). What opportunities there are for a women's ministry in her home! Look at some of the good works mentioned in verse 10. By way of contrast, great damage can be done by women who idle away their time (13,15). Widows supported by the church were expected to have a ministry of prayer (5). Such a hidden ministry is vital and many a servant of God is blessed and encouraged through the prayers and intercession of elderly Christians.

Elders are to be honoured and those set aside to full-time service must be adequately supported (17-18). Beware of listening to gossip about elders (Satan wants to destroy their reputation and so ruin their ministry). Any accusation against an elder must be substantiated by two or three witnesses. Those who have sinned must be publicly rebuked (18-20). Hands were laid on those set aside to serve the Lord in the church but they were only to be laid on those *whose good works ... are clearly evident* (22-25). **Good works cannot save us but the Lord expects to see them in the lives of all Christians.** Every Christian, young or old, rich or poor, should have *a reputation for good works* (cp. 6:18).

Godliness with contentment is great gain

The Roman world was full of slaves and questions were bound to be raised when slaves or their owners became Christians, in view of Galatians 3:28 (in Christ *there is neither slave nor free*). Slave owners were to treat their slaves with dignity (Ephesians 6:9) and slaves were to be better workers than they were before their conversion (1-2). Where the gospel flourishes, slavery withers and dies. These verses do have implications for us today, however. Christians should excel and be conscientious in their work *so that the name of God and his doctrine are not blasphemed* (1). We are not to have any fellowship with false teachers. They are proud and obsessed with disputes over words *from which come envy, strife, reviling, evil suspicions.* They suppose that religion (*'godliness'*) is a means of selfish gain and reject the words of Christ and *the doctrine which is according to godliness* (3-5).

Paul stresses the need for godliness throughout this letter (2:2; 4:7-8; 6:3,6,11). **If our teaching does not make us godly, we are going wrong.** *Godliness with contentment is great gain* (6). It is very dangerous, however, to be content without godliness. Many a contented sinner has slipped into hell! It is also a fact that many Christians are not content. Why is this? There is a sense in which we will never be fully content until our pilgrimage on earth is over and we are with our blessed Saviour in heaven. Many are discontented, however, because they are not godly. Over 350 years ago the Puritan Jeremiah Burroughs wrote a book (still available through Banner of Truth Trust publishers) entitled *The rare jewel of Christian contentment*. He writes, 'Christian contentment is that sweet, inward, quiet, gracious frame of spirit, which fully submits to and delights in God's wise and fatherly disposal in every condition.'

The great enemy of contentment is covetousness and the *desire to be rich* (9-10; cp. Hebrews 13:5). **We must flee these things and pursue the things that please the Lord** — *righteousness, godliness, faith, love, patience, gentleness* (11-12). Have you proved that *godliness with contentment is great gain?*

I know whom I have believed

Paul was thankful to God for *the genuine faith* ('sincere faith') of Timothy and recalled that this kind of faith had been seen in his mother and grandmother (5). Timothy's Jewish mother had become a Christian but his Gentile father had probably remained outside of Christ (Acts 16:1). **Eunice is a great example to any whose husband (or wife) is not a Christian.** This godly woman and her mother had taught Timothy the Scriptures (3:15) from his earliest years and he became an outstanding Christian and a beloved fellow-worker of the apostle Paul.

There is a great statement about our salvation in verses 9 and 10. Election (God's choice of individuals to salvation) is not based on our works but is by grace according to the purpose of God. We were chosen in Christ *before time began,* not because God foresaw any good works in us *but according to his own purpose and grace* ('grace' is the undeserved favour of God). Theologians describe this wonderful truth as 'unconditional election'. We have been saved and called with *a holy calling.* Christ through his death has abolished death (deprived it of its power) and *brought life and immortality to light through the gospel.* Our souls will go to heaven when we die and our bodies will be raised when Jesus comes again (cp. 1 Corinthians 15:5-55). What a glorious hope we have in Christ!

God had appointed Paul to be *a preacher, an apostle, and a teacher of the Gentiles* (11). As a servant of God he suffered, but he testified, *Nevertheless I am not ashamed, for I know whom I have believed and am persuaded that he is able to keep that which I have committed to him until that day* (12). It is important that we not only know what we believe, but that we also know whom we have believed (God). Paul stresses here his relationship with God. He was persuaded that God would keep all the precious things that he had committed to his care — his soul, his future, his friends, his work. Paul had such a great trust in his God and Saviour that he could face death with peace and assurance. **Commit your life, your ways, your problems and cares to him. He will never fail you, he cannot fail you, for he is God.**

A good soldier of Jesus Christ

Having written of the examples of Lois, Eunice, Onesiphorus and himself (chapter 1), Paul encouraged Timothy to *be strong in the grace that is in Christ Jesus* (1). He was to commit the teaching he had received from Paul to *faithful men* who would in turn become teachers of God's word (2). Paul went on to liken the Christian life and service to that of a soldier (3-4), an athlete (5) and a farmer (6). He reminded Timothy that Jesus Christ was raised from the dead so that God's elect might obtain the salvation which is in Christ Jesus with eternal glory (8,10). Paul was in chains for the gospel but he knew that the word of God is not chained (9).

We are involved in *the good warfare* (1 Timothy 1:18) against the world (4), the flesh (22) and the devil (26). *A good soldier of Jesus Christ* must endure hardship (3). We must not expect to have an easy time. *A good soldier of Jesus* will not get entangled *with the affairs of this life* (4). We may have to deny ourselves pleasures and enjoyments which are not in themselves sinful, but which may distract us from our warfare (1 Corinthians 6:12).

A good soldier will do all that he can to present himself *approved to God* so that there is nothing in his life of which he should be ashamed. He will rightly handle *the word of truth* (15); he will *depart from iniquity* (19) and *pursue righteousness, faith, love, peace* (22). *A good soldier is useful for the Master, prepared for every good work* (21). He is *gentle to all, able to teach, patient.* He is gracious and humble in his attitude to those who oppose the gospel (23-24).

Our supreme aim must be to please him who has enlisted us as his soldiers (4). Dare we be half-hearted when the Lord Jesus gave his life to save us? Surely, if we love him, we will be prepared to deny ourselves for him and to suffer for him. Let us consider the words of Paul in these scriptures and remember that success and fruitfulness in spiritual work do not come without hard toil or sacrifice.

Thoroughly equipped for every good work

The last days (1) are not limited to the time which immediately precedes the second coming of Christ. They refer to the time in which Paul lived until Christ returns (the gospel age; cp. Acts 2:17). There have been and there will continue to be perilous seasons which will have their climax in the revealing of the antichrist, the man of sin (2 Thessalonians 2:1-12). Verses 2 to 4 contain a list of dreadful sins which in many ways reflect the godless society around us. The first sin in the list is the love of self; other sins follow selfishness so that men become *lovers of money, boasters, proud, blasphemers, disobedient to parents, etc.* These sins are not only found among the godless. They are to be seen in the lives of religious people who are described as *having a form of godliness but denying its power* (5).

Paul reminded Timothy of his own teaching and manner of life, including the persecution he had suffered. We may not be imprisoned or called upon to die for our faith, but we must expect trouble in a hostile world. *All who desire to lead a godly life in Christ Jesus will suffer persecution* (12; cp. John 15:18-25; 16:33; 1 John 3:13). Paul urged Timothy to continue in the things he had learned from himself, and from Lois and Eunice (14; cp. 1:5). **We cannot emphasize enough the necessity of a thorough grounding in the Scriptures.** This is essential if we are to be godly people and if we are to be equipped to combat false teaching.

All Scripture is given by inspiration of God (i.e. 'God-breathed'). There are no errors in the Bible (this is known as 'the inerrancy of Scripture'). The Bible alone is the authority for our teaching. We must beware of those who add to Scripture from traditions which deny the gospel and those who subtract from it (e.g. who deny that it is God's word and reject the account of creation found in Genesis chapters 1 to 3, salvation through Christ alone, the bodily resurrection of Jesus, etc.). *All ... Scripture is profitable ... that the man of God may be complete, thoroughly equipped for every good work* (16-17). **How thoroughly equipped for every good work are you?**

I have fought the good fight

A gospel minister must know the word of God and preach it. The faithful preaching and teaching of God's word builds us up and helps keep us from error. *Preach the word*! (2-5). Paul comes to the end of his letter with a most moving statement of faith: *I am already being poured out as a drink offering, and the time of my departure is at hand* (6; cp. Philippians 2:17). In Old Testament times a drink offering was *poured out as a sweet aroma to the LORD* (Numbers 15:7). Paul was facing execution, but for him, death was not the dread end, but a departure for heaven; it was to be with Christ which is *gain ... which is far better* (Philippians 1:21,23).

Paul was *a good soldier* who had *fought the good fight*, the athlete had *finished the race* (cp. 2:3-5) and he awaited the victor's crown. The servant of the Lord had kept the faith and he was looking forward to receiving his heavenly reward (7-8). Demas had forsaken him and he was alone, except for Luke (10-11). Paul wanted Timothy to come urgently (9), not only because of his impending death, but if he were spared the winter, he would need warmth in his cold, damp prison cell. The cloak that he had left at Troas could be brought to him as well as his books and especially the parchments (13,21). Paul was a reader to the end and he wanted to encourage himself in the Scriptures (*the parchments*). He warned Timothy against Alexander the coppersmith who had been a bitter enemy (14-15).

Paul had felt his loneliness at his first court appearance (14-16). He was not alone however. *The Lord stood with me and strengthened me, so that the message might be preached* (17). He had fought the good fight and he knew that the Lord would preserve him *for his heavenly kingdom* (18). **Let us praise our great God who cares for us, preserves us, and who will never forsake us.** *To him be the glory for ever and ever. Amen!* Paul closes by giving Timothy some news of their fellow-workers and their present spheres of service, as well as sending greetings to some of his fellow-workers (19-22).

TITUS

Paul describes Titus as his true son (1:4; cp. 1 Timothy 1:2) and wrote to him at the same time as he wrote his first letter to Timothy (approximately AD 63). Titus, a Gentile (Galatians 2:3), was a faithful and trusted fellow-worker (cp. 2 Corinthians 2:13; 7:6-15; 12:18; 2 Timothy 4:10). Paul had left him in Crete to *set in order the things that are lacking, and appoint elders in every city* (1:5). This letter sets out the things necessary for a healthy church — godly elders, sound doctrine and godly living. Paul also wrote to urge Titus to come to him at Nicapolis as soon as Artemas or Tychicus arrived in Crete to take over from him (3:12).

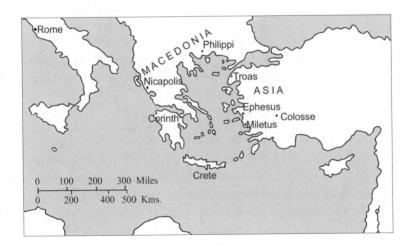

The faith of God's elect

Paul describes himself as *an apostle of Jesus Christ, according to the faith of God's elect* (1). The elect are those whom God was pleased to choose to salvation before time began. Let us think about this faith:

- *The faith of God's elect* produces a love for *the truth which is according to godliness* (1; cp. 1 Timothy 6:3). God has chosen us to be holy (Ephesians 1:4). Truth and godliness are inseparable. Truth embraces the great doctrines of the gospel.
- *The faith of God's elect* rests on the unchanging faithfulness of *God, who cannot lie* (2). We have the *hope of eternal life* which he *promised before time began* (2; cp. 2 Timothy 1:9). All the promises and threats in the Bible are true. If you are struggling in trial or perplexity, if you are beset by doubts, encourage yourself in the Lord by remembering that God cannot lie. He cannot deny his holy character (2 Timothy 2:13). He will bring you through!
- *The faith of God's elect* is committed to the faithful preaching (proclamation) of God's word (3). This faith will not bow to pressures which despise preaching and seek for entertainment in the church.

Paul had left Titus in Crete to do two things:

- He was to *set in order the things that are lacking* (5). The Greek translated *'set in order'* means 'to straighten out' and Titus was to deal with the things that remained to be done. Believers were to be gathered together to form churches under godly leadership.
- He was to *appoint elders in every city* (5). The *'elder'* (5) is also described as a *'bishop'* ('overseer', 7). An elder (or pastor) shepherds the flock of God (1 Peter 5:2).

The churches of Crete were being troubled by false teachers (10-16), who were not to be tolerated. Their mouths must be stopped (11) and they were to be sharply rebuked (13). Sound doctrine (9; 2:1) must be taught so that every Christian *may be sound in the faith* (13; cp. 2:2). The Greek word translated *'sound'* means 'healthy'. **Healthy doctrine should lead to a healthy faith. Do you have the precious faith of God's elect?**

That they may adorn the doctrine of God our Saviour

Titus was to teach and to be an example of one who embraced *sound* [healthy] *doctrine* (1,7-8). He was to reach all sections of the church in his pastoral work, encouraging young and old alike to lead godly lives (2-10). The older Christian man is to show in his life the kind of spiritual maturity that matches his age. He is to be *sober, reverent, temperate, sound in faith, in love, in patience* (2). Older men often lack patience, but they must look to the Lord to correct this deficiency (2). We must be *'sober'* ('serious-minded', 2,6,12) and beware of looking for religious excitement. This of course does not exclude joy and laughter in our lives, for walking with God brings great happiness. Older women may have a very useful ministry in teaching good things to the younger women in the church (3-5). This is a vital ministry in our churches but is only possible when the older women are loved and respected for their godliness. The young women should be willing to receive their help and teaching.

Godly living in the home and at work is essential if our witness is to be taken seriously by those outside the church. An inconsistent life will cause the word of God to be *'blasphemed'* (5; cp. 1 Timothy 6:1). Slaves were often very surly and untrustworthy but a Christian slave was able to have a very convincing testimony by being different (9-10). The same principle applies to all of us. Our lives must *adorn the doctrine of God our Saviour in all things.* Is this true of you? **Does your life make the Christian faith appear beautiful and attractive?**

The grace of God is described here as a teacher (12). It teaches us:

- To renounce *ungodliness and worldly lusts* (this includes immoral sexual desires, living for pleasure and being self-centred).
- To *live soberly, righteously, and godly* (12).
- To look *for the blessed hope and glorious appearing of our great God and Saviour Jesus Christ* (13). This verse is one of many which teach that the Lord Jesus is God (e.g. Romans 9:5; Philippians 2:6; Colossians 1:15-20; 2:9). This glorious hope is a great incentive to being holy (12,14; cp. 1 John 3:3). Do you think much about it?

Be careful to maintain good works

Paul commanded Titus to remind the Christians in Crete that as God's *special people* they were to be model citizens. Can the virtues listed in verses 1 and 2 be seen in your life? Are you *ready for every good work*? Do you refrain from speaking evil of others? Are you *peaceable, gentle, showing humility to all men*? Before God graciously saved us we were *once foolish* (ignorant of spiritual things), *disobedient* (rebels against God), *deceived* (believing the lies of Satan), *serving various lusts and pleasures* (slaves of our own sinful passions), and *living in malice and envy* (because of hatred in our hearts). It is only when we are saved that we realize the exceeding sinfulness of the human heart (3).

Verse 4 contains one of the great 'buts' of Scripture (cp. Ephesians 2:4): *But when the kindness and love of God our Saviour towards men appeared* (cp. 2:11, *the grace of God ... has appeared*). Man without God lives in malice, envy, and hatred (3), but God is kind.

The *faithful saying* (8) refers to the words in verses 4 to 7. We are not saved *by works of righteousness* (5) but we are saved to do good works. Paul urged Titus to *affirm constantly* these things (8) **We must always remember that free grace is not the enemy of good works. We must be kind to others because God is kind to us.** We are to be *ready for every good work* (1). Those who have believed in God *should be careful to maintain good works* (8). Good works flow out of a life which loves the Lord, which is grateful for his grace. We are warned not to tolerate false teachers or those who threaten the unity of the fellowship (9-11).

The apostle promised to send Artemas or Tychicus to Crete so that Titus could be released to go to him at Nicapolis where he was planning to spend the winter (12). Zenas and Apollos were probably the bearers of Paul's letter to Titus (13). Paul returns to the theme of good works in his closing greetings. *And let our people also learn to maintain good works, to meet urgent needs, that they may not be unfruitful* (14). **Is there an urgent need that you could meet by some good work? Is there someone you could help with a word of encouragement?**

JOEL & AMOS

We know little about **Joel** (which means 'Jehovah is God') except that he was the son of Pethuel (1:1). We do not know when he exercised his ministry; many evangelical scholars reckon that he prophesied during the reign of Joash, king of Judah (shortly after 835 BC). The land had been devastated by a plague of locusts (ch. 1) which God had sent in judgment. Joel urged the people to repent of their sin and he speaks of '*the day of the* LORD' (1:15; 2:1,11,31; 3:14). '*The day of the* LORD' refers to those times when God brings judgment upon sinners such as the plague of locusts in Joel's time (1:15), when Jerusalem is destroyed (Zephaniah 1:4,7), and when Christ comes again to judge the world (1 Thessalonians 5:2; 2 Peter 3:10-13). The outpouring of the Holy Spirit on the Day of Pentecost was a fulfilment of the prophecy by Joel (2:28-32; Acts 2:16-21).

Amos prophesied during the reigns of King Uzziah of Judah and King Jeroboam II of Israel (about 760 BC). He was a herdsman and a farmer of sycamore figs (1:1; 7:14). This fig tree (cp. Luke 19:4) must not be confused with the European sycamore tree. Amos prophesied to the northern kingdom (Israel), though he was from Tekoa (about twelve miles south of Jerusalem) in Judah. Both countries were enjoying an economic boom, but things were far from well. The rich grew richer, many of them owning several houses, but the poor grew poorer (3:15) and they were oppressed by the rich (2:6-7; 4:1). Justice was perverted by bribery (5:10-12). There was plenty of religion with great feast days, but it was corrupt (4:4-5; 5:21-23; 7:10-13).

Amos thundered out warnings of judgment against the people on account of their wickedness. His prophecy ends with a ray of hope, the restoring of the kingdom of David, the coming of Messiah to reign over his people (9:11-15; cp. Acts 15:13-17). You may wonder what relevance such a prophecy has for us almost 2800 years later? It has every relevance. The similarities between society in Amos' day and our day are quite striking and his prophecy contains vital lessons and warnings for us.

Whoever calls on the name of the LORD shall be saved

The word of the Lord came to Joel at a time when the land had been devastated by a plague of locusts which are described as God's army (11; cp. 1:1-7); this was an act of divine judgment upon the people. Such times of judgment are often called *'the day of the LORD'* (11). God called the people to repentance (12-17) with promises of blessing to those who heeded his call (18-27). True repentance involves more than tearing clothes; it results in sorrow over sin which cuts into our hearts (12-13). Joel did not take God's forgiveness for granted. He asks, *'Who knows if he will turn and relent, and leave a blessing behind him?'* (14; cp. Amos 5:15). When true religion is at a low ebb, God is reproached and the people ask, *'Where is their God?'* (15-17).

Peter quoted verses 28 to 32 in his sermon on the Day of Pentecost (Acts 2:16-21). Joel prophesied of the distant future when he wrote of the pouring out of the Holy Spirit in the last days (28-29; fulfilled at Pentecost). The prophet then gives us a glimpse of *the great and terrible day of the LORD* (30-32) when Jesus will come again as King and Judge of all the earth. That final *'day of the LORD'* will be a dreadful time for all who do not know the Lord Jesus Christ (2 Thessalonians 1:7-10; Revelation 9:6). If the Lord Jesus returned today, would you be ready?

There is a promise here for everyone who wants to be saved: *Whoever calls on the name of the LORD shall be saved* (32). Calling on the name of the Lord must involve repentance (cp. Acts 2:38) and trusting in God (Isaiah 50:10; John 1:12). We soon realize after calling on the name of the Lord, that he first called us (32; cp. Acts 2:39). **Have you called on the name of the Lord?** God promises that whoever calls on him will be saved and that they will receive the gift of the Holy Spirit (28-29; Acts 2:39). All Christians have the gift of the Holy Spirit, not just a select few (cp. Romans 8:9; Galatians 4:6). If you have called on God, you should be praising his name, for he has *dealt wondrously* with you (26).

Because they have despised the law of the LORD

Amos prophesied against the neighbours of Judah and Israel (1:1 - 2:3) but his own people had no reason to be smug or complacent; they were also wicked (4-16). Judah was not condemned for crimes against humanity but *because they have despised the law of the LORD and have not kept his commandments* (4). *Their lies* (4) refer to the idolatry and occult practices which took root in Judah when God's word was despised. The nation or individual who despise God's word will not keep his commandments. We have seen a dreadful decline in the western world because of this sin. The spiritual vacuum is being filled by the occult such as new-age practices, spiritism, astrology and witchcraft. False religion is a lie. May God have mercy on us!

The northern kingdom (Israel) was not only condemned for its idolatry, but also for oppressing the poor. The righteous and the poor were being sold into slavery and were being trampled into the dust by their oppressors (6-7). The new religion encouraged prostitution and all kinds of sexual immorality (8). God reminded the people of his mercy to their forefathers, but what had they done? Young men who had dedicated their lives to God as Nazirites (cp. Numbers 6:1-21) were being encouraged to take strong drink, so breaking their vows of abstinence, and the prophets of God were silenced (11-12; cp. 7:12-17).

God was weighed down by the burden of his people's sin (13; some translations, e.g. English Standard Version, render the verse to read that it is Jehovah who is pressing down upon his people). The Lord warned that he would destroy Judah and Israel by invading armies (5,13-16). When men refuse to hear God's word they have no excuse when judgment comes upon them. **Let the message of Amos be a warning to us all. We despise the law of the Lord at our peril! Let us search our own hearts to see if there be any such rebellion found in us.**

Prepare to meet your God

The Lord who is absolutely perfect demands that his people lead holy lives (1 Peter 1:15-16). The Lord chose Israel to be different from the other nations but she had fallen into the sins of those nations — idolatry, self-indulgence and the oppression of the poor. We read here, '*The Lord God has sworn by his holiness*' (2). He was affirming that as sure as he is holy he would visit the self-indulgent women of Samaria with judgment and disaster. Their husbands were oppressing the poor and crushing the needy in order to satisfy their opulent lifestyle. Amos did not mince his words. He called them '*cows of Bashan*' (1). Bashan was renowned for its fertile pasture land on which its fat cows gorged themselves. Amos prophesied that these women would be dragged away captive with hooks through their noses just as fish are drawn from the sea on hooks (2). This was fulfilled in 721 BC when the Assyrians led Israel away captive.

Bethel and Gilgal were two great centres of worship in Israel (Genesis 28:16-22; Joshua 5:9), but they had become debased with all kinds of idol worship. Amos mocked the song of the pilgrims as they went to worship their idols, '*Come to Bethel and transgress*' (4). These people loved their religious ceremony and sacrifices, but it was all so empty and vain. They had a religion without holiness which left them comfortable with their wickedness.

God sent Israel famine (6), drought (7), blight and locusts (9), plagues and war (10), and an earthquake (11) but they were deaf to his voice and rebellious. Look at the times that God says, '*Yet you have not returned to me*' (6,8,9,10,11). Israel had been '*like a firebrand plucked from the burning*' — charred and ugly, useless and hopeless, but there was an opportunity to repent and return to the Lord (11). The Lord again warned the people that judgment was coming: '*Therefore thus will I do to you, O Israel; and because I will do this to you, prepare to meet your God, O Israel!*' (12). **If you are not prepared in this day of grace to meet God in repentance, be prepared to meet him in judgment!**

'A famine ... of hearing the words of the LORD'

The Lord showed the prophet a basket of summer fruit and asked him, '*What do you see?*' (1-2). The Hebrew words for '*summer fruit*' and '*end*' (2) are very similar in sound. Ripe fruit needs to be gathered at once and Israel was like ripe fruit. Her sin demanded action. She was ripe for judgment because of her sin. The songs of worship in the temple would become cries of mourning. Dead bodies would be scattered everywhere. The shrieks of pain and the silence of the dead would confirm that God had kept his word to punish faithless and wicked Israel (3,10). God would not pass by his people in mercy any more (2). The rich oppressed the poor and the merchants hated the Sabbath because it interrupted their trade and their business rackets. They falsified their scales so that the poor, who were the victims of their deceit, were driven into slavery (4-6). The Lord would never forget what they were doing (7). He said, '*Shall not the land tremble for this?*' (8). Israel was ripe for judgment.

When God speaks to us through his word it is a great mercy. If we refuse to listen to God's word and obey it like Amaziah and Israel (chapter 7), it may well be that he will withdraw it from us. We will then be faced with the worst possible type of famine, not a famine of food or of water, but *a famine ... of hearing the words of the* LORD (11). What happens when such a famine comes upon a nation?

* There is a thirst that is never satisfied; the young are particularly vulnerable and without hope (12-13).
* There is an upsurge in false religion. The '*sin of Samaria*' refers to idol worship. People went on pilgrimages to Dan in the far north of the country to worship at the golden-calf shrine, and to the far south to Beersheba in Judah. The Lord warned that these false, corrupt religions would not save their followers from disaster (14).

Christian, prize your Bible! God's word is more precious than gold (Psalm 119:162). Pray that the Lord will be pleased to bless the preaching of his word this coming Lord's Day. Prepare your own heart to receive that word and be ready to obey it.

OBADIAH & JONAH

We do not know anything about the life of **Obadiah** whose book is the shortest in the Old Testament (where we find twelve men named Obadiah). Some scholars (and Jewish tradition) place Obadiah in the ninth century BC. Others believe that his prophecy against the Edomites came after the fall of Jerusalem in 586 BC. The twin brothers, Jacob and Esau, had little in common and never enjoyed an easy relationship (see Genesis chapters 25 to 36). Their descendants, the nations of Israel and Edom, became bitter enemies. The Edomites refused to allow the Israelites, who had solemnly promised not to take their crops or pasture, to pass through their country as they journeyed to Canaan (Numbers 20:14-21). Many years later David conquered the Edomites (2 Samuel 8:14) but they regained their freedom during the reign of Jehoram (2 Kings 8:20,22). They attacked Jerusalem during the reign of Ahaz (2 Chronicles 28:17). Edom fell into Arab hands in the fifth century BC, and was overrun by the Nabateans in the third century BC. Many Edomites fled to Judah during these centuries and were later incorporated into the Jewish nation during the time of John Hyrcanus.

Obadiah's message was one of wrath upon the wicked and unrepentant Edom. **The book of Jonah** shows the mercy of God to the wicked people of Nineveh who repented of their sin. The name 'Jonah' means a 'dove' but the prophet was a 'hawk' in his attitude to Gentiles. Like Amos he prophesied during the reign of Jeroboam II (793–753 BC). He not only prophesied to Nineveh, but also to the wicked northern kingdom (2 Kings 14:25). Jonah came from the village of Gath Hepher which was just a few miles north of Nazareth. The Lord Jesus used Jonah's three days and nights in the stomach of the great fish to illustrate his own death, burial and resurrection (Matthew 12:40-42; 16:4). We see in this book the sovereign power and greatness of God as he worked in miraculous ways to teach the reluctant prophet his will to save Nineveh. The key verse is *Salvation is of the LORD* (2:9). When God determines to save, no one can hinder his purposes, not even disobedient prophets.

The kingdom shall be the Lord's

The Edomites were a proud and arrogant people who lived in a rugged, mountainous land situated to the south of the Dead Sea. They felt secure in their mountain fortresses and could not believe that they would ever be overrun in battle (3; cp. Jeremiah 49:14-16). Their ancestor Esau is described as a *'profane person'* (Hebrews 12:16). The Greek word translated *'profane'* means 'without religion' or 'godless'. We never read in the Old Testament of Edomite gods or religion. They were secular in their outlook, priding themselves on their wisdom and might (8). The wisdom of Teman is mentioned in Jeremiah 49:7; one of Job's counsellors was Eliphaz from Teman (Job 2:11). God told Edom, *'The pride of your heart has deceived you'* (3) and he warned her that he would bring her down suddenly as a thief comes in the night. She would be utterly ruined and her wise men destroyed (*cut off,* 5,9). Her own allies would be God's instruments of judgment (7).

Verses 11 to 14 appear to describe the fall of Jerusalem to the Babylonians (cp. Psalm 137:7; Jeremiah 49:7-22). The Edomites were treacherous as well as proud. They gloated over the calamity of the Jews, plundered their possessions, and prevented those who fled from Jerusalem from making good their escape. Notice the repetition of the words, *'You should not have ... nor should you have'* (12-14). Edom richly deserved God's judgment and the Lord told them, *'As you have done, it shall be done to you'* (15; Galatians 6:7). The nation of Edom was utterly destroyed but Israel remains to this day.

The prophecy of Obadiah looks beyond the judgment of Edom and the return of the Jews from captivity to the everlasting reign of Christ our Saviour (cp. Revelation 11:15-18). *But on Mount Zion there shall be deliverance, and there shall be holiness* (17). The Lord Jesus will destroy all his enemies when he comes again (2 Thessalonians 1:7-9). Whenever we hear of the terrible atrocities and inhumanity of some totalitarian regimes or nations we must not despair. **God always has the last word!** *The kingdom shall be the Lord's* (21). Let this wonderful truth encourage you.

For you, O Lord, have done as it pleased you

The Lord told Jonah to go and to cry out against the great city of Nineveh, capital of Assyria, because of the wickedness of its people. Jonah did not want to go to Nineveh because he had little time for Gentiles and he did not care if they perished. *Jonah arose to flee to Tarshish from the presence of the Lord* (3). God had told him to go east to Nineveh but he was determined to go west to Tarshish (which may have been in Spain). He tried to do the impossible — to run away from God (cp. Psalm 139:7-12). At first all seemed to go well for the prophet and he found a ship just about to sail for Tarshish.

Trouble soon came to Jonah. The Lord sent a great tempest which threatened to destroy the ship (4). The heathen sailors called on their gods but they were useless to help. They then aroused the sleeping prophet, urging him to pray to his God (5-6). When they cast lots to determine the cause of their calamity, Jonah was singled out. He told them that he feared the Lord and was trying to run away from him (7-10). He suggested that they throw him overboard so that the sea would become calm but they tried to avoid such drastic action (11-13).

These Gentile sailors prayed to the living God and acknowledged his absolute sovereignty saying, *'For you, O Lord, have done as it pleased you'* (14). They also prayed that God would not hold them guilty if Jonah died. God's sovereign work is again seen in the statement of verse 17. *Now the Lord had prepared a great fish to swallow Jonah.* The Lord had prepared it! Scoffers reject the book of Jonah saying that it is impossible for a man to be swallowed by a fish or for a man to survive in the stomach of a fish for three days. Why should we think it strange that almighty God had prepared the fish and was able to keep Jonah alive inside it for three days? Jonah earnestly prayed from the stomach of the fish for deliverance. He confessed his trust in Jehovah: *'Salvation is of the Lord'* (2:9). God alone was able save him because only God could save and deliver him. **God who saved Jonah from the stomach of the fish, God who saved Nineveh, is able to save the most stubborn sinner.**

Now the word of the LORD came to Jonah the second time

The grace of God shines out in chapter 3 — restoring grace for a disobedient prophet and saving grace for a wicked city. Are you feeling miserable because you know that you have failed the Lord or disobeyed him? Do you despair of ever being used again by God? There is a word of hope here for you. *Now the word of the LORD came to Jonah the second time* (2). Jonah did not deserve a second chance, but the Lord did not cast him off. He graciously recommissioned him and sent him to Nineveh (2). God could have easily raised up another prophet but he wanted to use Jonah. **What grace! What patience! What love!**

Greater Nineveh (3) was a city with a circumference of about sixty miles. The wickedness of that city was great indeed and it was ripe for judgment (1:2) but *the people of Nineveh believed God* (5). The king and his subjects repented of their sin and cried to God (6-9). Though Jonah had no love for the Assyrians his preaching to them was an outstanding success. He was angry, however, that God had spared them and would have been far happier had God destroyed them (4:1-3). He went out of Nineveh to see what would become of it (4:5). He may have hoped for its destruction though the people had heeded his preaching.

The sulking, petulant prophet was in such a dreadful mood that he wanted to die (4:3,8). It was good for Jonah that God did not take him at his word. *The LORD God prepared a plant,* and *a worm,* and *a vehement east wind* (4:6-8). Jonah was very grateful for the plant that God had prepared, making it grow quickly to give him shelter. He was angry when the worm attacked it, causing it to wither so that he was exposed to the vehement wind and heat of the sun. Jonah again expressed a wish to die (4:8). God asked him, *'Is it right for you to be angry?'* The sinful prophet insisted that he was right to be angry, even if it killed him (4:4,9). Jonah had more pity for the plant than for the people of Nineveh (10) who would have perished in their ignorance but for *a gracious and merciful God, slow to anger and abundant in loving-kindness* (4:2). **If our hearts are filled with the love of God we will earnestly desire the salvation of those who are lost.**

Refresh my heart in the Lord

Philemon was a wealthy Christian who had been converted through Paul's ministry (19) and the church at Colosse met in his home (2). Apphia was probably his wife and Archippus, who was a leader in the Colossian church, his son (2; Colossians 4:17). Paul wrote this letter during his first imprisonment at Rome (Acts 28:30-31) to secure forgiveness for Onesimus, Philemon's runaway slave. He was expecting to be released from prison and hoped to visit Colosse (22).

'Onesimus' means 'profitable' but this slave had been unprofitable to Philemon (see Paul's play on his name in verse 11). He had stolen money or property from his master and had run away (18). Onesimus had found his way to Rome and while there came into contact with Paul. The apostle was in chains, but was greatly used of God and was able to preach the gospel to those guarding him and to visitors. Onesimus was wonderfully saved and Paul described him as *'my son ... whom I have begotten while in my chains'* (10). **The grace of God and his ways in providence are truly wonderful!**

When runaway slaves were caught they were often severely beaten or put to death. Onesimus was now dear to the heart of Paul, but he had to return to his master (12-14). This was no easy matter, though he was accompanied by Tychicus, a highly respected brother (Colossians 4:7-9). Paul was tender and tactful in his appeal to Philemon to forgive and to receive Onesimus. He appealed *'for love's sake'* and as the aged prisoner for his *'son'* in the faith (9-11). Philemon was known for his ministry of refreshing the saints (7) and Paul appealed, *Refresh my heart in the Lord* (20). He had been instrumental in Philemon's conversion and he reminded him of his indebtedness to him. He wanted Philemon to receive Onesimus as he would have received him (Paul). He asked his friend to put anything owed by the slave to his account (17-19). He was confident that Philemon would go beyond what was asked of him (20-21). **Are we prepared to forgive and to receive those who have wronged us (Colossians 3:13)?** Such an attitude is refreshing and a great blessing in any church.

HEBREWS & JAMES

Some believe that God inspired the apostle Paul to write **the letter to the Hebrews** but the Greek style here is very different from that of Paul. Moreover, in his letters Paul identifies himself in the opening greetings, but this is not found in Hebrews. Origen, one of the early Church Fathers said, 'Who it is who wrote the epistle, only God knows certainly.'

The letter was probably written between AD 60 and AD 70 (there is no indication in the letter that the Jewish sacrificial system had ceased owing to the destruction of the temple in AD 70). It was sent to Jewish Christians who were discouraged on account of persecution (10:32-36). They were in danger of drifting away from Christ and were lacking in Christian growth and maturity (2:1; 5:12-14). Some had ceased attending the meetings of the church (10:25) and were probably tempted to go back to Jewish ritual. We are shown how Christ, in his person and work, is far greater than the prophets, the angels and Moses. His work accomplished far more than Jewish sacrifices, for by his one sacrifice he has established a better covenant. Several passages give solemn warnings to the readers (2:1-4; 3:1 - 4:13; 6:4-8; 10:26-31; and 12:25-29).

Two of the twelve disciples had the name James but it is traditionally accepted that **the letter of James** was written by the half-brother of Jesus (Mark 6:3; Galatians 1:19). James was not a believer before the crucifixion of Christ (John 7:5). The Lord Jesus appeared to him after the resurrection (1 Corinthians 15:7) and he was in the upper room with Mary and his brothers on the Day of Pentecost (Acts 1:14). He became a leader of the church in Jerusalem (Acts 12:17; 15:13; 21:18; Galatians 2:9). James wrote his letter to Jewish Christians living outside of Palestine (1). He warns us against false religion, stressing that faith must be seen in action and showing how faith is to be worked out in our lives. *Faith without works is dead* (2:20) and though good works do not save us, they are an evidence of true faith (2:18).

God ... has in these last days spoken to us by his Son

God is not silent! *God who at various times ... spoke in time past to the fathers by the prophets has in these last days spoken to us by his Son* (1). *'The fathers'* are the people of ancient Israel who lived before the Lord Jesus came into the world. Those Israelites were more privileged than any other nation because God sent prophets to them to reveal his will for them, to teach them about God, and they prophesied the coming of a far greater prophet, the Messiah (the Christ). The prophets were highly esteemed by the Jews (Matthew 23:29-30).

God ... has in these last days spoken to us by his Son (2). How wonderful that he speaks to rebellious man, showing his great love in giving the Lord Jesus to die for us! The Lord Jesus Christ is far greater than the prophets. He is the fulfilment of their prophecies (Luke 24:44). In his ministry on earth the Lord Jesus astounded the people with his wisdom and his teaching. God the Father endorsed his ministry saying, *'This is my beloved Son. Hear him!'* (Mark 9:7). Are you listening for his voice as you read his word and when you hear it preached? Do you gladly obey the word of God when it challenges you or rebukes you?

God has spoken by his Son. He has nothing more to say to us by way of new revelation. The apostles taught what they had heard and learned from the Lord Jesus (Matthew 28:19-20; 1 Corinthians 11:23). It is most important that we understand that God has not sent any other prophet with new revelations since the Lord Jesus came into the world.

We see here more than fulfilment of the Old Testament prophets, however. These verses describe the surpassing greatness of Christ. He is the *brightness* (radiance) of God's glory and *the express image of his person* (3). He is the Creator of the universe (2,10; cp. Colossians 1:15-17) and he sustains all his creation by his powerful word. He ascended into heaven and is now at the right hand of God, reigning supreme over all the universe (3,13). If we can read Hebrews chapter 1 without seeing that Jesus is God, we are spiritually blind and in great darkness.

Jesus, who was made a little lower than the angels

We must all beware of drifting away from the Lord (1). Backsliding often begins with a slow drift away from God rather than with a headlong rush into sin. We soon begin to slip when we neglect private prayer and Bible reading. Our time of devotion and fellowship with the Lord is most important. *Therefore we must give all the more careful attention to the things we have heard* (margin reading of verse 1). We do not have to do anything to *neglect so great a salvation* (3). Just do nothing and drift through life without God!

The word spoken by angels (2) refers to the law given at Sinai (Galatians 3:19). If disobedience to the law, given by angels, was punished, how much more will those be punished who reject the gospel! The gospel of salvation was spoken by the Lord Jesus Christ who is *much better than the angels* (3; cp. 1:4). God confirmed the witness of the apostles *both with signs and wonders, with various miracles, and gifts of the Holy Spirit, according to his own will* (4).

Man was made *a little lower than the angels* but God chose him to rule over *the world to come* (the new heaven and the new earth; 5-8; cp. Psalm 8). The Lord Jesus left the glory of heaven to be *made a little lower than the angels* (9). *To taste death for everyone* (9) does not mean that everyone will be saved. Jesus is only the author of the salvation of the *'many sons'* whom he will bring to glory (10). We shall rule with the Lord Jesus (2 Timothy 2:12; Revelation 22:4-5). This is one of the reasons that our salvation is *'so great'*. How wonderful that God not only saves wretched, sinful men and women, but brings them into his glorious family and exalts them above angels!

The Lord Jesus conquered the devil and the power of death through his own death (14). He died *to make propitiation for the sins of the people,* turning God's holy wrath away from us by being punished in our place (17). **He did this to bring us to glory, to fulfil our destiny to rule with him over all things. Hallelujah! What a Saviour! He is worthy of our love, devotion and joyful obedience to his holy will.**

Let us therefore be diligent to enter that rest

This chapter has much to say about *'rest'* (see also 3:11,18-19). The rest spoken of is not a state of lazy inactivity. When God rested from his work of creation (4), it was rest from that particular work, the rest of accomplishment. He continues to work and to sustain his creation. The entrance of the Jews into Canaan brought them rest from the hardship of the wilderness wandering. Many of them did not enter into this rest through unbelief and rebellion (5-6; cp. 3:7-11). We are to fear lest we fail to come into God's rest because of unbelief (1-3).

'Rest' in verse 9 is translated from the Greek word meaning 'sabbath-rest'; this is the only place in Scripture where this word is found. This *'rest'* is for the people of God today. It is a *'rest'* which Joshua (same word as *'Jesus'* in Greek; cp. AV) was unable to give to the people who had entered Canaan (8). Matthew Henry describes this *'rest'* as a 'rest of grace' and a 'rest of glory':

- The 'rest of grace' brings us forgiveness of sin, cleansing, and peace with God. It brings the smile of God upon us and his peace ruling in our hearts (cp. Philippians 4:6-7,11). It is the 'rest' of open access to *the throne of grace where we may obtain mercy and find grace to help in time of need* (16).
- The 'rest of glory' awaits us in heaven, where we shall always be with the Lord (1 Thessalonians 4:17). In heaven *there shall be no more death, nor sorrow, nor crying; and there shall be no more pain* (Revelation 21:4).

The word of God is living and powerful (12). It exposes our thoughts and motives, it reveals the unbelief within us. The Christian life requires diligence, not carelessness. Have you entered the Christian rest? The Lord Jesus promised this rest to all who come to him and join (yoke) themselves to him in faith and obedience (Matthew 11:28-30). **We are warned that this rest can be missed through unbelief and disobedience (1-2,11). We all have to give an account of our lives to God (13) and we have no excuse for not entering his rest.** *Let us therefore be diligent to enter that rest* (11).

Such a high priest was fitting for us

In the Old Testament from the time of the exodus a man could only be a priest if he belonged to certain family groups within the tribe of Levi. The Lord Jesus could not be a Levitical priest because he was born into the tribe of Judah (14). He has a far greater priesthood, however, which is according to the order of Melchizedek *priest of the Most High God* (11,14-17; cp. 5:6). Melchizedek's origin and end are unknown and in this respect he was a 'type' of the Son of God, who had no beginning and will have no end (1-3). Melchizedek received tithes from Abraham and blessed him; it is the greater who blesses the lesser, and the lesser who gives tithes to the greater. Melchizedek was therefore greater than Abraham, and thus greater than Levi, who, as a descendant of Abraham, was in Abraham's loins when these events took place (4-10; cp. Genesis 14:18-20).

The Levitical priesthood and the law were imperfect, hence the need for something else to take their place (11,18-19). God ordained the Levitical priesthood to foreshadow that of Christ. We have already seen that the Lord Jesus, belonging to the order of Melchizedek, has a far greater priesthood. His priesthood is superior because:

- It was confirmed by the oath of God. The Levites did not have this oath (20-21).
- It is an everlasting and unchangeable priesthood (24-25).
- His person is superior. He *is holy, harmless, undefiled, separate from sinners, and has become higher than the heavens* (26).
- His work is perfect and his sacrifice complete. He does not need to offer up daily sacrifices. He offered himself up once for all on the cross at Calvary. Christ's sacrifice cannot be repeated (27).

We must never pray to God through Mary or the saints. We come to God the Father through the Lord Jesus Christ who loves us and prays for us (25). He is our perfect high priest, who made the perfect sacrifice to save us — *such a high priest was fitting for us* (26). **The Lord Jesus perfectly meets all our needs** and *he is also able to save to the uttermost* [completely] *those who come to God through him* (25).

A better covenant, which was established on better promises

The apostle stops to remind us of the main point of his message: we have a glorious high priest who is enthroned in heaven. He *is seated at the right hand of the throne of the Majesty in the heavens* (1; cp. 1:3). The Lord Jesus does not minister like a Levitical high priest in a sanctuary made by man such as the tabernacle or the temple. He ministers in the very presence of God in heaven (2). The priesthood, sacrifices and offerings of the Levitical order were but a shadow, a copy, of the heavenly priesthood of Christ (3-5).

Our great high priest has obtained a more excellent ministry than that of the Old Testament priests. The old covenant did not succeed because of the failure of the people to keep it (7-8). A new covenant was needed and promised (8-13). The Lord Jesus is the *mediator of a better covenant, which was established on better promises* (6; cp. 7:22). The new covenant is not sealed with the blood of sacrificial animals but by the precious blood of Christ (13:20). The Lord Jesus broke bread at the Last Supper as a symbol of his tortured body in which he bore our sins (1 Peter 2:24). He then took a cup of wine and said, *'This cup is the new covenant in my blood. This do, as often as you drink it, in remembrance of me'* (1 Corinthians 11:25).

All the Old Testament promises relating to the new covenant are for those who trust in Christ as their Saviour and Lord. This is shown in this chapter which quotes Jeremiah 31:31-34 with regard to the new covenant (8-12). These promises are far better than those of the old covenant (6). God puts his laws in our minds and writes them on our hearts (10). He enables us to know him and our sins he remembers no more (11-12). **When God forgives, he really does forget! Satan often rakes up our sinful past. If he is attacking you in this manner, come to God in prayer. Thank the Lord that he has forgiven you completely and that all Satan's accusations against you are futile (Romans 8:33-34).** There is no more condemnation for the child of God (Romans 8:1). Let us rejoice in the Lord and thank him for this *better covenant, which was established on better promises.*

By faith

This is one of the most encouraging chapters in the whole of the Bible. The previous chapter urges us: *'Let us hold fast the confession of our hope without wavering, for he who promised is faithful'* (10:23). The apostle now demonstrates how God has shown his faithfulness and he describes some of the exploits of godly people. *They died in faith, not having received the promises, but having seen them afar off, they were assured of them, embraced them, and confessed that they were strangers and pilgrims on the earth* (13). They confessed their hope! Look at all the sentences beginning *'By faith'* and be encouraged by the testimonies of these great men and women of faith. *The elders* ['ancients'] *obtained a good testimony* by faith (2; cp. verse 39). God bore testimony to their character, declaring that they were righteousness and that they pleased him (4-6).

What is faith? The English Standard Version of the Bible translates verse 1: *Now faith is the assurance of things hoped for, the conviction of things not seen.* This faith places its confidence in the promises of God, though we cannot presently see any fulfilment of them. The world says, 'Seeing is believing', but the Christian says, *'We walk by faith, not by sight'* (2 Corinthians 5:7). Thomas thought that seeing was believing and was afterwards ashamed of his unbelief (John 20:25-29). The Lord Jesus said to his disciples, *'Have faith in God'* (Mark 11:22). God delights in those who really trust in him and in his promises.

How can we have faith? If faith does not come by sight, how does it come? *Faith comes by hearing, and hearing by the word of God* (Romans 10:17). There it is! Pay close attention to the preaching of God's word. Read your Bible every day and obey it. Memorize passages of Scripture. **You will find your faith growing stronger and by faith you will persevere in the Christian life.** *Without faith it is impossible to please him* (6). We insult God if we refuse to trust him. He will never fail us. When we come to God we *must believe that he is, and that he is a rewarder of those who diligently seek him* (6).

The race that is set before us

The accomplishments of the great men and women described in chapter 11 bear witness to the fact that ordinary people can become extraordinary through faith in God. The Christian life is a race (1). The Greek word translated *'race'* (*'agon'*) was used to describe the contests in the Greek games. It means 'a struggle' and our English word 'agony' comes from it. *'Agon'* is also translated *'fight'* (1 Timothy 6:12; 2 Timothy 4:7). **The Christian life involves hard struggle, but we must succeed and we can. How are we to do this?**

- We must *lay aside every weight, and the sin which so easily ensnares us* (1). Notice the distinction between *'sin'* and *'weight'*. If we cling to sin, it will greatly hinder us or stop us in the Christian race. *'Every weight'* describes those things which are not wrong in themselves, but become wrong because they take a greater priority in our lives than is good for us. They weigh us down and handicap us in the race. Many a Christian has been ensnared through pornography that is so easily available on our computers and television; this is sinful and will ruin us. We must be ruthless with any sin in our lives and get rid of anything that encourages sinful thoughts. Indwelling sin will not quietly yield to our attacks upon it — there will be a struggle (4).
- We must beware of continually looking inward at ourselves. We must look to our great Saviour, the Lord Jesus, who endured great hardship and suffering to save us (2-3).
- We must not despise God's chastening (5-11); it is a token that he loves us; that we are his sons; and that the end result is good (6-11).
- We are to strengthen our spiritual limbs by spiritual exercise (12).
- We are to lead consistent Christian lives (13).
- We are to pursue peace with all men and holiness (14).

The Christian race is not easy, but the Lord Jesus *endured the cross and hostility from sinners against himself* (2-3) so that we could be in this race. He will never leave us nor forsake us. *Let us run with endurance the race that is set before us, looking unto Jesus, the author and finisher of our faith.*

Let brotherly love continue

We must never be so preoccupied with our struggles in the Christian 'race' that we forget others. *Let brotherly love continue* (1). We can show such love by opening our homes to entertain visitors. Abraham and Sarah once entertained angels when giving hospitality (2; cp. Genesis 18:1-16; 19:1). Christian love is also expressed in remembering those who are imprisoned for the sake of the gospel. The Lord Jesus not only gave us the new covenant, but also a new commandment, that we love one another as he has loved us (John 13:34-35; cp. 1 Thessalonians 4:9; 1 Peter 1:22; 1 John 3:16-19). Do look up these verses, think about them, and practise what they teach.

We live in a society where immorality and covetousness abound and verses 4 and 5 contain some timely warnings for us. *Marriage is honourable* but God will judge the immoral and adulterers. God has promised us, *'I will never leave you nor forsake you'* (5) What have we to fear when God is our helper and our Saviour does not change (6, 8)? Our lives must show a different quality from those of unbelievers. We must show brotherly love (1-3), we must keep ourselves pure (4) and we must be content (5).

Elders must be godly men who are able to teach the word of God (7; cp. 1 Timothy 3:1-7). They have an awesome responsibility to watch over your souls and they will have to give an account in the day of judgment (17). Do you welcome their admonition and correction when they lovingly seek to point out things that are wrong or are not helpful in your life? You are to *be submissive* though this is not popular in today's environment when most people want to do what is right in their own eyes. Do not grieve your pastor (elder) by backsliding or by coldness of heart. *Remember those who rule over you* (7).

The Book of Hebrews teaches us that the sacrifice of Christ is complete (7:27; 10:10,12). We do not have to offer animal sacrifices but there is the sacrifice of praise and of Christian benevolence (15-16). **May God make you complete in every good work (20-21).**

Let no one say when he is tempted, 'I am tempted by God'

After beginning his letter with a brief greeting, James makes what may appear to be an astonishing statement: *'My brethren, count it all joy when you fall into various trials'* (2). How can we consider it *'all joy'* when persecution, trouble, sickness and other trials come upon us?

- We must understand that God is always in control of all our circumstances. Trials belong to the *'all things'* that *work together for good* (Romans 8:28).
- The testing of our faith produces *patience* ('endurance'). This is essential to the process of making us *perfect and complete* (3-4). The word *'perfect'* means 'mature'; it has nothing to do with sinless perfection. Maturity does not come from chasing after sensational experiences, but in the school of affliction. Testing and chastening are for our profit, producing godly character (Romans 5:3-5; Hebrews 12:11). When you need wisdom in some perplexing trial, ask God for it, or for grace to help you in your need (5-8; cp. Hebrews 4:16).

We must distinguish between the testing of our faith (2-3,12) and temptation to sin (13-15). **God tests our faith but he does not tempt us to sin.** *Let no one say when he is tempted, 'I am tempted by God'* (13). The tendency to make excuses for sin and to shift the blame began in the Garden of Eden (Genesis 3:12-13). Some claim that they would not sin if God prevented them from being tempted. That will not do with God. Thousands of believers who have been providentially placed in circumstances where temptation comes upon them, have resolutely resisted it (e.g. Joseph — Genesis 39:7-12). Temptation rises from within ourselves through our sinful nature (14).

If we are to have the strength to face temptation and trial, we must forsake sin and *receive with meekness the implanted word* of God (21). We must *be doers of the word, and not hearers only* (22). We must apply the word of God to everyday living by obeying its teaching. If our religion is real, we will control the tongue, visit the needy and keep ourselves unspotted from the world (26-27). **How practical is your Christianity?**

I will show you my faith by my works

James pulls no punches in his letter but he is gentle. See how he addresses his readers: *'my brethren'* and *'my beloved brethren'* (1,5; cp. 1:2,19; 2:14; 3:1,10; 5:10,12). He now goes on to deal with favouritism in the church, and particularly with showing respect for some while ignoring others. He writes, *'Do not hold the faith of our Lord Jesus Christ ... with partiality'* (1). We must never despise those who are poor or those who are of a different race. James asks, *'Has not God chosen the poor of this world to be rich in faith and heirs of the kingdom which he promised to those who love him?'* (5).

God's *'royal law'* is *'You shall love your neighbour as yourself'* (8). This is a quotation from Leviticus 19:18 and verse 15 of the same chapter warns against showing partiality. Why is this called *'the royal law'*? Because it is the law of the kingdom of God to which all Christians belong and we must keep those laws. The royal law stands as a whole. To show partiality is to sin and this renders us guilty in the sight of God just as much as if we were adulterers or murderers (10-11). If our faith is real, we will not ignore the plight of any Christian among us who is poverty-stricken (15-16). If we lack compassion to those in need our faith is dead (17).

Some people believe that to look for works as an evidence of faith is a denial of the gospel. Others say that they are more interested in 'practical Christianity' and that what we believe and in whom we believe are not really important. **Both are wrong.** Faith without works is not true faith. *Faith by itself, if it does not have works, is dead* (17, repeated in verses 20 and 26). Works without faith will never save us. There are many kind, helpful and 'good' people who have no faith in Christ but they are sinners who need to be saved.

James challenges us, *'Show me your faith without your works, and I will show you my faith by my works'* (18). Saying that we believe in God is not enough to save us. *Even the demons believe — and tremble!* (19). **How is your faith working out?**

No man can tame the tongue

Pure religion involves not only good works, but also the control of the tongue (1:26-27). When we feel ill, the doctor may examine our tongue for an indication of what is wrong with us. The state of the tongue also reveals our spiritual condition. If we can control the tongue, we are able to control the whole body (2). Self-control is a fruit of the Holy Spirit (Galatians 5:23) and this must also include control of the tongue, which though it is small, is a very unruly member of the body. James shows how the tongue, a little member of the body, is able to do great damage. A small metal bit is used to control a strong horse and a great ship is turned by a very small rudder (3-4). The tongue is a little fire which can set a whole forest ablaze and hell knows its potential to cause great damage (5-6). **You may be able to control your temper, your sinful desires and passions, but how is it with your tongue?** *If anyone does not stumble in word, he is a perfect man* (2). Our Christian maturity is rather revealed by our ability to control our tongue.

We utter the most sublime words of praise with our tongues when we sing our psalms and hymns; with that same tongue which blesses God we curse men who have been made in the likeness of God (9). Many a church has been torn apart and destroyed by unruly tongues. *No man can tame the tongue* (8) so should we just give up trying? No! Remember that *the things which are impossible with men are possible with God* (Luke 18:27). How can we then, with God's help, control this unruly evil (8)? We must pause and think before we speak (cp. 1:19). We should remember that the Lord is the unseen listener of all that we say. *Let your speech always be with grace, seasoned with salt, that you may know how you ought to answer each one* (Colossians 4:6). Have you hurt others with your tongue? Apologize to them, ask the Lord to forgive you and be determined to control your tongue.

We must shun wicked behaviour which comes from wisdom inspired by demons (14-16) and seek that *wisdom that is from above which is first pure, then peaceable, gentle, willing to yield, full of mercy and good fruits* (17).

Friendship with the world is enmity with God

If we want to have pure religion, we must keep ourselves *'unspotted from the world'* (1:27). Worldliness is more than avoiding certain places or indulging in certain sins. It is a whole way of life which refuses to submit to God's rule. It is seen in such sins as self-seeking, covetousness, pride (2,6) and the love of pleasure rather than loving God (1,3; cp. 2 Timothy 3:4). Worldliness stifles spiritual desire and it fails to give lasting satisfaction (2-3). James makes it quite clear that a worldly Christian is guilty of spiritual adultery. The church is the bride of Christ (2 Corinthians 11:2; Revelation 19:7-9). He has purchased us at a tremendous price through his death on the cross and he demands our undivided loyalty. James asks, *'Do you not know that friendship with the world is enmity with God?'* (4). J. B. Phillips paraphrases this verse, 'You are like unfaithful wives, flirting with the glamour of this world, and never realising that to be the world's lover means becoming the enemy of God!' If you are worldly and refuse to obey God's word of challenge, you add further to your sin (17).

What is the answer to worldliness? It is the enjoyment of Christ through daily fellowship with him. We must resist the enticements of the world (remember Christian and Faithful at Vanity Fair in John Bunyan's *Pilgrim's Progress*). 'Don't let the world around you squeeze you into its own mould' (Romans 12:2 — J. B. Phillips). Think much about the greatness of God's love for you. Can you, dare you, be worldly, when Jesus gave his life to save you? *'Seek first the kingdom of God and his righteousness'* (Matthew 6:33) and you will find no joy or satisfaction like that of putting God first in your life. When you do this, the world will have very little attraction for you.

Our behaviour is worldly when we shut God out of our planning (13). James reminds us, *'You do not know what will happen tomorrow'* and that human life is *'a vapour'* (14; cp. Proverbs 27:1). If life is so short and uncertain, how foolish, arrogant and evil it is to boast of all that we will do without a submissive attitude to the will of God (16).

The effective, fervent prayer of a righteous man avails much

Worldliness may display itself in the pursuit of wealth. If anyone makes money by exploiting the poor or by resorting to injustice, he will not escape the judgment of God (1-6). The believer who desires to be rich is asking for spiritual trouble (1 Timothy 6:9). If your main goal in life is to be wealthy you can be sure that you will end up a spiritual pauper (cp. Revelation 3:17).

We must learn to be patient and to persevere in times of suffering. James reminds us of the example of the prophets, and of Job in particular (7-11). They were blessed for their perseverance. Just as faith without works is dead, so also faith without prayer is dead. Christians know times of trouble as well as joyfulness and we must look to the Lord in both situations. *'Is anyone among you suffering? Let him pray'* (13). **Prayer is a great but often neglected privilege.** How should we pray when in trouble? We must recognize that God is sovereign in all our circumstances and commit our way to him (Psalm 37:5,7-8). We should ask the Lord to deliver us but be prepared for whatever answer he gives (cp. 2 Corinthians 12:7-10). We should seek for his grace and help in our need (Hebrews 4:16).

What should we do when we are ill? We should seek the prayers of our church and call for the elders to pray for us. We should reflect on our lives and if we know that we have sinned, we must confess that sin and pray for forgiveness (14-16). Prayer must be with faith (*'the prayer of faith'*; cp. 1:6). Such faith cannot be worked up and it does not depend on feelings. Faith is a settled confidence in God and is also seen in submission to his will (cp. 4:15). Do you pray with faith? Prayer is vital in the Christian life. *The effective, fervent prayer of a righteous man avails much* (16). Elijah, *a man with a nature like ours,* with the same weaknesses, gave himself to prayer and he trusted in a great God to answer his prayers (17-18). **He was an ordinary man who obtained extraordinary results through prayer!** Let us remember to pray for backsliders and seek to restore them (19-20). Such efforts and prayers will avail much.

MICAH, NAHUM & HABAKKUK

Micah prophesied during the reigns of Jotham, Ahaz and Hezekiah (1). He was a country-dweller from Moresheth which lay near the border of Philistia and was a younger contemporary of the prophet Isaiah who prophesied in Jerusalem. The northern kingdom fell in 722 BC but was still standing when Micah prophesied (1:5-6). Micah warned that God would severely punish Judah and Israel for their wickedness. Their religion was corrupt (3:11) and the poor were oppressed by the rich (2:1-2,8-11; 3:1-3,9-11; 6:10-12; 7:1-6). Micah's name means 'Who is like Jehovah?' It points us to his message which shows the greatness of God's power (1:2-4) and of his pardoning grace (7:18). Micah prophesied that Christ would be born in Bethlehem (5:2-5).

Nahum prophesied against the Assyrian capital, Nineveh, over one hundred years after its people had repented at the preaching of Jonah. We cannot be sure of the date of Nahum's prophecy, but it is somewhere between the destruction of Thebes (No Amon, 3:8) in 661 BC and the fall of Nineveh in 612 BC. Nahum whose name means 'consolation' had a message of comfort for the people of Judah and there is an absence of any warning of judgment against them. The Lord assured them that he would destroy their cruel enemies, the Assyrians (1:15).

Habakkuk was probably a contemporary of Jeremiah, the date of his prophecy possibly being between the death of King Josiah (609 BC) and the time when Judah became a vassal to Babylon in the reign of King Jehoiakim (606 BC). It was certainly before God raised up the Chaldeans (Babylonians) as his instruments of judgment to punish Judah (1:6). The prophecy is not directly addressed to a nation but gives an account of the prayers of the perplexed prophet and the Lord's response. Habakkuk was baffled by the age-old questions, 'Why does God allow ... ?' and 'Why does God work in such and such a way if he is righteous?' His name means 'to cling' or 'to embrace' and here we find him clinging to God in his perplexity.

But we will walk in the name of the L<small>ORD</small> *our God for ever*

Verses 1 to 5 are almost identical to Isaiah 2:2-5. Micah prophesied of the Jews' captivity in Babylon and of their return from exile (10), but he also looked beyond this to *'the latter days'* (1). Verses 9 to 12 speak of the judgment that God was to bring at the hands of the Babylonians when Jerusalem would be in anguish like a woman in labour. Old Testament prophecy had an immediate application for the people of that particular time, but it also looked to the more distant future. I do not agree with those who believe that *'the latter days'* (1) refer to the restoration of Israel, to be ruled by Christ with Jerusalem as the centre of worship for the people of all nations. His glory is in his church, not in the nation of Israel (Ephesians 3:20-21). The church is God's temple where he dwells (1 Corinthians 3:16-17; Ephesians 2:19-22). The Lord Jesus indicated that there is now little significance in Jerusalem as a place of worship (John 4:21-22).

Peter, preaching at Pentecost, quotes from Joel and shows that *'the latter days'* refer to the gospel age (Acts 2:16-17; cp. Hebrews 1:1-2). Prophecies relating to Israel in the latter days and the conversion of Gentiles also point to the same age (Acts 15:16-17; Galatians 4:24-27; 6:16; Hebrews 12:22). God will gather a remnant of the Jews according to the election of grace and the Lord Jesus will reign over them in his church (6-8; Romans 11:5). **We have a wonderful future in Christ! Let us be determined to please him and to** *walk in the name of the* L<small>ORD</small> *our God for ever and ever* (5).

Chapter 5 contains the well-known prophecy of the birth of the Lord Jesus at Bethlehem, the city of David (2; cp. Matthew 2:4-6). His human descent came through the line of David, the shepherd-king of Israel. He was no ordinary babe however, but the eternal Son of God, *whose goings forth have been from of old, from everlasting* (cp. Luke 2:4; John 1:1-3). Jesus is the great Shepherd-King — *and he shall stand and feed his flock in the strength of the* L<small>ORD</small>. He is a caring, providing King, who gives his people peace, whose kingdom shall be *to the ends of the earth* (4; cp. Ephesians 2:14).

Because he delights in mercy

Micah here laments because of the lean spiritual times in which he lived. Just as summer fruits were difficult to find after Israel had gathered her harvest, so faithful men were few and far between (1-2). Jesus quoted verse 6 to show how following him can divide families and bring opposition from loved ones (Matthew 10:35-36). What are we to do when the spiritual outlook is bleak? We must do what Micah did! *'Therefore I will look to the LORD; I will wait for the God of my salvation; my God will hear me'* (7). We must look to the Lord and wait patiently for him (cp. Psalm 40:1). He will hear us. When Satan attacks us and appears to overwhelm us, we can affirm, *'Do not rejoice over me, my enemy; when I fall, I will arise; when I sit in darkness, the LORD will be a light to me'* (8). Micah confessed that God's dealings with his people are just and that he would vindicate his people who were taunted by their enemies (9-13).

Micah longed for better times for God's people and he prayed that God would lead them and feed them as a shepherd (14). The Lord answered him by promising to *show them marvellous things* just as he had done when he brought Israel out of Egypt (Exodus 14). The nations would see this and the fear of the Lord would come upon them (15-17).

Though God will surely punish those who refuse to turn from their sin, he is merciful to those who repent (18-19). Do you feel far away from God because of sin and failure? Do not wallow in despair. Come to God confessing your sin and repenting of it. He will accept you *because he delights in mercy.* He will cast your sins into the depths of the sea, never to remember them, *because he delights in mercy* (19; cp. Hebrews 10:16-17). Let these words *'because he delights in mercy'* ring in your heart. Praise the Lord with joyful singing *because he delights in mercy.* **Come to God's throne of grace with all your needs** *because he delights in mercy.* Let us proclaim to the needy world around us that God delights in mercy!

The LORD is good, a stronghold in the day of trouble

Assyria was brutal and cruel in its repression of its neighbouring nations. Nineveh was ripe for judgment because her repentance was short-lived and this later generation was vile and cruel (14; 3:1). The punishment of the Assyrians would be so complete that God would not need to strike them a second time (6,8-9). They would be gathered together as thorns, and burned as the dry straw which is left after the harvest (10). The wicked plotter against the Lord (11) was probably the Assyrian king, Ashur-banipal, who reigned from 669 to 626 BC. The Lord warned that he would destroy the gods of this vile man and would dig his grave (14). God promised Judah that he would break the yoke of Assyria (12-13; cp. Psalm 2:9). Verse 15 pictures a messenger coming over the mountain roads to Jerusalem to announce the good news of deliverance.

Listen to the message of the prophet of Jehovah. He tells us truths about God that are rarely heard from the pulpits of most churches — *God is jealous, and the LORD avenges; the LORD avenges and is furious. The LORD will take vengeance on his adversaries, he reserves wrath for his enemies* (2). God delays the time of judgment because he is slow to anger but he *will not at all acquit the wicked* (3). He allows the wicked time to repent. Sinners are foolish to despise God for his goodness in delaying to judge them (cp. Romans 2:4).

The jealousy of God (2) is of great comfort to his people. He is fiercely protective of those who belong to him, and any who seek to harm them, as Nineveh harmed his people of old, will surely come to grief (cp. 2 Kings 19:32-34). God avenges his elect (cp. Luke 18:7). *The LORD is ... great in power* (3). That great power is described in verses 3 to 6. Though God is severe in his judgment on unrepentant sinners (6), he is good to those who trust him and obey him (cp. Romans 11:22). **Christian, are you going through a time of trouble? Are problems and difficulties mounting up? Memorize verse 7 and rejoice in it!** *The LORD is good, a stronghold in the day of trouble; and he knows those who trust in him.*

Yet I will rejoice in the LORD

John Currid writes: 'The opening chapter of the book describes Habakkuk's lamentations, complaints and sorrows. Chapter 2 provides God's answer to him. And now in this final chapter, Habakkuk comes under great conviction, and he sings praises to the almighty, sovereign God of the universe. He now sings about the marvellous works of God that he had so recently questioned. His eyes had been opened to the majesty of God' (*The expectant prophet*, page 106).

The work of God was languishing and the spiritual outlook in Judah was very bleak. Habakkuk prayed, *O LORD, revive your work in the midst of the years! ... In wrath remember mercy* (2; the word 'wrath' here means 'trouble', 'trembling', 'commotion'). In the midst of the years of trouble he called on God, the righteous Judge, to have mercy on his people. He encouraged himself by thinking about the mighty works of God in former times (3-14). Whatever the trouble around us, we must never give up praying that God will revive his work.

The Lord had told Habakkuk, *'The just shall live by his faith'* (2:4); in these verses the prophet affirms his faith in God. Habakkuk's name means 'to cling'. He was prepared to cling to God even in a time of calamity because of failed harvests and the loss of livestock. He could say, *'Yet I will rejoice in the LORD, I will joy in the God of my salvation. The LORD God is my strength'* (18-19). Here is faith triumphant in times of testing, which clings to God and to his promises, and enables him to rejoice in the Lord.

When his wife Mary died in 1790 the hymn-writer John Newton confessed: 'The world seemed to die with her.' The grief-stricken pastor mounted his pulpit steps the Lord's Day following her death and preached from Habakkuk 3:17-19. Though numb with grief, he trusted in God. **Are you passing through some severe, perplexing trial? Cling to the Lord as Habakkuk did!** You will then *rest in the day of trouble* (16). The heavy feet will feel lighter; they will become *like deer's feet* (19), and your valley of trial will become a high hill of blessing as you joy in the God of your salvation.

ZEPHANIAH

Zephaniah prophesied during the reign of Josiah who was king from 640 to 609 BC (1:1). His ministry may have been used to encourage the young King Josiah in his reforming work when he purged the country of idolatry and restored the worship of Jehovah (2 Kings 22 and 23). Zephaniah means 'the Lord hides' which may indicate that he was born and hidden during the time of much slaughter in Manasseh's wicked reign (2 Kings 21:16). He may have been thinking about his own name when he appealed to the people of Judah, *'Seek the* LORD, *all you meek of the earth, who have upheld his justice. Seek righteousness, seek humility. It may be that you will be hidden in the day of the* LORD'*s anger'* (2:3).

Zephaniah warns of the coming of *the great day of the* LORD (1:14). Judgment would be visited on Judah and her wicked neighbours (1:4 - 3:8). Though he is a prophet of God's wrath (1:15-18), Zephaniah is also the prophet of God's tender care for his people. He concludes his prophecy with promises of blessing for the godly remnant of Israel (3:13); this also points to the church, the heavenly Jerusalem (3:14-20; cp. Galatians 4:26; Hebrews 12:22-24; Revelation 21:2,9-10).

He will rejoice over you with gladness ... with singing

Jerusalem is here described as a rebellious, unholy, oppressing city which would not receive correction and had not trusted in the Lord nor come near to him in prayer (1-2). The Lord condemned the princes and judges of Jerusalem (3). The prophets she recognized were false and are described as *'insolent, treacherous people'*. The priests were corrupt and had polluted the temple with their wickedness and had done violence to God's holy law (4).

The prophet speaks of God being in the *'midst'* of his people three times — being in their midst for judgment (5), and for blessing (15,17). *The LORD is righteous, he is in her midst* (5). Habakkuk ended his prophecy singing, *'Yet I will rejoice in the LORD, I will joy in the God of my salvation'* (Habakkuk 3:18). Zephaniah concludes his prophecy encouraging God's people to sing because of all that the Lord has done for them (14-15). Look at the precious promises that follow. *'He will rejoice over you with gladness, he will quiet you in his love, he will rejoice over you with singing'* (17). **Our God is a happy God, singing and rejoicing over us, tenderly caring for us.** It is too wonderful to take in. He gave his beloved Son to die for us, to save us from our sin. What amazing grace! What wondrous love!

Zephaniah concludes his prophecy with promises of blessing for the godly remnant of Israel (3:13) but these verses look beyond the restoration of captivity from Babylon (20) to the gospel age when people from all the nations will call upon the Lord and worship him (9-11). He points us to the glory of the church, the heavenly Jerusalem (14-20; cp. Galatians 4:26; Hebrews 12:22-24; Revelation 21:2,9-10). God's word for his church (Zion) is, *'Do not fear ... let not your hands be weak. The LORD your God is in your midst, the Mighty One, will save'* (16-17). Are you feeling discouragement from various trials? Take heart, battle on in the strength of the Lord and persevere in prayer. God loves you and delights in you. Wait for him and be patient.

1 & 2 PETER

The first letter of Peter was written to persecuted Jewish Christians who lived in the land that is now called Turkey. *The Dispersion* (1:1) was the term used to describe those Jews living outside Palestine. He wrote from *Babylon* (5:13) which probably referred to Rome (often called '*Babylon*' by early Christians; cp. Revelation chapters 17 and 18). The letter was probably written late AD 63 or early AD 64 before the Roman emperor Nero unleashed his great persecution against Christians. Silas, who had been involved with Paul in writing to the church at Thessalonica (1 Thessalonians 1:1; 2 Thessalonians 1:1), wrote this letter under the direction of Peter (5:12; 'Silvanus' is the Latin form of 'Silas').

Peter wrote to encourage Christians who had been *grieved by various trials* (1:6) and to prepare them for the *fiery trial* (4:12) which was soon to come upon them. He showed them how they should live at such times, encouraging them by the example of the Lord Jesus (2:21; 4:1). His sufferings were followed by glory (1:11,21) and so will ours be (4:13-14; 5:1,10).

Key words

Suffering:	1:11; 2:19-23; 3:14,17-18; 4:1,13,15,19; 5:1,10.
Glory:	1:11,21; 4:13-14; 5:1,4,10.
Precious:	1:7,19; 2:4,6,7; 3:4.

Peter wrote his **second letter** in AD 66 or 67 shortly before he was martyred (cp. 1:14-15). He reminded his first readers of the teaching of the prophets and the apostles (1:12-15; 3:1-2). He warned about the false teachers who were infiltrating the church. We are not to be surprised that in these last days there will be scoffers who scorn the promise of Christ's second coming. The apostle urges us to be holy and to be prepared for the return of Christ (3:10-14). His letter encourages us to *grow in the grace and knowledge of our Lord and Saviour Jesus Christ* (3:18).

A *living hope*

Peter writes to encourage persecuted Christians to persevere in the face of severe trials. He sets before them a feast of good things concerning God and our salvation. We read of election and sanctification, and of the precious blood of Christ, with which we are redeemed (2,18-19); the resurrection of Jesus Christ from the dead and the abundant mercy of God (3); our new birth (3,23); a glorious inheritance reserved for us in heaven (4) and the power of God to keep us until the return of Christ (5). The Old Testament prophets longed to know more of this great salvation of which they prophesied (10), and *which angels desire to look into* (12).

Each Person of the Trinity is involved in the work of our salvation (2). Every Christian is chosen by God the Father, sanctified (set apart to God) by the Holy Spirit and sprinkled by the blood of Christ for forgiveness and cleansing from sin. Peter reminds us that God the Father *has begotten us again to a living hope through the resurrection of Jesus Christ from the dead* (3). Peter's hopes had been crushed when Jesus was crucified but despair gave way to glorious joy after Jesus rose from the dead. Must the *various trials* which grieve us crush our hopes? Never! We serve a risen Saviour and we have *a living hope* (3). Our *faith and hope are in God* (21). The very thought of all that God has done for us caused Peter to burst out in praise to God (3).

How are we to live the Christian life? *Therefore gird up the loins of your mind* (13). In Bible times men often wore long robes which hindered them in work or battle. When preparing for action, they would gather up their robes and tuck them into their belts to facilitate movement (cp. 1 Kings 18:46). We are urged, *'Be sober* [level-headed], *and rest your hope fully upon the grace that is to be brought to you at the return of Christ'* (13). We must be *holy* for we have been redeemed at great cost with the precious blood of Christ (15-16,19). We are to *love one another fervently with a pure heart* (22). **We have a living hope and it is worth living for!**

His own special people

When we are born again we need spiritual food in order to grow. That food is *'the pure milk of the word'* of God (2). Growth is a vital part of life and if we have no desire to feed upon God's word, we are spiritually sick, or we are still dead in our sins. There is no such thing as instant maturity in Christ. The growing process goes on throughout our Christian lives. We must grow in the knowledge of God and his word, and we must become more Christlike in our lives, *laying aside all malice, all guile, hypocrisy, envy, and all evil speaking* (1). Peter's first readers knew rejection and persecution; he reminded them that the Lord Jesus had also been rejected by men but he is precious to God the Father and so are we (4-8).

The Lord Jesus Christ is precious to us (7) and we are special to him. *You are a chosen generation, a royal priesthood, a holy nation, his own special people, that you may proclaim the praises of him who called you out of darkness into his marvellous light* (9; cp. Deuteronomy 7:6-9). **Great responsibilities come with these great privileges.** We have been called out of darkness into God's marvellous light. We must proclaim his *praises* (virtues) by godly living. We are *pilgrims* bound for heaven and we must *abstain from fleshly lusts which war against the soul* (11). Spiritual warfare takes place in the flesh. We are not to yield to sinful desires.

We are to be God-fearing citizens beyond reproach in all our behaviour (12). We must obey the laws of our country (except when they contradict God's laws, Acts 5:29) even if rulers are evil (13-17). Remember, when Peter wrote his letter, the Roman emperor was the evil Nero. He urges slaves (*'servants'*) to be submissive to their masters and to bear mistreatment patiently, pointing them to the example of Christ in whose steps we are to follow (18-23). The Lord Jesus died for us so that we should die to sins and *live for righteousness* (24). We are his own special people, precious to God, and we should be proclaiming his praises. **Give thanks to God for all that he has done for you and show by the way that you live that he is precious to you.**

Sanctify the Lord God in your hearts

Our conduct must be honourable both within the home (1-7) and outside it (8-17). We must never forget that Jesus must be seen to be our Lord in the home, in the church, and in the world. Wives are to be submissive to their husbands but this in no way implies that they are inferior. They are equal in dignity; the difference lies in their God-given roles. Husbands must seek to understand their wives' needs and problems and give honour (respect) to them, loving them as Christ loved the church and gave himself for it (1,7; cp. Ephesians 5:23,25). If they neglect to do this their prayers will be hindered (7). A wife will not win her non-Christian husband by preaching at him, but by honouring God in her behaviour (1-2). He must be able to see that she is a much better person for being a Christian. If this is not apparent, how can she expect God to answer her prayers for him? *A gentle and quiet spirit ... is very precious in the sight of God* (4).

Peter writes, *'Sanctify* [set apart] *the Lord God in your hearts'* (15). **Do you do this?** Does it show in a desire to work for unity in your church? Does it show in compassion, in brotherly love, in tender-heartedness, in courteous behaviour (8)? Does it show in a refusal to get even and in blessing those who malign you (9)? Those who hate you may accuse you of doing evil and *revile your good conduct,* but you will have a good conscience towards God and know his blessing in suffering (13-17). We must not be intimidated by the threats of the ungodly but be ready to answer them, giving them a reason for the hope that is within us with meekness and in the fear of God (15). To be able to do this, we must know our Bibles and depend upon the Holy Spirit. The *'spirits in prison'* are those who refused to heed the words of the Holy Spirit through the preaching of Noah (19-20). They are now bound and awaiting judgment.

Christ suffered once for sins ... that he might bring us to God (18) so that we will *sanctify the Lord God in* our *hearts.* **As we do this, we will know his presence with us and we will enjoy his blessing.**

If you are reproached for the name of Christ

How are we to face suffering and at the same time live holy lives? Again, Peter urges us to use our minds. Biblical principles must be thought through and then worked out in our lives. *Therefore, since Christ suffered for us in the flesh, arm yourselves also with the same mind* (1; cp. 1:13). We must arm ourselves with this attitude, that we are not to live to please ourselves but to do the will of God (2). The old life must go! Immorality, unwholesome desires, drunkenness, wild parties, drunken orgies and idolatry have no place in the Christian life (3). Our former associates may misunderstand us and even speak evil of us (4), but they will have to give an account of their own lives to God (5). Verse 6 is difficult to understand and opinions are varied as to what it means. I believe that Peter is referring to those who responded to the gospel and suffered for Christ but are now dead.

What kind of people are we to be in uncertain and difficult times? We must be *serious and watchful* in our prayers (7). We must *above all things have fervent love for one another,* being ready to forgive and forget wrongs committed against us *for love will cover a multitude of sins* (8). We are to be cheerfully hospitable to others and be good stewards of the gifts that God has given to us (9-10).

We must not be surprised when *'the fiery trial'* comes upon us (12). Peter was probably preparing his readers for the terrible suffering that Nero was about to inflict upon them. Suffering in one form or another is part and parcel of the Christian life. We should not ask, 'Why is this happening to us?' but rather rejoice that we are privileged to partake of Christ's sufferings (13; cp. Acts 5:40-41). *If you are reproached for the name of Christ, blessed are you, for the Spirit of glory and of God rests upon you* (14). We should also rejoice knowing that though we share in Christ's sufferings, we will also share in his glory and we will *be glad with exceeding joy* (13; cp. 5:10; Romans 8:17-18). Suffering is not the end! **If you are being insulted by men because of your Christian faith, remember that the Lord loves you. Glorify God in suffering and commit your soul to his care in doing good (16,19).**

Casting all your care upon him, for he cares for you

The ability of a church to stand firm in times of trial and trouble depends much upon its elders. A well-taught and healthy flock (church) is better equipped to face difficulties and persecution than a church which receives little teaching. Elders must *shepherd* (pastor) the church. They are not to be eager to gain money, but rather, eager to serve God and his people (2). The office of elder has its own temptations and one that must always be resisted is the misuse of authority (lording it over church members, 3). Leadership must be by example, by serving. Elders are to lead God's people and must never drive them by harsh oversight. They are answerable to the Chief Shepherd (cp. Hebrews 13:17) who will richly reward faithful service. We must be prepared to submit to pastoral advice and to accept loving rebuke when we go wrong. Church membership is important. In becoming a member of a church, we are undertaking to submit to the leadership of that church and to play our part in its life and witness.

Young people must submit themselves to their elders and all of us must *be submissive to one another* (5). This is very difficult especially when we feel convinced that we are right and the other person is wrong. We must *be clothed with humility* and then the Lord will give us the necessary grace to submit to others.

Many of us face problems and troubles but we should remember that God knows all these things and he cares. Almighty God cares for us. No problem is too big for him to handle or too small to concern him. God knows about our troubles at home, problems at work, financial worries, heartache over unsaved loved ones. We need to remember verse 7: *Casting all your care upon him, for he cares for you.*

We must be sober and vigilant because Satan is prowling around like a roaring lion seeking to cause havoc in our lives, but we are able to resist him in the strength of Christ (8-9). **The Christian life is tough but God cares for us and 'his eternal glory' awaits us (10). What more could we desire?**

Exceedingly great and precious promises

God has given to us *exceedingly great and precious promises* which are found in the Holy Bible (4). We have these promises so that we may be partakers of the divine nature. To partake of the divine nature means to be *conformed to the image* of the Lord Jesus (Romans 8:29). We are no longer in bondage to the lusts of the flesh but are now free to be holy, free to love God, and to serve him (3-4; cp. John 8:34,36). *The knowledge of God and of Jesus our Lord* (2,3,8) is one of the Christian's great privileges. To know God the Father and his Son is to have *grace and peace* multiplied to us (2); it is to have eternal life and to be godly (3; cp. John 17:3).

The Lord has done great things for us. He has chosen us and called us but we must be very diligent to make our *calling and election sure* (10). How do we do this? We do this by having a practical faith and by leading a godly life (cp. James 2:18). If we do the things commanded in verses 5 to 10 we *will never stumble* and we will be sure of a wonderful welcome into *the everlasting kingdom* of the Lord Jesus Christ when we meet him at death, or when he returns (11). Peter knew that he was soon to die (*'put off my tent'* means departing from the body through death) and he was concerned to stress the importance of godly living. He used the words, *'remind ... reminding ... reminder'* (12-15) to show that he wanted the things commanded in verses 5 to 10 to be remembered and obeyed after his death. What are you doing to make *your calling and election sure* (10)?

Many professing Christians neglect God's word today and some prefer to listen to the ideas and heresies of self-proclaimed prophets. We have *the prophetic word made more sure* (19). The Scriptures are as a light shining in the darkness of this world exposing false teaching. The Bible is sufficient for all our guidance in matters of faith and practice. We do not need new revelations or so-called prophecies. **If we know God's word we will be spared much trouble and confusion. The Bible will never lose its power to guide us, build us up in our holy faith, bless us and inspire us.**

False teachers among you … destructive heresies

This is a very solemn and frightening chapter! Peter knows that he is soon to die (1:14) and he now warns us against the *destructive heresies … destructive ways* and *deceptive words* of false teachers. He writes of the severe judgment that God will bring upon these people (1-3). The apostle is vehement in his denunciation of false teachers. Is it any wonder that almost every New Testament book has warnings against false teachers and false teaching? The Lord Jesus and the apostles warn us against them (Matthew 7:15; 1 Timothy 4:1-3; Titus 3:9-11). False teaching is a greater threat to the church than persecution.

We may be aware of the heresies of the cults, but we must be on our guard against false teachers within our churches. They attract *many* to *follow their destructive ways* (2). We must never assume that a man is right because his teaching is popular. Do not be surprised that those who love truth are in the minority; this has always been the case. Heretics misuse Scripture to propagate their pernicious views. They are presumptuous and self-willed (10). They will exploit you and lead you astray if you tolerate them.

God did not spare the angels who sinned in rebelling against him before the world was made. He did not spare the ancient world of Noah's day or the wicked cities of Sodom and Gomorrah, and he will surely bring judgment on false teachers (4-11). We may be sorely tried by the wickedness of the ungodly and the blasphemies of false teachers, but *the Lord knows how to deliver the godly out of temptations* (or 'trials', 9-10). **Do you know and love truth enough to *contend earnestly for the faith* (Jude 3)?** False doctrine is often associated with wrong living (14). Balaam uttered sublime prophecies concerning God and his people but he was a wicked man (14-16; cp. Numbers chapters 22-24). *The wages of unrighteousness* may appear attractive for a time, but will bring terrible judgment (12-13). Verses 20 to 22 do not teach that a person can lose his salvation. Scripture is quite clear that this is not possible (the *'dog'* is still a dog, the *'sow'* is still a sow — there is no change in their nature). **God does not choose us to lose us!**

The Lord is not slack concerning his promise

Peter wrote his letter to stir up our *pure* [sincere] *minds* to make us mindful of the words of the prophets and the apostles (1-2). Many Christians in the early church were expecting the immediate return of Christ. They grew discouraged as persecution increased and Christ did not return as expected. Peter reminds us that the Lord Jesus and his apostles had warned of the scoffers who would taunt us with the question, *'Where is the promise of his coming? ... all things continue as they were from the beginning of creation'* (4). They hate the idea of judgment and assert that nothing changes. They wilfully forget that this is not true (5). God brought terrible judgment when he destroyed the world by flood because of its wickedness (5-6). Those who heard Noah had many years to repent of their sin (cp. Genesis 6:3) but they did not take him seriously. A thousand years is as one day with the Lord (8) who delays judgment to give sinners opportunity to repent.

Though scoffers may doubt that Christ will come again (4), *the Lord is not slack concerning his promise ... but is long-suffering* [patient] *toward us* (9). Jesus will come again just as he has promised! *'The day of the Lord'* is a term used for the return of Christ (10; cp. 1 Thessalonians 5:2; 2 Thessalonians 2:2). The earth and everything in it will be burned up in a massive conflagration (10,12). The coming judgment should have a sobering effect upon us. *What manner of persons ought you to be in holy conduct and godliness?* (11). Christians can look for the day of God, not with despair, but with a sense of great anticipation and joy. The Lord will create new heavens and a new earth in which righteousness dwells as he has promised (13; cp. Isaiah 65:17). We have a wonderful future! Let us be holy and godly (11,14; cp. 1 John 3:3). Are you looking forward to Christ's second coming?

Peter closes by reminding us that the greatest antidote to ungodliness and false teaching is for us to *grow in the grace and knowledge of our Lord and Saviour Jesus Christ* (17-18). **As you look back on your Christian life, are you able to trace and to see evidence of this growth?**

1, 2 & 3 JOHN

John outlived the other apostles and his letters may have been written as late as AD 90. His second and third letters are the shortest books of the New Testament. John wrote his Gospel to lead its readers to a life-giving faith in Christ (John 20:31). *These are written that you may believe that Jesus is the Christ, the Son of God, and that believing you may have life in his name* (John 20:31). He wrote his letters to strengthen believers in their assurance that they possessed eternal life and to show the evidence of true faith. *These things I have written to you who believe in the name of the Son of God, that you may know that you have eternal life* (1 John 5:13).

John's first readers had been deeply disturbed and unsettled in their faith by teachers of false doctrine. Some of these false teachers had once been in the church (2:19) and had undermined the assurance of some of those who were faithful, seeking to entice them away from the church (2:18,26). They are described as 'antichrists' (2:18) and 'false prophets' (4:1). They claimed to have a superior knowledge of God, but they were heretical in their beliefs about Christ's Person and they were ungodly in their behaviour. They denied that Jesus is the Christ, the Son of God (2:22; cp. 4:15; 5:5,10) who had come in the flesh to be the Saviour of the world (4:2,14). They claimed to love God but showed no love for believers (4:20). They claimed to be sinless but they did not keep Christ's commandments (1:8,10; 2:4). These false teachers had probably embraced some form of Gnostic teaching, one of the heresies that troubled the early church.

The Gnostics taught that matter is evil and spirit is good; thus the body is evil. By a special knowledge (Greek word for 'knowledge' = '*gnosis*'), only known to them, the human spirit could be released from its material prison and rise to God. They claimed that the Lord Jesus Christ would not have taken human flesh, because flesh is evil.

Key words: *love* (37 times); *life* (11 times); and *light* (5 times).

Our fellowship

John opens his Gospel and his first letter by pointing us to the Lord Jesus Christ who is *'the Word of life'* (1; cp. John 1:1,14). The Lord Jesus was there in the beginning. He has always existed! He took human flesh, coming into the world to save sinners (1 Timothy 1:15). John had been with Jesus during his ministry on earth so he wrote about someone he had seen, touched, heard and known (1-3). Jesus has ascended to heaven but this does not prevent us from having fellowship with him. John wrote, *'Truly our fellowship is with the Father and with his Son Jesus Christ'* (3).

To have *'fellowship'* (Greek, *'koinonia'*) is to have things in common, to share. To have fellowship with God and with his Son means to have peace with him and to know his love filling our lives; it is to enjoy his presence with us and to know his smile on us as he leads us and watches over us. To have fellowship with God means trusting in him and living to please him; it is to worship and praise him. To have fellowship with God is to rejoice in him and is expressed in our prayer life when we bring our thanksgiving and requests to him. To have fellowship with God leads to glorious joy and brings us into meaningful fellowship with other Christians (3-4,7). We share together the same desire for the glory of God, the same faith and destiny. **What more could we want? Christians are the most privileged people in all the world.**

The heretics who troubled John's first readers claimed to have a special knowledge of God but their strange beliefs and sinful behaviour denied this. *God is light and in him is no darkness at all* (5). There are conditions for fellowship with God:

- We must *walk in the light* and know the continual cleansing of the blood of Christ (7). If we walk in darkness, we cannot be in fellowship with God who is light (5-6).
- We must *confess our sins* (9). This means naming specific sins and seeking God's forgiveness. If we believe that we no longer sin, *we deceive ourselves* (8,10). When did you last confess to God a specific sin or failure in your life?

By this we know that we know him

God is *'faithful and just to forgive us our sins'* (1:9), but we must never have an easy-going attitude to sin. The very idea that we can continue with a sinful lifestyle because grace and forgiveness are free is emphatically denied in the Bible (Romans 6:1-2). The Lord Jesus Christ is our *Advocate with the Father* (1). As our *advocate* and great *high priest,* the Lord Jesus pleads our cause at the Father's right hand (Romans 8:34; Hebrews 1:3; 7:25; 8:1). *He himself is the propitiation for our sins* (2). A *'propitiation'* is a sacrifice which turns God's righteous anger away from us so that we receive mercy. Jesus is the propitiation *for the whole world* (2); this does not mean that everyone will be saved, but that Jew, Gentile and every race may be reached by God's mercy. God's anger is only turned away from those who belong to him, who are 'in Christ'.

We must beware of deceivers. If we belong to Christ, we have the promise of eternal life (24-27). How may we know that we truly know the Lord? John gives us three tests which are all found in this chapter and throughout his letter:

- The moral test: that we keep Christ's commandments (3). Our righteous Saviour paid a great price to save us and he expects much of us. We must keep his commandments and his word (4-5). Keeping God's word means walking as Jesus walked (6). If the love of God the Father is within us, we will not love the world and we will practise righteousness (15-17,29).
- The social test: that we love our fellow-Christians (8-11). If we have any hatred in our heart for other believers, we must question our salvation. Such hatred will cause us to grope in darkness and will cause ourselves and others to stumble.
- The theological test: that we believe that Jesus is the promised Messiah (Christ), the Son of God, and that he came into the world, taking human flesh (22-23; cp. 4:1-3).

Do you meet these three requirements? Do you know that you know him?

Children of God

When God saves us, he brings us into his family. *Behold what manner of love the Father has bestowed on us, that we should be called children of God!* (1). We are *children of God* because of his great love which he has lavished so freely upon us. We know that we shall be like the Lord Jesus when he returns, *for we shall see him as he is* (2). We will at last be perfect and will sin no more. We will have a body like his resurrection body (Philippians 3:21). There will be no more death, sorrow, crying or pain (Revelation 21:4). The truth of Christ's second coming is a great incentive to holy living. *Everyone who has this hope in him purifies himself, just as he is pure* (3; cp. 2 Peter 3:11).

The three tests of genuine Christianity are found throughout this chapter (e.g. 23-24). The Lord Jesus *was manifested* [came into the world] *to take away our sins* and *that he might destroy the works of the devil* (5,8). Sin is the work of the devil who *has sinned from the beginning.* It is *lawlessness,* being rebellion against God's holy law (4). Satan's power over the believer is broken. We are able to resist the devil and overcome his efforts to make us sin (James 4:7). If we are *children of God* we are *born of God* (9; cp. 2:29; 4:7; 5:1,4,18) and we will shun sin and practise righteousness. We will also love fellow-members of God's family (10-15). Brotherly love means being prepared to lay down our lives for another believer and helping a brother in need (16-18).

Christian assurance is the birthright of every child of God (19) but Satan is always busy seeking to undermine that assurance. We must never rely on the feelings of our heart but trust in our great God who is gracious and merciful to all who come to him. *If our heart condemns us, God is greater than our heart, and knows all things* (20). Obedience to God brings confidence towards him (21-22). When you feel discouraged or when you feel lonely as a Christian among ungodly people at work, college or school, **remember that you are a child of God and shine as a light in this dark world (Matthew 5:14-16; Ephesians 5:8).**

Perfect love casts out fear

Many Christians have been deceived by friendly, smooth-tongued false teachers. We must always keep the warnings of God's word fixed in our minds, especially when anyone comes with some new teaching or some new thing. *Beloved, do not believe every spirit, but test the spirits, whether they are of God* (1). Those who deny that Jesus is God the Son, who came to earth in the flesh, are false teachers who have *the spirit of the Antichrist* (2-3). These people are agents of the devil and *are of the world* (5; cp. 2 Corinthians 11:13-15).

These verses again return to the command of the Lord Jesus to love one another (cp. 2:7-11; 3:11-18). *Everyone who loves is born of God and knows God* (7). This does not mean that all who are loving belong to the Lord. That is contrary to the teaching of the Bible. John also stresses the need for correct belief in Christ and for obedience to God's commandments (15; cp. 3:22). *God is love* (8,16). This wonderful truth does not mean that he will not punish sinners. If God ignored human wickedness, we could not possibly trust in him because his justice would always be in doubt. God has manifested (shown) his love by sending his only begotten Son into the world to be our Saviour, *to be the propitiation for our sins,* turning his wrath away from us (9-10,14). No one has seen God at any time but the evidence that he lives in us can be seen when we love each other (12-13).

Fear involves torment. It saps our strength, it causes sleepless nights, it robs us of our joy and peace, but *perfect love casts out fear* (18). God is love and when his love is perfected (fulfilled) in us we will not allow anxious thoughts to blight our lives. On the night before he was crucified, the Lord Jesus said to his fearful disciples, *'Let not your heart be troubled, neither let it be afraid'* (John 14:27). **Child of God, your Saviour loves you and does not want you tormented by fear. If your mind is in turmoil with anxiety, come to him who is perfect in his love.** Repent of any sin that besets you and ask him to banish your fear and to fill you with his love and peace. He cares for you. He will never let you go, nor will he let you down.

The confidence we have in him

The three tests of Christian profession are again set out in these verses — our belief in Jesus as the Christ, the Son of God; our love for the children of God; and our obedience to his commandments. God brings us to new birth and it should be obvious that if we love him, we should also love our fellow-Christians who have also been *'begotten'* of God (1). The world hates us and we must not love it (2:15-17; 3:13). Our victory over the world and its ruler is assured (cp. 2:13-14). The phrase *'overcomes the world'* is repeated three times in verses 4 and 5. We have victory over the world because of:

- Our new birth. *Whatever is born of God overcomes the world* (4).
- *Our faith.* We trust in a great God who will never fail us (4).
- Our belief *that Jesus is the Son of God* (5).

The expression *'we know'* is repeated several times in this chapter (2,13,15,18,19,20). Satan wants to undermine our faith in Christ and John wrote his letter so that we would have assurance and know that we have eternal life (13). The Greek word translated *'confidence'* (14; cp. 2:28; 3:21) carries the idea of 'boldness in speech' (it is translated *'boldness'* in 4:17). *Now this is the confidence that we have in him, that if we ask anything according to his will, he hears us* (14-15). This promise is truly amazing but it does not mean that we can be like spoiled children, getting from God all that we want. We must ask *'according to his will'.* **We are more likely to pray in line with God's will if we love and obey him and if we love our fellow-Christians.** Unconfessed sin will hinder our prayers. We must walk in the light (1:7; cp. Psalm 66:18).

False gods are idols even though they may not be represented by images of wood, stone or metal. **Satan dangles all kinds of idols before us to draw us away from the true God.** There are the idols of false religions (such as the New Age), of materialism, or of seeking worldly advancement and the praise of men. There is much at stake. *Little children, keep yourselves from idols* (21).

Walking in truth

We cannot be sure whether *the elect lady* (1) is a specific individual or whether she is a church. The church is the bride of Christ and verse 13 may indicate that the *elect sister* is a sister church (cp. 1 Peter 5:13). John repeats the emphases found in his first letter: the necessity of correct views of Christ, that he is the Son of God who came in the flesh (7); love for fellow-Christians; and keeping God's commandments (5-6). John rejoiced greatly that he had found some who were *walking in truth* (4). **'Walking in truth' is more than believing the truth; it is living out the truth in our lives, loving one another and walking according to God's commandments.**

It is essential to walk in truth because *many deceivers have gone out into the world.* They refuse to accept that Jesus is God's promised Messiah who came in the flesh (7). John urges us, *'Look to yourselves that we do not lose those things we worked for'* (8). False teaching will spoil our life and witness if we allow it any entrance into our church. If we remain faithful, we will *receive a full reward* (8). The Greek word translated *'transgresses'* (9) means 'goes on ahead' or 'goes beyond'. Many false teachers have gone far beyond what the Bible teaches and they no longer remain in the doctrine of Christ. False teachers may appear to be sincere but they are antichrists (7). We must not entertain them in our homes or give them a hearing in our churches. If we do so, we identify with them in their evil deeds (10-11). These verses have been misused by some people to shun all contact with non-Christian relatives or friends. Our homes can be greatly used in winning people to Christ. Never invite false teachers such as Jehovah's Witnesses into your home unless they are seeking to know the truth. In such cases, involve a godly, well-taught Christian to meet them with you.

John recognized that paper and ink are a poor substitute for face to face fellowship (12). God's word is very precious but how wonderful it will be when we see our Saviour face to face in heaven (1 John 3:2; Revelation 22:4). **Our joy will then be complete!**

You do faithfully whatever you do

John wrote this letter to encourage his beloved friend Gaius (1). John prayed that Gaius would *prosper in all things and be in health* just as his soul prospered (2). Would it be safe to pray such a prayer for you? If your physical health were a reflection of your spiritual condition, in what kind of state would your body find itself? Gaius was a godly man but his church was spoiled by a man called Diotrephes, an ambitious power-seeker who loved to have the pre-eminence. He opposed John with malicious words and ordered church members not to give hospitality to visiting brethren. Those who dared to disobey him were put out of the church (9-10). Many a faithful saint has been grieved and hurt by petty tyrants who love to have the pre-eminence. We must always be careful to recognize leaders who love us and are eager to serve us rather than boost their own self-image.

John rejoiced greatly to hear that Gaius walked in the truth (3) and that he had given hospitality to visiting brethren and strangers, ignoring the threats of Diotrephes (5-6). Hospitality is a vital ministry (Matthew 10:40-42; Hebrews 13:2) which encourages visitors, the lonely, and others who may be seeking the Lord. When did you last open your home to give hospitality? Despite all the difficulties in the church, John commended Gaius, *'Beloved, you do faithfully whatever you do'* (5). What an example! We should always remember to do everything *as to the Lord* (Ephesians 6:7) so that we will honour him. **Are you an eager worker in the church, doing faithfully whatever you do?** Demetrius may have been one of the visiting brothers who needed hospitality but had been slandered by Diotrephes. John commended him as one who had *a good testimony from all* and he was faithful to the truth (12). What kind of testimony do you have?

In his closing greetings John writes, *'Peace to you'* (14). The apostle was mindful of the difficult circumstances surrounding his beloved friend. We can know God's peace in the most trying circumstances, even when our faith is sorely tested by the antics of someone who professes to know Christ.

JUDE

Jude identifies himself as the brother of James (1). In the early church, the only James (except the brother of John) known to everyone was the Lord's brother (Galatians 1:19). It seems therefore that Jude (or Judas) was the half-brother of the Lord Jesus (Matthew 13:55). These half-brothers of Jesus did not believe in him until after the resurrection (John 7:3-5; Acts 1:14). The warnings in Jude against false teachers (3-4) are very similar to those in 2 Peter chapter 2. John's first two letters also warn us again and again to be on our guard against false teaching.

These warnings are more relevant than ever. Some television evangelists and teachers are peddling all kinds of strange views and many thousands are being deceived. Some claim that the Holy Spirit is working through them to perform miracles and that he is speaking through them. Their claims are like their doctrine — highly questionable!

Contend earnestly for the faith

Jude's greeting gives a description of what it means to be a Christian. He wrote *to those who are called, sanctified by God the Father and preserved in Jesus Christ* (1). How does Jude pray for believers whose faith is under attack? He prays that God's choice blessings of *mercy, peace and love be multiplied* to them (2).

Jude had intended to write about our *common salvation* but the Holy Spirit directed him to exhort us *to contend earnestly for the faith which was once for all delivered to the saints* (3). Error never announces its coming to a church. False teachers creep in unnoticed and craftily spread their poison (4). Beware of those who claim to have 'new insights' and who bring new doctrines. They may appear to be godly, but they are not (4; cp. 2 Timothy 3:5-7). Jude not only urges pastors and other church leaders but **every** Christian *to contend earnestly for the faith.* Our word 'agonize' is derived from the Greek word translated 'contend'. It carries the idea of an athlete exerting himself to win his race. *The faith which was once for all delivered to the saints* is not negotiable. Our faith does not change with the times and we are not permitted to interpret Scripture in a way that denies its plain and obvious meaning. Some false teachers claim to be 'born again' and thus gain acceptance by unsuspecting Christians. **Confusion is all around us and you must** *contend earnestly for the faith.* **Are you able to do this?** If you feel insufficiently equipped for the battle, take time to give yourself to the study of God's word, and obey its teaching.

We must be vigilant and fight against error! Warren W. Wiersbe rightly observes that 'the Christian life is a battleground, not a playground'. We are in a fierce battle when we *contend earnestly for the faith* but we know that the Lord Jesus is able to keep us from stumbling into error and sin. When Jesus comes again, he will present us *faultless before the presence of his glory with exceeding joy* (24). This exceeding joy will last for ever because we will be with our Saviour in glory, and we will be perfect at last, never to sin again.

HAGGAI, ZECHARIAH & MALACHI

Haggai and Zechariah both prophesied during the reign of King Darius II of Persia, approximately 520 BC. Work on rebuilding the temple had ceased several years earlier on account of slander and opposition. These two men encouraged and challenged the Jews to restart their work on the temple (Ezra 5:1-2). Haggai's prophecies were given over a period of less than four months (1:1; 2:10,20). Zechariah had eight visions (1:7 - 6:8) and he also prophesied of Christ — of his entry into Jerusalem on a donkey (9:9); of his sufferings (12:10; 13:7); and of his second coming in great power (14:3-5).

Both Haggai and Zechariah repeatedly describe God as *'the LORD of hosts'*. It is a great comfort to know that though Satan and evil men oppose us, God and his mighty army of angels are on our side. Why should we fear?

The date of **Malachi's prophecy** is uncertain but it is likely that it was around the time of Nehemiah's return to Jerusalem from Babylon in 432 BC (both men deal with the problem of mixed marriages, the neglect of tithing, and of corrupt priests: Nehemiah 13:6-31; Malachi 2:1-11; 3:8). The name 'Malachi' means 'my messenger'. Three messengers are mentioned in his prophecy — the priest (2:7), the forerunner (3:1), and the Messenger of the covenant (3:1).

The exiles who had returned from Babylon fell into backsliding after the rebuilding of the temple and later the wall of Jerusalem. When we backslide, we become insensitive in our attitude to the Lord. The unfaithfulness of the Jews was quite frightening. As the Lord proclaimed his love for them, they had the audacity to reply, *'In what way have you loved us?'* (1:2). They questioned God in this manner on another six occasions (1:6; 1:7; 2:17; 3:7; 3:8; 3:13). Let us be determined to take the message of Malachi to heart so that we do not lose sight of our responsibility to honour God in our lives.

Consider your ways!

The rebuilding of the temple had been halted through enemy slander and opposition (Ezra 4:24) and fifteen years had passed without any attempt being made to restart the work. The discouraged people had fallen into spiritual lethargy and had become complacent, saying, *'The time has not come, the time that the* LORD's *house should be built'* (2). They had redirected their time, energy and money into building beautiful houses for themselves (4,9). Their excuse for neglecting God's house was, *'The time has not come.'* **We may have good intentions to give more of our time or money to God's work in the future, but such intentions rarely come to anything.** Satan is quite happy to see us have good intentions and neglect the work of God because *'the time has not come'.*

It is not sinful to improve our homes or to look for a better job. These things must not become priorities in our lives, however, lest they ensnare us and lead us into spiritual apathy and sin. If bettering ourselves means that we will be less useful in our local church or damage our family life, let us beware! The Lord Jesus said, *'Seek first the kingdom of God and his righteousness, and all these things shall be added to you'* (Matthew 6:33).

God sent drought and food shortages to the people because of their sinful neglect of his work (9-11). Haggai's message for them was, *'Consider your ways!'* (5,7). They took his message to heart and Zerubbabel the governor, and Joshua the high priest obeyed the voice of the Lord coming through the words of Haggai. *The people feared the presence of the* LORD and worked on the temple as Haggai continued to encourage them (12-15). When we read God's word or hear it preached, we must expect both rebuke and encouragement. If things are going wrong for us, maybe God is saying to us, *'Consider your ways!'* We must not make excuses that the time is not ripe for obedience to God. **The time has come for us to give ourselves wholeheartedly to the work of God.** As we obey him, we will increasingly know his awesome presence among us (12).

'Be strong' ... says the LORD, 'and work; for I am with you'

Zerubbabel, Joshua and the people had been working on the temple for almost four weeks when God gave Haggai another message for them (1-2; cp. 1:15). He encouraged them through the prophet, *'Yet now be strong ... and work; for I am with you'* (4). There were a few aged people who remembered the glory of the old temple before it was destroyed. They were discouraged as they observed that the new house of God would never match the old temple for splendour and beauty (3). We must beware of pining for 'the good old days' when there appeared to be greater blessing in the church.

The Lord promised, *'The glory of this latter temple shall be greater than the former'* (9). We must not look for God's glory and peace in magnificent temples or cathedrals (cp. John 4:21-22), but in his church, which is his temple (1 Corinthians 3:16; Ephesians 3:20-21). **We do well to learn the lessons from the past, but we must not fall into the error of living in the past so that we are useless in the present.** We have different challenges and opportunities from those of past generations. Who knows, God may be pleased to do a far greater work in our day than anything we could dare to imagine?

The Lord spoke again through the prophet two months later. God gave Haggai two messages, one for the priests and the other for Zerubbabel (10,20; cp. verse 1). He reminded the priests that the people had been polluted by their past disobedience and had seen little evidence of his blessing on them since they began the work (10-19). He promised that he would now begin to bless them (19). God encouraged Zerubbabel, telling him that he had chosen him, and that he would make him precious (*'a signet ring'*, 20-23). Zerubbabel foreshadows God's greater servant, the Lord Jesus (Isaiah 42:1; Acts 4:27,30) whose human descent is traced through him (Matthew 1:12). God has also chosen every Christian and we are precious in his sight. **Let us encourage ourselves in the Lord as we serve him.** *We are more than conquerors through him who loved us* (Romans 8:37).

Let us go with you, for we have heard that God is with you

Zechariah reminded the people that God had punished the Jews and sent them into exile because of their disobedience to his law (7:8-14). Jerusalem had known plenty of religious ceremony but little of truth and righteousness. The Lord said, *'I am zealous for Zion with great zeal'* (2; cp. 1:14). He cared very much for his people and his city. He promised to return to the city and dwell among her people so that Jerusalem would be called *'the City of Truth ... the Holy Mountain'* (3). There is a beautiful picture of a city which enjoyed peace and which was secure. The elderly would relax in those streets which had known bloodshed and had been in ruins following the Babylonian invasion. The city would be full of children, able to play safely in her streets (5). God's promise may have seemed too good to believe for many, but all things are possible with God (6).

Those rebuilding the temple were encouraged to let their hands be strong and not to fear (9,13; cp. Haggai 2:4). The Jews had been a curse among the nations but God would save Judah and Israel and they would be a blessing (13). The great blessing for the nations coming through Judah was the Lord Jesus Christ. God had been determined to punish sinning Israel but he was now determined to do good to Jerusalem (14-15). God reminded his people that he expected them to be righteous and to love truth (16-19).

God promised that many nations would come to seek him in Jerusalem (20-22). We should not look for a future glory for earthly Jerusalem, however. The prophecies relating to her coming glory are fulfilled in the church (Galatians 4:26-27; Ephesians 3:20-21). **Sinners will be encouraged to seek the Lord when they see the godly living of Christians and a love of truth and peace** (19). When we shine as lights in this dark world, there will be those who will say, *'Let us go with you, for we have heard that God is with you'* (21-23). Let us be Christlike, seeking always to please God. We will then know that he is with us and so will those who are not Christians, and we will enjoy the blessing of the Lord in our lives.

In what way have we despised your name?

The Lord had chosen Israel (descendants of Jacob) and had freely bestowed his love upon them, but the unfaithful and ungrateful Jews questioned that love for them (2). The Lord pointed out that the nation of Edom (descended from Jacob's twin brother, Esau), which had become Israel's treacherous foe, no longer existed (3-4). God had been merciful to his own people, though they had not deserved such grace. Malachi's fellow-Jews were lacking in the fear of God (6).

The third commandment forbids us to take the name of the Lord in vain (Exodus 20:7) and we pray in the Lord's prayer, *'Hallowed be your name'* (Matthew 6:9). The name of God is important because it reveals his character, e.g. *'El Shaddai'* = 'Almighty God' (Genesis 17:1). Malachi uses the title *'Yahweh Sabaoth'* (*'the* LORD *of hosts'*) more than twenty times in his prophecy. This title conveys the greatness and the sovereignty of God who rules over all the hosts or 'powers' in heaven and earth. God's name is great and to be feared (11,14). We should be overwhelmed with awe as we meditate upon the great and holy name of the Lord.

The priests had despised the name of the Lord and were insensitive to the seriousness of their sin. They asked, *'In what way have we despised your name?'* (6). The Lord then told them how they had despised his name. He rebuked them for offering to him blind, lame and sick animals (8,13-14) when they knew that only the best is good enough for God (e.g. Leviticus 1:3; 3:1; 4:3; 22:19-24). They were bringing offerings to God's altars which they would not dare to offer to their civil governor (8). How dare they treat God with such contempt?

We, too, despise God's name if we do not give to him the very best that we can offer. The Lord Jesus gave everything to save us. He was rich but he became poor (2 Corinthians 8:9). He is God but he took human flesh; he is King of kings but he took the form of a slave (Philippians 2:5-8). **The Lord will not accept our second-best. If we offer him second-rate service, we despise his great name.**

Prove me now ... says the LORD of hosts

Malachi prophesied the coming of John the Baptist and of Jesus Christ (1; cp. Matthew 11:10-11; Mark 1:1-3). When the Lord visits us in revival or in judgment, he comes to purge away sin (1-5). Why had God spared sinful Israel from destruction? We are told in verse 6: *'For I am the LORD, I do not change; therefore you are not consumed, O sons of Jacob.'* It is a great comfort to know in this world of change and decay that God is always the same. His infinite power will never diminish and his great faithfulness, mercy and love are always the same (cp. Hebrews 13:8).

Malachi prophesied to a backslidden people whom God called upon to return to him. They asked, *'In what way shall we return?'* (7). God told them that they had robbed him and they then asked, *'In what way have we robbed you?'* (8). He said that they had robbed him by neglecting to pay tithes and offerings (8). A tithe is a tenth of our income (cp. Genesis 28:22). The work of God languishes because many Christians do not face up to their responsibility to support it by giving generously. Let us gladly give as God has prospered us (1 Corinthians 16:2). If we are mean and miserly or neglect to give to the Lord's work, we are robbing God! No true Christian would ever dream of robbing a bank or stealing from his employer, but we may rob God by failing to support our church. We must be careful if we plead poverty. Paul found the most generous Christians to be the most poor (2 Corinthians 8:1-5). God challenges us: *'Try me now in this,'* says the LORD of hosts, *'if I will not open for you the windows of heaven and pour out for you such blessing that there will not be room enough to receive it'* (10).

Is your spiritual life dry? God does not change. He challenges **you** to prove him. Give to him generously and cheerfully out of a grateful and loving heart (2 Corinthians 9:6-7; cp. Luke 6:38). As the Lord pours out his blessing upon you, you will be able to talk of all his wondrous ways. He will listen with delight and hear you (16). **The unchanging God is near, just waiting for you to prove him! He is waiting to pour out blessings upon you, if you will only respond to his word.**

REVELATION

In the latter half of the first century AD the church suffered great persecution at the hand of Roman emperors Nero (from AD 64) and Domitian (AD 81-96). The book of Revelation is full of help and comfort for persecuted and suffering Christians. Satan and his helpers seem to be victorious over Christ and his church, but things are not what they seem. Jesus is Lord of lords and King of kings and he will overcome all his (and our) enemies (17:14; 19:11-21 — see William Hendriksen's commentary on Revelation, *More than conquerors,* pages 8-9).

Revelation is one of the most difficult books of the Bible to understand and because of this it is little read. Even the great Reformer John Calvin is reputed to have said that he did not write a commentary on the book of Revelation because he did not understand it! The problem that we face is that of interpreting the rich symbolism found in the book. Some symbols are clearly explained to us (e.g. the seven stars and the seven golden lampstands — 1:20) but others are open to widely differing interpretations. Many of the symbols come in groups of seven, e.g. seven seals, seven trumpets, seven bowls. The number seven which speaks of completeness is found 54 times in Revelation.

There are differing methods of interpreting the book of Revelation:

- **The Preterist View** which sees the book as having relevance only to the first century AD with no prediction of future events. This view can hardly be correct since the book calls itself a prophecy (1:3; 4:1).
- **The Historicist View** which sees Revelation as presenting the course of church history from the first century AD to the end of time. There are many variations within this view.
- **The Futurist View** which places all that is described after chapter 3 to things that will happen at the end of the age.
- **The Parallelist View** which sees the rich symbolism in the book as an expression of the conflict between God and Satan. There are seven parallel sections in the book, each spanning the entire Christian dispensation from the first to the second coming of

Christ. These seven sections fall into two divisions, chapters 1 to 11, and 12 to 22. I favour this view, which is held by many Bible scholars (including the late William Hendriksen). I have sought to interpret the symbols in the light of the teaching of the rest of the Bible. You may not agree with my views but please take the lessons of Revelation to heart.

Outline of Revelation (from Hendriksen)

A. The struggle on earth — chapters 1 - 11
The church persecuted by the world. The church is avenged, protected and victorious.

1. Christ in the midst of the seven golden lampstands: 1 - 3
2. The vision of heaven and the seven seals: 4 - 7
3. The seven trumpets of judgment: 8 - 11

B. The spiritual background of this struggle — chapters 12 - 22
This is a conflict between the Christ and the dragon (Satan) in which the Christ, and therefore his church, is victorious.

4. The woman and the Man-child persecuted by the dragon and his helpers (the beasts and the harlot):   12 - 14
5. The seven bowls of wrath: 15 - 16
6. The fall of the great harlot and of the beasts: 17 - 19
7. The judgment upon the dragon (Satan) followed by the new heaven and earth, new Jerusalem: 20 - 22

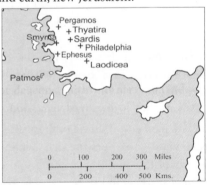

The Seven Churches of Asia (Revelation chapters 2 & 3)

To him who loved us

The title of this book is taken from its opening words, *'The Revelation of Jesus Christ'*. John's greeting is to the seven churches which are in Asia (4) but the message of the book is for every believer, as are the New Testament epistles (3; 22:18). The greeting is also from all three Persons of the Trinity, *'the seven Spirits'* speaking of the Holy Spirit in all his perfection (4). John's mention of the Lord Jesus Christ leads him to break out in adoration of his precious Saviour. Jesus is the eternal, almighty God, *the Alpha and the Omega* (first and last letters of the Greek alphabet), *the First and the Last* (8,11,17; 22:13); this is a title of God (Isaiah 44:6). In this doxology John ascribes glory *'to him who loved us'* (or 'loves us', 5-6). **The world may hate us and deride us but we are loved by the almighty King** who died on the cross to wash us and to free us from our sins *in his own blood* (4). He *has made us kings and priests to* God, and one day he will return for us (7).

John had been banished to the barren island of Patmos in the Aegean Sea (see map, page 405). It was about AD 96 when he wrote to his persecuted readers as their *brother and companion in tribulation, and in the kingdom and patience of Jesus Christ* (9). His persecutors had parted him from his church at Ephesus but they were not able to separate him from his Saviour (cp. Romans 8:35-37). He was able to worship God and to pray.

Verses 13 to 16 describe the Lord Jesus in all his splendour, majesty, power and burning purity. John was so overwhelmed by this vision of Christ that he *fell at his feet as dead* (17). The Lord Jesus is powerful, but oh, so tender. He laid his hand on the prostrate apostle and said to him, *'Do not be afraid, I am the First and the Last. I am he who lives, and was dead, and behold, I am alive for evermore. Amen. And I have the keys of Hades and death'* (17-18). Child of God, are you fearful? Remember who loves you and cares for you. **The Lord Jesus is in control of all your circumstances, and he still says to his troubled children, just as he said to John, *'Do not be afraid'*** (17).

You have left your first love

The messages to the seven churches (chapters 2 and 3) cover differing circumstances and problems still to be found in churches. In each church, except Laodicea, Christ finds something to commend. In five of the churches he finds something to criticize (the exceptions are Smyrna and Philadelphia). There is a similar pattern in each of the letters, with some slight variation:

1. The address. *'To the angel of the church in ...'.* (most scholars believe that the angel refers to the pastor or leader in each church).
2. Christ's self-designation (each time taken from 1:12-18), e.g. *'He who holds the seven stars in his right hand ...'*
3. Christ's commendation, *'I know your works ...'*
4. Christ's criticism, e.g. *'Nevertheless I have this against you ...'*
5. Christ's warning, e.g. *'Remember therefore ... or else ...'*
6. Christ's exhortation. *'He who has an ear, let him hear what the Spirit says to the churches'.*
7. Christ's promise, e.g. *'To him who overcomes I will give to eat from the tree of life.'*

There are four letters to different churches in chapter 2 but space restricts us to considering only the first letter. The Christians at Ephesus were commended for their perseverance in working for the Lord and for their intolerance of false teachers and wicked men (2-3,6). The Lord Jesus said to them, however, *'Nevertheless I have this against you, that you have left your first love'* (4). The church was sound in its doctrine and zealous in its work, but the sparkle had gone out of its love for Christ. **We may be highly respected in the church, we may even be elders or deacons, faithfully serving God week by week, but our love for the Lord may have grown cold so that we do not long for communion with him or delight in him.** It is possible to delight in God's work without delighting in God himself. If this is true of you, then hear the words of the Lord Jesus, *'Remember therefore from where you have fallen; repent and do the first works, or else ...'* (5). Have you left your first love?

Lukewarm

The church at Sardis had a reputation of being a live church. There is no mention of persecution or of heresy and they enjoyed peace, but it was the peace of the graveyard. The Lord Jesus said, *'You have a name that you are alive, but you are dead'* (1). He exhorted them, *'Be watchful, and strengthen the things which remain, that are ready to die'* (2). He urged them to remember how they had received and heard the truth and to repent (3). A church may be busy with all manner of activity and offer what is described as 'lively worship' while in reality it is dead; it may be correct in its doctrine but lacking in spiritual life.

The Lord had no rebuke for the church in Philadelphia. This church was not strong or influential but they had kept God's word and had remained faithful to Christ (8,10). Jesus promised them, *'I have set before you an open door, and no one can shut it'* (8). Even the persecuting Jews of the synagogue of Satan would be humbled and converted. We may suffer setbacks in the work for the Lord but it is a great encouragement to know that it is God who opens or closes doors.

Laodicea was a very prosperous city, important for banking, finance, clothing manufacture and for its eye-salve. The Laodicean church was wealthy, smug and complacent. They had deluded themselves into thinking that they were spiritually rich but they were poverty-stricken (17). They had sought happiness in earthly possessions but this had sapped their spiritual vitality and stifled their love for the Lord. The Lord Jesus was nauseated by their smug complacency. They were *'lukewarm'* and he was ready to spew them out of his mouth (16).

We may be sound in doctrine but lukewarm. We are lukewarm if we are not putting the Lord first in our lives, if we neglect Bible-reading and private prayer, if we have little enthusiasm to meet with God's people for worship and prayer. We are lukewarm if we are living a lie. **If you are lukewarm, you need to repent and to respond to the Lord as he knocks at the door of your heart (19-20).** Open the door! He will then revive you and bring you into sweet fellowship with himself.

You created all things, and by your will they exist

We now come to a new section of the Book of Revelation (chapters 4 to 7). John now sees another door, *a door standing open in heaven* and he hears the Lord Jesus, whose voice was like a trumpet (1:10). Jesus calls him up into heaven, *'Come up here, and I will show you things which must take place after this'* (1). John is again *in the Spirit* and he sees *a throne set in heaven* and the dazzling splendour and awesome beauty of the Lord, likened to different jewels (2-3).

He then sees twenty-four elders, each sitting upon a throne. They probably represent the church of both the Old and New Testament (there are twelve patriarchs of Israel and twelve apostles of the church, cp. 21:12-14). The four living creatures are cherubim (6-9; cp. Ezekiel 1:4-28; 10:20-22); these angelic beings guard the holy things of God (cp. Genesis 3:24; Exodus 25:20). Notice how often John mentions the throne of God in heaven (seventeen times in chapters 4 and 5). **The Lord God Almighty is sovereign over all the universe. He is in control of all our circumstances. His throne towers above all the trouble and turmoil around us and he is graciously working all things together for good (Romans 8:28).** *The LORD reigns, he is clothed in majesty* (Psalm 93:1). Alun Ebenezer writes, 'If you're a Christian this throne in heaven should encourage you too. Maybe you are really struggling at the moment and facing overwhelming temptation. Perhaps you're thinking of giving up. Remember this throne in heaven! The one who sits on it is all-powerful and majestic and you can call on him at any time' (*Revelation*, page 63; EP Books).

Much that is called 'worship' today is nothing of the kind. True worshippers are in awe as they adore and magnify the One who is holy and eternal (8; cp. Isaiah 6:3-5) and who created all things for his own glory (11; cp. John 1:3; Romans 11:36; Colossians 1:16; Hebrews 1:2; 11:3). Let us now worship and adore him. *'You are worthy, O Lord, to receive glory and honour and power; for you created all things, and by your will they exist and were created.'*

Worthy is the Lamb who was slain

John saw in the right hand of God the Father, *a scroll* (Greek = *'biblion'*; 1). The readers in the seven churches would have recognized that a *'biblion'* sealed with seven seals was a will and testament. When the testator died, his will was opened when possible in the presence of the seven witnesses who had sealed it. It was then read and its orders carried out. The scroll seen by John represents God's eternal plan and purpose for the whole universe and of all its creatures throughout history. If the scroll remained sealed, God's plan would not be carried out. A strong angel proclaimed with a loud voice (so that everyone in the universe could hear), *'Who is worthy to open the scroll and to loose its seals?'* (2). John *wept much* because no one in the entire universe was found worthy to open the scroll (3-4). None of the great saints are worthy, nor is Mary whom so many wrongly honour as 'the Queen of heaven'. Why is this? They are all weak, fallen sinners. The sinless angels who excel in strength are not worthy to open the scroll because they cannot possibly save sinners.

One of the elders comforted John, saying, *'Behold* [see] *the Lion of the tribe of Judah ... has prevailed* [conquered] *to open the scroll and to loose its seals'* (5). John then sees not a lion, but *a lamb as though it had been slain* (6). The seven horns signify his complete power and authority, and seven eyes indicate that he is filled with the Holy Spirit. John sees him approach the throne to take the scroll out of the right hand of God the Father (7). He has all authority to rule the universe according to God's eternal decree (Matthew 28:18; Philippians 2:9-11). **He has prevailed. He is worthy. To him be all our praise!**

The Lord Jesus was slain to redeem a people from every race (9). He is worthy to take the scroll and to open its seals because by his death and resurrection he has conquered Satan and all the dark forces of evil (Colossians 2:15; Hebrews 2:14; 1 John 3:8).

Worthy is the Lamb who was slain to receive power and riches and wisdom, and strength and honour and glory and blessing! (12).

The marriage supper of the Lamb

In chapter 18 John saw the fall of Babylon which symbolizes the fall of the godless world in which we live. He heard heaven rejoicing and praising God for defeating Babylon and for avenging his people who have been martyred (1-6). The word *'Alleluia'* (or 'Hallelujah') means 'praise Jehovah' and it is found four times in these verses (1,3,4,6).

John also heard rejoicing in heaven for the marriage of the Lamb (6-7). Marriage customs in Bible lands were elaborate compared with ours and those customs are reflected in the description of the marriage of the Lamb. In the betrothal the couple were legally husband and wife (cp. 2 Corinthians 11:2). Between the betrothal and the wedding feast there was an interval during which the groom paid a dowry to the bride's father. At the close of the interval the bride adorned herself in preparation to meet the groom. The groom, in his best clothes, walked in procession with his friends. He took the bride from her house and they returned in procession to his house or that of his parents (cp. Matthew 9:15; 25:1-13). The wedding feast included the marriage supper and the festivities which lasted for seven days or longer.

The church is betrothed to Christ who has purchased her with his own blood (Acts 20:28; Ephesians 5:25-27). The interval is the time between Christ's ascension to heaven and his second coming. During this period the bride makes herself ready to meet the Bridegroom (8; cp. 1 John 3:2-3). Our *'righteous acts'* do not save us, but they are evidence that we belong to Christ (8). The Lord Jesus is coming again with the angels (Matthew 25:31) to receive his bride the church. *'Blessed are those who are called to the marriage supper of the Lamb'* (9). What a day of rejoicing that will be! **Another supper is described in verses 11-21.** Our great Saviour, who is King of kings and Lord of lords (16), will destroy all his enemies and all who do not know him. This supper is terrifying indeed. **If you will be absent from the marriage supper of the Lamb, you will be present at the other supper. Which one do you expect to attend?**

The book of life

The interpretation of Revelation 20 is the subject of much disagreement and controversy. The main questions involved are:

- Will there be a literal millennium of one thousand years?
- Will there be two resurrections, one for the just and a later resurrection for the unjust?

The book of Revelation is full of symbolism and I agree with those Bible commentators who teach that the *'thousand years'* represents the gospel age in which we now live; this age will end when Christ returns to judge the world (11-15). The Lord Jesus bound Satan at his first coming (the binding of *the strong man* in Matthew 12:29 has the same Greek word as *'bound'* in verse two of this chapter). Satan fell as *lightning from heaven* (Luke 10:17-18; cp. John 12:20-32); this corresponds to verses 2 and 3. **Satan is bound and his power is limited; he is under the control of God.** He still deceives men and women but the Lord Jesus has triumphed over him (Colossians 2:15) and the gospel is being preached throughout the whole world.

Verses 7 to 9 refer to the battle of Armageddon (cp. 16:12-16; 19:19-21). Gog and Magog are first mentioned in Ezekiel chapter 38 where they symbolized Israel's great oppressor, the king of Syria, Antiochus Epiphanes, who was defeated by the Jews. Here, they also represent the enemies of God's people. At the end of the gospel age Satan and his allies will make their greatest ever attack on *the beloved city* (the church, 9). They will be defeated and will be cast into the lake of fire where *they will be tormented day and night for ever and ever* (10).

The first resurrection occurs when the souls of God's people are taken to be with the Lord when they die (5; cp. 2 Corinthians 5:8; Philippians 1:21-23). The resurrection of the body is when everyone who has ever lived will be raised at the return of Jesus (John 5:28-29; cp. Daniel 12:2-3; Matthew 25:31-46; Acts 24:15). We will be judged according to our works and all who are not written in *the book of life* will be cast into hell (12-15). **Is your name written in *the book of life*?**

Behold, I make all things new

This chapter tells us what heaven will be like and what we will be like in heaven. John saw *a new heaven and a new earth* for the old order had passed away (1; cp. Isaiah 65:17-19; 2 Peter 3:10,12). The church is described as *the holy city, New Jerusalem, coming down out of heaven from God, prepared as a bride adorned for her husband* (2). The Lord told John, *'Behold, I make all things new'* (5). The Greek word used for *'new'* in this chapter does not mean brand-new, but speaks of renewal and transformation. All will be transformed! God is with us now, but in heaven we will be much more aware of his presence, with no sin or suffering to disturb our fellowship with him (3). Look at the occurences of *'no more'* in verses 1 to 4.

* *There was no more sea* (1). The sea is a symbol of turmoil and unrest. The beast rose out of the sea (13:1) and wicked Babylon sat on many waters (17:1). *'No more sea'* — all our enemies and troubles will be gone.
* *'There shall be no more death, nor sorrow, nor crying; and there shall be no more pain, for the former things have passed away'* (4).

Heaven is not a vain hope! God said to John, *'Write, for these words are true and faithful'* (5). **Are you looking forward to going to heaven, to being with the Lord?** The alternative is too dreadful to contemplate. All kinds of unbelievers will have their part in the lake of fire (8). Are you thirsting to know God? You too can know him and enjoy him. He promises, *'I will give of the fountain of the water of life freely to him who thirsts'* (6). Come to the Lord Jesus and drink.

What will we be like in heaven? The church is described as *new Jerusalem* (2), as *holy Jerusalem* (10) and as *the bride, the Lamb's wife* (2,9). John sees the church in great splendour, having the glory of God (11). He had used the language of precious stones to describe the glory of God (4:2-4) and he now uses the same language to describe the glorified church which is radiant with that glory (18-21). If you are not a Christian and your name is not *written in the Lamb's book of life you will not be there* (27). **Oh, be sure that you are saved!**

They shall see his face

Adam's sin brought death to himself and all his descendants, and the ground was cursed (Genesis 3:17-19); he was driven out of Eden and kept from the tree of life (Genesis 3:24). In Christ all this will be restored. John now sees a pure, clear, sparkling *river of water of life, proceeding from the throne of God and of the Lamb ... and on either side of the river, was the tree of life'* (1-2). The tree of life and the water of life speak of our eternal life in Christ which comes from knowing him and the Father (John 17:3).

The glorious prospect of heaven may seem too good to be true, but it is no illusion. The angel said to John, *'These words are faithful and true'* (6; cp. 21:5). Heaven is a place of eternal rest from sin and suffering but it is not a place of idleness. We *shall serve* the Lord Jesus (3) and what joyful, satisfying service that will be! Heaven is a place of life and light — *there shall be no night there* (5). **We cannot now see the Lord Jesus (1 Peter 1:8) but we shall see him in all his matchless splendour in heaven.** *They shall see his face ... and they shall reign for ever and ever* (4-5). He will also greatly desire our beauty then, for we will be perfected (Psalm 45:11; cp. 1 John 3:2). Hallelujah!

There is a frightening finality about the words of verse 11 with no second chance to be right with God or to be cleansed from sin after we die. The unrighteous and the filthy will remain that way and they will be shut out of heaven for ever (15). The Lord Jesus will richly reward faithful service when he returns and will give access to the tree of life to those who keep his commandments (12-14).

There are words of encouragement here for any who desire to know Jesus as their Lord and Saviour. The Holy Spirit says, *'Come!'* The bride (the church) says, *'Come!'* **Are you thirsting for God? Come to Jesus and take the water of life freely (17).** The aged John, having had a glimpse of glory and all that awaits the children of God, prays, *'Even so, come, Lord Jesus!'* He couldn't wait to see his Saviour's face and to be with him in glory for ever!

Bibliography

Many of the recommended books can be downloaded to your computer, tablet or Kindle.

Commentaries on the whole Bible

Matthew Henry's *Commentary*. This well-loved commentary first published 350 years ago, has stood the test of time. Better to have the unabridged version rather than the concise version.

Rodger Crooks: *One Lord, One Plan, One People — A journey through the Bible from Genesis to Revelation* (Banner of Truth Trust). Written 350 years after Matthew Henry's *Commentary*, it introduces each book of the Bible by showing how they all focus on the Lord Jesus Christ.

Roger Ellsworth: *The Bible Book By Book* (Evangelical Press).

Old Testament Commentaries, book by book

John Currid: Seven volumes covering Genesis to Deuteronomy (Evangelical Press Study Commentaries).

Dale Ralph Davis: *Commentaries on Joshua, Judges, 1 & 2 Samuel, 1 & 2 Kings, Psalms 1 to 12* (Christian Focus). Davis really makes the Old Testament come alive. Highly commended.

Gordon Keddie: *According to Promise*. The message of the book of Numbers. Welwyn Commentary (Evangelical Press).

John Currid: *Strong and Courageous*. Joshua simply explained. Welwyn Commentary (Evangelical Press).

Gordon Keddie: *Even in Darkness*. Judges and Ruth simply explained. Welwyn Commentary (Evangelical Press).

Gordon Keddie: *Triumph of the King*. The message of 2 Samuel. Welwyn Commentary (Evangelical Press).

Andrew Stewart: *A Family Tree*. 1 Chronicles simply explained. Welwyn Commentary (Evangelical Press).

Andrew Stewart: *A House of Prayer*. The message of 2 Chronicles. Welwyn Commentary (Evangelical Press).

James Philip: *A Time to Build*. Studies in the Book of Ezra (Didasko Press).

Derek Thomas: *The Storm Breaks*. Job simply explained. Welwyn Commentary (Evangelical Press).

William Henry Green: *Conflict and Triumph — The argument of the Book of Job unfolded* (Banner of Truth Trust).

C. H. Spurgeon: *The Treasury of David*. Commentary on the Book of Psalms. I commend the seven-volume set rather than the one-volume abridged version.

Charles Bridges: *Psalm 119 — An exposition* (Banner of Truth Trust).

Charles Bridges: *Proverbs* (Banner of Truth Trust).

Charles Bridges: *Ecclesiastes* (Banner of Truth Trust).

Stuart Olyott: *A Life Worth Living and A Lord Worth Loving*. Ecclesiastes & Song of Solomon. Welwyn Commentary (Evangelical Press).

Derek Kidner: *A Time to Mourn, and a Time to Dance*. Ecclesiastes and the way of the world (Inter-Varsity Press).

Peter Masters: *The Mutual Love of Christ and His People*. An explanation of the Song of Solomon for personal devotions and Bible study groups (Wakeman Trust).

George Burrowes: *The Song of Solomon* (Banner of Truth Trust).

Alexander Stewart: *Jeremiah; The Man and His Work* (Knox Press).

Derek Thomas: *God Strengthens*. Ezekiel simply explained. Welwyn Commentary (Evangelical Press).

Stuart Olyott: *Dare to Stand Alone*. Read and enjoy the Book of Daniel. Welwyn Commentary (Evangelical Press).

James Philip: *By the Rivers of Babylon*. Studies in the Book of Daniel volumes 1 and 2 (Didasko Press).

Bibliography

Ray Beeley: *Wayward but Loved: A Commentary and Meditations on Hosea* (Banner of Truth Trust.

Ray Beeley: *The Roaring of the Lion: A Commentary on Amos* (Banner of Truth Trust).

J. A. Motyer: *The Day of the Lion: The message of Amos* (Inter-Varsity Press).

Dale Ralph Davis: *Micah* (Evangelical Press Study Commentary).

Hugh Martin: *Jonah* (Banner of Truth Trust).

D. Martyn Lloyd-Jones: *From Fear to Faith*. Studies in the Book of Habakkuk (Inter-Varsity Fellowship).

John Currid: *The Expectant Prophet*. Habakkuk simply explained. Welwyn Commentary (Evangelical Press).

Tim Shenton: *Habakkuk*. An expositional commentary (Day One).

T. V. Moore: *Haggai, Zechariah & Malachi* (Banner of Truth Trust).

John Benton: *Losing Touch with the Living God*. The message of Malachi. Welwyn Commentary (Evangelical Press).

New Testament Commentaries, book by book

D. Martyn Lloyd-Jones' sermons are excellent. Several sets have been published, especially by Banner of Truth Trust; these include sermons from John chapter one, Acts of the Apostles, Romans, Ephesians and 2 Peter.

William Hendriksen has written fine commentaries covering the following New Testament books: Matthew, Mark, Luke, John, Romans, Galatians, Ephesians, Philippians, Colossians & Philemon, 1 & 2 Thessalonians, 1 & 2 Timothy and Titus (Banner of Truth Trust).

J. C. Ryle: *Expository Thoughts on Matthew* (Banner of Truth Trust).

D. Martyn-Lloyd Jones: *Studies in the Sermon on the Mount*, 2 volumes (Inter-Varsity Fellowship).

J. C. Ryle: *Expository Thoughts on Mark* (Banner of Truth Trust).

J. C. Ryle: *Expository Thoughts on Luke*, 2 volumes (Banner of Truth Trust).

J. C. Ryle: *Expository Thoughts on John*, 3 volumes (Banner of Truth Trust).

Stuart Olyott: *The Gospel as it Really is.* Paul's Epistle to the Romans simply explained (Evangelical Press).

Charles Hodge: *1 and 2 Corinthians* (Sovereign Grace Publishers).

Paul Barnett: *The message of 2 Corinthians* (Inter-Varsity Press).

Stuart Olyott: *Alive in Christ.* Ephesians simply explained (Evangelical Press).

J. Philip Arthur: *Patience of Hope.* 1 and 2 Thessalonians simply explained. Welwyn Commentary (Evangelical Press).

J. Philip Arthur: *No Turning Back.* An exposition of the Epistle to the Hebrews (Grace Publications Trust).

Stuart Olyott: *I Wish Someone Would Explain Hebrews To Me!* (Banner of Truth Trust).

Thomas Manton: *The Epistle of James* (Banner of Truth Trust).

Alexander Nisbet: *1 & 2 Peter* (Banner of Truth Trust).

Ian Hamilton: *Let's study the Letters of John* (Banner of Truth Trust).

Thomas Manton: *Jude* (Banner of Truth Trust).

William Hendriksen: *More than Conquerors.* An interpretation of the Book of Revelation (Baker Books).

Alun Ebenezer: *Revelation* (Evangelical Press). This is a superb, easy to follow commentary, rich in practical application for Christians in the twenty-first century. If Alun writes any more commentaries, I would eagerly purchase them and read them.

The Tenderest Lover

The Tenderest Lover

THE EROTIC POETRY OF

Walt Whitman

EDITED AND WITH AN INTRODUCTION BY

Walter Lowenfels

ILLUSTRATIONS BY J. K. Lambert

DELACORTE PRESS
NEW YORK

Acknowledgements

To Lillian, who participated from beginning to
end; to Nan Braymer for her help all the way;
to Roger Asselineau, Harold Blodgett, Charles
Feinberg and Maxwell Geismar for reading the
introduction in manuscript, and for their
valuable suggestions; to Nancy E. Gross, my
editor, for her creativity in the final stages; and
to Manna Perpelitt for her devoted typing.

Walt Whitman Speaks to the Reader

Leaves of Grass is avowedly the song of Sex and Amativeness, and even Animality—though meanings that do not usually go along with those words are behind all, and will duly emerge; and all are sought to be lifted into a different light and atmosphere. . . . Difficult as it will be, it has become, in my opinion, imperative to achieve a shifted attitude from superior men and women toward the thought and fact of sexuality, as an element in character, personality, the emotions and a theme in literature. I am not going to argue the question by itself; it does not stand by itself. The vitality of it is altogether in its relations, bearings, significance—like the clef of a symphony. At last analogy the lines I allude to, and the spirit in which they are spoken, permeate all *Leaves of Grass,* and the work must stand or fall with them as the human body and soul must remain as an entirety.

from A BACKWARD GLANCE O'ER
TRAVELLED ROADS, 1889

I . . . sent out *Leaves of Grass* to arouse and set flowing in men's hearts and women's hearts, young and old (my present and future readers), endless streams of living, pulsating love and friendship, directly from them to myself, now and ever.

from THE PREFACE, 1876

I believe in the flesh and the appetites,
Seeing, hearing, feeling, are miracles, and each part and
     tag of me is a miracle.

Divine am I inside and out, and I make holy whatever I
     touch or am touched from,
The scent of these arm-pits aroma finer than prayer,
This head more than churches, bibles, and all the
     creeds.

If I worship one thing more than another it shall be the
     spread of my own body, or any part of it,
Translucent mould of me it shall be you!
Shaded ledges and rests it shall be you!
Firm masculine colter it shall be you!
Whatever goes to the tilth of me it shall be you!
You my rich blood! your milky stream pale strippings of
     my life!

Breast that presses against other breasts it shall be
  you!
My brain it shall be your occult convolutions!
Root of washed sweet-flag! timorous pond-snipe! nest of
  guarded duplicate eggs! it shall be you!
Mixed tussled hay of head, beard, brawn, it shall be
  you!
Trickling sap of maple, fibre of manly wheat, it shall be
  you!
Sun so generous it shall be you!
Vapors lighting and shading my face it shall be you!
You sweaty brooks and dews it shall be you!
Winds whose soft-tickling genitals rub against me it shall
  be you!
Broad muscular fields, branches of live oak, loving lounger
  in my winding paths, it shall be you!
Hands I have taken, face I have kissed, mortal I have ever
  touched, it shall be you.

from Section 24 of SONG OF MYSELF

Table of Contents

Calamus

Drum Taps

(*Civil War Poems, 1865–66*)

Afterlude

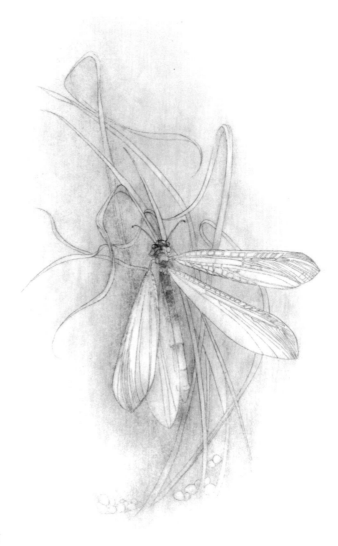

Walt Whitman's Many Loves

On June 30, 1865, Walt Whitman was fired from his job as a clerk in the Indian Bureau in Washington. His boss, Secretary of the Interior James Harlan, had been told that Whitman's poems were "indecent." He searched his desk, found a copy of *Leaves of Grass*. The next day Whitman got his pink slip.

Late in his life Whitman said: "When a man like Harlan does a thing like that we find generally that he is sincere, often deadly sincere, though a fiercely impossible bigot. Humanistically speaking the Bible and *Leaves of Grass* are in every way compatible."

Harlan was not the first person to be shocked by Whitman's verse, nor the last. Sixteen years later Whitman, who had never had a regular publisher, found one. In 1881 the Boston firm of Osgood brought out an edition of his poems. The book was selling well when the Society for the Prevention of Vice complained. The District Attorney notified the publisher that if the book was not withdrawn, he would be prosecuted for printing and selling obscene literature. The firm refused to fight the charge. The poet, then in his 60's, had to find another publisher.

Whitman has described a two-hour walk up and down the Boston Commons in 1860 with Emerson, who wanted him to make some deletions in the third edition of *Leaves of Grass,* then at the printer's: "During these two hours he was the talker and I the listener. It was an argument—statement, reconnoitering, review, attack, and pressing home (like an army corps in order, artillery, cavalry, infantry) of all that could be said against that part (and a main part) in the construction of my poems *Children of Adam*. . . . 'What have you to say to such things?' said E, pausing in conclusion. 'Only that while I can't answer them at all, I feel more settled than ever to adhere to my own theory, and exemplify it.' "

Attempts to censor writers are familiar in our century. But in Whitman's day, although Shakespeare and the Bible were widely sold in expurgated editions, he was exceptional among his own contemporaries in having to fight censorship throughout his life. It was not only his love poems that made Whitman a controversial figure. His style, free-flowing rhythms, lack of rhyme—his whole approach to people and to poetry was completely at variance with current fashions. His work was revolutionary, and he knew it: "I am the sworn poet of every dauntless rebel the world over. . . . My call is the call of battle. I nourish active rebellion."

Whitman did not write for erudite specialists. "In libraries I lie as one dumb, a gawk, or unborn, or dead." His aim was to reach the "divine average." These, he said, "inflate my throat." What has Whitman to offer them? His poems reflect many problems that affect us today—the social revolution, the sexual revolution, friendship between all nations, the vast potential of each individual, the significance of common people and, of course, youth: "I announce myriads of youths, beautiful, gigantic, sweet-bodied. . . ." But the term that unites all his work is love.

At 70 he told his young friend Horace Traubel about *Leaves of Grass*: "Sex is the root of it all: sex—the coming together of men and women: sex: sex."

In his younger days, at the height of his creative powers, he wrote: "Publish my name as that of the tenderest lover." Aside from his lifelong passion for everything human or unhuman ("I am eternally in love with you and with all my fellows upon the earth"), he was personally involved with few women and many young men. I have examined in manuscript the letters he received from soldiers he visited in Washington hospitals during the Civil War. They are intimate letters of love that Whitman kept all his life, as many other lovers have been known to do. "I can't find words to tell you the love their [sic] is in me for you," one young soldier writes. "You seemed like a father . . . but such has been the case with thousands of fellow soldiers," another says. And a mother tells him, in similar vein: "You have been more than a brother to James . . . and I still ask you to be a Father and Mother to him." Ten years after the war, a veteran wrote: "We have had a son borned since we heard from you. We call him Walter Whitman in honor of you, for love of you."

These passages are not to be found among the thousands of words written about Whitman's life, although they supply illuminating evidence of the real relations between Whitman and his "soldier-boys." "I believe no men ever loved each other as I and some of these poor wounded sick and dying men love each other," Whitman wrote his mother.

One soldier frequently referred to as a subject of Whitman's "perturbations" (Whitman's own word) is Tom Sawyer. In a letter to him Whitman tells how he said good-bye to their friend Lewey Brown: "When I came away he reached up his face, I put my arm around him and we gave each other a long kiss, half a minute long. . . ."

Yes, soldiers kissed him and he kissed them, and they loved each other. There was nothing furtive about it. "He loves everything and everybody," his lifelong friend John

Burroughs, the naturalist, reports. "I saw a soldier the other day stop on the street and kiss him."

In one of the many letters Whitman wrote asking for donations to help buy gifts and goodies for the wounded soldiers he was visiting and consoling, he wrote: "I pet them, some of them it does so much good, they are so faint and lonesome—at parting at night I sometimes kiss them right and left. The doctor tells me I supply the patients with a medicine all their drugs and bottles and powders are helpless to yield."

To his friend Abby Price, Whitman wrote: "How one gets to love them! There is little petting in the soldier's life in the field, but Abby, I know what is in their hearts. . . . What mutual attachments and how passing deep and tender these boys . . . love for them lives as long as I draw breath. . . . These soldiers know how to love, too, when they have the right person and the right love offered them. . . ."

His notes and journals reveal that he had hundreds of friends among "the roughs"—firemen, mechanics, New York bus drivers—in addition to the soldiers in Washington, but all we know about them is the kisses and hugs so often mentioned. Beyond this, we do not know what was implied when Whitman recorded in a notebook: "Friday night, October 11, 1862 . . . met a 19-year-old blacksmith David Wilson walking up Middaugh Street—slept with me. . . ." We do know that Whitman's kissses were not limited to young workers or soldiers. "He kissed me as if I were a girl," Whitman's friend John Burroughs observed.

Whitman's great postwar attachment to the young Washington streetcar conductor Peter Doyle suggests that his affairs were not physically consummated—at any rate, after he had passed his 30's. After Whitman's death, his letters to Doyle were published and Doyle was interviewed;

he confirmed the evidence of the correspondence that their devotion to each other was not sexual in the ordinary sense.

A personal friend of Whitman's, Thomas Donaldson, makes it clear (in *Walt Whitman, the Man*, Harpers, N.Y., 1896) that in his judgment Whitman put into his poems "the passionate love of comrades . . . not out of his experience but out of his loneliness."

In all the vast correspondence and notebooks that have survived, the only evidence of consummated homosexuality is in his poems. And yet, in referring to them, Whitman once wrote: "Doubtless I could not have perceived the universe or written one of the poems, if I had not freely given myself to comrades and to love."

In 1890, when Whitman was 71, John Addington Symonds, the English critic who wrote one of the first (and best) books on Whitman, wrote him that his poem *Calamus*, with its emphasis on love between men, suggested that Whitman was, like himself, "an unrepresentative" man. Whitman responded: "About the questions on *Calamus*, etc., they quite daze me. Love is only rightly to be construed by and within its own atmosphere and essential character. . . . That the *Calamus* part has ever allowed the possibility of such construction as mentioned is terrible. I am fain to hope that the pages themselves are not to be even mentioned for such gratuitous and quite at the time undreamed and unwished possibility of morbid inference—which are disavowed by me and seem damnable.

. . . My life, young manhood, mid-age, times South & c., have been jolly, bodily, and doubtless open to criticism. Though unmarried I have had six children—two are dead, one living Southern grandchild, fine boy, writes to me occasionally—circumstances (connected with their fortune and benefit) have separated me from intimate relations."

Scholars have agreed that these were dream children, like the others to whom he referred in a letter to his friend and disciple, Dr. Bucke, a year before his death: "I have two deceased children (young man & woman: illegitimate, of course) that I much desired to bury here with me—but have ab't abandoned the plan on account of angry litigation and fuss generally, and disinterment from down South."

In his letters, Whitman didn't hesitate late in his life to refer to youthful love affairs that all scholars agree were nonexistent. He did not, however, mention to his literary correspondents nor to anyone else the "Frenchy" we shall meet later, nor the mysterious "164," with whom, as we shall see, he seems to have had a desperate affair in Washington, 1868–70 (when Whitman was 50 and past his prime as poet).

Was there a woman in his life? The concordance to his poems shows that "woman" and "women" are among the words he used most frequently, but in his 73 years, there is no record of any stable love affair with any one man or woman.

His first poems were beginning to take shape when Whitman wrote an editorial (1853) about prostitution in which he said: "The plain truth is that nineteen out of twenty of the mass of American young men who live in or visit the great cities are more or less familiar with houses of prostitution and are customers to them. . . . Especially of the best classes of men under forty years of age, living in New York and Brooklyn, the mechanics, apprentices, sea-faring men, drivers of horses, butchers, machinists . . . the custom is to go among prostitutes as an ordinary thing. Nothing is thought of it—or rather the wonder is, how there can be any 'fun' without it?" The young workers Whitman mentioned are the kind who were his friends, and he seems to have written from personal experience.

"Singing what, to the Soul, entirely redeemed her," he wrote later in a poem, "the faithful one, the prostitute, who detained me when I went to the city. . . ."

In one of his notebooks (1862) Whitman identifies a friend, Frank Sweeny, as "the one I told the whole story to about Ellen Eyre." What was the story? After Whitman's death a letter came to light written to him by this lady. No one knows who she was, although there is some indication that "Ellen Eyre" was a young actress using an assumed name. Her letter reveals a passing affair with Whitman.

Tuesday, March 25, 1862

My Dear Mr. Whitman:

I fear you took me last night for a female privateer. It is time I was sailing under my true colors—but then today I assume you cared nothing piratical though I would joyfully have made your heart a captive. Women have an unequal chance in the world. Men are its monarchs, and "full many a rose is born to blush unseen and waste its sweetness on the desert air." Such I was resolved would not be the fate of the fancy I had long nourished for you. A gold mine may be found by the divining rod, but there is no such instrument for detecting in the crowded streets of a great city the unknown mine of latent affection a man may have unconsciously inspired in a woman's breast. I make these explanations in extenuation not by way of apology. My social position enjoins precaution and mystery and perhaps the enjoyment of my friends (friend's?) society is heightened while yielding to its fascination. I preserve my incognito, yet mystery lends an effable charm to love and when a woman is bent upon the gratification of her inclination she is pardonable if she still spreads the veil of decorum over her actions.

Hypocrisy is said to be the homage that sin pays to virtue, and yet I can see no vice in that generous sympathy in which we share our caprices with those who inspired us with tenderness. I trust you will think well enough of me soon to renew the pleasure you afforded me last p.m. and I therefore write to remind you that this is a sensible head as well as a sympathetic heart, both of which would gladly evolve with warmth for your diversion and comfort. You have already my whereabouts and hours. It shall only depend on you to make them yours and me the happiest of women.

I am always your sincerely,
Ellen Eyre

There is another mysterious unknown who makes a shadowy appearance in Whitman's life as "Frenchy." I came across a reference to her in a letter I found in the vast manuscript collection of Charles Feinberg, in Detroit, while I was engaged in research for *Walt Whitman's Civil War*. The letter is from Will H. Wallace, a surgeon Whitman probably knew from his earlier bohemian days in New York and apparently met again in the Washington hospitals. Wallace left Washington to work in General Hospital No. 3, in Nashville. From there he wrote Whitman, April 3, 1863: "I have five young ladies who act in the capacity of nurses—i.e., *one of them* is French, young and beautiful to set your eyes upon. Can you not visit us and note for yourself?"

Whitman's reply has not been found, but the following month Wallace wrote him again: "I am surprised at your frenchy leaving you in such a deplorable state, but you are not alone. I had to dismiss mine, to save the reputation of the hospital and your humble servant. . . ."

Was there a "Frenchy" or "Frenchies?" In his closing

years Whitman claimed in conversation with his young friend Traubel, who was recording every word: "I used to get love letters galore, those days, perfumed letters—from girls down there," and he showed Traubel a trifling gift that was made for him, he said, "by a clerk in Washington, a girl who was sweet on me."

Although Whitman's sexual affairs with women were not enduring, they were expressed on an emotional level that has made his poem "To a Common Prostitute" last over a hundred years:

> Be composed—be at ease with me—I am Walt Whit-
> man, liberal and lusty as Nature,
> Not till the sun excludes you do I exclude you . . .

A letter only recently discovered shows that Nelly O'Connor, wife of his closest friend, was deeply in love with him, not only as a poet, but as a man. Her husband, a writer and ardent abolitionist, wrote the pamphlet "The Good Gray Poet," defending Whitman's moral character from charges of "obscenity."

During his long stay in Washington, the O'Connor house was a second home to Whitman. It has long been thought that Mrs. O'Connor's emotion for him was no deeper than the love others in the Whitman circle felt for him. But it now appears that over the years Nelly O'Connor had fallen deeply in love with Whitman. In 1870, while on a visit to Providence, Nelly, in her 30's, wrote Whitman, then in his 50's:

> . . . It is good to feel so assured of one's love as not to need to express it, & it is very good to know that one's love is never doubted or questioned, & for these reasons it is I am sure that we do not write to each other. I al-

ways know that you know that I love you all the time, even though we should never meet again, my feeling could never change, and I am *sure* that you know it as well as I do.

I do flatter myself too, that *you* care for *me,*—not as I love you, because you are great and strong, and more sufficient unto yourself than any woman can be,—besides you have the great outflow of your pen which saves you from the need of personal love as one feels it who has no such resource.

You could not afford to love other than as the Gods love; that is to love *everybody*, but no one enough to be made unhappy, as to lose your balance . . .

It is only when I am away from you that I am conscious of how deeply you have influenced my life, my thoughts, my feelings, my views—*myself* in fact, in every way, you seem to have permeated my whole being. . . .

More than all your poems, more than all you ever can write, *you* are to me; yet they were very much to me before I knew you. It is good to have my love for them rounded by knowing you, and finding my feeling and thought about you justified. I have sometimes suffered very deeply, but I feel that I have been dealt with very kindly by, and had more than fullest compensation in the great privilege of knowing you, and being permitted to be with you as I have.

I hope that the good angels who take care of us will for long, long yet spare us to each other. And you must be very good and come often to see us. You must not neglect the golden opportunity of letting me love you and see you all that is possible. I think that I must have been very good at some time to have deserved such a blessing. . . .

Mrs. O'Connor's letter makes it obvious her love for Whitman differed from the affection he had for her. He never responded to Nelly O'Connor's confession that he had "permeated her whole being." It now appears that O'Connor had some inkling of how his wife felt about Whitman and that this knowledge played a role in the 10-year break in their friendship that arose when they differed about the role of black people after Emancipation.

In a notebook dated 1868, we meet the unnamed him or her * whom Whitman identified only by the number "16" or "164": "Cheating, childish abandonment of myself, fancying what does not really exist in another, but is all the time in myself alone—utterly deluded & cheated by *myself* & my own weakness (REMEMBER WHERE I AM MOST WEAK & most lacking.) Yet always preserve a kind spirit & demeanour to 16. But PURSUE HER NO MORE. . . .

"June 17. *It is* IMPERATIVE, that I obviate & remove myself (& my orbit) *at all hazards* (away from) this *incessant* (enormous) & enormous PERTURBATION. . . ."

And in 1870:

"July 15. To GIVE UP ABSOLUTELY & *for good, from this* present hour (all) this FEVERISH FLUCTUATING, useless undignified pursuit of 164. . . ."

Aside from his own poems celebrating Whitman's love and respect for women, the testimony that distinguished women have contributed is eloquent. A contemporary critic (Mary A. Chiltor, of Islip, Long Island) wrote in the *Saturday Press,* June 9, 1860: "I see him now as the apostle of purity who vindicates manhood and womanhood from

---

* Scholars have pointed out that erasures by Whitman make it hard to know whether the references are to a man or woman, whether "at different times he meant both him or her" (F. De Wolfe).

the charges of infamy, degradation and vice." And in the same magazine another woman writes (June 23): "Walt ennobles everything he writes about."

Mrs. Anne Gilchrist, an English literary personality and author of several books, wrote a powerful estimate of Whitman's work—the first serious essay on him by a woman. She fell in love with the poet across the Atlantic Ocean after reading *Leaves of Grass*. Mother of two grown children and a widow, Mrs. Gilchrist took Whitman's poems as a personal message addressed to her. After an exchange of letters, in which he urged her *not* to come, she nevertheless left England for the United States, to be his "mate."

Their relationship may shed some light on Whitman's ambivalence. Mrs. Gilchrist settled in Philadelphia with her son and daughter to be near Whitman. They became close friends—who never kissed. She found that the Whitman of the love poems and the Whitman who took the ferry from his Camden home to visit her were apparently unrelated.

If this lady, whose great love for Whitman drew her across the ocean, could not in Whitman's own presence penetrate his contradictions, how can we arrive at the final word, a century later, dealing not with a flesh-and-blood man, but with scraps of paper—letters, notes, poems?

In the course of his conversations with Traubel, Whitman hinted several times that he would one day tell him his Great Secret. If this concerned his love life, there is no record of his ever having divulged it; it remains shrouded in the ambiguity we seem to find everywhere.

What emerges appears to be a man who, like many other writers, lived one life in his books and another outside them. Whitman himself once told a visitor (Edward Carpenter): "I think there are truths which it is necessary to envelop or wrap up. . . . There is something in my nature, furtive like an old hen."

We arrive at some questions rather than at final answers. From the evidence, it would appear that Whitman probably had sexual relations with women—possibly even in his 50's. The direct evidence of sexual involvement with men is confined to poems written during his 30's. Why then the general impression that Whitman was exclusively homosexual?

The reasons may be summarized: (1) He did love hundreds of young men; he had particular attachments to several of them. This violates the normal cultural pattern, which concentrates on sex acts between men and women.

(2) Whitman never married.* He had no enduring relationship with anyone. The references to affairs with two or three unnamed women that I have unearthed from obscure sources are known only to a few Whitmaniacs. They are brought together here for the first time.

In notes for an undelivered lecture that were found after his death, he declared:

> I desire to say to you, and let you ponder well upon it, the fact that under present arrangement, the love and comradeship of a woman, of his wife, however welcome, however complete, does not and cannot satisfy the grandest requirements of a manly soul for love and comradeship,—The man he loves, he often loves with more passionate attachment than he ever bestows on any woman, even his wife.—Is it that the growth of love needs the free air—the seasons, perhaps more wildness more rudeness? Why is the love of women so invalid, so transient?

(3) Ever since his first book was published over a century ago and up to our own day, Whitman has been

---

* Late in her life Mrs. O'Connor remembered that in his Washington days, "Whitman upheld the modern theory of marriage being the true and ideal relation between the sexes."

attacked by some for writing immorally about sex—particularly about love between men. That has spread his reputation—as regards his sexuality—far beyond the circle of his readers. His contemporary, Whittier, is supposed to have thrown *Leaves* into the fire; only recently there was considerable protest when the new Camden-Philadelphia bridge was named in honor of the poet who used to cross the Delaware by ferry.

(4) The kind of young men to whom he was drawn were not his intellectual peers, but of "the roughs." This falls into a pattern with which we are familiar from the lives of other intellectuals who had homosexual experiences (Hart Crane is a recent example).

(5) Whitman's reputation for homosexuality lies in his poems. In them he not only described intimate physical contacts, but he announced himself a prophet of a new religion of love between men. This was to be the basis for fulfilling American democratic ideals: ". . . ideals of manly love . . . I will lift what has too long kept down these smoldering fires/I will give them complete abandonment/I will write the evangel-poem of comrades and of love."

The central question remains: How does the evidence of love in his poems relate to his personal experiences?

It is, I believe, unrealistic to try to find precise factual documentation about Whitman's love life in his poems, just as it would be to try to identify from them the particular workers in whose "labor of engines . . . and fields" he found "the eternal meanings."

Whitman's use of sexual love and imagery was deliberate and programmatic, rather than confessional and autobiographic. That, of course, is why he refused to censor it, even on his deathbed. It stood for a central theme in his work that he would not and could not allow to be eliminated; it was part of a prophetic program and a vision of a world-to-be dominated by love, freedom, equality—not only politically but sexually, and not only between but among the sexes.

The essential question is not what Whitman did in his private life. The only reason that it is of interest is because of what he did in his poems. There he elevated not only men but women, too, to a higher level than they had enjoyed in literature before. Whatever his experiences were, he turned them (at his best) into great verbal celebrations of human beings as individuals and *en masse*.

And yet, with all his love of many men and some women, none of them could satisfy his vast desire. There is one confession about this that I believe to be absolutely accurate. It is the passage in which he tells us that his big seminal affair was the universe: "The known universe has one complete lover, and that is the greatest poet. . . . He consumes an eternal passion. . . . He is no irresolute or suspicious lover—he is sure—he scorns intervals. . . . The sea is not surer of the shore, or the shore of the sea, than he is of the fruition of his love. . . ."

"Come closer to me," Whitman told his readers in a passage he deleted from "Song of Occupations": "Push close my lovers and take the best I possess,/Yield closer and closer and give me the best you possess."

This approach to you, the unknown reader, as well as to people he actually knew, was not a literary pose. It was the way he was alive to himself and came alive to others.

Whitman exuded a personal magnetism that evoked deep responses in many different kinds of people. He wanted to be a person, to be loved for himself, and not only as a poet. The familiar white-bearded face tells us nothing of the many and conflicting simultaneous lives he lived—wanting so much to be alive in every blade of grass and in every human relationship. He had tried many ways—journalist, lover, politician—finally he was driven to poems, "to make the works," as he jotted in an early notebook.

He wanted the personality he dramatized in *Leaves* to be all-inclusive, from suicides and prostitutes to lovers and heroes like John Brown. It is customary to stress his optimism and confidence; he was also the poet of death and despair and "down-hearted doubters, dull and excluded . . . I take my place among you as much as among any. . . ." He sublimated verbally his most profound emotional experiences. Sensitive to the nation's imperfections, injustices, corruptions, he was sustained by his faith in the development of "great individuals" as well as the "divine average."

He wanted to be honest about his experience; he tried to develop a unique technique for revealing himself, but if we grasp only his verbal magic apart from his complete personality, we miss an insight into the "you" he aimed to reach: "Whoever you are, now I place my hand upon you, that you be my poem. . . ."

What we get from Whitman is not like looking through a magnifying lens at an enlarged figure of a man. It is rather a human being seen through a prism that breaks up his image into many colors and shapes. "Amid all the blab whose echoes recoil upon me I have not once had the least idea who or what I am./But before all my arrogant poems the real Me still stands yet untouched, untold, altogether unreached. . . ."

"Poets to come," Whitman wrote in 1860, "not today is to justify me and answer what I am for,/But you. . . ." Today an anthology could be made of young poets whose work Whitman has inspired: "We look at him after a hundred years of turning away," Robert Mezey wrote recently. "The poets he called to follow are alive and following. He has sons at last."

Poems often seem to be crowded out of the reading market by stories, philosophy, history, politics, science fiction, criticism, and other prose. There is one niche they still try to occupy—the secrets. Whitman opened up some of them, not just the old-time secrets—love, life, liberty, and the pursuit of peace—but the peculiar secret of being alive in his own generation. That is one of the things that keeps Whitman's poems alive, for the sacredness of being alive in our own time is what contemporary poems are all about: "The direct trial of him who would be the greatest poet is today."

Whitman's poems serve as a bridge to get you across nowhere. They bring into the collapsing fragments of a universe that each one of us sees only in his own broken bits the totality which all humanity taken together completes. That, I believe, is the Whitman vision. The way we grasp it is not through some miraculous osmosis, but through the way he put together common words, those little nuggets of reality. Yesterday's rhymes would not do for Whitman because he was rejecting yesterday's commonplaces.

The "I" in Whitman is not just the unique personality of the author. The "I" is identified with all human beings. Whitman's greatest poems are never completely fulfilled. They are always aspiring to be completed in the reader. The drive of the poems is toward a humanity where each will be completely alive to every experience we witness or observe. This is the essence of Whitman's many loves, each of us alive in everyone else. Thus, his belief in immortality, his references to "delicious death," and the continual emphasis "that all men ever born are also my brothers . . . and the women my sisters and lovers. . . ." People themselves, individually and *en masse*, are to be the living poems. The poet's role is to indicate that and then "wheel and hurry back into darkness."

THE
POEMS

RECORDERS AGES HENCE

Recorders ages hence,
Come, I will take you down underneath this impassive ex-
      terior, I will tell you what to say of me,
Publish my name and hang up my picture as that of the
      tenderest lover,
The friend the lover's portrait, of whom his friend his
      lover was fondest,
Who was not proud of his songs, but of the measureless
      ocean of love within him, and freely poured it
      forth,
Who often walked lonesome walks thinking of his dear
      friends, his lovers,
Who pensive away from one he loved often lay sleepless
      and dissatisfied at night,
Who knew too well the sick, sick dread lest the one he
      loved might secretly be indifferent to him,
Whose happiest days were far away through fields, in
      woods, on hills, he and another, wandering
      hand in hand, they twain apart from other men,
Who oft as he sauntered the streets curved with his arm
      the shoulder of his friend, while the arm of his
      friend rested upon him also.

Male and Female!

I pass so poorly with paper and types, I must pass with
      the contact of bodies and souls. . . .
O you robust, sacred!
I cannot tell you how I love you;
All I love America for, is contained in men and women
      like you.
When the psalm sings instead of the singer,
When the script preaches instead of the preacher,
When the pulpit descends and goes instead of the carver
      that carved the supporting-desk,
When I can touch the body of books, by night or by day,
      and when they touch my body back again,

When the holy vessels, or the bits of the eucharist, or the
 lath and plast, procreate as effectually as the
 young silver-smiths or bakers, or the masons in
 their over-alls,
When a university course convinces like a slumbering
 woman and child convince,
When the minted gold in the vault smiles like the night-
 watchman's daughter,
When warrantee deeds loafe in chairs opposite, and are
 my friendly companions,
I intend to reach them my hand, and make as much of
 them as I do of men and women like you.

from SONG OF OCCUPATIONS

I will sing the song of companionship,
I will show what alone must finally compact these,
I believe these are to found their own ideal of manly love,
　　　　indicating it in me,
I will therefore let flame from me the burning fires that
　　　　were threatening to consume me,
I will lift what has too long kept down those smouldering
　　　　fires,
I will give them complete abandonment,
I will write the evangel-poem of comrades and of love,
For who but I should understand love with all its sorrow
　　　　and joy?
And who but I should be the poet of comrades? . . .

What do you seek so pensive and silent?
What do you need camerado?
Dear son do you think it is love?

Listen dear son—listen America, daughter or son,
It is a painful thing to love a man or woman to excess,
　　　　and yet it satisfies, it is great,
But there is something else very great, it makes the whole
　　　　coincide,
It, magnificent, beyond materials, with continuous hands
　　　　sweeps and provides for all.

from STARTING FROM PAUMANOK

Camerado, I give you my hand!
I give you my love more precious than money,
I give you myself before preaching or law;
Will you give me yourself? will you come travel with me?
Shall we stick by each other as long as we live?

from S O N G   O F   T H E   O P E N   R O A D

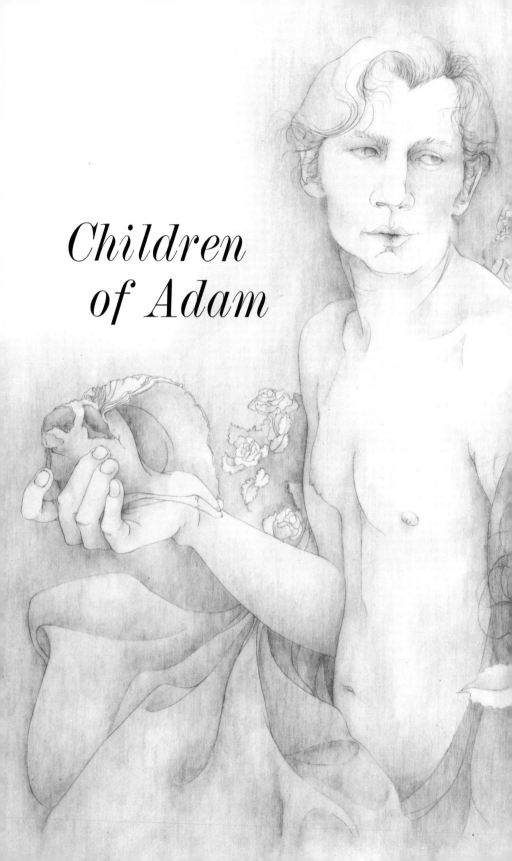

*Children
of Adam*

TO THE GARDEN THE WORLD

To the garden the world anew ascending,
Potent mates, daughters, sons, preluding,
The love, the life of their bodies, meaning and being,
Curious here behold my resurrection after slumber,
The revolving cycles in their wide sweep having brought
        me again,
Amorous, mature, all beautiful to me, all wondrous,
My limbs and the quivering fire that ever plays through
        them, for reasons, most wondrous,
Existing I peer and penetrate still,
Content with the present, content with the past,
By my side or back of me Eve following,
Or in front, and I following her just the same.

From pent-up aching rivers,
From that of myself without which I were nothing,
From what I am determined to make illustrious, even if I
      stand sole among men,
From my own voice resonant, singing the phallus,
Singing the song of procreation,
Singing the need of superb children and therein superb
      grown people,
Singing the muscular urge and the blending,
Singing the bedfellow's song, (O resistless yearning!
O for any and each the body correlative attracting!
O for you whoever you are your correlative body! O it,
      more than all else, you delighting!)
From the hungry gnaw that eats me night and day,
From native moments, from bashful pains, singing them.
Seeking something yet unfound though I have diligently
      sought it many a long year,
Singing the true song of the soul fitful at random,
Singing what to the Soul, entirely redeemed her, the faith-
      ful one, the prostitute, who detained me when
      I went to the city;
Singing the song of prostitutes;
Renascent with grossest Nature or among animals,
Of that, of them and what goes with them my poems in-
      forming,
Of the smell of apples and lemons, of the pairing of birds,
Of the wet of woods, of the lapping of waves,
Of the mad pushes of waves upon the land, I them chant-
      ing,
The overture lightly sounding, the strain anticipating,
The welcome nearness, the sight of the perfect body,

The swimmer swimming naked in the bath, or motionless
on his back lying and floating,
The female form approaching, I pensive, love-flesh tremu-
lous aching,
The divine list for myself or you or for any one making,
The face, the limbs, the index from head to foot, and
what it arouses,
The mystic deliria, the madness amorous, the utter aban-
donment,
(Hark close and still what I now whisper to you,
I love you, O you entirely possess me,
O that you and I escape from the rest and go utterly off,
free and lawless,
Two hawks in the air, two fishes swimming in the sea not
more lawless than we;)
The furious storm through me careering, I passionately
trembling,
The oath of the inseparableness of two together, of the
woman that loves me and whom I love more
than my life, that oath swearing,
(O I willingly stake all for you,
O let me be lost if it must be so!
O you and I! what is it to us what the rest do or think?
What is all else to us? only that we enjoy each other and
exhaust each other if it must be so;)
From the master, the pilot I yield the vessel to,
The general commanding me, commanding all, from him
permission taking,
From time the programme hastening, (I have loitered too
long as it is,)
From sex, from the warp and from the woof,
(To talk to the perfect girl who understands me—the girl
of The States,

To waft her to these from my own lips—to effuse them
        from my own body;)
From privacy, from frequent repinings alone,
From plenty of persons near and yet the right person not
        near,
From the soft sliding of hands over me and thrusting of
        fingers through my hair and beard,
From the long sustained kiss upon the mouth or bosom,
From the close pressure that makes me or any man drunk,
        fainting with excess,
From what the divine husband knows, from the work of
        fatherhood,
From exultation, victory and relief from the bedfellow's
        embrace in the night,
From the act-poems of eyes, hands, hips and bosoms,
From the cling of the trembling arm,
From the bending curve and the clinch,
From side by side the pliant coverlet off-throwing,
From the one so unwilling to have me leave, and me just
        as unwilling to leave,
(Yet a moment O tender waiter, and I return,)
From the hour of shining stars and dropping dews,
From the night a moment I emerging flitting out,
Celebrate you act divine and you children prepared for,
And you stalwart loins.

I SING THE BODY ELECTRIC

1

I sing the body electric,
The armies of those I love engirth me and I engirth them,
They will not let me off till I go with them, respond to
      them,
And discorrupt them, and charge them full with the charge
      of the soul.
Was it doubted that those who corrupt their own bodies
      conceal themselves?
And if those who defile the living are as bad as they who
      defile the dead?
And if the body does not do fully as much as the soul?
And if the body were not the soul, what is the soul?

2

The love of the body of man or woman balks account, the
      body itself balks account,
That of the male is perfect, and that of the female is
      perfect.

The expression of the face balks account,
But the expression of a well-made man appears not only in
      his face,
It is in his limbs and joints also, it is curiously in the joints
      of his hips and wrists,
It is in his walk, the carriage of his neck, the flex of his
      waist and knees, dress does not hide him,
The strong sweet quality he has strikes through the cotton
      and broadcloth,
To see him pass conveys as much as the best poem, per-
      haps more,

You linger to see his back, and the back of his neck and
  shoulder-side.

The sprawl and fulness of babes, the bosoms and heads of
  women, the folds of their dress, their style as
  we pass in the street, the contour of their shape
  downwards,
The swimmer naked in the swimming-bath, seen as he
  swims through the transparent green-shine, or
  lies with his face up and rolls silently to and
  fro in the heave of the water,
The bending forward and backward of rowers in row-
  boats, the horseman in his saddle,
Girls, mothers, house-keepers, in all their performances,
The group of laborers seated at noon-time with their open
  dinner kettles, and their wives waiting,
The female soothing a child, the farmer's daughter in the
  garden or cow-yard,
The young fellow hoeing corn, the sleigh-driver driving
  his six horses through the crowd,
The wrestle of wrestlers, two apprentice-boys, quite grown,
  lusty, good-natured, native-born, out on the
  vacant lot at sundown after work,
The coats and caps thrown down, the embrace of love and
  resistance,
The upper-hold and under-hold, the hair rumpled over
  and blinding the eyes;
The march of firemen in their own costumes, the play of
  masculine muscle through clean-setting trow-
  sers and waist-straps,
The slow return from the fire, the pause when the bell
  strikes suddenly again, and the listening on the
  alert,
The natural, perfect, varied attitudes, the bent head, the
  curved neck and the counting;

Such-like I love—I loosen myself, pass freely, am at the
mother's breast with the little child,
Swim with the swimmers, wrestle with wrestlers, march in
line with the firemen, and pause, listen,
count. . . .

5

This is the female form,
A divine nimbus exhales from it from head to foot,
It attracts with fierce undeniable attraction,
I am drawn by its breath as if I were no more than a help-
less vapor, all falls aside but myself and it,
Books, art, religion, time, the visible and solid earth, and
what was expected of heaven or feared of hell,
are now consumed,
Mad filaments, ungovernable shoots play out of it, the
response likewise ungovernable,
Hair, bosom, hips, bend of legs, negligent falling hands all
diffused, mine too diffused,
Ebb stung by the flow and flow stung by the ebb, love-flesh
swelling and deliciously aching,
Limitless limpid jets of love hot and enormous, quivering
jelly of love, white-blow and delirious juice,
Bridegroom night of love working surely and softly into
the prostrate dawn,
Undulating into the willing and yielding day,
Lost in the cleave of the clasping and sweet-fleshed day.

This the nucleus—after the child is born of woman, man
is born of woman,
This the bath of birth, this the merge of small and large,
and the outlet again.

Be not ashamed women, your privilege encloses the rest,
and is the exit of the rest,
You are the gates of the body, and you are the gates of the
soul.

The female contains all qualities and tempers them,
She is in her place and moves with perfect balance,
She is all things duly veiled, she is both passive and active,
She is to conceive daughters as well as sons, and sons as
well as daughters.

As I see my soul reflected in Nature,
As I see through a mist, One with inexpressible complete-
ness, sanity, beauty,
See the bent head and arms folded over the breast, the
Female I see.

6

The male is not less the soul nor more, he too is in his
place,
He too is all qualities, he is action and power,
The flush of the known universe is in him,
Scorn becomes him well, and appetite and defiance become him well,
The wildest largest passions, bliss that is utmost, sorrow
that is utmost become him well, pride is for
him,
The full-spread pride of man is calming and excellent to
the soul,
Knowledge becomes him, he likes it always, he brings
every thing to the test of himself,

Whatever the survey, whatever the sea and the sail he
strikes soundings at last only here,
(Where else does he strike soundings except here?)

The man's body is sacred and the woman's body is sacred,
No matter who it is, it is sacred—is it the meanest one in
the laborers' gang?
Is it one of the dull-faced immigrants just landed on the
wharf?
Each belongs here or anywhere just as much as the well-off,
just as much as you,
Each has his or her place in the procession.

(All is a procession,
The universe is a procession with measured and perfect
motion.)

Do you know so much yourself that you call the slave or
dull-faced ignorant?
Do you suppose you have a right to a good sight, and he or
she has no right to a sight?
Do you think matter has cohered together from its diffuse
float, and the soil is on the surface, and water
runs and vegetation sprouts,
For you only, and not for him and her?

7

A man's body at auction,
I help the auctioneer, the sloven does not half know his
business.

Gentlemen look on this wonder,
Whatever the bids of the bidders they cannot be high
enough for it,

For him the globe lay preparing quintillions of years without one animal or plant,
For him the revolving cycles truly and steadily rolled.

In this head the all-baffling brain,
In it and below it the makings of heroes.

Examine these limbs, red, black, or white, they are cun-
           ning in tendon and nerve,
They shall be stripped that you may see them.
Exquisite senses, life-lit eyes, pluck, volition,
Flakes of breast-muscle, pliant backbone and neck, flesh
           not flabby, good-sized arms and legs,
And wonders within there yet.

Within there runs blood,
The same old blood! the same red-running blood!
There swells and jets a heart, there all passions, desires,
           reachings, aspirations,
(Do you think they are not there because they are not
           expressed in parlors and lecture-rooms?)

This is not only one man, this the father of those who
           shall be fathers in their turns,
In him the start of populous states and rich republics,
Of him countless immortal lives with countless embodi-
           ments and enjoyments.

How do you know who shall come from the offspring of
           his offspring through the centuries?
(Who might you find you have come from yourself, if you
           could trace back through the centuries?)

8

A woman's body at auction,
She too is not only herself, she is the teeming mother of
           mothers,

She is the bearer of them that shall grow and be mates to
the mothers.

Have you ever loved the body of a woman?
Have you ever loved the body of a man?

Do you not see that these are exactly the same to all in all
nations and times all over the earth?
If anything is sacred the human body is sacred,
And the glory and sweet of a man is the token of manhood
untainted,
And in man or woman a clean, strong, firm-fibred body, is
more beautiful than the most beautiful face.

Have you seen the fool that corrupted his own live body?
or the fool that corrupted her own live body?
For they do not conceal themselves, and cannot conceal
themselves.

9

O my body! I dare not desert the likes of you in other men
and women, nor the likes of the parts of you,
I believe the likes of you are to stand or fall with the likes
of the soul, (and that they are the soul,)
I believe the likes of you shall stand or fall with my poems,
and that they are my poems,
Man's, woman's, child's, youth's, wife's, husband's, mother's, father's, young man's, young woman's
poems,
Head, neck, hair, ears, drop and tympan of the ears,
Eyes, eye-fringes, iris of the eye, eyebrows, and the waking
or sleeping of the lids,
Mouth, tongue, lips, teeth, roof of the mouth, jaws, and
the jaw-hinges,

Nose, nostrils of the nose, and the partition,
Cheeks, temples, forehead, chin, throat, back of the neck,
neck-slue,
Strong shoulders, manly beard, scapula, hind-shoulders,
and the ample side-round of the chest,
Upper-arm, armpit, elbow-socket, lower-arm, arm-sinews,
arm-bones,
Wrist and wrist-joints, hand, palm, knuckles, thumb, fore-
finger, finger-joints, finger-nails,
Broad breast-front, curling hair of the breast, breast-bone,
breast-side,
Ribs, belly, backbone, joints of the backbone,
Hips, hip-sockets, hip-strength, inward and outward round,
man-balls, man-root,
Strong set of thighs, well carrying the trunk above,
Leg-fibres, knee, knee-pan, upper-leg, under-leg,
Ankles, instep, foot-ball, toes, toe-joints, the heel;
All attitudes, all the shapeliness, all the belongings of my
or your body or of any one's body, male or
female,
The lung-sponges, the stomach-sac, the bowels sweet and
clean,
The brain in its folds inside the skull-frame,
Sympathies, heart-valves, palate-valves, sexuality, ma-
ternity,
Womanhood and all that is a woman, and the man that
comes from woman,
The womb, the teats, nipples, breast-milk, tears, laughter,
weeping, love-looks, love-perturbations and
risings,
The voice, articulation, language, whispering, shouting
aloud,
Food, drink, pulse, digestion, sweat, sleep, walking, swimming,

Poise on the hips, leaping, reclining, embracing, arm-
        curving and tightening,
The continual changes of the flex of the mouth, and
        around the eyes,
The skin, the sunburned shade, freckles, hair,
The curious sympathy one feels when feeling with the
        hand the naked meat of the body,
The circling rivers the breath, and breathing it in and out,
The beauty of the waist, and thence of the hips, and
        thence downward toward the knees,
The thin red jellies within you or within me, the bones
        and the marrow in the bones,
The exquisite realization of health;
O I say these are not the parts and poems of the body only,
        but of the soul,
O I say now these are the soul!

A woman waits for me, she contains all, nothing is lacking,
Yet all were lacking if sex were lacking, or if the moisture
    of the right man were lacking.

Sex contains all, bodies, souls,
Meanings, proofs, purities, delicacies, results, promulga-
    tions,
Songs, commands, health, pride, the maternal mystery, the
    seminal milk,
All hopes, benefactions, bestowals, all the passions, loves,
    beauties, delights of the earth,
All the governments, judges, gods, followed persons of the
    earth,
These are contained in sex as parts of itself and justifica-
    tions of itself.

Without shame the man I like knows and avows the de-
    liciousness of his sex,
Without shame the woman I like knows and avows hers.

Now I will dismiss myself from impassive women,
I will go stay with her who waits for me, and with those
    women that are warm-blooded and sufficient
    for me,
I see that they understand me and do not deny me,
I see that they are worthy of me, I will be the robust hus-
    band of those women.

They are not one jot less than I am,
They are tanned in the face by shining suns and blowing
    winds,
Their flesh has the old divine suppleness and strength,
They know how to swim, row, ride, wrestle, shoot, run,
    strike, retreat, advance, resist, defend them-
    selves,

They are ultimate in their own right—they are calm, clear,
    well-possessed of themselves.

I draw you close to me, you women,
I cannot let you go, I would do you good,
I am for you, and you are for me, not only for our own
    sake, but for others' sakes,
Enveloped in you sleep greater heroes and bards,
They refuse to awake at the touch of any man but me.

It is I, you women, I make my way,
I am stern, acrid, large, undissuadable, but I love you,
I do not hurt you any more than is necessary for you,
I pour the stuff to start sons and daughters fit for these
    States, I press with slow rude muscle,
I brace myself effectually, I listen to no entreaties,
I dare not withdraw till I deposit what has so long accu-
    mulated within me.

Through you I drain the pent-up rivers of myself,
In you I wrap a thousand onward years,
On you I graft the grafts of the best-loved of me and
    America,
The drops I distil upon you shall grow fierce and athletic
    girls, new artists, musicians, and singers,
The babes I beget upon you are to beget babes in their
    turn,
I shall demand perfect men and women out of my love-
    spendings,
I shall expect them to interpenetrate with others, as I and
    you interpenetrate now,
I shall count on the fruits of the gushing showers of them,
    as I count on the fruits of the gushing showers
    I give now,
I shall look for loving crops from the birth, life, death,
    immortality, I plant so lovingly now.

SPONTANEOUS ME

Spontaneous me, Nature,
The loving day, the mounting sun, the friend I am happy
with,
The arm of my friend hanging idly over my shoulder,
The hillside whitened with blossoms of the mountain ash,
The same late in autumn, the hues of red, yellow, drab,
purple, and light and dark green,
The rich coverlet of the grass, animals and birds, the
private untrimmed bank, the primitive apples,
the pebble-stones,
Beautiful dripping fragments, the negligent list of one
after another as I happen to call them to me or
think of them,
The real poems, (what we call poems being merely pictures,)
The poems of the privacy of the night, and of men like me,
This poem drooping shy and unseen that I always carry,
and that all men carry,
(Know once for all, avowed on purpose, wherever are men
like me, are our lusty lurking masculine
poems.)
Love-thoughts, love-juice, love-odor, love-yielding, love-
climbers, and the climbing sap,
Arms and hands of love, lips of love, phallic thumb of
love, breasts of love, bellies pressed and glued
together with love,
Earth of chaste love, life that is only life after love,
The body of my love, the body of the woman I love, the
body of the man, the body of the earth,
Soft forenoon airs that blow from the south-west,
The hairy wild-bee that murmurs and hankers up and
down, that grips the full-grown lady-flower,

curves upon her with amorous firm legs, takes his will of her, and holds himself tremulous and tight till he is satisfied;

The wet of woods through the early hours,

Two sleepers at night lying close together as they sleep, one with an arm slanting down across and below the waist of the other,

The smell of apples, aromas from crushed sage-plant, mint, birch-bark,

The boy's longings, the glow and pressure as he confides to me what he was dreaming,

The dead leaf whirling its spiral whirl and falling still and content to the ground,

The no-formed stings that sights, people, objects, sting me with,

The hubbed sting of myself, stinging me as much as it ever can any one,

The sensitive, orbic, underlapped brothers, that only privileged feelers may be intimate where they are,

The curious roamer the hand roaming all over the body, the bashful withdrawing of flesh where the fingers soothingly pause and edge themselves,

The limpid liquid within the young man,

The vexed corrosion so pensive and so painful,

The torment, the irritable tide that will not be at rest,

The like of the same I feel, the like of the same in others,

The young man that flushes and flushes, and the young woman that flushes and flushes,

The young man that wakes deep at night, the hot hand seeking to repress what would master him,

The mystic amorous night, the strange half-welcome pangs, visions, sweats,

The pulse pounding through palms and trembling encir-
cling fingers, the young man all colored, red,
ashamed, angry;
The souse upon me of my lover the sea, as I lie willing
and naked,
The merriment of the twin babes that crawl over the grass
in the sun, the mother never turning her vigilant eyes from them,
The walnut-trunk, the walnut-husks, and the ripening or
ripened long-round walnuts,
The continence of vegetables, birds, animals,
The consequent meanness of me should I skulk or find
myself indecent, while birds and animals never
once skulk or find themselves indecent,
The great chastity of paternity to match the great chastity
of maternity,
The oath of procreation I have sworn, my Adamic and
fresh daughters,
The greed that eats me day and night with hungry gnaw,
till I saturate what shall produce boys to fill
my place when I am through,
The wholesome relief, repose, content,
And this bunch plucked at random from myself,
It has done its work—I toss it carelessly to fall where it
may.

ONE HOUR TO MADNESS AND JOY

One hour to madness and joy! O furious! O confine me
    not!
(What is this that frees me so in storms?
What do my shouts amid lightnings and raging winds
    mean?)

O to drink the mystic deliria deeper than any other man!
O savage and tender achings! (I bequeath them to you, my
    children,
I tell them to you, for reasons, O bridegroom and bride.)

O to be yielded to you whoever you are, and you to be
    yielded to me in defiance of the world!
O to return to Paradise! O bashful and feminine!
O to draw you to me, to plant on you for the first time the
    lips of a determined man.

O the puzzle, the thrice-tied knot, the deep and dark pool,
    all untied and illumined!
O to speed where there is space enough and air enough at
    last!
To be absolved from previous ties and conventions, I from
    mine and you from yours!
To find a new unthought-of nonchalance with the best of
    Nature!
To have the gag removed from one's mouth!
To have the feeling to-day or any day I am sufficient as I
    am.

O something unproved! something in a trance!
To escape utterly from others' anchors and holds!

To drive free! to love free! to dash reckless and dangerous!
To court destruction with taunts, with invitations!

To ascend, to leap to the heavens of the love indicated to
      me!
To rise thither with my inebriate soul!

To be lost if it must be so!
To feed the remainder of life with one hour of fulness and
      freedom!
With one brief hour of madness and joy.

OUT OF THE ROLLING OCEAN
THE CROWD

Out of the rolling ocean the crowd came a drop gently to
    me,
Whispering *I love you, before long I die,*
I have traveled a long way merely to look on you to touch
    you,
For I could not die till I once looked on you,
For I feared I might afterward lose you.

Now we have met, we have looked, we are safe,
Return in peace to the ocean my love,
I too am part of that ocean my love, we are not so much
    separated,
Behold the great rondure, the cohesion of all, how perfect!
But as for me, for you, the irresistible sea is to separate us,
As for an hour carrying us diverse, yet cannot carry us
    diverse forever;
Be not impatient—a little space—know you I salute the air,
    the ocean and the land,
Every day at sundown for your dear sake my love.

AGES AND AGES
RETURNING AT INTERVALS

Ages and ages returning at intervals,
Undestroyed, wandering immortal,
Lusty, phallic, with the potent original loins, perfectly
       sweet,
I, chanter of Adamic songs,
Through the new garden the West, the great cities calling,
Deliriate, thus prelude what is generated, offering these,
       offering myself,
Bathing myself, bathing my songs in Sex,
Offspring of my loins.

WE TWO, HOW LONG
WE WERE FOOLED

We two, how long we were fooled,
Now transmuted, we swiftly escape as Nature escapes,
We are Nature, long have we been absent, but now we
      return,
We become plants, trunks, foliage, roots, bark,
We are bedded in the ground, we are rocks,
We are oaks, we grow in the openings side by side,
We browse, we are two among the wild herds spontaneous
      as any,
We are two fishes swimming in the sea together,
We are what locust blossoms are, we drop scent around
      lanes mornings and evenings,
We are also the coarse smut of beasts, vegetables, minerals,
We are two predatory hawks, we soar above and look
      down,
We are two resplendent suns, we it is who balance our-
      selves orbic and stellar, we are as two comets,
We prowl fanged and four-footed in the woods, we spring
      on prey,
We are two clouds forenoons and afternoons driving over-
      head,
We are seas mingling, we are two of those cheerful waves
      rolling over each other and interwetting each
      other,
We are what the atmosphere is, transparent, receptive,
      pervious, impervious,
We are snow, rain, cold, darkness, we are each product and
      influence of the globe,
We have circled and circled till we have arrived home
      again, we too,
We have voided all but freedom and all but our own joy.

O HYMEN! O HYMENEE!

O hymen! O hymenee! why do you tantalize me thus?
O why sting me for a swift moment only?
Why can you not continue? O why do you now cease?
Is it because if you continued beyond the swift moment
        you would soon certainly kill me?

I AM HE THAT ACHES WITH LOVE

I am he that aches with amorous love;
Does the earth gravitate; does not all matter, aching,
      attract all matter?
So the body of me to all I meet or know.

NATIVE MOMENTS

Native moments—when you come upon me—ah you are
  here now,
Give me now libidinous joys only,
Give me the drench of my passions, give me life coarse and
  rank,
To-day I go consort with Nature's darlings, to-night too,
I am for those who believe in loose delights, I share the
  midnight orgies of young men,
I dance with the dancers and drink with the drinkers,
The echoes ring with our indecent calls, I take for my
  love some prostitute—I pick out some low per-
  son for my dearest friend,
He shall be lawless, rude, illiterate, he shall be one con-
  demned by others for deeds done,
I will play a part no longer, why should I exile myself
  from my companions?
O you shunned persons, I at least do not shun you,
I come forthwith in your midst, I will be your poet,
I will be more to you than to any of the rest.

ONCE I PASSED THROUGH
A POPULOUS CITY

Once I passed through a populous city imprinting my
      brain for future use with its shows, architec-
      ture, customs, traditions,
Yet now of all that city I remember only a woman I cas-
      ually met there who detained me for love of me,
Day by day and night by night we were together—all else
      has long been forgotten by me,
I remember I say only that woman who passionately clung
      to me,
Again we wander, we love, we separate again,
Again she holds me by the hand, I must not go,
I see her close beside me with silent lips sad and tremulous.

I HEARD YOU SOLEMN-SWEET PIPES OF THE ORGAN

I heard you solemn-sweet pipes of the organ as last Sunday
    morn I passed the church,
Winds of autumn, as I walked the woods at dusk I heard
    your long-stretched sighs up above so mourn-
    ful,
I heard the perfect Italian tenor singing at the opera, I
    heard the soprano in the midst of the quartet
    singing;
Heart of my love! you too I heard murmuring low through
    one of the wrists around my head,
Heard the pulse of you when all was still ringing little
    bells last night under my ear.

AS ADAM EARLY IN THE MORNING

As Adam early in the morning,
Walking forth from the bower refreshed with sleep,
Behold me where I pass, hear my voice, approach,
Touch me, touch the palm of your hand to my body as I
       pass,
Be not afraid of my body.

Calamus

IN PATHS UNTRODDEN

In paths untrodden,
In the growth by margins of pond-waters,
Escaped from the life that exhibits itself,
From all the standards hitherto published, from the
    pleasures, profits, conformities,
Which too long I was offering to feed my soul,
Clear to me now standards not yet published, clear to me
    that my soul,
That the soul of the man I speak for rejoices in comrades,
Here by myself away from the clank of the world,
Tallying and talked to here by tongues aromatic,
No longer abashed, (for in this secluded spot I can re-
    spond as I would not dare elsewhere,)
Strong upon me the life that does not exhibit itself, yet
    contains all the rest,
Resolved to sing no songs to-day but those of manly attach-
    ment,
Projecting them along that substantial life,
Bequeathing hence types of athletic love,
Afternoon this delicious Ninth-month in my forty-first
    year,
I proceed for all who are or have been young men,
To tell the secret of my nights and days,
To celebrate the needs of comrades.

Scented herbage of my breast,

Leaves from you I glean, I write, to be perused best afterwards,

Tomb-leaves, body-leaves growing up above me above
death,

Perennial roots, tall leaves, O the winter shall not freeze
you delicate leaves,

Every year shall you bloom again, out from where you
retired you shall emerge again;

O I do not know whether many passing by will discover
you or inhale your faint odor, but I believe a
few will;

O slender leaves! O blossoms of my blood! I permit you
to tell in your own way of the heart that is
under you,

O burning and throbbing—surely all will one day be accomplished;

O I do not know what you mean there underneath yourselves, you are not happiness,

You are often more bitter than I can bear, you burn and
sting me,

Yet you are beautiful to me you faint-tinged roots, you
make me think of death,

Death is beautiful from you, (what indeed is finally beautiful except death and love?)

O I think it is not for life I am chanting here my chant of
lovers, I think it must be for death,

For how calm, how solemn it grows to ascend to the atmosphere of lovers,

Death or life I am then indifferent, my soul declines to
prefer,

(I am not sure but the high soul of lovers welcomes death
		most,)
Indeed O death, I think now these leaves mean precisely
		the same as you mean,
Grow up taller sweet leaves that I may see! grow up out of
		my breast!
Spring away from the concealed heart there!
Do not fold yourself so in your pink-tinged roots timid
		leaves!
Do not remain down there so ashamed, herbage of my
		breast!
Come I am determined to unbare this broad breast of
		mine, I have long enough stifled and choked;
Emblematic and capricious blades I leave you, now you
		serve me not,
I will say what I have to say by itself,
I will escape from the sham that was proposed to me,
I will sound myself and comrades only, I will never again
		utter a call only their call,
I will raise with it immortal reverberations through the
		States,
I will give an example to lovers to take permanent shape
		and will through the States,
Through me shall the words be said to make death exhil-
		arating.
Give me your tone therefore O death, that I may accord
		with it,
Give me yourself, for I see that you belong to me now
		above all, and are folded inseparably together,
		you love and death are,
Nor will I allow you to balk me any more with what I was
		calling life,

For now it is conveyed to me that you are the purports
essential,
That you hide in these shifting forms of life, for reasons,
and that they are mainly for you,
That you beyond them come forth to remain, the real
reality,
That behind the mask of materials you patiently wait, no
matter how long,
That you will one day perhaps take control of all,
That you will perhaps dissipate this entire show of appear-
ance,
That may-be you are what it is all for, but it does not last
so very long,
But you will last very long.

WHOEVER YOU ARE HOLDING ME
NOW IN HAND

Whoever you are holding me now in hand,
Without one thing all will be useless,
I give you fair warning before you attempt me further,
I am not what you supposed, but far different.

Who is he that would become my follower?
Who would sign himself a candidate for my affections?

The way is suspicious, the result uncertain, perhaps de-
        structive,
You would have to give up all else, I alone would expect
        to be your sole and exclusive standard,
Your novitiate would even then be long and exhausting,
The whole past theory of your life and all conformity to
        the lives around you would have to be aban-
        doned,
Therefore release me now before troubling yourself any
        further, let go your hand from my shoulders,
Put me down and depart on your way. . . .

Or else, only by stealth, in some wood, for trial,
Or back of a rock, in the open air,
(For in any roofed room of a house I emerge not—nor in
        company,
And in libraries I lie as one dumb, a gawk, or unborn, or
        dead,)
But just possibly with you on a high hill—first watching
        lest any person, for miles around, approach
        unawares,
Or possibly with you sailing at sea, or on the beach of the
        sea, or some quiet island,
Here to put your lips upon mine I permit you.

With the comrade's long-dwelling kiss, or the new husband's kiss,
For I am the new husband, and I am the comrade.

Or, if you will, thrusting me beneath your clothing,
Where I may feel the throbs of your heart, or rest upon
your hip,
Carry me when you go forth over land or sea;
For thus, merely touching you, is enough—is best,
And thus, touching you, would I silently sleep and be
carried eternally.

But these leaves conning, you con at peril,
For these leaves, and me, you will not understand,
They will elude you at first, and still more afterward—I
will certainly elude you,
Even while you should think you had unquestionably
caught me, behold!
Already you see I have escaped from you.

For it is not what I have put into it that I have written
this book,
Nor is it by reading it you will acquire it,
Nor do those know me best who admire me and vaunt-
ingly praise me,
Nor will the candidates for my love (unless at most a very
few) prove victorious,
Nor will my poems do good only, they will do just as much
evil, perhaps more,
For all is useless without that which you may guess at many
times and not hit, that which I hinted at;
Therefore release me and depart on your way.

FOR YOU O DEMOCRACY

Come, I will make the continent indissoluble,
I will make the most splendid race the sun ever shone
        upon,
I will make divine magnetic lands,
        With the love of comrades,
        With the life-long love of comrades.

I will plant companionship thick as trees along all the
        rivers of America, and along the shores of the
        great lakes, and all over the prairies,
I will make inseparable cities with their arms about each
        other's necks,
        By the love of comrades,
        By the manly love of comrades,

For you these from me, O Democracy, to serve you ma
        femme!
For you, for you I am trilling these songs.

THESE I SINGING IN SPRING

These I singing in spring collect for lovers,
(For who but I should understand lovers and all their
    sorrow and joy?
And who but I should be the poet of comrades?)
Collecting I traverse the garden the world, but soon I pass
    the gates,
Now along the pond-side, now wading in a little, fearing
    not the wet,
Now by the post-and-rail fences where the old stones
    thrown there, picked from the fields, have
    accumulated,
(Wild-flowers and vines and weeds come up through the
    stones and partly cover them, beyond these I
    pass,)
Far, far in the forest, or sauntering later in summer, before
    I think where I go,
Solitary, smelling the earthy smell, stopping now and then
    in the silence,
Alone I had thought, yet soon a troop gathers around me,
Some walk by my side and some behind, and some embrace
    my arms or neck,
They the spirits of dear friends dead or alive, thicker they
    come, a great crowd, and I in the middle,
Collecting, dispensing, singing, there I wander with them,
Plucking something for tokens, tossing toward whoever is
    near me,
Here, lilac, with a branch of pine,
Here, out of my pocket, some moss which I pulled off a
    live-oak in Florida as it hung trailing down,
Here, some pinks and laurel leaves, and a handful of sage,
And here what I now draw from the water, wading in the
    pond-side,

(O here I last saw him that tenderly loves me, and returns
again never to separate from me,
And this, O this shall henceforth be the token of comrades,
this calamus-root shall,
Interchange it youths with each other! let none render it
back!)
And twigs of maple and a bunch of wild orange and chest-
nut,
And stems of currants and plum-blows, and the aromatic
cedar,
These I compassed around by a thick cloud of spirits,
Wandering, point to or touch as I pass, or throw them
loosely from me,
Indicating to each one what he shall have, giving something to each;
But what I drew from the water by the pond-side, that I
reserve,
I will give of it, but only to them that love as I myself am
capable of loving.

NOT HEAVING
FROM MY
RIBBED BREAST ONLY

Not heaving from my ribbed breast only,
Not in sighs at night in rage dissatisfied with myself,
Not in those long-drawn, ill-suppressed sighs,
Not in many an oath and promise broken,
Not in my wilful and savage soul's volition,
Not in the subtle nourishment of the air,
Not in this beating and pounding at my temples and
      wrists,
Not in the curious systole and diastole within, which will
      one day cease,
Not in many a hungry wish told to the skies only,
Not in cries, laughter, defiances, thrown from me when
      alone far in the wilds,
Not in husky paintings through clinched teeth,
Not in sounded and resounded words, chattering words,
      echoes, dead words,
Not in the murmurs of my dreams while I sleep,
Nor the other murmurs of these incredible dreams of every
      day,
Nor in the limbs and senses of my body that take you and
      dismiss you continually—not there,
Not in any or all of them O adhesiveness! O pulse of my
      life!
Need I that you exist and show yourself any more than in
      these songs.

OF THE
TERRIBLE DOUBT OF
APPEARANCES

Of the terrible doubt of appearances,
Of the uncertainty after all, that we may be deluded,
That may-be reliance and hope are but speculations after
      all,
That may-be identity beyond the grave is a beautiful fable
      only,
May-be the things I perceive, the animals, plants, men,
      hills, shining and flowing waters,
The skies of day and night, colors, densities, forms,
      may-be these are (as doubtless they are) only
      apparitions, and the real something has yet to
      be known,
(How often they dart out of themselves as if to confound
      me and mock me!
How often I think neither I know, nor any man knows,
      aught of them,)
May-be seeming to me what they are (as doubtless they in-
      deed but seem) as from my present point of
      view, and might prove (as of course they
      would) nought of what they appear, or nought
      anyhow, from entirely changed points of view;
To me these and the like of these are curiously answered
      by my lovers, my dear friends,
When he whom I love travels with me or sits a long while
      holding me by the hand,
When the subtle air, the impalpable, the sense that words
      and reason hold not, surround us and pervade
      us,
Then I am charged with untold and untellable wisdom, I
      am silent, I require nothing further,

I cannot answer the question of appearances or that of
     identity beyond the grave,
But I walk or sit indifferent, I am satisfied,
He ahold of my hand has completely satisfied me.

HOURS CONTINUING

Hours continuing long, sore and heavy-hearted,
Hours of the dusk, when I withdraw to a lonesome and
    unfrequented spot, seating myself, leaning my
    face in my hands;
Hours sleepless, deep in the night, when I go forth, speed-
    ing swiftly the country roads, or through the
    city streets, or pacing miles and miles, stifling
    plaintive cries;
Hours discouraged, distracted—for the one I cannot con-
    tent myself without, soon I saw him content
    himself without me;
Hours when I am forgotten, (O weeks and months are
    passing, but I believe I am never to forget!)
Sullen and suffering hours! (I am ashamed—but it is use-
    less—I am what I am;)
Hours of my torment—I wonder if other men ever have
    the like, out of the like feelings?
Is there even one other like me—distracted—his friend, his
    lover, lost to him?
Is he too as I am now? Does he still rise in the morning,
    dejected, thinking who is lost to him? and at
    night, awaking, think who is lost?
Does he too harbor his friendship silent and endless? har-
    bor his anguish and passion?
Does some stray reminder, or the casual mention of a name,
    bring the fit back upon him, taciturn and de-
    pressed?
Does he see himself reflected in me? In these hours, does
    he see the face of his hours reflected?

WHEN I HEARD
AT THE CLOSE OF THE DAY

When I heard at the close of the day how my name had
    been received with plaudits in the capitol, still
    it was not a happy night for me that followed,
And else when I caroused, or when my plans were accom-
    plished, still I was not happy,
But the day when I rose at dawn from the bed of perfect
    health, refreshed, singing, inhaling the ripe
    breath of autumn,
When I saw the full moon in the west grow pale and dis-
    appear in the morning light,
When I wandered alone over the beach, and undressing
    bathed, laughing with the cool waters, and saw
    the sun rise,
And when I thought how my dear friend my lover was on
    his way coming, O then I was happy,
O then each breath tasted sweeter, and all that day my
    food nourished me more, and the beautiful
    day passed well,
And the next came with equal joy, and with the next at
    evening came my friend,
And that night while all was still I heard the waters roll
    slowly continually up the shores,
I heard the hissing rustle of the liquid and sands as di-
    rected to me whispering to congratulate me,
For the one I love most lay sleeping by me under the same
    cover in the cool night,
In the stillness in the autumn moonbeams his face was in-
    clined toward me,
And his arm lay lightly around my breast—and that night
    I was happy.

ARE YOU THE NEW PERSON
DRAWN TOWARD ME?

Are you the new person drawn toward me?
To begin with take warning, I am surely far different from
        what you suppose;
Do you suppose you will find in me your ideal?
Do you think it is so easy to have me become your lover?
Do you think the friendship of me would be unalloyed
        satisfaction?
Do you think I am trusty and faithful?
Do you see no further than this façade, this smooth and
        tolerant manner of me?
Do you suppose yourself advancing on real ground toward
        a real heroic man?
Have you no thought O dreamer that it may be all maya,
        illusion? O the next step may precipitate you!
O let some past deceived one hiss in your ears, how many
        have pressed on the same as you are pressing
        now,
How many have fondly supposed what you are supposing
        now—only to be disappointed.

ROOTS AND LEAVES
THEMSELVES ALONE

Roots and leaves themselves alone are these,
Scents brought to men and women from the wild woods
    and pond-side,
Breast-sorrel and pinks of love, fingers that wind around
    tighter than vines,
Gushes from the throats of birds hid in the foliage of trees
    as the sun is risen,
Breezes of land and love sent from living shores to you on
    the living sea, to you O sailors!
Frost-mellowed berries and Third-month twigs offered
    fresh to young persons wandering out in the
    fields when the winter breaks up,
Love-buds put before you and within you whoever you
    are,
Buds to be unfolded on the old terms,
If you bring the warmth of the sun to them they will open
    and bring form, color, perfume, to you,
If you become the aliment and the wet they will become
    flowers, fruits, tall branches and trees.

NOT HEAT FLAMES UP AND CONSUMES

Not heat flames up and consumes,
Not sea-waves hurry in and out,
Not the air delicious and dry, the air of ripe summer,
      bears lightly along white down-balls of myriads
      of seeds,
Wafted, sailing gracefully, to drop where they may;
Not these, O none of these more than the flames of me,
      consuming, burning for his love whom I love,
O none more than I hurrying in and out;
Does the tide hurry, seeking something, and never give
      up? O I the same,
O nor down-balls nor perfumes, nor the high rain-emitting
      clouds, are borne through the open air,
Any more than my soul is borne through the open air,
Wafted in all directions O love, for friendship, for you.

TRICKLE DROPS

Trickle drops! my blue veins leaving!
O drops of me! trickle, slow drops,
Candid from me falling, drip, bleeding drops,
From wounds made to free you whence you were prisoned,
From my face, from my forehead and lips,
From my breast, from within where I was concealed, press
      forth red drops, confession drops,
Stain every page, stain every song I sing, every word I say,
      bloody drops,
Let them know your scarlet heat, let them glisten,
Saturate them with yourself all ashamed and wet,
Glow upon all I have written or shall write, bleeding drops,
Let it all be seen in your light, blushing drops.

WHO IS NOW READING THIS?

Who is now reading this?

May-be one is now reading this who knows some wrong-
doing of my past life,
Or may-be a stranger is reading this who has secretly loved
me,
Or may-be one who meets all my grand assumptions and
egotisms with derision,
Or may-be one who is puzzled at me.

As if I were not puzzled at myself!
Or as if I never deride myself! (O conscience-struck! O
self-convicted!)
Or as if I do not secretly love strangers! (O tenderly, a
long time, and never avow it;)
Or as if I did not see, perfectly well, interior in myself,
the stuff of wrong-doing,
Or as if it could cease transpiring from me until it must
cease.

Of him I love day and night I dreamed I heard he was
 dead,
And I dreamed I went where they had buried him I love,
 but he was not in that place,
And I dreamed I wandered searching among burial-places
 to find him,
And I found that every place was a burial-place;
The houses full of life were equally full of death, (this
 house is now,)
The streets, the shipping, the places of amusement, the
 Chicago, Boston, Philadelphia, the Manna-
 hatta, were as full of the dead as of the living,
And fuller, O vastly fuller of the dead than of the living;
And what I dreamed I will henceforth tell to every person
 and age,
And I stand henceforth bound to what I dreamed,
And now I am willing to disregard burial-places and dis-
 pense with them,
And if the memorials of the dead were put up indifferently
 everywhere, even in the room where I eat or
 sleep, I should be satisfied,
And if the corpse of any one I love, or if my own corpse,
 be duly rendered to powder and poured in the
 sea, I shall be satisfied,
Or if it be distributed to the winds I shall be satisfied.

CITY OF ORGIES

City of orgies, walks and joys,
City whom that I have lived and sung in your midst will
        one day make you illustrious,
Not the pageants of you, not your shifting tableaus, your
        spectacles, repay me,
Not the interminable rows of your houses, nor the ships
        at the wharves,
Nor the processions in the streets, nor the bright windows
        with goods in them,
Nor to converse with learned persons, or bear my share
        in the soiree or feast;
Not those, but as I pass O Manhattan, your frequent and
        swift flash of eyes offering me love,
Offering response to my own—these repay me,
Lovers, continual lovers, only repay me.

Behold this swarthy face, these gray eyes,
This beard, the white wool unclipped upon my neck,
My brown hands and the silent manner of me without
   charm;
Yet comes one a Manhattanese and ever at parting kisses
   me lightly on the lips with robust love,
And I on the crossing of the street or on the ship's deck
   give a kiss in return,
We observe that salute of American comrades land and
   sea,
We are those two natural and nonchalant persons.

I SAW IN LOUISIANA
A LIVE-OAK GROWING

I saw in Louisiana a live-oak growing,
All alone stood it and the moss hung down from the
    branches,
Without any companion it grew there uttering joyous
    leaves of dark green,
And its look, rude, unbending, lusty, made me think of
    myself,
But I wondered how it could utter joyous leaves standing
    alone there without its friend near, for I knew
    I could not,
And I broke off a twig with a certain number of leaves
    upon it, and twined around it a little moss,
And brought it away, and I have placed it in sight in my
    room,
It is not needed to remind me as of my own dear friends,
(For I believe lately I think of little else than of them.)
Yet it remains to me a curious token, it makes me think
    of manly love;
For all that, and though the love-oak glistens there in
    Louisiana solitary in a wide flat space,
Uttering joyous leaves all its life without a friend a lover
    near,
I know very well I could not.

TO A STRANGER

Passing stranger! you do not know how longingly I look
    upon you,
You must be he I was seeking, or she I was seeking, (it
    comes to me as of a dream,)
I have somewhere surely lived a life of joy with you,
All is recalled as we flit by each other, fluid, affectionate,
    chaste, matured,
You grew up with me, were a boy with me or a girl with
    me,
I ate with you and slept with you, your body has become
    not yours only nor left my body mine only,
You give me the pleasure of your eyes, face, flesh, as we
    pass, you take of my beard, breast, hands, in
    return,
I am not to speak to you, I am to think of you when I sit
    alone or wake at night alone,
I am to wait, I do not doubt I am to meet you again,
I am to see to it that I do not lose you.

WHEN I PERUSE
THE CONQUERED FAME

When I peruse the conquered fame of heroes and the
     victories of mighty generals, I do not envy the
     generals,
Nor the President in his Presidency, nor the rich in his
     great house,
But when I hear of the brotherhood of lovers, how it was
     with them,
How together through life, through dangers, odium, un-
     changing, long and long,
Through youth and through middle and old age, how
     unfaltering, how affectionate and faithful they
     were,
Then I am pensive—I hastily walk away filled with the
     bitterest envy.

We two boys together clinging,
One the other never leaving,
Up and down the roads going, North and South excursions
making,
Power enjoying, elbows stretching, fingers clutching,
Armed and fearless, eating, drinking, sleeping, loving,
No law less than ourselves owning, sailing, soldiering,
thieving, threatening,
Misers, menials, priests alarming, air breathing, water
drinking, on the turf or the sea-beach dancing,
Cities wrenching, ease scorning, statues mocking, feeble-
ness chasing,
Fulfilling our foray.

A GLIMPSE

A glimpse through an interstice caught,
Of a crowd of workmen and drivers in a bar-room around
       the stove late of a winter night, and I unre-
       marked seated in a corner,
Of a youth who loves me and whom I love, silently ap-
       proaching and seating himself near, that he
       may hold me by the hand,
A long while amid the noises of coming and going, of
       drinking and oath and smutty jest,
There we two, content, happy in being together, speaking
       little, perhaps not a word.

EARTH, MY LIKENESS

Earth, my likeness,
Though you look so impassive, ample and spheric there,
I now suspect that is not all;
I now suspect there is something fierce in you eligible to
   burst forth,
For an athlete is enamoured of me, and I of him,
But toward him there is something fierce and terrible in
   me eligible to burst forth,
I dare not tell it in words, not even in these songs.

WHAT THINK YOU
I TAKE MY PEN IN HAND?

What think you I take my pen in hand to record?
The battle-ship, perfect-modeled, majestic, that I saw pass
    the offing to-day under full sail?
The splendors of the past day? or the splendor of the night
    that envelops me?
Or the vaunted glory and growth of the great city spread
    around me?—no;
But merely of two simple men I saw to-day on the pier in
    the midst of the crowd, parting the parting of
    dear friends,
The one to remain hung on the other's neck and passion-
    ately kissed him,
While the one to depart tightly pressed the one to remain
    in his arms.

SOMETIMES WITH ONE I LOVE

Sometimes with one I love I fill myself with rage for fear
    I effuse unreturned love,
But now I think there is no unreturned love, the pay is
    certain one way or another,
(I loved a certain person ardently and my love was not
    returned,
Yet out of that I have written these songs.)
Doubtless I could not have perceived the universe, or
    written one of my poems, if I had not freely
    given myself to comrades, to love.

TO A WESTERN BOY

Many things to absorb I teach to help you become eleve of
mine;
Yet if blood like mine circle not in your veins,
If you be not silently selected by lovers and do not silently
select lovers,
Of what use is it that you seek to become eleve of mine?

FAST-ANCHORED ETERNAL O LOVE!

Primeval my love for the woman I love,
O bride! O wife! more resistless, more enduring than I
    can tell, the thought of you!
Then separate, as disembodied, the purest born,
The ethereal, the last athletic reality, my consolation,
I ascend—I float in the regions of your love, O man,
O sharer of my roving life.

AMONG THE MULTITUDE

Among the men and women the multitude,
I perceive one picking me out by secret and divine signs,
Acknowledging none else, not parent, wife, husband,
       brother, child, any nearer than I am,
Some are baffled, but that one is not—that one knows me.

Ah lover and perfect equal,
I meant that you should discover me so by faint indirec-
       tions,
And I when I meet you mean to discover you by the like
       in you.

O YOU WHOM I OFTEN
AND SILENTLY COME

O you whom I often and silently come where you are
    that I may be with you,
As I walk by your side or sit near, or remain in the same
    room with you,
Little you know the subtle electric fire that for your sake
    is playing within me.

THAT SHADOW MY LIKENESS

That shadow my likeness that goes to and fro seeking a
      livelihood, chattering, chaffering,
How often I find myself standing and looking at it where
      it flits,
How often I question and doubt whether that is really me;
But among my lovers and caroling these songs,
O I never doubt whether that is really me.

FULL OF LIFE NOW

Full of life now, sweet-blooded, compact, visible,
I, forty years old the eighty-third year of the States,
To one a century hence or any number of centuries hence,
To you yet unborn these, seeking you.

When you read these I that was visible am become in-
        visible,
Now it is you, compact, visible, realizing my poems, seeking
        me,
Fancying how happy you were if I could be with you and
        become your lover;
Be it as if I were with you. (Be not too certain but I am
        now with you.)

TO A COMMON PROSTITUTE

Be composed—be at ease with me—I am Walt Whitman,
    liberal and lusty as Nature,
Not till the sun excludes you do I exclude you,
Not till the waters refuse to glisten for you and the leaves
    to rustle for you, do my words refuse to glisten
    and rustle for you.

My girl I appoint with you an appointment, and I charge
    you that you make preparations to be worthy
    to meet me,
And I charge you that you be patient and perfect till I
    come.

Till then I salute you with a significant look that you do
    not forget me.

Unfolded out of the folds of the woman man comes unfolded, and is always to come unfolded,

Unfolded only out of the superbest woman of the earth is to come the superbest man of the earth,

Unfolded out of the friendliest woman is to come the friendliest man,

Unfolded only out of the perfect body of a woman can a man be formed of perfect body,

Unfolded only out of the inimitable poems of woman can come the poems of man, (only thence have my poems come;)

Unfolded out of the strong and arrogant woman I love, only thence can appear the strong and arrogant man I love,

Unfolded by brawny embraces from the well-muscled woman I love, only thence come the brawny embraces of the man.

Unfolded out of the folds of the woman's brain come all the folds of the man's brain, duly obedient,

Unfolded out of the justice of the woman all justice is unfolded,

Unfolded out of the sympathy of the woman is all sympathy;

A man is a great thing upon the earth and through eternity, but every jot of the greatness of man is unfolded out of woman;

First the man is shaped in the woman, he can then be shaped in himself.

THE SLEEPERS

1

I wander all night in my vision,
Stepping with light feet, swiftly and noiselessly stepping
and stopping,
Bending with open eyes over the shut eyes of sleepers,
Wandering and confused, lost to myself, ill-assorted, con-
tradictory,
Pausing, gazing, bending, and stopping.

How solemn they look there, stretched and still,
How quiet they breathe, the little children in their cradles.

The wretched features of ennuyés, the white features of
corpses, the livid faces of drunkards, the sick-
gray faces of onanists,
The gashed bodies on battle-fields, the insane in their
strong-doored rooms, the sacred idiots, the
newborn emerging from gates, and the dying
emerging from gates,
The night pervades them and infolds them.

The married couple sleep calmly in their bed, he with his
palm on the hip of the wife, and she with her
palm on the hip of the husband,
The sisters sleep lovingly side by side in their bed,

The men sleep lovingly side by side in theirs,
And the mother sleeps with her little child carefully
wrapped.

The blind sleep, and the deaf and dumb sleep,
The prisoner sleeps well in the prison, the runaway son
sleeps,

The murderer that is to be hung next day, how does he
    sleep?
And the murdered person, how does he sleep?

The female that loves unrequited sleeps,
And the male that loves unrequited sleeps,
The head of the money-maker that plotted all day sleeps,
And the enraged and treacherous dispositions, all, all
    sleep.

I stand in the dark with drooping eyes by the worst-suffer-
    ing and the most restless,
I pass my hands soothingly to and fro a few inches from
    them,
The restless sink in their beds, they fitfully sleep.

Now I pierce the darkness, new beings appear,
The earth recedes from me into the night,
I saw that it was beautiful, and I see that what is not the
    earth is beautiful.

I go from bedside to bedside, I sleep close with the other
    sleepers each in turn,
I dream in my dream all the dreams of the other dreamers,
And I become the other dreamers.

I am a dance—play up there! the fit is whirling me fast!

I am the ever-laughing—it is new moon and twilight,
I see the hiding of douceurs, I see nimble ghosts whichever
    way I look,
Cache and cache again deep in the ground and sea, and
    where it is neither ground nor sea.

Well do they do their jobs those journeymen divine,
Only from me can they hide nothing, and would not if
    they could,

I reckon I am their boss and they make me a pet besides,
And surround me and lead me and run ahead when I walk,
To lift their cunning covers to signify me with stretched
    arms, and resume the way;
Onward we move, a gay gang of blackguards! with mirth-
    shouting music and wild-flapping pennants of
    joy!

I am the actor, the actress, the voter, the politician,
The emigrant and the exile, the criminal that stood in the
    box,
He who has been famous and he who shall be famous after
    to-day,
The stammerer, the well-formed person, the wasted or
    feeble person.

I am she who adorned herself and folded her hair expec-
    tantly,
My truant lover has come, and it is dark.

Double yourself and receive me darkness,
Receive me and my lover too, he will not let me go with-
    out him.

I roll myself upon you as upon a bed, I resign myself to
    the dusk.

He whom I call answers me and takes the place of my lover,
He rises with me silently from the bed.

Darkness, you are gentler than my lover, his flesh was
    sweaty and panting,
I feel the hot moisture yet that he left me.

My hands are spread forth, I pass them in all directions,
I would sound up the shadowy shore to which you are
    journeying.

Be careful darkness! already what was it touched me?
I thought my lover had gone, else darkness and he are one,
I hear the heart-beat, I follow, I fade away.

O hotcheeked and blushing! O foolish hectic!
O for pity's sake, no one must see me now! my clothes
were stolen while I was abed,
Now I am thrust forth, where shall I run?

Pier that I saw dimly last night when I looked from the
windows,
Pier out from the main, let me catch myself with you and
stay, I will not chafe you;
I feel ashamed to go naked about the world,
And am curious to know where my feet stand, and what
is this flooding me, childhood or manhood,
and the hunger that crosses the bridge between.

The cloth laps a first sweet eating and drinking,
Laps life-swelling yolks, laps ear of rose-corn, milky and
just ripened:
The white teeth stay, and the boss-tooth advances in darkness,
And liquor is spilled on lips and bosoms by touching
glasses, and the best liquor afterward.

2

I descend my western course, my sinews are flaccid,
Perfume and youth course through me and I am their
wake.

It is my face yellow and wrinkled instead of the old
woman's,
I sit low in a straw-bottom chair and carefully darn my
grandson's stockings.

It is I too, the sleepless widow looking out on the winter
    midnight,
I see the sparkles of starshine on the icy and pallid earth.

A shroud I see and I am the shroud, I wrap a body and lie
    in the coffin,
It is dark here under ground, it is not evil or pain here,
    it is blank here, for reasons.

(It seems to me that everything in the light and air ought
    to be happy,
Whoever is not in his coffin and the dark grave let him
    know he has enough.)

3

I see a beautiful gigantic swimmer swimming naked
    through the eddies of the sea,
His brown hair lies close and even to his head, he strikes
    out with courageous arms, he urges himself
    with his legs,
I see his white body, I see his undaunted eyes,
I hate the swift-running eddies that would dash him head-
    foremost on the rocks.

What are you doing unruffianly red-trickled waves?
Will you kill the courageous giant? will you kill him in the
    prime of his middle age?

Steady and long he struggles,
He is baffled, banged, bruised, he holds out while his
    strength holds out,
The slapping eddies are spotted with his blood, they bear
    him away, they roll him, swing him, turn him,
His beautiful body is borne in the circling eddies, it is
    continually bruised on rocks,
Swiftly and out of sight is borne the brave corpse.

4

I turn but do not extricate myself,
Confused, a past-reading, another, but with darkness yet.

The beach is cut by the razory ice-wind, the wreck-guns
    sound,
The tempest lulls, the moon comes floundering through
    the drifts.

I look where the ship helplessly heads end on, I hear the.
    burst as she strikes, I hear the howls of dismay,
    they grow fainter and fainter.

I cannot aid with my wringing fingers,
I can but rush to the surf and let it drench me and freeze
    upon me.

I search with the crowd, not one of the company is washed
    to us alive,
In the morning I help pick up the dead and lay them in
    rows in a barn. . . .

6

. . . Now Lucifer was not dead—or if he was, I am his
    sorrowful terrible heir;
I have been wronged—I am oppressed—I hate him that
    oppresses me,
I will either destroy him, or he shall release me.

Damn him! how he does defile me.
How he informs against my brother and sister, and takes
    pay for their blood,
How he laughs when I look down upon the bend after the
    steamboat that carries away my woman.

Now the vast dusk bulk that is the whale's bulk, it seems
    mine,
Warily, sportsman! though I lie so sleepy and sluggish,
    my tap is death.

7

A show of the summer softness—a contact of something
    unseen—an amour of the light and air,
I am jealous and overwhelmed with friendliness,
And will go gallivant with the light and air myself. . . .

Peace is always beautiful,
The myth of heaven indicates peace and night.
The myth of heaven indicates the soul,
The soul is always beautiful, it appears more or it appears
    less, it comes or it lags behind,
It comes from its embowered garden and looks pleasantly
    on itself and encloses the world,
Perfect and clean the genitals previously jetting, and per-
    fect and clean the womb cohering,
The head well-grown proportioned and plumb, and the
    bowels and joints proportioned and plumb.

The soul is always beautiful,
The universe is duly in order, every thing is in its place,
What has arrived is in its place and what waits shall be in
    its place,
The twisted skull waits, the watery or rotten blood waits,
The child of the glutton or venerealee waits long, and the
    child of the drunkard waits long, and the
    drunkard himself waits long,
The sleepers that lived and died wait, the far advanced are
    to go on in their turns, and the far behind
    are to come on in their turns,

The diverse shall be no less diverse, but they shall flow
and unite—they unite now.

8

The sleepers are very beautiful as they lie unclothed,
They flow hand in hand over the whole earth from east
to west as they lie unclothed,
The Asiatic and African are hand in hand, the European
and American are hand in hand,
Learned and unlearned are hand in hand, and male and
female are hand in hand,
The bare arm of the girl crosses the bare breast of her
lover, they press close without lust, his lips
press her neck,
The father holds his grown or ungrown son in his arms
with measureless love, and the son holds the
father in his arms with measureless love,
The white hair of the mother shines on the white wrist
of the daughter,
The breath of the boy goes with the breath of the man,
friend is inarmed by friend,

The scholar kisses the teacher and the teacher kisses the
scholar, the wronged is made right,
The call of the slave is one with the master's call, and the
master salutes the slave,
The felon steps forth from the prison, the insane becomes
sane, the suffering of sick persons is relieved,
The sweatings and fevers stop, the throat that was un-
sound is sound, the lungs of the consumptive
are resumed, the poor distressed head is free,
The joints of the rheumatic move as smoothly as ever, and
smoother than ever,
Stiflings and passages open, the paralyzed become supple,

The swelled and convulsed and congested awake to themselves in condition,
They pass the invigoration of the night and the chemistry
of the night, and awake.
I too pass from the night,
I stay a while away O night, but I return to you again and
love you.

Why should I be afraid to trust myself to you?
I am not afraid, I have been well brought forward by you,
I love the rich running day, but I do not desert her in
whom I lay so long,
I know not how I came of you and I know not where I go
with you, but I know I came well and shall go
well.

I will stop only a time with the night, and rise betimes,
I will duly pass the day O my mother, and duly return to
you.

Not you will yield forth the dawn again more surely than
you will yield forth me again.
Not the womb yields the babe in its time more surely than
I shall be yielded from you in my time.

TO YOU

Whoever you are, I fear you are walking the walk of
dreams,
I fear these supposed realities are to melt from under your
feet and hands,
Even now your features, joys, speech, house, trade, man-
ners, troubles, follies, costume, crimes, dissipate
away from you,
Your true soul and body appear before me,
They stand forth out of affairs, out of commerce, shops,
work, farms, clothes, the house, buying, selling,
eating, drinking, suffering, dying.

Whoever you are, now I place my hand upon you, that
you be my poem,
I whisper with my lips close to your ear,
I have loved many women and men, but I love none better
than you.

O I have been dilatory and dumb,
I should have made my way straight to you long ago,
I should have blabbed nothing but you, I should have
chanted nothing but you.

I will leave all and come and make the hymns of you,
None has understood you, but I understand you,
None has done justice to you, you have not done justice
to yourself,

None but has found you imperfect, I only find no imper-
fection in you,
None but would subordinate you, I only am he who will
never consent to subordinate you,
I only am he who places over you no master, owner, better,
God, beyond what waits intrinsically in yourself.

Painters have painted their swarming groups and the centre-figure of all,
From the head of the centre-figure spreading a nimbus of gold-colored light,
But I paint myriads of heads, but paint no head without its nimbus of gold-colored light,
From my hand from the brain of every man and woman it streams, effulgently flowing forever.

O I could sing such grandeurs and glories about you!
You have not known what you are, you have slumbered upon yourself all your life,
Your eyelids have been the same as closed most of the time,
What you have done returns already in mockeries,
(Your thrift, knowledge, prayers, if they do not return in mockeries, what is their return?)

The mockeries are not you,
Underneath them and within them I see you lurk,
I pursue you where none else has pursued you,
Silence, the desk, the flippant expression, the night, the accustomed routine, if these conceal you from others or from yourself, they do not conceal you from me,
The shaved face, the unsteady eye, the impure complexion, if these balk others they do not balk me,
The pert apparel, the deformed attitude, drunkenness, greed, premature death, all these I part aside.

There is no endowment in man or woman that is not tallied in you,
There is no virtue, no beauty in man or woman, but as good is in you,
No pluck, no endurance in others, but as good is in you,
No pleasure waiting for others, but an equal pleasure waits for you.

As for me, I give nothing to any one except I give the like
carefully to you,
I sing the songs of the glory of none, not God, sooner than
I sing the songs of the glory of you.

Whoever you are! claim your own at any hazard!
These shows of the East and West are tame compared to
you,
These immense meadows, these interminable rivers, you
are immense and interminable as they,
These furies, elements, storms, motions of Nature, throes
of apparent dissolution, you are he or she who
is master or mistress over them,
Master or mistress in your own right over Nature, elements, pain, passion, dissolution.

The hopples fall from your ankles, you find an unfailing
sufficiency,
Old or young, male or female, rude, low, rejected by the
rest, whatever you are promulges itself,
Through birth, life, death, burial, the means are provided, nothing is scanted,
Through angers, losses, ambition, ignorance, ennui, what
you are picks its way.

I AM NOT CONTENT

I am not content now with a mere majority . . .
I must have the love of all men and all women,
If there be one left in any country who has no faith in
me, I will travel to that country, and go to
that one.

AFTER DEATH

Now when I am looked upon, I will hold level
I lean upon my left elbow—I take ten thousand lovers,
    one after another by my right hand.

OUT OF THE CRADLE ENDLESSLY ROCKING

Out of the cradle endlessly rocking,
Out of the mocking-bird's throat, the musical shuttle,
Out of the boy's mother's womb, and from the nipples of
    her breasts,
Out of the Ninth-month midnight,
Over the sterile sands and the fields beyond, where the
    child leaving his bed wandered alone, bare-
    headed, barefoot,
Down from the showered halo,
Up from the mystic play of shadows twining and twisting
    as if they were alive,
Out from the patches of briers and blackberries,
From the memories of the bird that chanted to me,
From your memories sad brother, from the fitful risings
    and fallings I heard,
From under that yellow half-moon late-risen and swollen
    as if with tears,
From those beginning notes of yearning and love there in
    the mist,
From the thousand responses of my heart never to cease,
From the myriad thence-aroused words,
From the word stronger and more delicious than any,
From such as now they start the scene revisiting,
As a flock, twittering, rising, or overhead passing,
Borne hither, ere all eludes me, hurriedly,
A man, yet by these tears a little boy again,
Throwing myself on the sand, confronting the waves,
I, chanter of pains and joys, uniter of here and hereafter,
Taking all hints to use them, but swiftly leaping beyond
    them,
A reminiscence sing.
Once Paumanok,
When the lilac-scent was in the air and Fifth-month grass
    was growing,

Up this seashore in some briers,
Two feathered guests from Alabama, two together,
And their nest, and four light-green eggs spotted with
        brown,
And every day the he-bird to and fro near at hand,
And every day the she-bird crouched on her nest, silent,
        with bright eyes,
And every day I, a curious boy, never too close, never dis-
        turbing them,
Cautiously peering, absorbing, translating.

Shine! shine! shine!
Pour down your warmth, great sun!
While we bask, we two together.

Two together!
Winds blow south, or winds blow north,
Day come white, or night come black,
Home, or rivers and mountains from home,
Singing all time, minding no time,
While we two keep together.

Till of a sudden,
May-be killed, unknown to her mate,
One forenoon the she-bird crouched not on the nest,
Nor returned that afternoon, nor the next,
Nor ever appeared again.

And thenceforward all summer in the sound of the sea,
And at night under the full of the moon in calmer weather,
Over the hoarse surging of the sea,
Or flitting from brier to brier by day,
I saw, I heard at intervals the remaining one, the he-bird,
The solitary guest from Alabama.

Blow! blow! blow!
Blow .up sea-winds along Paumanok's shore;
I wait and I wait till you blow my mate to me.

Yes, when the stars glistened,
All night long on the prong of a moss-scalloped stake,
Down almost amid the slapping waves,
Sat the lone singer wonderful causing tears.

He called on his mate,
He poured forth the meanings which I of all men know.

Yes my brother I know,
The rest might not, but I have treasured every note,
For more than once dimly down to the beach gliding,
Silent, avoiding the moonbeams, blending myself with the
    shadows,
Recalling now the obscure shapes, the echoes, the sounds
    and sights after their sorts,
The white arms out in the breakers tirelessly tossing,
I, with bare feet, a child, the wind wafting my hair,
Listened long and long.

Listened to keep, to sing, now translating the notes,
Following you my brother.

Soothe! soothe! soothe!
Close on its wave soothes the wave behind,
And again another behind embracing and lapping, every
    one close,
But my love soothes not me, not me.

Low hangs the moon, it rose late,
It is lagging—O I think it is heavy with love, with love.

O madly the sea pushes upon the land,
With love, with love.

O night! do I not see my love fluttering out among the
    breakers?
What is that little black thing I see there in the white?

Loud! loud! loud!
Loud I call to you, my love!
High and clear I shoot my voice over the waves,
Surely you must know who is here, is here,
You must know whom I am, my love.

Low-hanging moon!
What is that dusky spot in your brown yellow?
O it is the shape, the shape of my mate!
O moon do not keep her from me any longer.

Land! land! O land!
Whichever way I turn, O I think you could give me my
　　　　mate back again if you only would,
For I am almost sure I see her dimly whichever way I look.

O rising stars!
Perhaps the one I want so much will rise, will rise with
　　　　some of you.

O throat! O trembling throat!
Sound clearer through the atmosphere!
Pierce the woods, the earth,
Somewhere listening to catch you must be the one I want.

Shake out carols!
Solitary here, the night's carols!
Carols of lonesome love! death's carols!
Carols under that lagging, yellow, waning moon!
O under the moon where she droops almost down into the
　　　　sea!
O reckless despairing carols.

But soft! sink low!
Soft! let me just murmur,
And do you wait a moment you husky-noised sea,

*For somewhere I believe I heard my mate responding to
    me,*
So faint, I must be still, be still to listen,
*But not altogether still, for then she might not come
    immediately to me.*

Hither my love!
Here I am! here!
With this just-sustained note I announce myself to you,
This gentle call is for you my love, for you.

Do not be decoyed elsewhere,
That is the whistle of the wind, it is not my voice,
That is the fluttering, the fluttering of the spray,
Those are the shadows of leaves.

O darkness! O in vain!
O I am very sick and sorrowful.

*O brown halo in the sky near the moon, drooping upon
    the sea!*
O troubled reflection in the sea!

O throat! O throbbing heart!
And I singing uselessly, uselessly all the night.

O past! O happy life! O songs of joy!
In the air, in the woods, over fields,
Loved! loved! loved! loved! loved!
But my mate no more, no more with me!
We two together no more.

The aria sinking,
All else continuing, the stars shining,
The winds blowing, the notes of the bird continuous
    echoing,
With angry moans the fierce old mother incessantly moan-
    ing,

On the sands of Paumanok's shore gray and rustling,
The yellow half-moon enlarged, sagging down, drooping,
the face of the sea almost touching,
The boy ecstatic, with his bare feet the waves, with his
hair the atmosphere dallying,
The love in the heart long pent, now loose, now at last
tumultuously bursting,
The aria's meaning, the ears, the soul, swiftly depositing,
The strange tears down the cheeks coursing,
The colloquy there, the trio, each uttering,
The undertone, the savage old mother incessantly crying,
To the boy's soul's questions sullenly timing, some drowned
secret hissing,
To the outsetting bard.

Demon or bird! (said the boy's soul,)
Is it indeed toward your mate you sing? or is it really to
me?
For I, that was a child, my tongue's use sleeping, now I
have heard you,
Now in a moment I know what I am for, I awake,
And already a thousand singers, a thousand songs, clearer,
louder and more sorrowful than yours,
A thousand warbling echoes have started to life within
me, never to die.

O you singer solitary, singing by yourself, projecting me,
O solitary me listening, never more shall I cease perpetuat-
ing you,
Never more shall I escape, never more the reverberations,
Never more the cries of unsatisfied love be absent from
me,
Never again leave me to be the peaceful child I was before
what there in the night,
By the sea under the yellow and sagging moon,
The messenger there aroused, the fire, the sweet hell
within,

The unknown want, the destiny of me.

O give me the clew! (it lurks in the night here some-
        where,)
O if I am to have so much, let me have more!

A word then, (for I will conquer it,)
The word final, superior to all,
Subtle, sent up—what is it?—I listen;
Are you whispering it, and have been all the time, you sea
        waves?
Is that it from your liquid rims and wet sands?

Whereto answering, the sea,
Delaying not, hurrying not,
Whispered me through the night, and very plainly before
        daybreak,
Lisped to me the low and delicious word death,
And again death, death, death, death,
Hissing melodious, neither like the bird nor like my
        aroused child's heart,
But edging near as privately for me rustling at my feet,
Creeping thence steadily up to my ears and laving me
        softly all over,
Death, death, death, death, death.

Which I do not forget,
But fuse the song of my dusky demon and brother,
That he sang to me in the moonlight on Paumanok's gray
        beach,
With the thousand responsive songs at random,
My own songs awaked from that hour,
And with them the key, the word up from the waves,
The word of the sweetest song and all songs,
That strong and delicious word which, creeping to my feet,
(Or like some old crone rocking the cradle, swathed in
        sweet garments, bending aside,)
The sea whispered me.

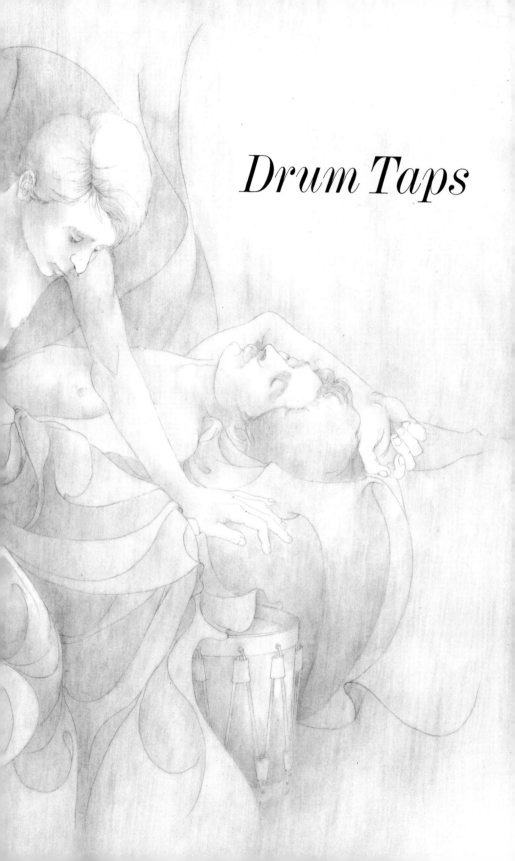

Drum Taps

VIGIL STRANGE I KEPT
ON THE FIELD ONE NIGHT

Vigil strange I kept on the field one night;
When you my son and my comrade dropped at my side
that day,
One look I but gave which your dear eyes returned with
a look I shall never forget,
One touch of your hand to mine O boy, reached up as you
lay on the ground,
Then onward I sped in the battle, the even-contested
battle,
Till late in the night relieved to the place at last again I
made my way,
Found you in death so cold dear comrade, found your
body son of responding kisses, (never again on
earth responding,)
Bared your face in the starlight, curious the scene, cool
blew the moderate night-wind,
Long there and then in vigil I stood, dimly around me the
battlefield spreading,
Vigil wondrous and vigil sweet there in the fragrant silent
night,
But not a tear fell, not even a long-drawn sigh, long, long
I gazed,
Then on the earth partially reclining sat by your side
leaning my chin in my hands,
Passing sweet hours, immortal and mystic hours with you
dearest comrade—not a tear, not a word,
Vigil of silence, love and death, vigil for you my son and
my soldier,
As onward silently stars aloft, eastward new ones upward
stole,

Vigil final for you brave boy, (I could not save you, swift
        was your death,
I faithfully loved you and cared for you living, I think we
        shall surely meet again,)
Till at latest lingering of the night, indeed just as the
        dawn appeared,
My comrade I wrapped in his blanket, enveloped well his
        form,
Folded the blanket well, tucking it carefully over head and
        carefully under feet,
And there and then and bathed by the rising sun, my son
        in his grave, in his rude-dug grave I deposited,
Ending my vigil strange with that, vigil of night and
        battlefield dim,
Vigil for boy of responding kisses, (never again on earth
        responding,)
Vigil for comrade swiftly slain, vigil I never forget, how as
        day brightened,
I rose from the chill ground and folded my soldier well in
        his blanket,
And buried him where he fell.

AS I LAY WITH MY HEAD
IN YOUR LAP CAMERADO

As I lay with my head in your lap camerado,
The confession I made I resume, what I said to you and
the open air I resume,
I know I am restless and make others so,
I know my words are weapons full of danger, full of death,
For I confront peace, security, and all the settled laws, to
unsettle them,
I am more resolute because all have denied me than I
could ever have been had all accepted me,
I heed not and have never heeded either experience, cau-
tions, majorities, nor ridicule,
And the threat of what is called hell is little or nothing to
me,
And the lure of what is called heaven is little or nothing to
me;
Dear camerado! I confess I have urged you onward with
me, and still urge you, without the least idea
what is our destination,
Or whether we shall be victorious, or utterly quelled and
defeated.

THE WOUND-DRESSER

1

An old man bending I come among new faces,
Years looking backward resuming in answer to children,
Come tell us old man, as from young men and maidens
    that love me,
(Aroused and angry, I'd thought to beat the alarum, and
    urge relentless war,
But soon my fingers failed me, my face drooped and I
    resigned myself,
To sit by the wounded and soothe them, or silently watch
    the dead;)
Years hence of these scenes, of these furious passions, these
    chances,
Of unsurpassed heroes, (was one side so brave? the other
    was equally brave;)
Now be witness again, paint the mightiest armies of earth,
Of those armies so rapid so wondrous what saw you to tell
    us?
What stays with you latest and deepest? of curious panics,
Of hard-fought engagements or sieges tremendous what
    deepest remains?

2

O maidens and young men I love and that love me,
What you ask of my days those the strangest and sudden
    your talking recalls,
Soldier alert I arrive after a long march covered with
    sweat and dust,

In the nick of time I come, plunge in the fight, loudly
      shout in the rush of successful charge,
Enter the captured works—yet lo, like a swift-running
      river they fade,
Pass and are gone they fade—I dwell not on soldiers' perils
      or soldiers' joys,
(Both I remember well—many of the hardships, few the
      joys, yet I was content.)

But in silence, in dreams' projections,
While the world of gain and appearance and mirth goes
      on,
So soon what is over forgotten, and waves wash the im-
      prints off the sand,
With hinged knees returning I enter the doors, (while for
      you up there,
Whoever you are, follow without noise and be of strong
      heart.)

Bearing the bandages, water and sponge,
Straight and swift to my wounded I go,
Where they lie on the ground after the battle brought in,
Where their priceless blood reddens the grass the ground,
Or to the rows of the hospital tent, or under the roofed
      hospital,
To the long rows of cots up and down each side I return,
To each and all one after another I draw near, not one
      do I miss,
An attendant follows holding a tray, he carries a refuse
      pail,
Soon to be filled with clotted rags and blood, emptied,
      and filled again.

I onward go, I stop,
With hinged knees and steady hand to dress wounds,

I am firm with each, the pangs are sharp yet unavoidable,
One turns to me his appealing eyes—poor boy! I never
    knew you,
Yet I think I could not refuse this moment to die for you,
    if that would save you.

3

On, on I go, (open doors of time! open hospital doors!)
The crushed head I dress, (poor crazed hand tear not the
    bandage away,)
The neck of the cavalry-man with the bullet through and
    through I examine,
Hard the breathing rattles, quite glazed already the eye,
    yet life struggles hard,
(Come sweet death! be persuaded O beautiful death!
In mercy come quickly.)

SONG OF MYSELF

1

I celebrate myself, and sing myself,
And what I assume you shall assume,
For every atom belonging to me as good belongs to you.

I loafe and invite my soul,
I lean and loafe at my ease observing a spear of summer
    grass.

2

Houses and rooms are full of perfumes, the shelves are
    crowded with perfumes,
I breathe the fragrance myself and know it and like it,
The distillation would intoxicate me also, but I shall not
    let it.

The atmosphere is not a perfume, it has no taste of the
    distillation, it is odorless,
It is for my mouth forever, I am in love with it,
I will go to the bank by the wood and become undisguised
    and naked,
I am mad for it to be in contact with me.

The smoke of my own breath,
Echoes, ripples, buzzed whispers, love-root, silk-thread,
    crotch and vine,
My respiration and inspiration, the beating of my heart,
    the passing of blood and air through my lungs,
The sniff of green leaves and dry leaves, and of the shore
    and dark-colored sea-rocks, and of hay in the
    barn,

The sound of the belched words of my voice loosed to the
eddies of the wind,
A few light kisses, a few embraces, a reaching around of
arms,
The play of shine and shade on the trees as the supple
boughs wag,
The delight alone or in the rush of the streets, or along
the fields and hill-sides,
The feeling of health, the full-noon trill, the song of me
rising from bed and meeting the sun.

Have you reckoned a thousand acres much? have you
reckoned the earth much?
Have you practised so long to learn to read?
Have you felt so proud to get at the meaning of poems?

Stop this day and night with me and you shall possess the
origin of all poems,
You shall possess the good of the earth and sun, (there are
millions of suns left,)
You shall no longer take things at second or third hand,
nor look through the eyes of the dead, nor
feed on the spectres in books,
You shall not look through my eyes either, nor take things
from me,
You shall listen to all sides and filter them from your self.

3

I have heard what the talkers were talking, the talk of the
beginning and the end,
But I do not talk of the beginning or the end.

There was never any more inception than there is now,
Nor any more youth or age than there is now,

And will never be any more perfection than there is now,
Nor any more heaven or hell than there is now.
Urge and urge and urge,
Always the procreant urge of the world.
Out of the dimness opposite equals advance, always sub-
stance and increase, always sex,
Always a knit of identity, always distinction, always a
breed of life.

To elaborate is no avail, learned and unlearned feel that
it is so.

Sure as the most certain sure, plumb in the uprights, well
entretied, braced in the beams,
Stout as a horse, affectionate, haughty, electrical,
I and this mystery here we stand.

Clear and sweet is my soul, and clear and sweet is all that
is not my soul.

Lack one lacks both, and the unseen is proved by the seen,
Till that becomes unseen and receives proof in its turn.

Showing the best and dividing it from the worst age vexes
age,
Knowing the perfect fitness and equanimity of things,
while they discuss I am silent, and go bathe
and admire myself.

Welcome is every organ and attribute of me, and of any
man hearty and clean,
Not an inch nor a particle of an inch is vile, and none
shall be less familiar than the rest.

I am satisfied—I see, dance, laugh, sing;
As the hugging and loving bed-fellow sleeps at my side
through the night, and withdraws at the peep
of the day with stealthy tread,

Leaving me baskets covered with white towels swelling
the house with their plenty,
Shall I postpone my acceptation and realization and
scream at my eyes,
That they turn from gazing after and down the road,
And forthwith cipher and show me to a cent,
Exactly the value of one and exactly the value of two, and
which is ahead?

4

Trippers and askers surround me,
People I meet, the effect upon me of my early life or the
ward and city I live in, or the nation,
The latest dates, discoveries, inventions, societies, authors
old and new,
My dinner, dress, associates, looks, compliments, dues,
The real or fancied indifference of some man or woman I
love,
The sickness of one of my folks or of myself, or ill-doing
or loss or lack of money, or depressions or
exaltations,
Battles, the horrors of fratricidal war, the fever of doubtful
news, the fitful events;
These come to me days and nights and go from me again,
But they are not the Me myself.

Apart from the pulling and hauling stands what I am,
Stands amused, complacent, compassionating, idle, uni-
tary,
Looks down, is erect, or bends an arm on an impalpable
certain rest,
Looking with side-curved head curious what will come
next,

Both in and out of the game and watching and wondering
      at it.

Backward I see in my own days where I sweated through
      fog with linguists and contenders,
I have no mockings or arguments, I witness and wait.

5

I believe in you my soul, the other I am must not abase
      itself to you,
And you must not be abased to the other.

Loafe with me on the grass, loose the stop from your throat,
Not words, not music or rhyme I want, not custom or lec-
      ture, not even the best,
Only the lull I like, the hum of your valvèd voice.

I mind how once we lay such a transparent summer morn-
      ing,
How you settled your head athwart my hips and gently
      turned over upon me,
And parted the shirt from my bosom-bone, and plunged
      your tongue to my bare-stripped heart,
And reached till you felt my beard, and reached till you
      held my feet.

Swiftly arose and spread around me the peace and knowl-
      edge that pass all the argument of the earth,
And I know that the hand of God is the promise of my
      own,
And I know that the spirit of God is the brother of my
      own,
And that all the men ever born are also my brothers, and
      the women my sisters and lovers,
And that a kelson of the creation is love,

And limitless are leaves stiff or drooping in the fields,
And brown ants in the little wells beneath them,
And mossy scabs of the worm fence, heaped stones, elder,
mullein and poke-weed.

6

A child said *What is the grass?* fetching it to me with full
hands,
How could I answer the child? I do not know what it is
any more than he.

I guess it must be the flag of my disposition, out of hope-
ful green stuff woven.

Or I guess it is the handkerchief of the Lord,
A scented gift and remembrancer designedly dropped,
Bearing the owner's name someway in the corners, that we
may see and remark, and say *Whose?*

Or I guess the grass is itself a child, the produced babe of
the vegetation.

Or I guess it is a uniform hieroglyphic,
And it means, Sprouting alike in broad zones and narrow
zones,
Growing among black folks as among white,
Kanuck, Tuckahoe, Congressman, Cuff, I give them the
same, I receive them the same.

And now it seems to me the beautiful uncut hair of graves.

Tenderly will I use you curling grass,
It may be you transpire from the breasts of young men,
It may be if I had known them I would have loved them,
It may be you are from old people, or from offspring
taken soon out of their mothers' laps,
And here you are the mothers' laps.

This grass is very dark to be from the white heads of old
    mothers,
Darker than the colorless beards of old men,
Dark to come from under the faint red roofs of mouths.
O I perceive after all so many uttering tongues,
And I perceive they do not come from the roofs of mouths
    for nothing.

I wish I could translate the hints about the dead young
    men and women,
And the hints about old men and mothers, and the off-
    spring taken soon out of their laps.

What do you think has become of the young and old men?
And what do you think has become of the women and
    children?

They are alive and well somewhere,
The smallest sprout shows there is really no death,
And if ever there was it led forward life, and does not wait
    at the end to arrest it,
And ceased the moment life appeared.

All goes onward and outward, nothing collapses,
And to die is different from what any one supposed, and
    luckier.

7

Has any one supposed it lucky to be born?
I hasten to inform him or her it is just as lucky to die, and
    I know it.

I pass death with the dying and birth with the new-washed
    babe, and am not contained between my hat
    and boots,
And peruse manifold objects, no two alike and everyone
    good,

The earth good and the stars good, and their adjuncts all
good.

I am not an earth nor an adjunct of an earth,
I am the mate and companion of people, all just as immor-
tal and fathomless as myself,
(They do not know how immortal, but I know.)

Every kind for itself and its own, for me mine male and
female,
For me those that have been boys and that love women,
For me the man that is proud and feels how it stings to be
slighted,
For me the sweet-heart and the old maid, for me mothers
and the mothers of mothers,
For me lips that have smiled, eyes that have shed tears,
For me children and the begetters of children.

Undrape! you are not guilty to me, nor stale nor discarded,
I see through the broadcloth and gingham whether or no,
And am around, tenacious, acquisitive, tireless, and can-
not be shaken away.

8

The little one sleeps in its cradle,
I lift the gauze and look a long time, and silently brush
away flies with my hand.

The youngster and the red-faced girl turn aside up the
bushy hill,
I peeringly view them from the top.

The suicide sprawls on the bloody floor of the bedroom,
I witness the corpse with its dabbled hair, I note where
the pistol has fallen.

The blab of the pave, tires of carts, sluff of boot-soles, talk
     of the promenaders,
The heavy omnibus, the driver with his interrogating
     thumb, the clank of the shod horses on the
     granite floor,
The snow-sleighs, clinkink, shouted jokes, pelts of snow-
     balls,
The hurrahs for popular favorites, the fury of roused
     mobs,
The flap of the curtained litter, a sick man inside borne
     to the hospital,
The meeting of enemies, the sudden oath, the blows and
     fall,
The excited crowd, the policeman with his star quickly
     working his passage to the centre of the crowd,
The impassive stones that receive and return so many
     echoes,
What groans of over-fed or half-starved who fall sunstruck
     or in fits,
What exclamations of women taken suddenly who hurry
     home and give birth to babes,
What living and buried speech is always vibrating here,
     what howls restrained by decorum,
Arrests of criminals, slights, adulterous offers made, ac-
     ceptances, rejections with convex lips,
I mind them or the show or resonance of them—I come
     and I depart. . . .

21

I am the poet of the Body and I am the poet of the Soul,
The pleasures of heaven are with me and the pains of hell
     are with me,

The first I graft and increase upon myself, the latter I
    translate into a new tongue.

I am the poet of the woman the same as the man,
And I say it is as great to be a woman as to be a man,
And I say there is nothing greater than the mother of men.

I chant the chant of dilation or pride,
We have had ducking and deprecating about enough,
I show that size is only development.

Have you outstripped the rest? are you the President?
It is a trifle, they will more than arrive there every one,
    and still pass on.

I am he that walks with the tender and growing night,
I call to the earth and sea half-held by the night.

Press close bare-bosomed night—press close magnetic
    nourishing night!
Night of south winds—night of the large few stars!
Still nodding night—mad naked summer night.

Smile O voluptuous cool-breathed earth!
Earth of the slumbering and liquid trees!
Earth of departed sunset—earth of the mountains misty-
    topped!
Earth of the vitreous pour of the full moon just tinged with
    blue!
Earth of shine and dark mottling the tide of the river!
Earth of the limpid gray of clouds brighter and clearer for
    my sake!
Far-swooping elbowed earth—rich apple-blossomed earth!
Smile, for your lover comes.

Prodigal, you have given me love—therefore I to you give
    love!

O unspeakable passionate love.

Thruster holding me tight and that I hold tight,
We hurt each other as the bridegroom and the bride hurt
    each other. . . .

24

Walt Whitman, an American, one of the roughs, a kosmos,
Disorderly, fleshy, sensual, eating, drinking and breeding,
No sentimentalist, no stander above men and women or
    apart from them,
No more modest than immodest.

Unscrew the locks from the doors!
Unscrew the doors themselves from their jambs!

Whoever degrades another degrades me,
And whatever is done or said returns at last to me.

Through me the afflatus surging and surging, through me
    the current and index.

I speak the pass-word primeval, I give the sign of democ-
    racy,
By God! I will accept nothing which all cannot have their
    counterpart of on the same terms.

Through me many long dumb voices,
Voices of the interminable generations of prisoners and
    slaves,
Voices of prostitutes and of deformed persons,
Voices of the diseased and despairing and of thieves and
    dwarfs,
Voices of cycles of preparation and accretion,
And of the threads that connect the stars, and of wombs
    and of the father-stuff,
And of the rights of them the others are down upon,

Of the deformed, trivial, flat, foolish, despised,
Fog in the air, beetles rolling balls of dung.

Through me forbidden voices,
Voices of sexes and lusts, voices veiled and I remove the
veil,
Voices indecent by me clarified and transfigured.

I do not press my fingers across my mouth,
I keep as delicate around the bowels as around the head
and heart,
Copulation is no more rank to me than death is.

I believe in the flesh and the appetites,
Seeing, hearing, feeling, are miracles, and each part and
tag of me is a miracle.

Divine am I inside and out, and I make holy whatever I
touch or am touched from,
The scent of these arm-pits aroma finer than prayer,
This head more than churches, bibles, and all the creeds.

If I worship one thing more than another it shall be the
spread of my own body, or any part of it,
Translucent mould of me it shall be you!
Shaded ledges and rests it shall be you!
Firm masculine colter it shall be you!
Whatever goes to the tilth of me it shall be you!
You my rich blood! your milky stream pale strippings of
my life!
Breast that presses against other breasts it shall be you!
My brain it shall be your occult convolutions!
Root of washed sweet-flag! timorous pond-snipe! nest of
guarded duplicate eggs! it shall be you!
Mixed tussled hay of head, beard, brawn, it shall be you!
Tricking sap of maple, fibre of manly wheat, it shall be
you!

Sun so generous it shall be you!
Vapors lighting and shading my face it shall be you!
You sweaty brooks and dews it shall be you!
Winds whose soft-tickling genitals rub against me it shall
be you!
Broad muscular fields, branches of live oak, loving lounger
in my winding paths, it shall be you!
Hands I have taken, face I have kissed, mortal I have ever
touched, it shall be you.

I dote on myself, there is that lot of me and all so luscious,
Each moment and whatever happens thrills me with joy,
I cannot tell how my ankles bend, nor whence the cause
of my faintest wish,
Nor the cause of the friendship I emit, nor the cause of
the friendship I take again.

That I walk up my stoop, I pause to consider if it really be,
A morning-glory at my window satisfies me more than the
metaphysics of books.

To behold the day-break!
The little light fades the immense and diaphanous
shadows,
The air tastes good to my palate.

Hefts of the moving world at innocent gambols silently
rising, freshly exuding,
Scooting obliquely high and low.

Something I cannot see puts upward libidinous prongs,
Seas of bright juice suffuse heaven.

The earth by the sky staid with, the daily close of their
junction,
The heaved challenge from the east that moment over my
head,

The mocking taunt, See then whether you shall be master! . . .

26

Now I will do nothing but listen,
To accrue what I hear into this song, to let sounds contribute toward it.

I hear bravuras of birds, bustle of growing wheat, gossip of
flames, clack of sticks cooking my meals,
I hear the sound I love, the sound of the human voice,
I hear all sounds running together, combined, fused or
following,
Sounds of the city and sounds out of the city, sounds of
the day and night,
Talkative young ones to those that like them, the loud
laugh of work-people at their meals,
The angry base of disjointed friendship, the faint tones
of the sick,
The judge with hands tight to the desk, his pallid lips pro-
nouncing a death-sentence,
The heave'e'yo of stevedores unloading ships by the
wharves, the refrain of the anchor-lifters,
The ring of alarm-bells, the cry of fire, the whirr of swift-
streaking engines and hose-carts with pre-
monitory tinkles and colored lights,
The steam-whistle, the solid roll of the train of approaching cars,
The slow march played at the head of the association
marching two and two,
(They go to guard some corpse, the flag-tops are draped
with black muslin.)

I hear the violoncello, ('tis the young man's heart's complaint,)

I hear the keyed cornet, it glides quickly in through my
    ears,
It shakes mad-sweet pangs through my belly and breast.

I hear the chorus, it is a grand opera,
Ah this indeed is music—this suits me.

A tenor large and fresh as the creation fills me,
The orbic flex of his mouth is pouring and filling me full.

I hear the trained soprano, she convulses me like the cli-
    max of my love-grip;
The orchestra whirls me wider than Uranus flies,
It wrenches unnamable ardors from my breast,
It throbs me to gulps of the farthest down horror,
It sails me, I dab with bare feet, they are licked by the
    indolent waves,
I am exposed, cut by bitter and poisoned hail,
Steeped amid honeyed morphine, my windpipe squeezed
    in the fakes of death,
Let up again to feel the puzzle of puzzles,
And that we call Being.

27

To be in any form, what is that?
(Round and round we go, all of us, and ever come back
    thither,)
If nothing lay more developed the quahaug in its callous
    shell were enough.

Mine is no callous shell,
I have instant conductors all over me whether I pass or
    stop,
They seize every object and lead it harmlessly through me.

I merely stir, press, feel with my fingers, and am happy,

To touch my person to some one else's is about as much as
    I can stand.

28

Is this then a touch? quivering me to a new identity,
Flames and ether making a rush for my veins,
Treacherous tip of me reaching and crowding to help
    them,
My flesh and blood playing out lightning to strike what is
    hardly different from myself,
On all sides prurient provokers stiffening my limbs,
Straining the udder of my heart for its withheld drip,
Behaving licentious toward me, taking no denial,
Depriving me of my best as for a purpose,
Unbuttoning my clothes, holding me by the bare waist,
Deluding my confusion with the calm of the sunlight and
    pasture-fields,
Immodestly sliding the fellow-senses away,
They bribed to swap off with touch and go and graze at
    the edges of me,
No consideration, no regard for my draining strength or
    my anger,
Fetching the rest of the herd around to enjoy them a while,
Then all uniting to stand on a headland and worry me.
The sentries desert every other part of me,
They have left me helpless to a red marauder,
They all come to the headland to witness and assist against
    me.

I am given up by traitors,
I talk wildly, I have lost my wits, I and nobody else am the
    greatest traitor,
I went myself first to the headland, my own hands carried
    me there.

You villain touch! what are you doing? my breath is tight
    in its throat,
Unclench your floodgates, you are too much for me.

29

Blind loving wrestling touch, sheathed hooded sharp-
    toothed touch!
Did it make you ache so, leaving me?

Parting tracked by arriving, perpetual payment of perpet-
    ual loan,
Rich showering rain, and recompense richer afterward.
Sprouts take and accumulate, stand by the curb prolific
    and vital,
Landscapes projected masculine, full-sized and
    golden. . . .

31

I believe a leaf of grass is no less than the journey-work of
    the stars,
And the pismire is equally perfect, and a grain of sand,
    and the egg of the wren,
And the tree-toad is a chef-d'œuvre for the highest,
And the running blackberry would adorn the parlors of
    heaven,
And the narrowest hinge in my hand puts to scorn all
    machinery,
And the cow crunching with depressed head surpasses any
    statue,
And a mouse is miracle enough to stagger sextillions of
    infidels. . . .

32

I think I could turn and live with animals, they are so
placid and self-contained,
I stand and look at them long and long.

They do not sweat and whine about their condition,
They do not lie awake in the dark and weep for their sins,
They do not make me sick discussing their duty to God,
Not one is dissatisfied, not one is demented with the mania
of owning things,
Not one kneels to another, nor to his kind that lived thou-
sands of years ago,
Not one is respectable or unhappy over the whole earth.

So they show their relations to me and I accept them,
They bring me tokens of myself, they evince them plainly
in their possession.

I wonder where they get those tokens,
Did I pass that way huge times ago and negligently drop
them?
Myself moving forward then and now and forever,
Gathering and showing more always and with velocity,
Infinite and omnigenous, and the like of these among
them,
Not too exclusive toward the reachers of my remem-
brancers,
Picking out here one that I love, and now go with him on
brotherly terms.

A gigantic beauty of a stallion, fresh and responsive to
my caresses,
Head high in the forehead, wide between the ears,
Limbs glossy and supple, tail dusting the ground,
Eyes full of sparkling wickedness, ears finely cut, flexibly
moving.

His nostrils dilate as my heels embrace him,
His well-built limbs tremble with pleasure as we race
        around and return.

I but use you a minute, then I resign you, stallion,
Why do I need your paces when I myself out-gallop them?
Even as I stand or sit passing faster than you. . . .

40

Flaunt of the sunshine I need not your bask—lie over!
You light surfaces only, I force surfaces and depths also.
Earth! you seem to look for something at my hands,
Say, old top-knot, what do you want?

Man or woman, I might tell how I like you, but cannot,
And might tell what it is in me and what it is in you, but
        cannot,
And might tell that pining I have, that pulse of my nights
        and days.

Behold, I do not give lectures or a little charity,
When I give I give myself.

You there, impotent, loose in the knees,
Open your scarfed chops till I blow grit within you,
Spread your palms and lift the flaps of your pockets,
I am not to be denied, I compel, I have stores plenty and
        to spare,
And any thing I have I bestow.

I do not ask who you are, that is not important to me,
You can do nothing and be nothing but what I will infold
        you.

To cotton-field drudge or cleaner of privies I lean,
On his right cheek I put the family kiss,

And in my soul I swear I never will deny him.

On women fit for conception I start bigger and nimbler
    babes,
(This day I am jetting the stuff of far more arrogant re-
    publics.)

To any one dying, thither I speed and twist the knob of
    the door,
Turn the bed-clothes toward the foot of the bed,
Let the physician and the priest go home.

I seize the descending man and raise him with resistless
    will,
O despairer, here is my neck,
By God, you shall not go down! hang your whole weight
    upon me.

I dilate you with tremendous breath, I buoy you up,
Every room of the house do I fill with an armed force,
Lovers of me, bafflers of graves.

Sleep—I and they keep guard all night,
Not doubt, not decease shall dare to lay finger upon you,
I have embraced you, and henceforth possess you to my-
    self,
And when you rise in the morning you will find what I tell
    you is so. . . .

45

O span of youth! ever-pushed elasticity.
O manhood, balanced, florid and full.

My lovers suffocate me,
Crowding my lips, thick in the pores of my skin,
Jostling me through streets and public halls, coming naked
    to me at night,

Crying by day *Ahoy!* from the rocks of the river, swinging
     and chirping over my head,
Calling my name from flower-beds, vines, tangled under-
     brush,
Lighting on every moment of my life,
Bussing my body with soft balsamic busses,
Noiselessly passing handfuls out of their hearts and giving
     them to be mine.

Old age superbly rising! O welcome, ineffable grace of
     dying days!

Every condition promulges not only itself, it promulges
     what grows after and out of itself,
And the dark hush promulges as much as any.

I open my scuttle at night and see the far-sprinkled sys-
     tems,
And all I see multiplied as high as I can cipher edge but
     the rim of the farther systems.

Wider and wider they spread, expanding, always expand-
     ing,
Outward and outward and forever outward.

My sun has his sun and round him obediently wheels,
He joins with his partners a group of superior circuit,
And greater sets follow, making specks of the greatest in-
     side them.

There is no stoppage and never can be stoppage,
If I, you, and the worlds, and all beneath or upon their
     surfaces, were this moment reduced back to a
     pallid float, it would not avail in the long run,
We should surely bring up again where we now stand,
And surely go as much farther, and then farther and far-
     ther.

A few quadrillions of eras, a few octillions of cubic
      leagues, do not hazard the span or make it
      impatient,
They are but parts, any thing is but a part.

See ever so far, there is limitless space outside of that,
Count ever so much, there is limitless time around that.

My rendezvous is appointed, it is certain,
The Lord will be there and wait till I come on perfect
      terms,
The great Camerado, the lover true for whom I pine will
      be there. . . .

49

And as to you Death, and you bitter hug of mortality, it is
      idle to try to alarm me.

To his work without flinching the accoucheur comes,
I see the elder-hand pressing receiving supporting,
I recline by the sills of the exquisite flexible doors,
And mark the outlet, and mark the relief and escape.

And as to you Corpse I think you are good manure, but
      that does not offend me,
I smell the white roses sweet-scented and growing.

I reach to the leafy lips, I reach to the polished breasts of
      melons.

And as to you Life I reckon you are the leavings of many
      deaths,
(No doubt I have died myself ten thousand times before.)

I hear you whispering there O stars of heaven,
O suns—O grass of graves—O perpetual transfers and pro-
      motions,

If you do not say any thing how can I say any thing?

Of the turbid pool that lies in the autumn forest,
Of the moon that descends the steeps of the soughing twi-
light,
Toss, sparkles of day and dusk—toss on the black stems that
decay in the muck,
Toss to the moaning gibberish of the dry limbs.

I ascend from the moon, I ascend from the night,
I perceive that the ghastly glimmer is noonday sunbeams
reflected,
And debouch to the steady and central from the offspring
great or small. . . .

51

The past and present wilt—I have filled them, emptied
them,
And proceed to fill my next fold of the future.

Listener up there! what have you to confide to me?
Look in my face while I snuff the sidle of evening,
(Talk honestly, no one else hears you, and I stay only a
minute longer.)

Do I contradict myself?
Very well then I contradict myself,
(I am large, I contain multitudes.)

I concentrate toward them that are nigh, I wait on the
door-slab.

Who has done his day's work? who will soonest be through
with his supper?
Who wishes to walk with me?

Will you speak before I am gone? will you prove already
too late?

52

The spotted hawk swoops by and accuses me, he complains
    of my gab and my loitering.

I too am not a bit tamed, I too am untranslatable,
I sound my barbaric yawp over the roofs of the world.

The last scud of day holds back for me,
It flings my likeness after the rest and true as any on the
    shadowed wilds,
It coaxes me to the vapor and the dusk.
I depart as air, I shake my white locks at the runaway sun,
I effuse my flesh in eddies, and drift it in lacy jags.

I bequeath myself to the dirt to grow from the grass I
    love,
If you want me again look for me under your boot-soles.

You will hardly know who I am or what I mean,
But I shall be good health to you nevertheless,
And filter and fibre your blood.

Failing to fetch me at first keep encouraged,
Missing me one place search another,
I stop somewhere waiting for you.

RESPONDEZ

Respondez! Respondez!
Let every one answer! Let those who sleep be waked! Let
    none evade!
(Must we still go on with our affectations and sneaking?
Let me bring this to a close—I pronounce openly for a
    new distribution of roles,)
Let that which stood in front go behind! and let that
    which was behind advance to the front and
    speak!
Let murderers, thieves, bigots, fools, unclean persons, offer
    new propositions!
Let the old propositions be postponed!
Let faces and theories be turned'inside out! Let meanings
    be freely criminal, as well as results!
Let there be no suggestion above the suggestion of drudg-
    ery!
Let none be pointed toward his destination! (Say! do you
    know your destination?)
Let trillions of men and women be mocked with bodies
    and mocked with Souls!
Let the love that waits in them, wait! Let it die, or pass
    still-born to other spheres!
Let the sympathy that waits in every man, wait! or let it
    also pass, a dwarf, to other spheres!
Let contradictions prevail! Let one thing contradict an-
    other! and let one line of my poems contradict
    another!
Let the people sprawl with yearning aimless hands! Let
    their tongues be broken! Let their eyes be
    discouraged! Let none descend into their hearts
    with the fresh lusciousness of love!
Let the theory of America be management, caste, com-
    parison! (Say! what other theory would you?)

Let them that distrust birth and death lead the rest! (Say! why shall they not lead you?)

Let the crust of hell be neared and trod on! Let the days be darker than the nights! Let slumber bring less slumber than waking-time brings!

Let the world never appear to him or her for whom it was all made!

Let the heart of the young man exile itself from the heart of the old man! and let the heart of the old man be exiled from that of the young man!

Let the sun and moon go! Let scenery take the applause of the audience! Let there be apathy under the stars!

Let freedom prove no man's inalienable right! Every one who can tyrannize, let him tyrannize to his satisfaction!

Let none but infidels be countenanced!

Let the eminence of meanness, treachery, sarcasm, hate, greed, indecency, impotence, lust, be taken for granted above all! Let writers, judges, governments, households, religions, philosophies, take such for granted above all!

Let the worst men beget children out of the worst women!

Let priests still play at immortality!

Let Death be inaugurated!

Let nothing remain upon the earth except the ashes of teachers, artists, moralists, lawyers, and learned and polite persons!

Let him who is without my poems be assassinated!

Let the cow, the horse, the camel, the garden-bee—Let the mud-fish, the lobster, the mussel, eel, the sting-ray, and the grunting pig-fish—Let these, and the like of these, be put on a perfect equality with man and woman!

Let churches accommodate serpents, vermin, and the

corpses of those who have died of the most filthy of diseases!

Let marriage slip down among fools, and be for none but fools!

Let men among themselves talk and think obscenely of women! and let women among themselves talk and think obscenely of men!

Let every man doubt every woman! and let every woman trick every man!

Let us all, without missing one, be exposed in public, naked, monthly, at the peril of our lives! Let our bodies be freely handled and examined by whoever chooses!

Let nothing but copies, pictures, statues, reminiscences, elegant works, be permitted to exist upon the earth!

Let the earth desert God, nor let there ever henceforth be mentioned the name of God!

Let there be no God!

Let there be money, business, imports, exports, custom, authority, precedents, pallor, dyspepsia, smut, ignorance, unbelief!

Let judges and criminals be transposed! Let the prison-keepers be put in prison! Let those that were prisoners take the keys! (Say! why might they not just as well be transposed?)

Let the slaves be masters! Let the masters become slaves!

Let the reformers descend from the stands where they are forever bawling! Let an idiot or insane person appear on each of the stands!

Let the Asiatic, the African, the European, the American and the Australian, go armed against the murderous stealthiness of each other! Let them sleep armed! Let none believe in good-will!

Let there be no unfashionable wisdom! Let such be scorned and derided off from the earth!

Let a floating cloud in the sky—Let a wave of the sea—Let
one glimpse of your eye-sight upon the land-
scape or grass—Let growing mint, spinach,
onions, tomatoes—Let these be exhibited as
shows at a great price for admission!
Let all the men of These States stand aside for a few
smouchers! Let the few seize on what they
choose! Let the rest gawk, giggle, starve, obey!
Let shadows be furnished with genitals! Let substances be
deprived of their genitals!
Let there be wealthy and immense cities—but through
any of them, not a single poet, saviour, knower,
lover!
Let the infidels of These States laugh all faith away! If
one man be found who has faith, let the rest
set upon him! Let them affright faith! Let
them destroy the power of breeding faith!
Let the she-harlots and the he-harlots be prudent! Let
them dance on, while seeming lasts! (O seeming! seeming! seeming!)
Let the preachers recite creeds! Let them teach only what
they have been taught!
Let the preachers of creeds never dare to go meditate
candidly upon the hills, alone, by day or by
night! (If one ever once dare, he is lost!)
Let insanity have charge of sanity!
Let books take the place of trees, animals, rivers, clouds!
Let the daubed portraits of heroes supersede heroes!
Let the manhood of man never take steps after itself! Let
it take steps after eunuchs, and after consump-
tive and genteel persons!
Let the white person tread the black person under his
heel! (Say! which is trodden under heel, after
all?)
Let the reflections of the things of the world be studied

in mirrors! Let the things themselves continue
    unstudied!
Let a man seek pleasure everywhere except in himself! Let
    a woman seek happiness everywhere except in
    herself! (Say! what real happiness have you
    had one single time through your whole life?)
Let the limited years of life do nothing for the limitless
    years of death! (Say! what do you suppose
    death will do, then?)

SO LONG

To conclude, I announce what comes after me.

I remember I said before my leaves sprang at all,
I would raise my voice jocund and strong with reference
    to consummations.

When America does what was promised,
When each part is peopled by free people,
When through these States walk a hundred millions of
    superb persons,
When the rest part away for superb persons and contribute
    to them,
When breeds of the most perfect mothers denote America,
Then to me and mine our due fruition.

I have pressed through in my own right,
I have sung the body and the soul, war and peace have I
    sung, and the songs of life and death,
And the songs of birth, and shown that there are many
    births.

I have offered my style to every one, I have journeyed with
    confident step;
While my pleasure is yet at the full I whisper *So long!*
And take the young woman's hand and the young man's
    hand for the last time.

I announce natural persons to arise,
I announce justice triumphant,
I announce uncompromising liberty and equality,
I announce the justification of candor and the justification
    of pride.

I announce that the identity of these States is a single
    identity only,

I announce the Union more and more compact, indis-
     soluble,
I announce splendors and majesties to make all the pre-
     vious politics of the earth insignificant.
I announce adhesiveness, I say it shall be limitless, un-
     loosened,
I say you shall yet find the friend you were looking for.

I announce a man or woman coming, perhaps you are the
     one, (*So long!*)
I announce the great individual, fluid as Nature, chaste,
     affectionate, compassionate, fully armed.

I announce a life that shall be copious, vehement, spiritual,
     bold,
I announce an end that shall lightly and joyfully meet its
     translation.

I announce myriads of youths, beautiful, gigantic, sweet-
     blooded,
I announce a race of splendid and savage old men.

O thicker and faster—(*So long!*)
O crowding too close upon me,
I foresee too much, it means more than I thought,
It appears to me I am dying.

Hasten throat and sound your last,
Salute me—salute the days once more. Peal the old cry
     once more.

Screaming electric, the atmosphere using,
At random glancing, each as I notice absorbing,
Swiftly on, but a little while alighting,
Curious enveloped messages delivering,
Sparkles hot, seed ethereal down in the dirt dropping,
Myself unknowing, my commission obeying, to question
     it never daring,

To ages and ages yet the growth of the seed leaving,
To troops out of me arising, they the task I have set
    promulging,
To women certain whispers of myself bequeathing, their
    affection me more clearly explaining,
To young men my problems offering—no dallier I—I the
    muscle of their brains crying,
So I pass, a little time vocal, visible, contrary,
Afterward a melodious echo, passionately bent for, (death
    making me really undying,)
The best of me then when no longer visible, for toward
    that I have been incessantly preparing.

What is there more, that I lag and pause and crouch ex-
    tended with unshut mouth?
Is there a single final farewell?

My songs cease, I abandon them,
From behind the screen where I hid I advance personally
    solely to you.

This is no book,
Who touches this touches a man,
(Is it night? are we here together alone?)
It is I you hold and who holds you,
I spring from the pages into your arms—decease calls me
    forth.

O how your fingers drowse me,
Your breath falls around me like dew, your pulse lulls the
    tympans of my ears,
I feel immerged from head to foot;
Delicious, enough.

Enough O deed impromptu and secret,
Enough O gliding present—enough O summed-up past.

Dear friend whoever you are take this kiss,
I give it especially to you, do not forget me,
I feel like one who has done his work—I progress on,
The unknown sphere, more real than I dreamed, more
        direct, darts awakening rays about me—*So long!*
Remember my words—I love you—I depart from materials,
I am as one disembodied, triumphant, dead.

Afterlude

The Modality

Whitman once described *Leaves of Grass* as a "modality of but fragments"—a clue to the strange way the book was put together. Its shape changed as he added new poems. The original volume bore no title, nor did the individual poems. Now it takes a variorum edition of three large volumes to follow the transformation in the text from 12 poems to over 400. And this transformation represented nine versions by the author over the 36 years between the birth of the book and its Deathbed edition.

The nine editions that Whitman put through the press were not just literary exercises. They reveal his lifework as an adventure in self-discovery. The poet who thought he was recording how it felt to be alive in his particular epoch transcends the epoch. His writings about the Civil War were not just North *vs* South, they were all the young men who fight and get wounded and die in wars. It is this universal quality that has raised Whitman to the level of other towering figures—not excluding Homer or Dante or Tu Fu.

One attribute Whitman shares with Homer is his ability to nod. Ralph Waldo Emerson was one of the first Whitmaniacs to detect this. A few days after the first, 1855, edition, Emerson wrote Whitman: "I greet you at the beginning of a great career." He never withdrew that judgment, but later commented privately: "I expected Whitman to write the songs of a nation, not the inventories," and described him as "half-alligator, half song thrush . . . a mixture of the *Bhagavad-Gita* and the *New York Herald*."

Today the consensus of specialists who have mastered Whitman's entire work is that the texture is extremely uneven. One early biographer (Canby) wrote: "Nobody ever read or should attempt to read *Leaves* from cover to cover."

The Tenderest Lover is intended for anyone to read. In several ways it is a unique selection: Although Whitman's erotic poems have been discussed throughout the world for over a century, they have never before been published by themselves in a single volume. Poems are included that Whitman published at one time or another but later omitted from his final selection. Also included are several poems that were found among his papers after his death.

Most of the poems in *The Tenderest Lover* were selected from the nine editions he published during his lifetime. Our text, however, is unexpurgated; erotic lines and passages that Whitman changed or deleted have been restored. I chose what I considered most representative in the changing versions. The one criterion was Whitman's poetic genius as reflected in his own words.

Whitman suspected that others would come along and edit him. "In the long run the world will do as it pleases with the book. I am determined to have the world know what I was pleased to do."

Often he improved the text; sometimes I believe he did not. For example, he omitted from the "modality" his entire poem "Respondez," a great diatribe against things as they are—Whitman as King Lear. "Let insanity have charge of sanity . . . O days! O lands! in every public and private corruption!/Smothered in thievery, impotence, shamelessness. . . ." He never explained why he discarded it; I include it as a poem of love. Only his passion for the country he wanted the United States to be could evoke such a diatribe against what it was.

The changes he himself made were not major; the poems he excluded did not affect the overall impact of *Leaves*. Whether his poem "Once I Passed Through a Populous City" was inspired by a man or a woman is not basic. In a manuscript version he never published, he wrote: "Now of all that city I remember only the man who wandered with me there, for love of me. . . ." In the published text he remembered only "a woman I casually met there who detained me for love of me." What is intrinsic to the poem is not the sex of the loved one but the love itself that is "all I remember, all else has been forgotten by me."

Whitman was a prophet of today's sexual revolution. He broke all verbal barriers as he expressed his passion for men and women, their bodies and all their acts. He was consumed not only by the act but also by the idea of love and its vast potentialities for the individual and for all humanity.

Except for three poems addressed to soldiers during the Civil War, the poems in *The Tenderest Lover* were all written during the first five years of his poetic career. Our book might have been called "The Young Whitman." In his love poems, youth speaks to youth of all ages, across all centuries and languages.

Whitman's longest poem and, in the opinion of most critics, his greatest, was originally untitled. Later it was called "Song of Myself." This is included, in a shortened version, as representative of Whitman's overall genius and "love that is all earth to lovers—love that mocks time and space."

My selection is not designed to replace *Leaves of Grass* but to induce readers to try the complete Whitman and discover for themselves all that he has to offer. My experience has been that you do not just read Whitman once and become a devotee. It is an affair of many stages, quarrels, rebuffs, renewed passion until you finally realize what he was talking about when he asked: "Shall we stick by each other as long as we live?"

Sources for the Text

In order not to interrupt the reading of the poems, foot-
notes have been eliminated. The main sources for the
text of *The Tenderest Lover* are the three following editions of *Leaves of Grass:* the first edition, 1855; the third,
1860; and the ninth, or Deathbed edition, 1891–92—the
last that Whitman himself saw through the press. They
are referred to here as 1st, 3rd, and DB, for Deathbed.

Unless otherwise specified, this text is from the DB
edition. However, in the following poems a different reading has been used:

"From Pent-Up Aching Rivers": 15th, 16th, 43rd, and
44th lines, 3rd.

"I Sing the Body Electric": 17th line of 6th section, 1st.
2nd line of 7th section in DB did not appear in 1st and is
omitted. 5th and 6th lines of 7th section, 1st.

"Native Moments": 7th line, 3rd.

"Scented Herbage of My Breast": 8th and 25th lines,
3rd.

"Whoever You Are Holding Me Now in Hand": 13th
line, 3rd.

"Hours Continuing": 3rd. The entire poem was never
reprinted by Whitman.

"Are You the New Person Drawn Toward Me?": Last
2½ lines appeared only in 3rd.

"Who Is Now Reading This?": Appeared only in 3rd.

"Sometimes with One I Love": Last line appeared only
in 3rd.

"Fast-Anchored Eternal O Love!": 3rd. DB version is considerably changed.

"Full of Life Now": 1st and 7th lines, the words "sweet-blooded" and "lover" appeared only in 3rd.

"The Sleepers": Last 11 lines of 1st section, 1st. In 6th section, 17 lines from DB were deleted and 8 lines from 1st were added. Last 2 lines of 8th section appeared only in 1st.

"I Am Not Content" and "After Death" are manuscript poems Whitman never published. They first appeared in *Notes and Fragments*, 1899, edited by R. M. Bucke.

"Out of the Cradle Endlessly Rocking": 3rd line appeared only in 3rd.

"Song of Myself": Last 2 lines of 21st section appeared in 1st. First 2 and 14th lines of 24th section follow text of 1st. Last 9 lines of 26th section appeared in 1st. This poem has been considerably shortened.

"Respondez": After his 1876 edition, Whitman eliminated this poem, which first appeared in the 1856 edition.

"So Long!": 5th, 44th, 54th, and last 4 lines, 3rd.

In his early editions Whitman spelled out past participles, as in "spelled." Later he abbreviated, "spell'd." Our text uses the unabbreviated form throughout.

Chronology

From the facsimile of a handwritten document in *Leaves of Grass,* David McKay, Philadelphia, 1900.

1819—May 31
Born at West Hills, Long Island, State of New York—second child of Walter and Louisa (born Van Velsor) Whitman, 1820, '21, '22, '23 continued at West Hills.

1824
Moved to Brooklyn. Went to public school. 1831, tended in lawyer's office. Then in doctor's. In 1834 went into printing office to learn typesetting.

1838
Teaching country schools in Suffolk county. Continued at it partly in Queens county for three years. Then starts a weekly paper *The Long Islander* at Huntington, L.I.

1840
Back in New York City. Working at printing and journalistic writing. In 1846 and '47 edits the *Eagle* newspaper in Brooklyn.

1848
Goes to New Orleans as an editor on the staff of *The Crescent* newspaper. Afterward travels south and southwest.

1850
Returns north. Publishes *The Freeman* newspaper in Brooklyn. Then works at building houses and selling them.

1855

Issues *Leaves of Grass,* 1st edition, small 4to, 95 pp. In 1856, 2nd edition, 16mo, 384 pp. In 1860, 3rd edition, 12mo, 456 pp. Boston.

1862

Goes down to the Secession War Fields. Begins his ministration to the wounded in the hospitals and after battles, and continues at them steadily for three years. In 1865 gets an appointment as Department Clerk.

1867

Publishes 4th edition of *Leaves of Grass* including "Drum Taps." In 1871, 5th edition.

1873

Prostrated by paralysis at Washington. Starts for Atlantic seashore by order of the physician. Breaks down badly at Philadelphia and takes up quarters in Camden, N.J., where he has remained up to date, for over fifteen years.

1876

Sixth, or Centennial, issue of *Leaves of Grass* with another volume, *Two Rivulets,* of prose and poems alternately. In 1881, 7th edition of *Leaves of Grass* published by Osgood & Co., Boston.

1882

Eighth issue of *Leaves of Grass* published by David McKay, Philadelphia. Also *Specimen Days,* a prose and autobiographic volume.

1888

Mr. Whitman is now in his 70th year. He is almost entirely disabled physically, through the paralysis from his persistent army labors in 1863 and '64, but is now just printing, we hear, a little volume of additional prose and verse called *November Boughs.* He resides in Mickle St., Camden, N.J.[1]

[1] On March 26, 1892, four years aftter this last entry, Walt Whitman died in the Mickle Street house.

This book was set in
Baskerville and Torino types by
Brown Bros. Linotypers, Inc.
It was printed by
Halliday Lithograph Corporation
and was bound by
Montauk Book Mfg. Co., Inc.
Designed by Larry Kamp